D0408684

BURT FRANKLIN: BIBLIOGRAPHY & REFERENCE 400
Essays in Literature & Criticism 114

ENGLISH TALES AND ROMANCES

A LIST OF ENGLISH TALES
AND PROSE ROMANCES PRINTED
BEFORE 1740

By ARUNDELL ESDAILE

PART I. 1475–1642.

PART II. 1643–1739.

BURT FRANKLIN
NEW YORK

Published by LENOX HILL Pub. & Dist. Co. (Burt Franklin)
235 East 44th St., New York, N.Y. 10017
Originally Published: 1912
Reprinted: 1971
Printed in the U.S.A.

S.B.N.: 8337-10680
Library of Congress Card Catalog No.: 79-150148
Burt Franklin: Bibliography and Reference 400
Essays in Literature and Criticism 114

Reprinted from the original edition in the Wesleyan University
Library.

PREFACE.

THE following list of English Tales and Romances is divided into two parts, the first containing all books which appeared up to the year 1642, the outbreak of the Civil War, the second containing all books which first appeared between that date and 1740. This plan has been adopted, primarily in order that Part I may fall into line with the Lists of English Plays and Translations from the Classics already issued by the Society; and secondarily in the hope that the division of the mass of material may sensibly diminish the incongruous juxtapositions inevitable in any author-catalogue, and may thus bring into light the historical perspective, which is still to a great extent, and would otherwise have been entirely, obscured by the alphabetical arrangement under the authors' names.

It may be well to add here that in the references to libraries, etc., given at the end of each entry, the following order of precedence is observed : (1) British Museum, (2) Bodleian, (3) University Library, Cambridge, (4) any other public library, preferably in England, (5) catalogued and accessible private libraries, such as the Bridgewater or Huth collections (the latter now no longer appropriate to this category), (6) other private libraries, and (7), failing an accessible copy, a reference to some authority for the book's present or past existence. A reference to a library means that a copy has not been found in a library higher in the list (as regards the later period a reference to a source placed lower may not always exclude the presence of a copy in the University Library, Cambridge);

but it does not imply that copies may not exist in any or all of the classes named below it ; thus, " B.M." does not mean that the book may not also be in " Bodl." or " U.L.C.," but " U.L.C." does mean that it is not in " B.M." or " Bodl."   But I am not so sanguine as to suppose that I have been quite consistent.

In the time, by now unduly protracted, in which this compilation has been accumulating in my hands, I have experienced my full share of that " mutual help and comfort," which it is the honourable tradition of librarians and other students of literature to afford.   Of the Society's two Hon. Secretaries it is Mr. Pollard who first suggested and assisted the commencement of the collection, and Mr. McKerrow who has edited the result. Our Treasurer, Mr. Graves, very kindly gave me entries for books preserved at Britwell, and Mr. Collmann settled some queries relating to them for me.   Dr. Henry Thomas gave useful help in dealing with translations from the Spanish.   At Oxford and Cambridge I owe thanks to most members of the libraries' staffs, but especially to Miss F. O. Underhill of the Bodleian, and at Cambridge to Mr. C. E. Sayle of the University Library, and for Pepysian entries to Mr. S. Gaselee ; while Mr. Martin Hardie has helped me with notes on books in the Forster and Dyce collections at South Kensington, and Mr. W. K. Dickson with the Arbuthnot tracts in the Advocates' Library.   At a rather early stage Professor F. Ives Carpenter, of Chicago, examined the whole of my material, and made many additions ; and my proofs of Part I were very kindly read by Professor Friedrich Brie, of Freiburg, who, I hope, found in them some suggestions, in return for those that he made, towards his forthcoming work on that period.

INTRODUCTION.

A LIST of earlier English Tales and Romances may seem at first sight to have a well-defined scope; but on many sides it needs definition, and it is necessary to draw round it frontier-lines, which, like those of kingdoms, are at times natural and at times arbitrary. Even the distinction between prose and verse becomes occasionally, as in some mixed Elizabethan pamphlets, not very easy to follow; this limitation, by excluding the early-printed mediæval verse-romances, has very much reduced both the labour and the value of this list. A harder line to draw is that between books of tales and books of anecdotes. Jest-books are only included when they have at least one unity, that of a single hero; this admits *Howleglas* and the *Jests* of Skelton and Peele, among others, which border too closely on the picaresque stories to be excluded. Fables are also admitted. But the most essential limitation lies in the fact that these are *early* English Tales and Romances. The adjective *early*, like other adjectives, is relative; it was necessary to find some closing limit of date if possible less arbitrary than others. This limit was really fixed for me at 1740 by the critics, more numerous perhaps than eminent, who have called Richardson's *Pamela*, which appeared in that year, the first English novel; the Society now has before it, as a corrective to this opinion, a sufficiently substantial list of the English novels which preceded the first. But a better limit, as increased familarity with the material shews, would have been the Revolution of 1688, or if a year could have been chosen, about a decade earlier, 1675 perhaps, the bicentenary of Caxton's Troy book. The long French romances had run their course, and the flood of scandalous novelettes had not begun. The consolation for the presence of these and other valueless trifles must be found in headings such as those of Bunyan, Defoe, and Swift.

The discussion of the date at which such a collection as this should end might well be interminable; but the date at which it should begin is simple; it begins with the first book printed in the English language. Caxton did well in choosing the tale of Troy divine for the first work of his press. For the period of nearly three centuries that we are now concerned with his version of it never lost hold of the English mind. His Bruges edition was followed by Wynkyn de Worde's of 1502-3, then, after a long gap which we must suppose to have been filled by lost editions of de Worde, Copland and East as well as by Copland's extant edition of 1553, it was reissued by Creede in 1596, "newly corrected, and the English much amended." After this there followed at regular intervals no fewer than eighteen editions, and in 1728 it was rewritten, being distinguished by the title *the New History of the Trojan Wars*, and a drama on the subject added. Caxton's next choice was not so happy; from Le Fevre's *Recueil* he turned to the same author's *History of Jason*, of his version of which there are only two extant editions, the second being printed in 1492 at Antwerp by Gerard Leeu. The mediæval *Godfrey of Bouillon*, which followed in 1481, was never reprinted; but *Reynard the Fox*, which appeared in the same year, was a better selection; for a reprint by Caxton himself survives, Pynson printed it twice, probably near the turn of the century, and then, after one surviving edition and two appearances in the licences of the Stationers' Company (in 1560 and 1586), it reappears in 1620, like the Troy book revised, and was constantly reprinted to the end of the period. Degulleville's allegory, *The Pilgrimage of the Soul*, 1483, came next, but was not reprinted. Caxton's success with the famous beast-fable of Reynard may perhaps have contributed to encourage him to return to this kind of book, which he did in the next year, 1484, by translating and printing the fables of Æsop; but the celebrity of Æsop as an elementary Latin reading-book (almost the only amusing one then known) makes it rather to be wondered at that it did not precede the others. Caxton's version, which also contains the fables of Avianus, Alphonso and Poggio ("Poge the Florentine"), held the field for a century, and was printed so late as 1700 among all the rival versions which multiplied as time went on, from that "in tru Ortŏgraphy with Grammar-nŏtz" by William Bullokar in 1585 to those by Hoole and L'Estrange. In the next year, 1485, came three mediæval romances, *Charles the Great*, which was not reprinted, *Paris and Vienne*, and, most important of all Caxton's prose books, Malory's *Morte d'Arthur*, the only perfect copy of which has recently changed hands. *Paris and Vienne* was reprinted at Antwerp by Gerard Leeu in 1492, and by Wynkyn de Worde and Pynson early in the next century, and then (though it was licensed in 1586) no edition is extant till those of Mainwaring's Jacobean version, of which there were three editions between 1621 and 1650. Malory's book had a more continuous popularity, unless the explanation of the fact that a greater number of editions of it are extant be merely that its greater bulk has preserved more copies from destruction; it was reprinted in 1498, 1529, 1557, twice about 1580, and, once more, in the revision of 1634. Except for two editions of a chapbook abridgement by the industrious John Shurley, entitled *Britain's Glory*, which appeared just half a century later, in 1684, this was the last to be heard of Malory till his revival in the nineteenth century.

After this valuable gift to English readers, Caxton produced only three more books which concern this list; they are all undated, but all were printed about 1489 or 1490. These are two more mediæval romances, *Blanchardine and Eglantine* and *The Four Sons of Aymon*, and *Eneydos*, a condensation in prose of the Aeneid. This last was never reprinted, so far as we know, but we have an edition of *Blanchardine and Eglantine* by Wynkyn de Worde and then, as in the case of so many of these early books, two revised editions at the end of the sixteenth century, while of *The Four Sons of Aymon* there were reprints in 1504 and 1554 and licences in 1581–2 and 1598–9, whether more than merely provisional there is no copy extant to tell us.

On the whole, then, we may say that our first printer showed good judgment of the public favour as well as good personal taste when he selected his books for printing. Only *Godfrey of Bouillon*, *Charles the Great*, *Eneydos*, and Degulleville's *Pilgrimage of the Soul* were not reprinted; though the last was re-written in verse thirty years later, and one, Lefevre's *Jason*, did not survive the fifteenth century. All the rest were really popular, and form a noble contribution to our national literature.

Caxton's followers, Wynkyn de Worde, Pynson, Wyer, and Copland, produced for the most part, apart from their reprints, less important books; it is not easy to see why Caxton did not himself venture on some of them, which were certain of a sale, though of course it is always quite possible that he did and that his editions of them are lost to us. This is specially the case with Mandevile's *Ways to the Holy Land*, which would have paired not unworthily with the *Morte d'Arthur*; apparently it was left to Wynkyn de Worde, whose edition of 1499 is the first known. Indeed, with Caxton's business, his mantle as producer of romances had fallen on de Worde; we owe to him *The Three Kings of Cologne* and *Robert the Devil*, both about 1500, *The Destruction of Jerusalem* (of which, however, there is an edition, also undated, by Pynson), *Ponthus of Galyce*, 1511, *Helyas*, 1512, *Joseph of Arimathea*, the *Gesta Romanorum*, and the *Seven Wise Masters*, all undated but of about this time, the last two being surely notable omissions on the part of Caxton, and *Oliver of Castile*, 1518. The most striking feature of this list is perhaps its complete mediævalism. Renaissance literature has not begun in England yet, except for More's *Utopia* and Elyot's *Book of the Governor*, not much of an exception, for the former was published abroad in Latin in 1518, and the latter's interest for us is confined to the presence in it of Boccaccio's tale of Titus and Gisippus. Before the turn of the fashion, which came rather after the middle of the century, we have a few more older books to chronicle. Jan van Doesborgh printed five of these at Antwerp in about 1520, three of them translations from Teutonic tales of secondary importance, *Frederick of Jennen*, *Mary of Nemmegen*, and *The Parson of Kalenborowe*, the other two being the mediæval story which tells "the lyfe of Virgilius and of his deth and many maruayles that he dyd in "his lyfe tyme by whychcrafte and nygramansy thorowgh the helpe of the "deuyls of hell," and the more important German jest-book of *Till Eulenspiegel* or *Howleglas*, both of which were reprinted, the latter twice, by Copland; *Howleglas* also reappeared after a long effacement in 1720, entitled, in the picaresque fashion which it had in some sense heralded, *The German Rogue*.

At about this time, in 1521, Pepwell printed Christine de Pisan's allegorical *City of Ladies*, and ten or fifteen years later Wyer printed her *Hundred Histories of Troy*; but both these books belonged to the age that was passing away, and not to that which was opening, and neither is known to have been reprinted. But among the English men of letters of this generation there is one who faces both ways. This is John Bourchier, Lord Berners, now most celebrated for his version of Froissart, but who also translated not only that favorite Renaissance moralist, Guevara, but, more to our purpose now, two mediæval romances; these are *Arthur of Little Britain*, first printed in about 1535 and revised in 1581, and the beautiful story of *Huon de Bordeaux*, which reached a third edition in 1601; to these must be added another translation, San Pedro's short allegorical story, *The Castle of Love*. *The Castle of Love* escaped the fate of the same author's *Arnalt and Lucenda*, which was published in 1575 as a text-book of Italian, with English and Italian versions on opposite pages, by Claude Desainliens, a teacher of languages, who anglicised his name to Hollyband. The same fate had earlier attended another Spanish love-story, Juan de Flores' "Historie of Aurelio and of Isabell, daughter of the Kinge of Schotlande, nyeuly translatede in foure langagies, Frenche, Italien, Spanishe, and Inglishe," published at Antwerp (which probably accounts for the spelling) in 1556. This story was licensed in England in 1556, in French, Italian, and English, and again in

1588 in the four languages ; it was reprinted at Brussels in 1608, and a new English version appeared in 1606 under the title of "A Paire of Turtle Doves: or the Tragicall History of Bellora and Fidelio," which has been attributed in error to Greene and is here identified.

Copland, for all his industry, added only one tale, that was not a mere reprint, to the national stock, and even this was itself an old story, being the *Historia de duobus amantibus* of Aeneas Silvius. A secular production for one who was to be a Pope, it belongs to the class of Boccaccio's *novelle* ; beside it stand the version of Boccaccio's Titus and Gisippus in Elyot's *Book of the Governor*, and two translations in verse, his *Tancred and Sigismund*, long known on the Continent in the Latin version by Leonardo Bruni Aretino, and Bandello's *Romeus and Juliet*. These three tales, though not products of the new age, may perhaps be taken as marking the transition in the taste of English readers, and pointing their attention to Italy.

The half-century that followed was in the West of Europe and not least in England the age of the Italian supremacy ; yet the number of Italian romances or novels translated or adapted for English readers was not so large as might be expected. The *Decameron* itself was not published in English as a whole until the end of James I's reign, though an attempt by John Wolfe to produce an edition of the original Italian was vetoed by authority. The explanation of the comparative slightness of the output of translations may perhaps be suggested by this incident of Wolfe's projected edition of the *Decameron* in its native tongue ; for the great majority of educated Englishmen could read Italian, and preferred to read their Boccaccio and Bandello in Italian, much as most people of our time prefer to read Anatole France in French.

To turn to what did find its way into English, there was a version in 1592 of the first half of the celebrated *Hypnerotomachia*, with not impossibly unworthy imitations of the woodcuts. The regular books of novels began with Painter's *Palace of Pleasure*, 1566, which was followed in succession by Fenton's *Tragical Discourses*, 1567, Guicciardini's *Garden of Pleasure*, 1573, Pettie's *Petite Pallace of Pettie his Pleasure*, 1576, Wotton's *Courtly Controversy of Cupid his Cautels* (which is a Pentameron), 1578, *Rich his Farewell to Military Profession*, 1581, Whetstone's *Heptameron*, 1582, and Warner's *Pan his Syrinx*, 1584. These regulars were reinforced by light-armed allies, books of mixed genre, containing letters and verses, such as Gascoigne's *Posies*, 1572, which contains an original roman-à-clef in the Italian manner, Tilney's *Discourse of Duties in Marriage*, 1568, Whetstone's *Rock of Regard*, 1576, and other books of the kind.

Though some of these collections were reprinted in the last decade of the century, and Marguerite de Navarre's *Heptameron*, which may be classed with its Italian sources, was not translated till 1592, yet the fashion yielded very quickly to the conquering progress of Lyly's *Euphues*. This strange and attractive book had just that originality which can be combined with popular success, the original combination of familiar but scattered qualities. Its balanced antitheses and assonances were already popular in Pettie, where they waited in the rough the polish that only the very young stylist of self-conscious culture often cares to give. The pithy proverbs were the stock in trade of the ordinary Englishman. The extreme morality appealed to the growing Puritanism of the time. The classical and pseudo-classical allusions served to attract the scholarly, and still more no doubt those who liked to think themselves so. And the constant discussions of education, of friendship, of love, of most other things, were in the taste of a generation of readers that knew Hoby's *Castiglione* and Elyot's *Governor*. The success of *Euphues* was immense. It appeared in 1578, and was constantly reprinted for nearly half a century. But early in its career it had rivals, in the shape of the short pastoral and other tales by Greene and Lodge, which followed its appearance closely, while a decade later it was overshadowed by Sidney's *Arcadia*. Sydney despised Euphuism as

> talking of beasts, birds, fishes, flies,
> playing with words and idle similes,

though he was but substituting for it a convention as artificial; but Greene and Lodge were as much influenced by Lyly in style, as they (and Sidney) were by the Greek pastoral romances; and they both adopt the moralising vein, especially on their title-pages. And both sometimes also placed on their title-pages catch-penny appeals to the popularity of *Euphues*: Greene has *Euphues his Censure to Philautus*, and *Menaphon, Camilla's alarum to slumbering Euphues*, while Lodge, besides *Euphues' Shadow, the Battle of the Senses*, gave his famous *Rosalynde* the sub-title, in 1612 transformed into the first title, of *Euphues' Golden Legacy*. Anthony Munday followed their example in *Zelauto*. It may be worth while to see, by means of an abstract of a chronological table which I had the curiosity to make, how the popularity of Greene and Lodge lived and died with that of Lyly.

Euphues appeared in 1578 and had gone through four editions by 1582. In 1583 Greene published his *Mamillia*, in 1584 Lodge appeared, and Greene brought out four more books, in 1585 came one Greene, in 1587 no fewer than five, in 1588, 1589, and 1590 two, in 1590 also Lodge's *Rosalynde*, in 1591 a Greene and a Lodge, in 1592, the year of Greene's death, three of his and Lodge's *Euphues' Shadow*, in 1593 and 1596 a Lodge each. Twenty-nine books by the three had been published by 1596; many had already been reprinted, while eleven had been weeded out by popular judgment, and had appeared for the last time, among these being all Lodge's except *Rosalynde*. After 1601 there is a short gap, *Rosalynde and Euphues* appearing in 1604 and three Greenes in 1605, *Euphues* and a Greene in 1606, three in 1607, two in 1608, and five in 1609, these years seeing three expire; the years 1610–1613 produced one apiece, 1614 two, 1615 one; in 1616 and 1617 there was a revival, nine being reprinted. These, the only survivors of the original 28, were *Euphues, Rosalynde*, and, of Greene's, beside *Pandosto*, which had a green old age before it, *Arbasto, Ciceronis Amor, Euphues' Censure to Philautus*, Greene's *Groats worth of Wit, Menaphon, Philomela*, and *Never Too Late*. In 1626 *Arbasto* disappears, in 1628 *Ciceronis Amor*, in 1631 *Philomela* and *Never Too Late*, in 1634 *Menaphon* and *Euphues' Censure to Philautus*, in 1636 *Euphues*, in 1637 Greene's *Groats worth of Wit*, and in 1642

Rosalind. After that year, the year of the outbreak of the Civil War, none of these books were reprinted except *Pandosto*, called in its later editions (of which there were not less, and probably many more, than twenty-four), *Dorastus and Fawnia.* This one tale alone had been found to suit the taste of different generations ; the rest suffered the common fate at last. That Lyly at least was being forgotten between 1630 and 1640 we can see from the address to the reader which Edward Blount the publisher prefixed to his edition of Lyly's plays in 1632.

" Reader, I haue (for the loue I beare to Posteritie) dig'd vp the Graue of a Rare and Excellent Poet, whom Queene Elizabeth then heard, Graced, and Rewarded. These Papers of his, lay like dead Laurels in a Churchyard ; but I have gathered the scattered branches vp, and by a Charme (gotten from Apollo) made them greene againe, and set them vp as Epitaphes to his memory.

" A sinne it were to suffer these Rare Monuments of wit, to be couered in Dust, and a shame, such conceipted Comedies, should be Acted by none but wormes . . . Our Nation are in his debt for a new English which hee taught them. *Euphues* and his *England* began first, that language : All our Ladies were then his Schollers ; And that Beautie in Court, which could not Parley Euphueisme, was as little regarded : as shee which now there, speakes not French."

It is clear that Blount himself was in Lyly's debt for an English by then far from new, and still more clear that, though he is referring to the Comedies, and though *Euphues* had been printed in the preceding year and was to be printed once again four years later, yet he was a forgotten author revived in consideration of the interest which the past generation had found in him.

Euphuism was only a phase in our literature ; Arcadianism left a deeper mark. The *Arcadia* was printed eighteen times between 1590 and 1725 ; it was continued in 1607 and 1613 by Gervase Markham, in 1624 by Richard Beling, whose Sixth Book is included in all later editions, in 1651 by Anne Weamys. An abstract appeared in 1701 and the whole story was modernised in 1725. Moreover the story of Argalus and Parthenia, besides being versified by Francis Quarles, was separately adapted as a chapbook in 1672 and frequently reprinted in the next generation. The *Arcadia* also has the distinction of having been early translated into French and having deeply influenced the sentimental romances of the next half century. Montemayor's *Diana*, which had influenced the *Arcadia*, was translated in 1598; and an imitation, Lady Mary Wroth's *Countess of Montgomery's Urania*, followed in 1621. That the "sweetness long drawn out" of this pastoral-heroical tale was found so grateful on the literary palate of the seventeenth century is as strange to us as it is true ; partly perhaps the fame of the Countess of Pembroke may account for it, but more the magic of the name of Sidney, immortalised by an early and heroic death before the book was published, a name which an Englishman even now rarely hears but he "finds his heart moved more than with a trumpet." But the French romances were even more popular, and the chief factor in the popularity of the school is rather to be found in the new elaboration of the theme of sentiment, more complex than the passions described in the Italian *novelle* or the purely heroic romances.

The mention of the last recalls our attention to the generation preceding Sidney. While the mediæval romances were still being reprinted for old-fashioned readers, a newer group had sprung up on the Continent and reached England when one would expect them to, that is not until the countries of their origin were wearying of them, and were ready to enjoy their condemnation to the flames by Don Quixote's housekeeper. It is true that extracts from *Amadis de Gaule* were translated as early as 1567; but the beginning of this fashion in England was the translation of Diego Ortuñez de Calahorra's *Espejo de Principes*, which began in 1578 and was not completed till 1601 ; in 1588 the Amadis and Palmerin cycles began to be translated with bewildering rapidity and profusion ; *Bellianis* came in 1598, and imitations were soon put out by Markham, Middleton, and Forde. Forde's three absurd romances were *Parismus*, with its sequel *Parismenos*, 1598–9, *Ornatus and Artesia*, 1607, and *Montelion*, of which no edition earlier than 1633 survives. They were all popular, *Parismus* being printed over twenty times before 1740, and a third part was added not much before 1700. It is noteworthy that their heroes come from far afield, distance being favourable to the marvels of romance. Parismus was "the renowned Prince of Bohemia," the scene of the History of Ornatus and Artesia is laid in Phrygia, and Montelion, Knight of the Oracle, was "son to the renowned Persicles, King of Assyria." Even Forde's absurdities, however, were exceeded by those of Richard Johnson, whose most famous *History of the Champions of Christendom*, appearing in 1596–7, two years before *Parismus*, held first place in the estimation of simple readers well into the eighteenth century.

Romance, which expresses the desire to escape from real life, was suffering eclipse, or rather, perhaps, running into new moulds; the novel, which represents an acceptance of real life, was being born. There had been an element of realism in the Italian *novelle*, but the old contrast of tragedy, which represents men as better than they are, and comedy, which represents them as worse than they are, was now strikingly seen in the contrast between the impossible hero of romance and the impossible rogue of the picaresque novel. The origin of the picaresque is an enquiry not to be undertaken here. In England, the first signs of it are to be seen in the welcome accorded to the jests of Skelton, Scoggin, and Eulenspiegel, and Harman's *Caveat for Common Cursetors*. But these were only slight things, evidence that the public was ready. The celebrated Spanish story of Lazarillo de Tormes was licensed in 1568–9, and went through many editions; a second part followed in 1596, and another, "The Pursuit of the History," by Juan de Luna, in 1631. Lazarillo produced a clever imitation in Nashe's *Unfortunate Traveller*, published in 1594, in which the rogue's adventures are laid in Italy, and mixed up with romantic legends about the poet Surrey and his fair Geraldine. Nashe's book is an interesting and individual performance, but produced no imitators. Rabelais' *Gargantua*, probably regarded with the same eye as the jest-books and picaresque stories, was licensed in 1594, but no copy is known, and Urquhart was not yet born. In 1622 and 1623 two more Spanish books were translated and published here, Cespedes y Meneses' *Gerardo* and Aleman's *Guzman de Alfarache*.

Gerardo was only revived once, in 1653; but Gusman, or, as he was more often called, the Spanish Rogue, had a long life and a numerous progeny. He was reprinted in 1630 and 1634, epitomized in 1655, and again reprinted in 1656 and 1661, and newly translated in 1707 and 1708. In 1652, George Fidge published his work "The English Gusman; or The History of that Unparallel'd Thief James Hind"; Hind was the celebrated highwayman who had been hanged the year before, and whom another pamphlet calls the Yorkshire Rogue. In 1665 Richard Head, the biographer of the celebrated Mother Ursula Shipton, produced the first part of *The English Rogue*, which was continued and ultimately completed in five parts by Francis Kirkman, the bookseller. This book continued the exposure of thieves' life and language which Greene and Dekker had begun in pamphlets not noticed here, and enjoyed a popularity far beyond its deserts. Seven years later the French imitation of Gusman, by Charles de Fieux, "The French Rogue, or The Life of Monsieur Ragoue de Versailles," was translated, perhaps by John Shurley, and twice reprinted by 1704. *The Dutch Rogue* of Lebechea was translated in 1685. In 1706 came "The Scotch Rogue, or the Life and Actions of Donald McDonald, a Highland Scot." There was an Irish rogue, by name Teague O'Dively, and *Howleglas* was reproduced in 1720 as *The German Rogue*.

These early attempts at realism, working side by side with the idealism of romance, culminate in the last decade of the sixteenth century in a very curious product, not the least fruitful even of that time. This is the democratisation of fiction in the trade-novels of Deloney, Johnson, and others. The romances, old and new, were at least expensive from their mere bulk, and they were probably also above the heads of the commonalty. Euphuism and Arcadianism were essentially courtly fashions. The men of the new school were men of the people; their corypheus, Thomas Deloney, was "the balletting silk-weaver of Norwich." They knew the popular need, and they met it. Deloney's tales approximate to the jest-book type, but they tell the stories, not of rogues, but of the great names of the shoe-makers' and clothiers' trades; Valens glorifies Hawkwood as a member of the Merchant Taylors; Johnson tells the stories of the Nine Worthies of London; Roberts, those of the Six Merchants of Devonshire; the story of Dick Whittington, of which no edition is known till 1656, may have originally belonged to this group; Robin Hood and George a Green are heroes after the people's own heart; Johnson's *Tom a Lincoln* is King Arthur's son and the Red Rose Knight, but is no more aloof than Robin Hood. *Faustus* and *Friar Bacon* combine the jest-book, the story of wonder, and the pious warning; no wonder that they were popular. The level of literature in these books may not be high. An educated taste soon wearies of them, except in the terrible climax of *Faustus* or *Friar Rush*, or, for humour, in the Slawkenbergian story of Margaret's wooing in *Thomas of Reading*. But the prentice at the shop bench had not an educated taste; and we may be sure that he often had *The Gentle Craft* or *Jack of Newbury* on his knees under the table and read it when his master's or mistress's eye was not on him, and would in the intervals turn back to drudgery with the delightful dream of following in the footsteps of those heroes of his craft.

The first third of the seventeenth century produced few notable English books; we have some share, perhaps, in the *Euphormion* and *Argenis* of John Barclay, a cosmopolitan Scotsman of the type of the admirable Crighton, though they were first published abroad and in Latin. The *Argenis* is the starting point for the political romances of the next generation. But a few outstanding books, apart from the Spanish rogues, were translated in the reign of James I. Don Quixote began to appear in 1612 and was completed in 1620, perhaps in 1615; it is pleasant to think that Shakespeare, in his retirement at Stratford, may have read the first part at least. The *Exemplary Novels* followed in 1640. Both took firm hold of the English reader. The *Decameron*, long over-due, was translated in 1620–25; it was several times reprinted, and in 1702 was, as the title-page phrases it, "adapted to the Gust of this present Age." Richard Bernard's *Isle of Man*, 1626, a legal-religious allegory, acquires some importance in the light of Bunyan's allegories; and Reynolds' celebrated collection of deterrent stories, *God's Revenge against Murder* (1621–3) enjoyed great popularity ; it was perhaps suggested by Beard's *Theatre of God's Judgments*, which had appeared in 1597. But the political strife that was to end in the Civil War was more and more distracting men's minds from such frivolities as romance-writing, and we find that, though the old favourites went on being reprinted, the output of new tales between 1630 and 1660 was by comparison very slight.

Of original writing from 1630 to 1650 there was extraordinarily little. Bishop Godwin's *Man in the Moon* appeared in 1638, and is perhaps the first philosophical romance ; Richard Braithwaite published three novels in 1640 and 1641 ; Howell's *Dodona's Grove* and Hart's *Alexto and Angelica* both came in 1640 ; after these until 1650 there is only Baron's 'Ερωτοπαίγνιον, 1647. There was, however, a rather larger bulk of translation. Cervantes' *Exemplary Novels* were translated and printed in 1640 ; Machiavelli's *Belphegor* in 1647, and a number of less important tales, such as those by Bishop Camus, Biondi, Perez de Montalvan, and Boisrobert. In 1647 a more definite group of romances began to invade England ; these were the artificial and enormously long French stories, pseudo-historical, pseudo-pastoral, pseudo-heroic, pseudo-romantic. The first to come was Gomberville's *Polexander* ; in 1652 it was followed by the first instalments of Calprenède's *Cassandra* and *Cleopatra*, and by Mademoiselle de Scudéry's *Ibrahim* ; in the next year began the latter's *Artamenes, or the Grand Cyrus*, in 1655 her *Clelia*, in 1662 Calprenède's *Pharamond*, and so late as 1677 Mademoiselle de Scudéry's *Almahide*. From 1652 to the first two or three years of the Restoration these books, appearing part by part, loaded the press ; and country ladies like Dorothy Osborne found not only leisure and patience but also interest enough to read and discuss them. What that literary "man in the street," Francis Kirkman, who was moreover an expert in romances, thought of them, may be seen in his dedication to his translation of *Clerio and Lozia*, 1652 : "No Nation ever could glory in such Playes, as the most learned and incomperable Johnson, the copious Shakespear, or the ingenuous Fletcher compos'd; but I beleeve the French for amorous language, admirable invention, high atchievements, honorable Loves, inimitable constancy, are not to be equalled." Naturally their success produced some imitations. Roger Boyle's *Parthenissa* was commenced in 1654, and never finished; "the bluidy Mackenzie" published in 1660 the first part of his *Aretina, or the Serious Romance*, but, becoming immersed in matters of even greater seriousness, published no more; in 1664 John Bulteel produced his *Birinthea*. The French romances were moreover turned to edification by Nathaniel Ingelo in his clumsy allegory of *Bentivolio and Urania*, 1660, which took the public fancy enough to reach a fourth edition in 1682, and the historical element in them was turned to topical interest in two or three political romances. Of these one, *Cloria and Narcissus* or *The Royal Romance*, 1653, is described on the title-page as being "imbellished with divers politicall notions, and singular remarks of moderne transactions," and Braithwaite's *Panthalia*, 1659, also called "The Royal Romance," was "a discourse stored with infinite variety in relation to State-Government."

If they produced imitations, they also produced parodies. Sorel's *Lysis or the Extravagant Shepherd* ridiculed the false pastoral as *Don Quixote* had ridiculed false heroic; it was translated so early as 1653, and was followed in 1656 by a native English parody, Holland's *Don Zara del Fogo*. But these did not prove fatal. There were some reprints of Calprenède and Scudéry in the seventies; *Cassandra* was even reprinted so late as 1725, and these romances figure in the lady's boudoir described in the *Spectator*. But their real triumph was over by 1680. Perhaps Subligny's *Mock-Clelia*, 1678, and Scarron's *Comical Romance*, 1676, may have helped their fall; but they fell by their own weight. Such an extreme of fashion must be followed by its converse; the picaresque burst out again, and the day of the romance in twelve folio books gave way to that of the duodecimo novel in a hundred and fifty pages. The first workers of this reform were Jean Regnauld de Segrais and the Comtesse de Lafayette, whose *Zaïde* and more celebrated *Princess of Cleves* were translated in 1678 and 1679. For the next twenty years novelettes flowed from the press in a constant stream. Their authors imitated Madame de Lafayette's brevity, but they were not so well able to imitate her truth to nature or her delicacy. A large number are gross ; and their grossness is rendered more offensive by the artificial courtliness of their manner. Indeed of these stories of intrigue very much the more readable are those "novels of the cloak and the sword," more often of Spanish than of French origin, in which the main motive is not in the successful climax of the intrigue, but in the vicissitudes and dangers of its progress. Some of the worst are historical, or relate to living persons, and retail scandals that were no doubt all as well known at the time as a few still are. And as well as novels in which truth masquerades as fiction there were those in which fiction masquerades as truth. In fact, in this generation biography and fiction are divided by such an indeterminate line that the present compiler has sometimes turned in doubt to the love passages for a test, and only included the book if they were narrated in detail. [1]

But side by side with the story which was its own reward there was beginning to be a novel of ideas. The early attempts at this are scattered, but we can follow two threads, the allegory and the satire by a story of travel. The first allegory to appear in English was Caxton's version of Degulleville's *Pilgrimage of the Soul*, and Christine de Pisan's *City of Ladies*, 1521, San Pedro's *Castle of Love* [1548 ?], the *Hypnerotomachia*, 1592, and de Cartigny's *Voyage of the Wandering Knight*, in their different ways, contributed to the tradition. A much more influential book than any of these was Richard Bernard's *Isle of Man, or the legall proceeding in Manshire against sinne*, a dull and over-elaborated allegory in legal phraseology, which may have suggested *The Holy War* and the trial in *Pilgrim's Progress ;* it reached a sixteenth edition in 1683. In the middle of the century the spirit of allegory is seen in *Nova Solyma*, 1648, which has been rashly attributed to Milton, and is now known to be by Samuel Gott, and

(1) The authorship of many French novels of this period may be found in the bibliography which forms part 2 of *De l'Usage des Romans*, by "le Comte Gordon de Percel," *i.e.*, Nicolas Lenglet du Fresnoy.

in Bayly's *Herba Parietis*, 1650, the title of which is worth quoting more at length : "Herba Parietis : or, The Wall-Flower. As it grew out of the Stone-Chamber belonging to the Metropolitan Prison of London, called Newgate. Being a History which is partly True, partly Romantick, Morally Divine. Written by Thomas Bayly, D.D., whilst he was a Prisoner there. Capiant qui capere possunt." A more regular allegory is Ingelo's *Bentivolio and Urania*, already mentioned as turning the long French romances to purposes of edification, which appeared at the height of their success, in the year of Restoration. Five years later Simon Patrick published his *Parable of the Pilgrim*, which was popular, reaching a sixth edition in 1687. Every older allegory has been called the origin of *Pilgrim's Progress*, even the never-translated *Colombelle et Volontairette ;* and *The Parable of the Pilgrim* is not last of the claimants. Bunyan owes, perhaps, no more to Patrick than the central idea of *Pilgrim's Progress*, but it is hard to believe that he does not owe him that ; and it is worth noticing that the three allegories which were alive when his tale appeared all disappeared before its advance within a few years, *Bentivolio and Urania* (which, however, probably fell with the fall of the books it was built on, and was never read at all by Bunyan's uncourtly public) in 1682, *The Isle of Man* in 1683, and *The Parable of the Pilgrim* in 1687. The first part of *The Pilgrim's Progress* itself was published in 1678, and the second part in 1684. Its success was immediate, and the booksellers' hacks did not neglect the opportunity. In 1682 one T.S. anticipated Bunyan with *The Second Part of the Pilgrim's Progress*, which also is "Exactly Described under the Similitude of a Dream" ; the third edition of this was printed in 1684, when the imitation was no doubt superseded by the true second part. In 1692–3 appeared a third part, which enjoyed almost as great a popularity for a time as the first two, a thirteenth edition being brought out in 1738. It is anonymous when examined, but at a first glance seems to be attributed to Bunyan, his name being skilfully and prominently brought into the title-page in the words "To which is added the Life and Death of John Bunyan, Author of the First and Second Parts," in which strict verbal truthfulness is combined with a strong *suggestio falsi*, the name John Bunyan being printed in very large letters.   A parallel case to this is found in *Gillian of Croydon*, 1727, of which the title reads " The Pleasant and Delightful History of Gillian of Croydon.   Containing . . . the tragical History of William and Margaret [and also, I may add, the celebrated ballad] Illustrated with suitable Cuts.   The Whole done much after the same method as those celebrated novels BY MRS. ELIZA HAYWOOD."

Honest imitations followed in Dunton's *Pilgrim's Guide from the Cradle to the Grave*, and *Hue and Cry after Conscience : or the Pilgrim's Progress by Candlelight*, 1685, and an anonymous *Progress of the Christian Pilgrim*, 1700.

Bunyan's two other allegories had appeared between the two parts of *The Pilgrim's Progress*, *The Life and Death of Mr. Badman* in 1680, and *The Holy War* in 1682 ; both were often reprinted, but without becoming household classics.   In *Pilgrim's Progress* the high-water mark of allegory had been reached, and (though we must remember *The Tale of a Tub*) Bunyan has had almost fewer followers than predecessors.

So with travels.   The acknowledged masterpiece of the genre, *Gulliver's Travels*, had behind it a considerable ancestry.   More's *Utopia*, not translated into its author's native tongue until 1551, was before its time. The seventeenth century was a more reflective period than the sixteenth ; Europe began to have leisure to contemplate the new knowledge and the new ideas.   We find the growth of intellectual romance corresponds. Political ideas appear in Barclay's *Argenis*, already mentioned ; and satire is seen in *Mundus Alter et Idem*, attributed to Bishop Hall, which was published in 1609 and revived quite late in the century, and in Erycius Puteanus' *Comus*, Louvain, 1611, and Oxford, 1634, and in the licensing of Petronius in 1631.   The Utopia was imitated by Bacon in his *New Atalantis*, posthumously published in 1626, by Hartlib in his discourse, devoid of narrative, of the island of Macaria, 1641, and by Harrington

in *Oceana*, 1656. Unknown but sublunary lands afforded good sport, no
doubt, for constitution-builders and satirists; but Bishop Francis Godwin's
Man in the Moon, 1638, and Bishop John Wilkins' *Discovery of a World
in the Moon*, 1638, which is not a narrative, went further and were not
without fruit; for the latter was translated into French in 1656, and
probably suggested to "that famous Wit and Cavaleer of France," Cyrano
de Bergerac, the idea of his satire Σεληναρχία, *or the Government of the
World in the Moon*, which was translated in 1659 and again in 1687. To
return to earth, another imaginary voyage, Vairasse d'Allais' *History of the
Sevarites*, was translated in 1675 (and later reprinted as vol. 3 of *Gulliver's
Travels*), Barnes' *Gerania* appeared in the same year; Schooten's *Hairy
Giants* came some time after 1671, and Gabriel·de Foigny's *New Discovery
of Terra Australis Incognita*, under the name of Jacques Sadeur, in 1693;
while satires on the Jansenists and the disciples of Descartes respectively
were brought over to England in *A Relation of the Country of Jansenia*, 1668,
by a père Zacharie, calling himself Louis Fontaines, and Daniel's *Voyage
to the World of Cartesius*, 1692. But all these are pale beside the
immortal *Gulliver's Travels*, which followed at the distance of a generation.
Several voyages were published soon after *Gulliver*, but all were imitations
by Grub Street hacks, now, as in the time of Bunyan, watching the public
fancy. Bennet's *Memoirs of the Court of Lilliput, Written by Captain
Gulliver*, 1727, *A Voyage to Cacklogallinia . . . by Captain Samuel Brunt*,
also 1727, and McDermot's *Trip to the Moon*, reprinted from a lost Dublin
edition in 1728, need only be mentioned as examples.

Allegory and satire had each produced a masterpiece not even now
rivalled. The novel meanwhile was gaining ground as an instrument for
the expression of ideas more subtle than either because more concealed.
The first true masterpiece of the tale in which the ideas are presented to
the mind only by implication is of course Defoe's *Robinson Crusoe*. But
before the appearance in 1719 of the masterpiece, the necessary material
had been gathered and the art to work in it had been practised by many
hands. Realism of characterisation, incident and diction, was at first

found only in picaresque stories, and there in a more or less debased form ; in the middle of the seventeenth century everything else was put into the background by the artificial idealism of the French Court romances, but realism, when it returned to favour, was greatly reinforced by reaction, and in Defoe's day had been gaining ground for a generation. Defoe's literary reform was not to rebel against the conventions of Scudéry and Calprenède, [1] but to convert the mere dull probability of the contemporary tale into narratives that should not only convince, but should also fascinate. The line between fiction and falsehood is a fine one, and no man ever trod it with more agility than Defoe. That Swift could, had he chosen to be possible as well as probable, have made men believe in Captain Lemuel Gulliver's relation, is surely in some part because Defoe had seven years earlier made them believe in that of Robinson Crusoe. Nevertheless, in style, Defoe's debt to his predecessors is slight ; his own experience as a journalist explains his skill, even better than Swift's experience as a pamphleteer explains his. Nor can we find any clear origin of his happiest idea, any Robinsoniads before Robinson. He may have seen *The Isle of Pines*, 1668, attributed to Henry Nevile, a dull little fiction, narrating how one George Pine and a few other persons had been cast on a desert island, and, multiplying with a rapidity worthy of Zola's *Fécondité*, had organised their society. There is no reason to think that this fugitive pamphlet influenced Defoe, but, as we have seen, the idea of imaginary travel was familiar at the time. The travel-story, the rogue-story and the philosophical story were the chief elements in his art. His larger contributions to the rogue story were to follow *Robinson Crusoe*, though he had served his apprenticeship for writing them in his earlier journalistic pamphlets on condemned criminals, and in *The Compleat Mendicant* ; moreover the genre had greatly increased in power and dignity with the advent of Le Sage, whose *Gil Blas* was by now to be read in English. It has been said that the good love to hear of nothing so much as of the

(1) This is the impression conveyed by M. Jusserand in his pamphlet *Le Roman Anglais et la Réforme littéraire de Daniel Defoe*, 1887.

wicked ; for the pious tradesfolk of his day Defoe's tales of guilt and his shallow moralisings were exquisitely calculated. But once, in *Robinson*, he gave expression to profounder ideas. A man, separated from other men, when once his material necessities are provided for, must think, and Robinson tells us, to our complete conviction, what his thoughts were. This conception of the spiritual growth of an isolated mind may possibly have been suggested by an Oriental tale. Abú Bakr ibn Al-Tufail's story of Hai Ebn Yokdan, which was published in Arabic and Latin as *Philosophus Autodidactus* in 1671, was translated from the Latin into English in 1674 "for a general service," and translated twice again, in 1686 and 1708, the latter time as *The Improvement of Human Reason*, besides being abridged and appended to a chap-book edition of Greene's *Dorastus and Fawnia* in 1696. As its Western titles show, this story is that of a mind isolated from birth, and its achievement of natural religion. The growth of this idea at the time may account for the story's evident popularity ; but that popularity, in spite of the abridgement of 1696, must have been among educated men. Defoe's public was not familiar with free-thinking ideas, and we find that natural religion appears only in Friday, and is combated by Crusoe, whose progress is all towards the Christian verities. Natural religion is for Defoe the religion of the natural man, but not therefore a criterion of truth. In short, if he was influenced by *Hai Ebn Yokdan*, it was by way of opposition. What is perhaps an echo of both may be found in the anonymous story of *Autonous*, 1736.

The doctrine of the noble savage, it may be mentioned, had been proclaimed by Mrs. Aphra Behn in *Oroonoko*, so long before Rousseau as 1688. The earlier half of this novel, turning on intrigue, is in the artificial French style of her other novels ; but, for the latter half, when the African prince is a slave to his inferiors, the authoress drew on her early experience in Surinam, and her evident sincerity almost conceals even the apparent absurdity of her theme. But Defoe, without her experience, had a genius for probability, and the delusion of the noble savage, if he knew of it, did not impose on him.

Like Bunyan and Swift, Defoe had no worthy successor, not even in his later self; but all three left their mark on later writing. The man with an allegory, a satire, almost any idea, to express could now express it easily and attractively in the form of a narrative; new ground was conquered for literature. But side by side with this newer growth, the old mundane story of incident and sentiment went on. On the one side Le Sage and the Spanish novelists developed the qualities of wit and truth to nature, without which the story of incident and adventure cannot rise high in the degrees of true literature; on the other hand, the French novel of sentiment found a master in Marivaux, whose *Paysan parvenu* (*Milord*) was translated in 1735, and *Marianne* in 1736–42, the English version of the latter being only known from the announcements in *The Gentleman's Magazine*. There is no reason to suppose that Richardson owed anything of his *Pamela* to *Marianne*, though he may have read it. We know how the immediate suggestion of the book came to him; but the similarity of the two books shows how, independently of consciousness, a current idea may enter the mind.

On the other hand, the circumstance that *Pamela* is written in a series of letters has been claimed as original in Richardson; but this is far from being the case. Though his early practice in writing love-letters for young ladies is enough to account for his choice of form, even if he had not originally set out to write disconnected letters, only adding the story as an afterthought, yet the novel by letters was well known before his day. Letters occur, of course, in Euphues and the heroic romances; but they are not used for telling the story. The growth of biography in the latter half of the seventeenth century probably suggested the application of the method to fiction; but the most important single influence is to be found in the celebrated *Letters of a Nun to a Cavalier*, translated by L'Estrange in 1678, and doubtfully included here with the certainly fictitious sequels, *Seven Portuguese Letters*, 1681, and *The Cavalier's Answers*, 1683. In 1683 Mrs. Behn published her *Love Letters between a Nobleman and his Sister* (sister-in-law), and in 1686 appeared an anonymous love-story in letters,

Love's Posy. Mrs. Manley's *Letters,* 1696, reprinted in 1725 as *A Stage-Coach Journey to Exeter,* include a letter in imitation of the Portuguese Nun, by a Major Pack, and suggest Fielding's use of the road and its incidents. Her more characteristic *Court Intrigues,* 1711, and her follower Mrs. Haywood's *Bath Intrigues,* 1725, are in the same form. In 1702, Tom Brown wrote *The Adventures of Lindamira* in twenty-four letters; this was reprinted in 1713. Here was tradition enough.

But these, except the Nun, were small achievements. The success of *Pamela* in 1740 opens a new chapter in the story of the English novel, and closes our period; but the more virile, if less subtle, story of incident was also to find its great reformer. Curiously enough, the masterpiece of one style was to be the opportunity for that of the other. Richardson's *Pamela* was made to be parodied, and its parody followed close in Fielding's *Joseph Andrews.* But it was only a parody in its inception; when once its author's genius had been drawn into the way of the novel, the future was secure. Yet the two opposed styles persisted. In France the Abbé Prévost fused these apparently discordant elements of strength and sweetness in his *Manon Lescaut,* 1731 (which was apparently not translated till much later); but no one heeded the example, at least in England. For that we had to wait for Scott.

Note.—PART I. The following lost books are probably prose tales, but some may be plays.

ALBION'S QUEEN.

The Famous Historie of Albion's Queene. *W. W. for T. Pauier.* 1601. 4°. 𝔅.𝔏.

Hazlitt, II. 5.

ALERANE.

The Strange Fortune of Alerane : Or, My Ladies Toy. By H. M. of the Middle Temple in London. *V. S[ims] for M. L[ownes].* 1605. 4°.

B.M. (title only ; Bagford 5927, 239).

APOLLONIUS AND CAMILLA.

The historye of Apolonius and Camilla.

Licensed to J. Perryn, 9 Oct., 1587 (*Stat. Reg.*, ii. 476).

AVERELL, WILLIAM.

The History of Charles and Julia, 1581.

Licensed to J. Charlwood, 4 Jan., 1581–2 (*Stat. Reg.*, ii. 386).
Hazlitt, I. 18.

BROOME, STEPHEN.

The mery historye of Steven Broome, howe he becam pope of Rome.

Licensed to R. Jones, 9 Feb., 1579–80 (*Stat. Reg.*, ii. 365).

CLEOMENES AND JULIET.

The renowmed historie of Cleomenes and Juliet.

Licensed to H. Jackson, 14 Oct., 1577 (*Stat. Reg.*, ii. 318).

EDWARD.

The pleasant history of Edward Lord of Lancaster, knight of the holy crosse, with his aduentures, &c.

Licensed to J. Danter, 5 March, 1593 (*Stat. Reg.*, ii. 628).

FREDERIGO.

The historye of the life and fortune of Don Frederigo di Terra noua.

Licensed to J. Roberts, 1 Oct., 1599 (*Stat. Reg.*, iii. 148).

HISTORIEN.

Lxxi Lustige Historien.

Licensed to E. White, 7 Aug., 1590 (*Stat. Reg.*, ii. 557).

HONORA.

Honora, containing a most Pleasant History Deciding a Controversy between English modesty and Spanish pride. 1597. 4°.

Hazlitt, H. 570.

PARNESUS.

Parnesus his Loue to the Three Bohemian Ladies, &c.

Licensed to G. Vincent, 7 Sept., 1605 (*Stat. Reg.*, iii. 300).

SORORIPHILUS.

Sororiphilus and Fraticola.

Licensed to R. Blore, 5 Oct., 1601 (*Stat. Reg.* iii. 192).

TALE OF A TUB.

A Tale of a Tubb or a Gallamanfrey of Merriment by N : D :

Licensed to F. Grove, 16 Jan., 1637–8 (*Stat. Reg.*, iv. 405).

TWO ITALIAN KNIGHTS.

The strange aduentour of two Italian Knights.

Licensed to H. Kirkham, 19 April, 1577 (*Stat. Reg.*, ii. 311).

URANO.

The moste famous and delightfull history of Vrano otherwise called the Grene knighte and the bewtifull Princess Beroshia, Daughter to Lucius Kinge of Brittaine, &c.

Licensed to F. Burton, 12 Sept., 1605 (*Stat. Reg.*, iii. 300).

VINCENTIO AND MARGARET.

Vincentio and Margaret.

Licensed to V. Sims, 26 Nov., 1605 (*Stat. Reg.*, iii. 305).

WHARTON'S NOVEL.

Whartons Nouel.

Licensed to H. Kirkham, 19 April, 1577 (*Stat. Reg.*, ii. 311).

WOLNER, RICHARD.

Pleasaunte tayles of the lyf of Rychard Wolner, &c.

Licensed to H. Denham, 1568 (*Stat. Reg.*, i. 364)

ADDENDA AND CORRIGENDA.

PART I.

Chaucer's *Tale of Melibeus*, in the *Canterbury Tales* [1478?], [1484?], [1493?], 1498, 1526, and the *Works*, 1532, 1542, [1545?], 1561, 1598, 1602, 1687, and 1721. All are in the British Museum.

PART II.

The Countess of Salisbury is by d'Argence.

Grimmelshausen's *Simplicissimus* is stated by Miss C. Morgan (*Rise of the Novel of Manners*, p. 200), an untrustworthy authority, to have been advertised by Baldwin in February, 1688. It does not appear in the *Term Catalogues*.

PART I.

(1475—1642.)

ENGLISH TALES AND ROMANCES.

PART I. (1475—1642).

ACHILLES TATIUS.

The most delectable and plesant Historye of Clitophon and Leucippe from the Greek of Achilles Statius . . . by W. B. [*For T. Creede?*] 1577 [1597].

Licensed to T. Creede, 5 April, 1597 (*Stat. Reg.* iii. 82).
Priv. Lib. Hazlitt, H. 593; cf. *Times*, 10 Feb., 1905.

[A different version.] The Loves of Clitophon and Leucippe. A most elegant History, written in Greeke by Achilles Tatius: And now Englished. *W. Turner, Oxford.* 1638. 8⁰.

Translated by A. H.
B.M. (11340. a. 9.).

[A different version.] The Amours of Clitophon and Leucippe. Illustrated, in Six Novels. . . . . Written in Greek, By Achilles Tatius. Now first rendred into English, *etc. For T. Bickerton.* 1720. 12⁰.

Bodl. (Douce CC. 137).

AENEAS SYLVIUS.

[Eurialus and Lucresia. *J. van Doesborgh, Antwerp.*] 4⁰. 𝕭.𝕷.
Signet (frag.).

The goodly History of the moste noble and beautyful Ladye Lucres of Scene in Tuskan, & of her louer Eurialus verye pleasaunt and delectable vnto the reder. *J. Kynge.* 1560. 8⁰. 𝕭.𝕷.
B.M. (Huth 51).

[Another edition.] *W. Copland.* 1567. 8⁰. 𝕭.𝕷.
Pepys 29 (3).

[Another edition.] [*W. Copland?*] 4⁰. 𝕭.𝕷.
B.M. (C. 21. c. 65).

[Another edition ?]

Licensed to T. Norton in 1569–70 (*Stat. Reg.* i. 409).

[A different version.]   The Moste Excellente Historie, of Euryalus and Lucresia.   *T. Creede, and are to be solde by W. Barley.*   1596.   4°.

The Latin dedication to Charles Blunt is signed W. Braunche.

B.M. (12612. c. 10).

[A different version.]   The Historie of Eurialus and Lucretia.   Written in Latine by Eneas Sylvius ; And translated into English by Charles Allen, Gent.   *T. Cotes, for W. Cooke.*   1639.   12°.

B.M. (E. 1378/1).

[A different version.]   The Amours of Count Schlick.   1708.   *See* (in Part II) LA MOTHE, Marie Catherine.   Hipolytus Earl of Douglas.

AESOP.

[Esopes Fables in Greeke.]

Licensed to Bishop and Newbery, 3 July, 1591 (*Stat. Reg.* ii. 587).

Esopus cum commento optimo et morali.   *R. Pynson.*   1502.   4°.   𝕭.𝕷.

B.M. (C. 40. e. 32).

[Another edition.]   Fabule Esopi cum commento.   *W. de worde.*   1503.   4°.   𝕭.𝕷.

B.M. (C. 38. d. 1).

[Another edition.]   *W. de worde.*   1516.   4°.

J.R.L.

[A different version.]   Aesopi Phrygis et vita ex maximo Planude desumpta & fabellæ iucundissimæ : quarū interpretes hi sunt. Gulielmus Goudanus. Hadrianus Barlandus. Erasmus Roterodamus. Aulus Gellius. Laurentius Valla. Angelus Politianus. Petrus Crinitus. Ioānes Antonius Campanus. Plinius secūdus Nouocamēsis. Anianus Gulielmus Hermanus. Nicolaus Gerbellius Phorcensis. Laurentius Abstemius. Rimicius.   Index omnes fabulas indicabit.   Addite sunt his quædam iucūdæ ac honestæ fabellæ, selecte ex omnibus facetijs Pogii Florentini, oratoris eloquentiss.   *W. de Worde.*   1535.   8°.

Bodl. (Douce A. 57).

Aesopi Fabulae.   *T. Marsh.*   1580.   8°.

Herbert, p. 868.

Æsopi Phrygis Fabulæ Jam recenter ex collatione optimorum exemplarium emendatius excusæ, *etc. Ex Academiæ celeberrimæ typographeo : Cantabrigiæ.* 1655. 8°.

B.M. (12305. b. 19).

[Another edition.] *J. Hayes : Cantabrigiæ.* 1670. 8°.
B.M. (012305. de. 1).

[Another edition.] *Ex Typographia Societatis Stationariorum.* 1691. 8°.
B.M. (12304. ccc. 35).

[Another edition.] Ab Infinitis pene Mendis repurgatæ, etc. *T. Hodgkin, pro Societate Stationariorum.* 1711. 8°.

B.M. (12305. aa. 14).

Fabularum Æsopicarum delectus. *E Theatro Sheldoniano, Oxford.* 1698. 8°.

B.M. (637. i. 13/2).

[Caxton's version.] *Begin :* Here begynneth the book of the subtyl historyes and Fables of Esope whiche were translated out of Frensshe in to Englysshe by wylliam Caxton at westmynstre In the yere of our Lorde . M.CCCC.lxxxiij. *W. Caxton, Westminster.* 1484. Fol. 𝕭.𝕷.
B.M. (C. 11. c. 17).

[Another edition.] *R. Pynson.* Fol. 𝕭.𝕷.
B.M. (IB. 55523), imperf.

[Another edition.] *R. Pynson.* Fol.
Priv. Lib., imperf.

[Another edition.] *L. Andrewe.* Fol.
Herbert, 1786, frag.

[Another edition.] [*W. Myddelton.*] 8°. 𝕭.𝕷.
Bodl. (Douce A. 40).

[Another edition.] *W. Powell.* 1551. 8°. 𝕭.𝕷.
Ashburnham. *Book Prices Current,* 1897.

[Another edition.] *W. Powell.* 8°.
Hazlitt, VII. 3.

[Another edition.] *I. Walley.* 8°. 𝕭.𝕷.
U.L.C. (Syn. 8. 56. 119), the title mutilated.

[Another edition.] *H. Wykes for J. Waley.* 8°. 𝕭.𝕷.

B.M. (12304. aaa. 32), the imprint cut away from the title-page.

[Another edition ?]

Licensed to Robert Waley, March 7, 1590/91 (*Stat. Reg.*, ii. 576).

[Another edition.] Æsop, Avicen [*sic*?], Alphonce and Poge's Fables. 1611.

Heber, v. 18.

[Another edition.] 𝕭.𝕷.

Bodl. (8°. B. 468. Linc.), imperf.

[Another edition.] *For A. Hebb.* 1634. 8°. 𝕭.𝕷.

B.M. (636. b. 38).

[Another edition.] *F. B. for A. Hebb.* 1647. 8°.

B.M. (12305. bb. 14).

[Another edition.] *J. Owsley and P. Lillicrap, for A. Roper.* 1658. 12°.

B.M. (E. 1889).

[Another edition.] *Sold by T. Fabian.* 1676. 12°.

Term Cat., i. 261.

[Another edition.] With near 200 cuts. [*For G. Conyers?*] 1700.

Term Cat., iii. 178.

[Bullokar's version.] AEsopź Fabl'ź in tru Ortŏgraphy with Grammar nótz . Her-yntoo ar al'so įooinęd the short sentenčez of the wýz Cato im-printęd with lýk form and order: bóth of which Autorź ar translátę out-of Latin intoo Énglish By William Bullokar. *E. Bollifant.* 1585, 8°. 𝕭.𝕷.

B.M. (C. 58. c. 23).

[Sturtevant's version.] The Etymologist of Æsop's Fables, Containing the construing of his Latine fables into English : Also The Etymologist of Phaedrus fables, containing the construing of Phaedrus (a new found ye auncient Author) into English, verbatim, Both very necessarie helps for young schollers. Compiled by Simon Sturtevant. *R. Field for R. Dexter.* 1602. 8°.

U.L.C. (Syn. 8. 60. 22).

[Brinsley's version.]

Licensed 7 Sept., 1617 (*Stat. Reg.* iii. 613).

[Another edition.] Esops Fables Translated both Grammatically, and also in propriety of our English phrase ; and, euery way, in such sort as may be most profitable for the Grammar-schoole, *etc.* *I. D. for T. Man.* 1624. 8°.

B.M. (C. 27. d. 11/3).

[Peacham's version.] Aesops Fables, with the Fables of Phaedrus Moralized, Translated . . . for the use of Grammar Schooles . . . Published by H. P. *I. L. for A. Hebb,* 1646. 8°.

B.M. (12304. a. 24/1).

[A different version.] Aesops Fables, with their Moralls, in Prose and verse Grammatically translated. Illustrated with Pictures, *etc.* *R. D. for P. Eglesfield.* 1651. 12°.

B.M. (12305. aaa. 27).

[Another edition.] *For F. Eglesfield.* 1670. 12°.
Term Cat., i. 28.

[Another edition.] The thirteenth Edition corrected. *For R. Bentley J. Phillips, H. Rhodes, and J. Taylor.* 1696. 12°.
Term Cat., ii. 572.

[Another edition.] The eighteenth edition, exactly corrected by W. D. 1721. 8°.
Dyce.

[Philipott's version.] Aesop's Fables, with his Life : in English, French and Latin. The English by Tho. Philipott Esq. ; the French and Latin by Rob. Codrington M.A. Illustrated with One hundred and Twelve Sculptures by Francis Barlow. *W. Godbid, and are to be sold by Ann Seile and E. Powell.* 1666. Fol.

The engraved title gives the date 1665, and Barlow as the publisher.

B.M. (637. k. 3).

[Ayres' version.] Mythologia Ethica : or, Three Centuries of Æsopian Fables. In English Prose. Done from Æsop, Phædrus, Camerarius . . . By Philip Ayres, Esq. *For T. Hawkins.* 1689. 8°.

B.M. (637. f. 13).

[L'Estrange's version.]   Fables of Aesop And other Eminent Mythologists, with Morals and Reflexions.   By Sir Roger L'Estrange, Kt.   *For R. Sare, T. Sawbridge, B. Took, M. Gillyflower, A. & J. Churchil, and J. Hindmarsh.* 1692.   Fol.

    B.M. (12304. l. 16).

[Another edition.]   The Second Edition Corrected and Amended.   *For R. Sare, B. Took, M. Gillyflower, A. & J. Churchil, J. Hindmarsh, and G. Sawbridge.*   1694.   Fol.

    B.M. (85. l. 1).

[Another edition.]   The Third Edition Corrected and Amended.   *For R. Sare, B. Took, M. Gillyflower, A. & J. Churchil, G. Sawbridge, and H. Hindmarsh.*   1699.   Fol.

    B.M. (12304. l. 11).

[Another edition.]   The Fourth Edition Corrected and Amended.   *For A. and J. Churchil, R. Sare, T. Goodwin, M. Wotton, D. Brown, J. Nicholson, G. Sawbridge, B. Tooke, G. Strahan.*   1704.   Fol.

    Term Cat., iii. 403.

[Another edition.]   The Sixth Edition Corrected.   *For R. Sare, A. and J. Churchil, D. Brown, T. Goodwin, M. Wotton, J. Nicholson, G. Sawbridge, B. Tooke, and G. Strahan.*   1714.   8°.

    B.M. (12304. cc. 31).

[Another edition.]   The Seventh Edition Corrected.   *For D. Brown, R. Sare, A. Roper, T. Norris, A. Bettesworth, G. Strahan, E. Valentine, T. Wotton, and S. Took.*   1724.   8°.

    B.M. (637. g. 40).

[Another edition.]   The Eighth Edition Corrected, *etc.*   *For A. Bettesworth, C. Hitch, G. Strahan, R. Gosling, R. Ware, J. Osborn, S. Birt, B. Motte, C. Bathurst, D. Browne, and J. Hodges.*   1738.   8°.

    Bodl. (Douce A. 500).

[Part 2 of L'Estrange's version.]   Fables and stories moralized.   Being a Second Part of the Fables of Æsop, And other Eminent Mythologists, &c. By Sir Roger L'Estrange, Kt.   Vol. II.   The Fourth Edition.   *For J. and J. Knapton, R. Williamson, T. Wotton, D. Brown, and T. Osborne.*   1730.   8°.

    Bodl. (Douce A. 501).

[Hoole's version.] Aesop's Fables, English and Latin . . . By Charles Hoole, *etc.* *R. E. for the Company of Stationers.* 1700. 8º.

B.M. (12304. aaa. 41).

[Another edition.] *J. Read for the Company of Stationers.* 1731. 12º.

B.M. (12305. aa. 2).

[Locke's version.] Aesops Fables, in English and Latin, Interlineary, for the Benefit of those who not having a Master Would Learn Either of these Tongues. With Sculptures. *For A. & J. Churchil,* 1703. 8º.

B.M. (1211. h. 33).

[Another issue.] The Second Edition. With Sculptures. By John Locke, Gent. *For A. Bettesworth.* 1723. 8º.

B.M. (1211. h. 38).

[Toland's version.] The Fables of Aesop. With the Moral Reflexions of Monsieur Baudoin. Translated from the French, *etc.* *For T. Leigh and D. Midwinter.* 1704. 8º.

B.M. (12304. ee. 40).

[Jackson's version.] A New Translation of Æsop's Fables, Adorn'd with Cutts . . . by . . . Christopher Van Sycham . . . By Joseph Jackson, *etc.* *For T. Tebb.* 1708. 12º.

Bodl. (Douce A. 118).

[Another edition.] Second Edition with Additions. By J. J., Gent. *For T. Tebb and T. King.* 1715. 12º.

B.M. (12304. aaa. 43).

[Croxall's version.] Fables of Aesop and Others. Newly done into English . . . Illustrated with Cutts, *etc.* *For J. Tonson and J. Watts.* 1722. 8º.

B.M. (C. 70. c. 9).

[Another edition.] The Third Edition, Improved. *For J. Tonson, and J. Watts.* 1731. 12º.

B.M. (12305. aaa. 34).

[Another version?] Aesop's Fables. *For H. Woodgate and S. Brooks.*
Woodgate and Brooks' list, in *Argalus and Parthenia.*

[Crouch's Part 2.] AEsop's Fables in Prose and Verse, the Second Part : collected from Antient and Modern Authors, with Pictures and proper morals to every Fable. Several applicable to the present time. By R. B. *For N. Crouch.* 1696.

> *Term Cat.*, ii. 596.

ALBERTI, LEON BATTISTA.

Amorous Fiammetta. *See* BOCCACCIO, Giovanni.

ALBION'S QUEEN.

[The famous Historie of Albions Queene.] *W. W. for T. Pauier.* 1601. 4°. 𝔅.𝔏.

> Priv. Lib. (imperf., wants title-page).

ALEMAN, MATEO.

The Rogue: Or The Life of Guzman de Alfarache. Written in Spanish by Matheo Aleman, *etc. For E. Blount.* 1622. Fol. 2 vols.

> Translated by James Mabbe ("Diego Puede-Ser"). Vol. 2 has the imprint "G. E. for E. Blount."
> Bodl. (M. 4. 10 Art.).

[Another edition.] *For E. Blount.* 1623. Fol. 2 vols.

> B.M. (12403. bb. 1).

[Another edition.] *W. Turner, Oxford, for R. Allot.* 1630. Fol.

> B.M. (12403. b. 16).

[Another edition.] To which is added the Tragi-Comedy of Calisto and Melibea, represented in Celestina. The third Edition corrected. *R.B. for R. Allot.* 1634, 33, 31. Fol.

> B.M. (635. l. 12).

[Another edition.] The Rogue: Or The Life of Guzman de Alfarache, the Witty Spaniard. In Two Parts. Written in Spanish, by Matheo Aleman . . . The Fifth and last Edition, corrected. *J. C. for P. Chetwind ; and are to be sold by T. Johnson.* 1656, 55. 8°. 2 vols.

> Vol. 2 has the imprint "Printed by H. Hills."
> Bodl. (Wood 305).

[Another edition?] Guzman de Alfarache. The fifth Edition. *H. Marsh,* [1661 ?].

> Marsh's list.

[A different version.] The Life of Guzman d'Alfarache : or, The Spanish Rogue. To which is added, The Celebrated Tragi-Comedy, Celestina. In Two Volumes. Written in Spanish by Mateo Aleman. Done into English from the New French Version, and compar'd with the Original. By several Hands. Adorn'd with Sculptures by Gaspar Bouttats. *For R. Bonwick, W. Freeman, T. Goodwin, J. Walthoe, M. Wotton, J. Nicholson, S. Manship, R. Parker, B. Tooke, and R. Smith,* 1708, 1707. 8°. 3 vols.

Celestina is in a separate volume, dated, like vol. 2, 1707. The contents of vol. 2, however, include ' Celestina, or the Spanish Bawd, p. 381.'

B.M. (12490. e. 5).

[Another edition of Book i., chapter viii.] The Loves of Osmin and Daraxa. Translated from the French. 1721.

[Another edition]. 1729. *See* CROXALL, Samuel. A Select Collection of Novels, vol. vi.

[Another edition of Book iii., chapter ii.] The Amour of Count Palviano and Eleonora. Translated from the French, 1721.

[Another edition.] 1729. *See* CROXALL, Samuel. A Select Collection of Novels, vol. v.

[An abridgement.] The Rogue : or, The Excellencie of History displayed, the Notorious Life of that Incomparable Thief, Guzman de Alfarache, the Witty Spaniard. Written originally in Spanish, by Matheo Aleman . . . And from the same Epitomiz'd into English, by A. S. Gent. *J. C. for the Author ; and are to be sold by T. Johnson and S. Chatfield.* 1655. 8°.

Bodl. (Douce A. 433).

[Another edition.] The Spanish Rogue, or, The Life of Guzman de Alfarache . . . In two Parts, *etc. For T. Smith.* 12°.

B.M. (12490. aa. 20).

AMADIS OF GAUL.

The moste excellent and pleasaunt Booke, entituled : The treasurie of Amadis of Fraunce. Conteyning eloquente orations, pythie Epistles, learned Letters, and feruent Complayntes . . . Translated out of Frenche into English. *H. Bynneman for T. Hacket* [1567/8]. 4°. 𝕭.𝕷.

Extracts from *Amadis*, translated by Thomas Paynell.

B.M. (C. 34. e. 62).

[The first Book of Amadis of Gaule. Discoursing the Aduentures and Loue of many Knightes and Ladies, as well of the Realme of great Brittayne, as sundry other Countries, &c.] 4°. 𝔅.𝔏.

Translated by Anthony Munday from the French.

Books 1–4 were licensed to E. Allde, 15 Jan., 1588/9 (*Stat. Reg.* ii., 514), books 2–5 to J. Wolfe, 10 April, 1592 (*Stat. Reg.* ii. 607), books 2–12 to A. Islip and W. Moring, 16 Oct., 1594 (*Stat. Reg.* ii. 662), and book 13 ("the first parte of the Historye of Don Silves de Silva") to W. White, 29 May, 1609 (*Stat. Reg.* iii. 410). The numeration of books is that of the French series.

B.M. (C. 57. e. 30), imperf., wanting title = Hazlitt, H. 7 (1595)?

The Seconde Booke of Amadis de Gaule. Containing the description, wonders, and conquest of the Firme-Island . . . . Englished by L. P. *For C. Burbie.* 1595. 4°. 𝔅.𝔏.

L. P. is Lazarus Pyot, *i.e.,* Anthony Munday.

B.M. (C. 39. e. 11).

The Ancient, Famous and Honourable History of Amadis de Gaule . . . Written in French by the Lord of Essars, Nicholas de Herberay, *etc. N. Okes,* 1619, 1618. Fol. 4 vols.

Books 1–4. Vols. 3 and 4 are dated 1618. The dedications are signed A. M. [*i.e.,* Anthony Munday.]

B.M. (C. 21. d. 3).

The Fifth Book of the Most Pleasant and Delectable History of Amadis De Gaule, *etc. T. J. for A. Kembe and C. Tyus.* 1664. 4°. 𝔅.𝔏.

B.M. (1075. f. 6).

The Famous and Renowned History of Amadis de Gaule . . . Being the sixt Part never before Published. Translated out of French into English, by Francis Kirkman. *Jane Bell,* 1652. 4°.

B.M. (1075. l. 7), the date cut away. Hazlitt, H. 8.

Amadis of Gaule. The Seventh Book. 1694. 4°. 𝔅.𝔏.

Books 7 and 8 are announced as in preparation in the advertisement of Tyus' Book 5, 1664 (printed in *Palladine,* 1664).

Hazlitt, H. 8.

The most Excellent and Famous History Of the Most Renowned Knight Amadis of Greece, Surnam'd The Knight of the Burning Sword, son to Lisvart of Greece, and the Fair Onoloria of Trebisond . . . By a Person of Quality. *For J. Deacon and J. Blare.* 1693. 4°.

Book 7. Also advertised by B. Deacon in his ed. of *The Seven Champions.*

Huth Sale, i. no. 136.

[A reissue.] *For J. Deacon and J. Blare.*   1694.   4°.   𝕭.𝕸.
   B.M. (G. 10490).

[An abridgement?] The History of Amadis de Gaul.   *For T. Passinger.*   4°.
Passinger's list (in *Valentine and Orson*, 1685).

[An abridgement.] The History of Amadis de Gaul.   *For E. Tracy.*   4°.
Tracy's list (in *Valentine and Orson*).

[Another edition?]   The Famous and Delightful History of the Renowned
and Valiant Prince Amadis de Gaule . . .   The Whole now Abridg'd by
J. S. Gent.   *For J. Gwillim.*   1702.   12°.
   J. S. is John Shurley.
      B.M. (12450. aaa. 13).

See (in Part II) FLORES, *Don.*

ANEAU, BARTHÉLÉMI.

Αλεκτωρ.   The Cock.   Containing the first part of the most excellent, and
Mytheologicall Historie of the valorous Squire Alector ;   Sonne to the
Renowned Prince Macrobius Franc-Gal ; and to the Peerelesse Princesse
Priscaraxe, Queene of High Tartary.   *T. Orwin, and are to be solde by
E. White.*   1590.   4°.   𝕭.𝕸.
      Hazlitt, I. 9 ; Lowndes 44.

ANTON, ROBERT.

Moriomachia.   *S. Stafford.*   1613.   4°.   𝕭.𝕸.
      B.M. (C. 40. e. 58).

APOLLONIUS.

Kynge Appolyn of Thyre.   *W. de Worde.*   1510.   4°.   𝕭.𝕸.
      Devonshire.

[The most excellent pleasant and variable historie of the strange aduentures
of prince Apollonius Lucina his wife and Tharsa his Daughter.]
   Licensed to W. Howe, 17 July, 1576 (*Stat. Reg.*, ii. 301).

[Another edition.]   The Patterne of painefull Aduentures : Containing the
most excellent, pleasant, and variable Historie of the strange accidents that
befell vnto Prince Apollonius, the Lady Lucina his wife, and Tharsia his
daughter.   Wherein the vncertaintie of this world, and the fickle state of

man's life are liuely described.   Gathered into English by Laurence Twine
Gentleman.   *V. Simmes for the Widow Newman.*   [1594?]   4°.   𝕭.𝕷.

    B.M. (Huth 43).

[Another edition.]   Translated into English by T. Twine Gent.   *V. Sims.*
1607.   4°.   𝕭.𝕷.

[Another edition?]

Licensed to Mistress Griffin and J. Haviland, 7 June, 1621 (*Stat. Reg.*, iv. 55.)

See WILKINS, George.

APULEIUS, LUCIUS.

The xi Bookes of the Golden Asse, Conteininge the Metamorphosie of
Lucius Apuleius, enterlaced with sondrie pleasaunt and delectable Tales, with
an excellent Narration of the Marriage of Cupido and Psiches, set out in the
iiij. v. and vi Bookes.   Translated out of Latine into Englishe by William
Adlington.   *H. Wykes* 1566.   4°.   𝕭.𝕷.

The Latin was licensed to the partners in the English Stock, 22 June, 1631 (*Stat. Reg.*,
iv. 255).
    B.M. (C. 21. b. 31).

[Another edition.]   *W. How for A. Veale.*   1571.   4°.   𝕭.𝕷.

    B.M. (244. k. 23).

[Another edition.]   *T. East for A. Veale.*   1582.   8°.   𝕭.𝕷.

    B.M. (12410. aa. 42).

[Another edition.]   *V. Symmes.*   1596.   4°.   𝕭.𝕷.

    B.M. (C. 34. h. 39).

[Another edition?]

Licensed to C. Knight, 26 June, 1600.   (*Stat. Reg.*, iii. 164.)

[Another edition?]

"Translated by W. S." (=W. A. ?).   Licensed to J. Thomas, 12 July, 1637.   (*Stat.
Reg.* ii. 389.)

[Another edition.]   *T. Harper for T. Alchorn.*   1639.   4°.   𝕭.𝕷.

See (in Part II) MONTE SOCIO, Carlo de.

ARCADIAN PRINCESS.   *See* SILESIO, Mariano.

ARGALUS AND PARTHENIA.   *See* SIDNEY, Sir Philip.

ARIANA. *See* Desmarets de Saint Sorlin, Jean.

ARNALT AND LUCENDA. *See* San Pedro, Diego de.

ARTHUR OF LITTLE BRITAIN.

Arthur of Brytayn. The hystory of the moost noble and valyaunt knyght Arthur of lytell brytayne, translated out of frensshe in to englisshe by the noble Iohan bourghcher knyght lorde Barners, newly Imprynted. *R. Redborne.* Fol. 𝕭.𝕷.

J.R.L.

[Another edition.] The History of the Most Noble and valyant Knyght Arthur of Little Britaine, Translated out of French into English By the Noble Iohn Bourghchere Knight Lord Berners. *T. East.* [1581.] 4°. 𝕭.𝕷.

Licensed to East, 12 March, 1581–2.
Hazlitt, H. 14.

AUDIGUIER, Vital d'.

Lisander and Calista, a tragi-comical History. 1621. Fol.

Hazlitt, H. 336.

[Another edition.] A Tragi-Comicall History of our Times, under the borrowed names of Lisander, And Calista. *H. L[ownes] for G. Latham.* 1627. Fol.

Translated by W. D.
Licensed to Latham, 25 Aug., 1626. (*Stat. Reg.*, iv. 166.)
B.M. (12612. i. 8).

[Another edition.] *R. Y. for G. Latham.* 1635. Fol.
Priv. Lib.

[Another edition.] *For R. Lownes.* 1652. 8°.
B.M. (12611. de. 20).

Love and Valour : Celebrated in the person of the Author, by the name of Adraste. Or, The divers affections of Minerva. One part of the unfained story of Lisander and Caliste ; Translated out of the French by W. B[arwick]. *T. Harper, for T. Slater.* 1638. 4°.

In two parts ; Part 2 is entitled "Divers Amorous Epistles wrote by the Author to the same Lady, during the time mentioned in the precedent story, and not therein spoke of."
B.M. (12512. c. 1).

AURELIA. *See* Whetstone, George.

AVERELL, WILLIAM.

A Dyall for dainty Darlings, rockt in the Cradle of Securitie.   A Glasse for all Disobedient Sonnes to looke in.   A Myrrour for vertuous Maydes.   A Booke right excellent, garnished with many woorthy examples, and learned aucthorities, most needefull for this tyme present.   Compiled by W. Auerell, Student in Diuinitie, and Schoolemaister in London.   *For T. Hackette.* 1584.   4°.   𝕭.𝕷.

B.M. (C. 37. c. 7).

Foure notable Histories, applyed to foure worthy examples: As, 1.   A Diall for daintie darlings.   2. A spectacle for negligent Parents.   3. A glasse for disobedient Sonnes.   4. And a myrrour for virtuous Maydes.   Whereunto is added a Dialogue, expressing the corruptions of this age.   A booke right excellent and profitable, garnished with many learned authorities, necessary for this time present.   Written by W. A.   *For T. Hacket.*   1590.   4°.   𝕭.𝕷.

Hazlitt, I. 18.

AYMON.

[The Four Sons of Aymon.]   [*W. Caxton. Westminster,* 1489 ?]   Fol. 𝕭.𝕷.

J.R.L., imperf.

[Another edition.]   The right pleasant and goodly historie of the foure Sonnes of Aimon.   *W. de Worde.*   1504.   Fol.   𝕭.𝕷.

T. Osborne's Comarque Sale Catalogue, no. 1629 (Hazlitt, VII. 423).   U.L.C. (Syn. 7. 50. 9/6, 7) frag.   *Cf.* the colophon of Copland's edition of 1554.

[Another edition.]   The right plesaunt and goodly Historie of the foure sonnes of Aimon, the which for the excellent endytyng of it, and for the notable Prowes and great vertues that were in them: is no les pleasaunt to rede, then worthy to be knowen of all estates bothe hyghe and lowe. *W. Copland, for T. Petet.*   1554.   Fol.   𝕭.𝕷.

The colophon reads: "Here finissheth the hystory of the noble ℭ valiaunt knyght Reynawde of Mountawban, and his three brethern.   Imprinted at London by Wynkyn de worde, the . viii. daye of maye, and yᵉ yere of our lorde . M.CCCCC.iiii . . . And now Emprinted in the yere of our Lorde . M.CCCCC. liiii. the vi . daye of Maye, by Wylliam Copland, for Thomas Petet"; in the Bridgewater copy: ". . . And now Imprinted in the yere of our Lorde . M.CCCCC. liiii. the vi daye of maye, By Wylliam Copland, dwellyng in Fletestrete at the Signe of the Rose Garland, for Iohn Waley."

B.M. (C. 12. i. 7).

Licensed to T. East, 12 March, 1581-2, and to T. Purfoot, sen., 5 Feb., 1598-9; the last part to J. Wolfe, 22 Feb., 1598-9 (*Stat. Reg.* ii. 408, iii. 137, 139).

B., R. *See* BERNARD, Richard.

BACON, FRANCIS.

[The New Atlantis: in] Sylva Sylvarvm: or A Naturall Historie. In ten centvries. Written by the right Honourable Francis Lo. Verulam Viscount S⁺· Alban. Published after the Authors death, By William Rawley Doctor of Diuinitie, late his Lordships Chaplaine. *J. H[aviland] for W. Lee.* 1626. Fol.

> The engraved title is dated 1627.
> Bodl. (List. D. 2).

[Another edition.] *J. H[aviland] for W. Lee.* 1627. Fol.
> B.M. (G. 2449).

[Another edition.] The second Edition. *J. H[aviland] for W. Lee.* 1628. Fol.
> Hazlitt, II. 24.

[Another edition.] *J. H[aviland] for W. Lee.* 1631. Fol.
> Hazlitt, II. 24.

[Another edition.] *J. Haviland for W. Lee.* 1635. Fol.
> B.M. (442. g. 5).

[Another edition.] The fifth Edition. *J. Haviland, for W. Lee.* 1639. Fol.
> B.M. (535. k. 11).

[Another edition.] The sixt Edition. *J. F. for W. Lee.* 1651. Fol.
> B.M. (442. g. 6).

[Another edition.] The Seventh Edition. *A. M. for W. Lee, and are to be sold . . . by T. Johnson.* 1658. Fol.
> B.M. (535. i. 11.)

[Another edition.] New Atlantis. A Work unfinished. Written by the Right Honorable, Francis, Lord Verulam, Viscount St. Alban. *T. Newcomb.* 1659. 4°.
> Issued as a supplement to *Mr. Bushell's Abridgment Of the Lord Chancellor Bacon's Philosophical Theory in Mineral Prosecutions,* 1659.
> B.M. (G. 19405/2).

[Another edition.] New Atlantis. Begun by the Lord Verulam, Viscount St. Albans: And Continued by R. H., *etc. For J. Crooke.* 1660. 8°.
> B.M. (E. 1797/2).

[Another edition : in] Sylva Sylvarum . . . The Eighth Edition, *etc. J. F. and S. G. for W. Lee, and are to be sold by T. Williams.* 1664. Fol.

B.M. (730. l. 40).

[Another edition.] The Ninth and Last Edition, *etc. J. R. for W. Lee.* 1670. Fol.

B.M. (986. g. 14).

[Another edition.] The Tenth Edition, *etc. S. G. and B. Griffin for T. Lee.* 1676. Fol.

B.M. (730. l. 41).

[Another edition]. Whereunto is added . . . The new Atlantis . . . The Eleventh Edition. *Sold by D. Brown and R. Sare.* 1684. Fol.

Term. Cat., ii. 105.

[Another edition : in] Francisci Baconi . . . Opera Omnia, *etc. R. Gosling.* 1730. Fol. 4 vols.

The New Atlantis is in Vol. 3.

B.M. (12268 k. 1).

[A continuation.] *See* (in Part II.) GLANVILL, Joseph.

BACON, FRIAR.

[The Historye of Fryer Bacon and Fryer Boungaye.]

Licensed to E. White, 14 May, 1594 (*Stat. Reg.* ii. 649).

[Another edition.]

Licensed to F. Grove, 12 Jan., 1623/4 (*Stat. Reg.* iv. 110).

[Another edition.] The Famous Historie of Fryer Bacon. Containing the wonderfull things that he did in his Life : Also the manner of his Death ; With the Liues and Deaths of the two Coniurers, Bungye and Vandermast, *etc. G. P. for F. Groue.* 1627. 4°. 𝔅.𝔏.

B.M. (1077. e. 58).

[Another edition.] *E. A. for F. Groue.* 1629. 4°. 𝔅.𝔏.

Bridgewater.

[Another edition.] *E. A. for F. Groue.* 4°. 𝔅.𝔏.

Licensed, with *Robin Goodfellow*, to H. Gosson, 23 March, 1630–31 (*Stat. Reg.*, iv. 250). Hazlitt, H. 21. Thoms, *Early English Prose Romances*.

[Another edition.] *T. C.* 1640. 4°. 𝕭.𝕷.
  Priv. Lib.

[Another edition.] *E. Cotes, for F. Grove.* 1661. 4°. 𝕭.𝕷.
  B.M. (12612. e. 2).

[Another edition.] *E. Cotes, and are to be sold by T. Passinger.* 1666.
4°. 𝕭.𝕷.
  B.M. (12430. c. 14).

[Another edition.] *M. Clark, and are to be sold by T. Passenger.* 1679.
4°. 𝕭.𝕷.
  Pepys, 1192 (13).

[Another edition.] *For T. Passenger.* 1682. 4°.
  Term Cat. i. 480.

[Another edition.] *For M. W[otton ?].* 1683. 12°. 𝕭.𝕷.
  Bodl. (Wood 707/1),

[Another edition.] *For W. Thackery, and C. Bates.* 4°. 𝕭.𝕷.
  B.M. (12613. c. 17).

[Another edition.] The Most Famous History of the Learned Fryer
Bacon; shewing his Parentage and Birth, *etc.* *T. Norris At the sign of the
Looking-glass on London Bridge.* 4°.
  Dealer's list. Identical with the following?

[Another edition.] *T. Norris ; And Sold by M. Deacon.* 4°.
  Hazlitt, VII. 18.

[Another edition.] *For R. Deacon.* 4°.
  Hazlitt, II. 22. Also advertised by B. Deacon in his ed. of *The Seven Champions.*

[Another edition.] *For T. Norris.* 4°.
  B.M. (1077. g. 32).

The History of Fryer Bacon : The Second Part : Being a most true and
exact relation of the most famous and merry Exploits of . . . Miles Wagner,
etc. For J. Blare. 8°. 𝕭.𝕷.
  Bodl. (Wood 707).

BALDWIN, William.

A Maruellous Hystory intituled Beware the Cat. 1561. 8°. 𝕭.𝕷.
  Ritson, *Bibl. Poet,* p. 118.

[Another edition.] Conteynyng diuerse wounderfull and incredible matters. Very pleasant and mery to read.   *W. Gryffyth.*   1570.   8°.   𝕭.𝕷.

Corser, *Collect. Anglo-Poet,* i. 108, a fragment of 4 leaves.

[Another edition.]   *E. Allde.*   1584.   8°.   𝕭.𝕷.

B.M. (Huth 66), imperf., wanting title.

[Another edition.]   *For Jane Bell.*   1652.   8°.
Bagford frag.

The mirrour of mirrours, or all the tragedys of the mirrour for magistrates abbreuiated in breefe histories in prose.   Very necessary for those that haue not the cronicle.   *For J. Roberts.*

Warton, ed. Hazlitt, iv. 209.

BARCLAY, JOHN.

[Argenis.]

Licensed, in 8°, to "the partenors in the Latten stocke," 29 June, 1622 (*Stat. Reg.* iv. 72), the second part (in Latin?) to Islip, 18 Jan., 1626–7 (*Stat. Reg.* iv. 172).

[Another edition?]

Ioannis Barclaii Argenis.   Editio novissima.   Cum Clave, *etc.   I. L. impensis T. Huggins: Oxoniae.*   1634.   12°.

B.M. (12410. a. 32).

[Another edition.]   Editio ultima Correctior & Emendatior.   *J. Hayes, Impensis J. Creed: Cantabrigiae.*   1673.   8°.

B.M. (12403. a. 9).

[Ben Jonson's version.]

Licensed to *E. Blount,* 2 Oct., 1623 (*Stat. Reg.* iv. 105).

[Long's version.]   Barclay his Argenis : or, The Loves of Poliarchus and Argenis : Faithfully translated out of Latine into English, By Kingesmill Long Gent.   *G. P. for H. Seile.*   1625.   Fol.

Long's version was licensed to Seile, 1 Jan., 1624/5 (*Stat. Reg.* iv. 133).
B.M. (12403. g. 12).

[Another edition.]   Barclay his Argenis, or, The Loves of Polyarchus & Argenis.   Faithfully Translated out of Latin into English by Kingsmill Long Esquire.   The Second Edition, Beautified with Pictures.   Together with a Key Præfixed to vnlock the whole Story.   *For H. Seile.*   1636.   4°.

B.M. (838. c. 1).

[Le Grys' version.] Iohn Barclay his Argenis, Translated out of Latine into English: The Prose vpon His Maiesties Command: By Sir Robert Le Grys, Knight: And the Verses by Thomas May, Esquire. With a Clauis annexed, *etc.* *F. Kyngston for R. Meighen and H. Seile.* 1628. 4°.

U.L.C. (Adams 6. 62. 7).

[Another edition.] *F. Kyngston for R. Meighen and H. Seile.* 1629. 4°.

B.M. (839. d. 40).

An Epitome of the History of Faire Argenis and Polyarchus, Extracted out of the Latin, and put in French, by that Great and Famous Writer, M. N. Coeffeteau Bishop of Marseilles. And translated out of the French into English by a yong Gentlewoman, *etc.* *E. G. for H. Seile.* 1640. 8°.

Translated by Judith Man.
Priv. Lib.

Euphormionis Lusinini, Sive Ioannis Barclaii Partes quinq₅, *etc.* *I.L. Impensis H. Cripps: Oxoniae.* 1634. 12°.

B.M. (836. a. 4).

BEARD, Thomas.

The Theatre of Gods Iudgements: Or, A Collection of Histories out of Sacred, Ecclesiasticall, and prophane Authours, concerning the admirable Iudgements of God vpon the transgressours of his commandements. Translated out of French, and augmented by more than three hundred Examples, by Th. Beard. *A. Islip.* 1597. 4°.

B.M. (4404. i. 7).

[Another edition.] The Theatre of Gods Iudgements. Wherein is repre-sented the admirable iustice of God against all notorious Sinners . . . Collected out of Sacred, Ecclesiasticall, and prophane Histories: Now secondly printed, and augmented with at least two Centuries of examples. By the first Author thereof, Thomas Beard, *etc.* *A. Islip.* 1612. 4°.

B.M. (4376. aa. 3).

[Another edition.] Reuised and augmented. Now thirdly printed, and encreased with many more Examples, *etc.* *A. Islip, for M. Sparke.* 1631. 4°.

B.M. (1364. a. 5).

[Another edition.] Collected . . . by . . . Thomas Beard . . . and Tho. Taylor . . . The fourth Edition, With Additions. *S. I. & M. H. and are to be sold by T. Whitaker.* 1648. Fol.

B.M. (G. 19651).

BELING, RICHARD.

A Sixth Booke to the Countesse of Pembrokes Arcadia.   *See* SIDNEY, *Sir* Philip.

BELLEFOREST, FRANÇOIS DE.
  The Hystorie of Hamblet.   *R. Bradocke for T. Pauier.*   1608.   4°.   𝕭.𝕿.
    T.C.C. (Capell, S. 33. 3).

BELLIANIS.
  The Honour of Chiualrie.   Set downe in the most Famous Historie of the Magnanimous and Heroike Prince Don Bellianis : Sonne vnto the Emperour Don Bellaneo of Greece.   Wherein are described, the straunge and dangerous Adventures that him befell.   With his loue towards the Princesse Florisbella : Daughter vnto the Souldan of Babylon.   Englished out of Italian by L. A.   *T. Creede,* 1598.   4°.   𝕭.𝕿.
    B.M. (Huth 60).

  [Another edition.]   The Honour of Chivalry : Or the famous and delectable History of Don Bellianis of Greece . . .   Translated out of Italian, *etc.*   *B. Alsop.*   1650.   4°.
    B.M. (12450. e. 16).

  [Another version.]   The second Part.   Illustrated with Pictures.   Now newly written in English by F. K., *etc.*   *T. Johnson.*   1664.   4°.   𝕭.𝕿.
    F. K. is Francis Kirkman.
    An edition, "printed for Charles Tyus," was advertised in *Palladine,* 1664, the second part being then in the press.
    Bridgewater.

  [Another edition.]   The Famous and Delectable History of Don Bellianis of Greece, or, the Honour of Chivalry . . .   Now newly writen, by Francis Kirkman.   *For F. Kirkman.*   1673, 71, 72.   4°.   𝕭.𝕿.
    B.M. (C. 39. d. 43).

  [Another edition.]   The Honour of Chivalry, or The Famous and Delectable History of Don Bellianis of Greece.   *For T. Passenger.*   1678.   4°.
    Term Cat., i. 316.

  [Another edition.]   *For T. Passinger.*   1683.   4°.   3 parts, 2 vols.   𝕭.𝕿.
    Part 1 of the 1650 version.   The second and third parts are written by J. Shurley.
    B.M. (12403. a. 30).

[Another edition.]   *For E. Tracy.*   1703.   4°.

B.M. (12410. f. 20).

[An abridgement.]   The Honour of Chivalry: Or, The Renowned and Famous History of Don Bellianis of Greece, *etc.*   *W. O[nley].*   4°.

Bodl. (Douce R. 528).

[Another edition.]   The Honour of Chivalry: Or the Famous and Delectable History of Don Bellianis of Greece ...   Translated out of Italian, *etc.* *For J. S[tarkey?].*   8°.

B.M. (12450. b. 10).

BELLORA AND FIDELIO.   *See* FLORES, Juan de.

BERNARD, RICHARD.

The Isle of Man: Or, The Legall Proceeding in Man-shire against Sinne. Wherein, by way of a continued Allegorie, the chiefe Malefactors disturbing both Church and Common Wealth, are detected and attached ...   By R. B., Rector of Batcomb, Somers.   The fourth Edition much enlarged. *For E. Blackmore.*   1627.   12°.

Licensed to Blackmore, 4 Nov., 1626 (*Stat. Reg.*, iv. 169).
B.M. (1018. b. 19).

[Another edition.]   The fifth Edition much enlarged.   *For E. Blackmore.* 1628.   12°.

Hazlitt, II. 47.

[Another edition.]   The seventh Edition.   [*F. Kyngston?*] *for E. Blackmore.*   1630.   12°.

U.L.C. (Syn. 8. 63. 30/1).

[Another edition.]   The eighth Edition.   *G. M[iller] for E. Blackmore.* 1632.   12°.

U.L.C. (Syn. 8. 63. 289).

[Another edition.]   The tenth Edition.   *I. H[aviland] for E. Blackmore.* 1635.   12°.

U.L.C. (Syn. 8. 63. 125).

[Another edition.]   The eleventh Edition.   *G. M. for E. Blackmore.* 1640.   12°.

B.M. (4413. a. 9).

[Another edition.] The Twelfth Edition. *J. D. for E. Blackmore.* 1648. 12°.
U.L.C. (2. 76. 1).

[Another edition.] The Thirteenth Edition. *For N. Ranew.* 1659. 12°.
B.M. (4409. bb. 4).

[Another edition.] The Fourteenth Edition. *T. Milbourn for T. S. and
are to be sold by J. Wright.* 1668. 12°.
B.M. (4401. aa. 38).

[Another edition.] The Fifteenth Edition. *For J. Wright and T. Sawbridge.* 1676. 12°.
Term Cat., i. 262.

[Another edition.] The Sixteenth Edition. *T. M.* 1683. 12°.
B.M. (856. a. 19).

BETTIE, W.
The Historie of Titana and Theseus . . . Written by W. Bettie. *For
R. Bird.* 1636. 4°. 𝖁.𝖑.
B.M. (12410. bb. 11).

BEWARE THE CAT. *See* BALDWIN, William.

BIDPAI.
The Morall Philosophie of Doni : drawne out of the auncient writers. A
worke first compiled in the Indian tongue, and afterwardes reduced into
diuers other languages : and now lastly englished out of Italian by Thomas
North, *etc.* *H. Denham.* 1570. 4°. 𝖁.𝖑.

"Wytty fayned saynges of men, beastes and fowles marylized," licensed to H. Bynneman
in 1569-70 (*Stat. Reg.*, i. 399), may refer to the Fables of Bidpai, or to the *Dialogi
Creaturarum.*
Bodl. (Douce S. 195).

[Another edition.] *S. Stafford.* 1601. 4°. 𝖁.𝖑.
B.M. (C. 33. f. 2).

[A different version.] The Fables of Pilpay, A Famous Indian Phyloso-
pher : Containing many useful Rules for the Conduct of Humane Life.
Made English, and Address'd to his Highness the Duke of Gloucester. *For
D. Brown, C. Connigsby* [*sic*]*, D. Midwinter and T. Leigh.* 1699. 12°.
B.M. (243. e. 8).

See DIALOGI CREATURARUM.

BIONDI, GIOVANNI FRANCESCO.

Donzella Desterrada, or, The Banish'd Virgin. Written originally in Italian : By Cavalier Gio. Francesco Biondi . . . Divided into three Bookes : and Englished by I. H. of Graies Inne, Gent. *T. Cotes for H. Mosley.* 1635. Fol.

Translated by James Hayward.
B.M. (12470. k. 10).

[Another edition.] *For Anne Moseley* [1663 ?].

Anne Moseley's list, 1663.

Eromena, or, Love and Revenge. Written originally in the Thoscan tongue, by Cavalier Gio. Francesco Biondi . . . Divided into six Books. And now faithfully Englished, by Ia. Hayward, of Graies-Inne, Gent. *R. Badger, for R. Allot.* 1632. Fol.

B.M. (12470. k. 9).

[Another edition.] Love and Revenge. An excellent Romance, in Six Books. Written by Cavalier Biondi. Englished by James Hayward, of Gray's Inn, Gent. The Second Edition. 1690.

Term Cat., ii. 316.

BLANCHARDINE AND EGLANTINE.

Begin : Here begynneth the table of the victoryous prynce Blanchardyn, sone of the noble Kyng of Fryse, etc. [*W. Caxton : Westminster*, 1489 ?]. Fol. 𝕭.𝕷.

J. R. L., imperf.

[A different version.] The Moste Pleasaunt Historye of Blanchardine Sonne to the King of Friz ; & the faire Lady Eglantine, Queene of Tormaday (surnamed) the proud Ladye in Loue. *For W. Blackewall.* 1595. 4°. 𝕭.𝕷. 2 vols.

The title of part 2 bears the ascription "By P T G Gent," *i.e.*, Thomas Pope Goodwin.
Britwell.

[Another edition.] By P. T. G. Gent. *G. Shaw, for W. Blackwall.* 1597. 4°.

The dedication is signed Thomas Pope Goodwine.
Public Library, Hamburg, part 1 only (Hazlitt, I. 40).

BLOOD FOR BLOOD. *See* REYNOLDS, John.

BOCCACCIO, Giovanni.

Amorous Fiammetta.   Wherein is sette downe a catologue [*sic*] of all and singuler passions of Loue and iealosie, incident to an enamored yong Gentlewoman, with a notable caueat for all women to eschewe deceitfull and wicked Loue, by an apparant example of a Neapolitan Lady, her approued & long miseries, and wyth many sounde dehortations from the same.   First wrytten in Italian by Master Iohn Boccace, the learned Florentine, and Poet Laureat. And now done into English by B. Giouano de M. Temp., *etc.*   *I. C. for T. Gubbin and T. Newman.*   1587.   4°.   𝕭.𝕷.

Sometimes attributed to Leon Battista Alberti.   The translator was Bartholomew Yong of the Middle Temple.
B.M. (C. 57. b. 46).

The Decameron Containing An hundred pleasant Nouels.   Wittily discoursed, betwene seauen Honourable Ladies, and three Noble Gentlemen. *I. Iaggard.*   1620.   Fol.   2 vols.

Licensed to W. Jaggard, 22 March, 1620, but the license was recalled by the Archbishop of Canterbury (*Stat. Reg.* iii. 667).   An Italian edition had been licensed to John Wolfe, 13 Sept., 1587 (*Stat. Reg.* ii. 475).
B.M. (86. k. 2).

[Another edition.]   The Modell of Wit, Mirth, Eloquence, and Conuersation.   Framed in Ten Dayes, of an hundred curious Pieces, by seuen Honourable Ladies and three Noble Gentlemen.   Preserued to Posterity by the Renowned Iohn Boccacio, the first Refiner of Italian prose : And now translated into English.   *I. Iaggard, for M. Lownes.*   1625.   Fol.

The first five Days.
B.M. ; Bodl. (Douce B. Subt. 277).

[Another edition.]   *T. Cotes.*   1634.   8°.

Hazlitt, H. 41.

[Another edition.] . . . The Fourth Edition.   *E. Cotes.*   1657, 1655.   12°. 2 vols.

B.M. ; Priv. Lib.

[Another edition.]   The Novels and Tales of the Renowned John Boccacio, The first Refiner of Italian Prose : containing A hundred curious Novels . . . The Fifth Edition, much Corrected and Amended.   *For A. Churchill.*   1684.   Fol.   2 parts.

B.M. (634. l. 6).

[A different version, abridged.]   Il Decamerone, One Hundred Ingenious Novels :   Written by John Boccacio, The first Refiner of the Italian

Language. Now done into English, and accommodated to the Gust of the present Age. *For J. Nicholson, J. Knapton, and B. Tooke.* 1702. 8°.

B.M. (12470. e. 4).

[Another edition.] Il Decamerone : Or, Decads, Consisting of One Hundred Ingenious Novels : Written by John Boccacio, First Refiner of the Italian Language. Now newly done into English, and accommodated to the Gust of the present Age ; with an Argument and Moral added to each Novel. The Second Edition, Carefully Corrected and Amended. *For J. Nicholson, J. Knapton, and B. Tooke.* 1722. 8°.

B.M. (12470. d. 25).

Titus and Gisippus.

See ELYOT, *Sir* Thomas. The boke named the Gouernour.

Giorn. x. Nov. 8 of the *Decameron*.

[Ninfale Fiesolano.] A Famous tragicall discourse of two lovers, Affrican and Mensola, their lives, infortunate loves, and lamentable deaths, to-gether with the ofspring of the Florentines. A History no lesse pleasant then full of recreation and delight. Newly translated out of Tuscan into French by Anthony Guerin [Guercin] domino Creste, And out of French into English by Jo. Goubourne. *J. R[oberts] for W. Blackman.* 1597. 4°. 𝕭.𝕷.

Hazlitt, H. 234.

[Philocolo.] [A pleasant disport of diuers Noble Personages.] *A. Ieffes, and are to be solde . . . by T. Woodcocke.* 1566. 8°. 𝕭.𝕷.

Bodl. (Tanner 515), imperf.

[Another edition.] A pleasaunt disport of diuers Noble Personages. Written in Italian by M. Iohn Boccace Florentine and Poet Laureat. in his Boke which is entituled Philocopo. And nowe Englished by H. G. *H. Bynneman, for R. Smyth and N. England.* 1567. 4°. 𝕭.𝕷.

B.M. (C. 57. c. 35).

[Another edition.] Thirtene most plesant and delectable Questions, entituled A disport of diuers noble personages Written in Italian by M. Iohn Bocace, Florentine and Poet Laureate, in his Booke named Philocopo. Englished by H. G. *H. Bynneman for R. Smyth.* 1571. 8°. 𝕭.𝕷.

Bodl. (Tanner 133).

[Another edition.] *A. J[effes] and are to be sold by T. Woodcock.* 1587. 8°. 𝕭.𝕷.

B.M. (C. 12. d. 13).

BOISROBERT, François le Metel de.

[The History of Annaxander [*sic*] and Orazia. An Indian story. Translated out of French into English by William Duncomb.]

Licensed to S. Waterson, 13 Nov., 1639 (*Stat. Reg.* iv. 488).

For the version of 1657, *see* in Part II.

BORDE, Andrew. *See* Scoggin, John.

BRAITHWAITE, Richard.

Ar't asleepe Husband? A Boulster Lecture; Stored With all variety of witty jeasts, merry Tales, and other pleasant passages; Extracted, from the choicest flowers of Philosophy, Poesy, antient and moderne History. Illustrated with Examples of incomparable constancy, in the excellent History of Philocles and Doriclea. By Philogenes Panedonius. *R. Bishop, for R. B. or his Assignes.* 1640. 8°.

Licensed to Bishop, 25 Nov., 1639 (*Stat. Reg.* iv. 490).
Some copies are printed " by R. Bishop, for R. Best."
     B.M. (1081. d. 2).

[Another edition.] The Two Lancashire Lovers: Or the Excellent History of Philocles and Doriclea ... By Musaeus Palatinus. *E. Griffin for R. B[est] or his Assignes.* 1640. 8°.

     B.M. (12613. b. 25).

The Penitent Pilgrim. *I. Dawson, and are to be sold by I. Williams.* 1641. 12°.

     B.M. (C. 37. b. 37).

See also in Part II.

BRETON, Nicholas.

Grimellos Fortunes, with his Entertainment in his trauaile, *etc.*   *For E. White.* 1604. 4°. 𝕭.𝕷.

     B.M. (12330. b. 24).

[The Miseries of Mauillia.]

Assigned to Creede by W. Wright, 20 Oct., 1596 (*Stat. Reg.* iii. 72).

The Miseries of Mauillia. The most vnfortunate Ladie, that euer liued. First found by the said Author N. Breton Gentleman. *T. Creede.* 1599. 4°. 𝕭.𝕷.

     B.M. (C. 27. b. 14/4).

The Strange Fortunes of Two Excellent Princes : in their liues and loues, to their equall Ladies in all the titles of true honour. *P. Short, for N. Ling.* 1600. 4°. 𝔅.𝔏.
    Bodl. (Wood 321/1).

BREWER, THOMAS.
The Life and Death of the merry Deuill of Edmonton ... By T. B. *T. P[avier] for F. Faulkner.* 1631. 4°. 𝔅.𝔏.
Signed at the end Tho: Brewer.
    B.M. (C. 39. c. 18).

C., H. *See* CHETTLE, Henry; FOREST OF FANCY.

C., W. *See* EGERIA; FRAGOSA.

CALANTHROP AND LUCILLA. *See* KENNEDY, John.

CAMUS, JEAN PIERRE.
Admirable Events : Selected out of Foure Bookes, Written in French by the Right Reverend, John Peter Camus, Bishop of Belley. Together with morall Relations, written by the same Author. And translated into English by S. Du Verger. *T. Harper for W. Brooks.* 1639. 4°.
Some copies have the imprint "T. Harper for A. Roper."
    U.L.C., Syn. 7. 63. 112 ["for W. Brooks"]; Bodl. (Douce C. 233) ["for A. Roper"].

Diotrephe. Or, An Historie of Valentines. Written in French by the Right Reverend Iohn Peter Camus, *etc.* *T. Harper.* 1641.
    B.M. (12511. aa. 36).
See also Part II.

CARTIGNY, JEAN DE.
The Voyage of the Wandering Knight. Deuised by Iohn Carthenie, a Frenchman : and translated out of French into English, by William Goodyear of South-hampton Merchant. *T. East.* 1581. 4°. 𝔅.𝔏.
    Priv. Lib.

[Another edition.] Shewing al the course of mans life, how apt he is to follow vanitie, and how hard it is for him to attaine to Vertue. Deuised by Iohn Carthenie, a French man : and translated out of French into English, by W. G., of South-hampton, Merchant. A worke worthie of reading, and dedicated to the right Worshipfull, Sir Francis Drake, knight. *T. Este.* 1607. 4°. 𝔅.𝔏.
    B.M. (1077. f. 8).

[Another edition.] Shewing the whole course of Mans life, *etc.   W. Stansby.*
4°. 𝕭.𝕷.
     B.M. (G. 536).

[Another edition.]   *T. Snodham.*   4°.   𝕭.𝕷.
     B.M. (C. 25. f. 5).

[Another edition.]   *R. Bishop, and are to be sold by W. Gilbertson.*   1650.
4°.   𝕭.𝕷.
     Bodl. (4°. Rawl. 269).

[Another edition.]   1661.   4°.
     Hazlitt, H. 76.

[Another edition.]   *E. Crouch.*   1670.   4°.   𝕭.𝕷.
     Hazlitt, H. 76.

CAUSSIN, Nicolas.
     The Unfortunate Politique, First written in French By C. N.   Englished
by G. P.   *L. Lichfield, for I. Godwin : Oxford,* 1639.   8°.
     The subtitle is "The Life of Herod."   The author is alluded to (as "Causinus") in the
     Preface.
     B.M. (12512. a. 13).

CAWWOOD THE ROOK.
     [Cawwood the Rook.]
     Licensed to F. Grove, 23 July, 1638 (*Stat. Reg.* iv. 425).

     The Pleasant History of Cawwood the Rooke, or the Assembly of Birds,
with the Severall Speeches which the Birds made to the Eagle, in hope to
have the Government in his absence : and lastly, how the Rooke was
banished ; with the Reason why crafty Fellowes are called Rookes.   As also
fit Morrals and Expositions added to every Chapter.   *T. C. for F. Grove.*
1640.   4°.   𝕭.𝕷.
     B.M. (Huth 83).

[Another edition.]   *R. I. for F. Grove.*   1656.   4°.   𝕭.𝕷.
     B.M. (1080. i. 62).

[Another edition].   *For I. Wright, I. Clarke, W. Thackeray and T.
Passinger.*   1683.   4°.   𝕭.𝕷.
     B.M. (12403. aaa. 3).

[Another edition.]   4°.   𝕭.𝕷.
     Bodl. (Douce R. 528), imperf.

[Another edition.] *W. O[nley].* 4°.

> Bodl. (Douce R. 528).

See REYNARD THE FOX. 1735.

CELESTINA.

The Delightful History of Celestina the Faire : Daughter to the King of Thessalie . . . Done out of French into English. *A. I. for W. Barley,* 1596. 4°. 𝕭.𝕷.

> B.M. (1077. e. 9).

CERVANTES, SAAVEDRA, MIGUEL DE.

[Shelton's version. Part 1.] The History of the Valorous and Wittie Knight-Errant, Don Quixote Of the Mancha. Translated out of the Spanish. *W. Stansby, for E. Blount and W. Barret.* 1612. 4°.

> Part I. The dedication is signed Thomas Shelton.
> B.M. (C. 57. c. 39).

[Another edition. Parts 1, 2.] The History of Don Quichote. *For E. Blounte.* 1620. 4°. 2 vols.

> Both parts have engraved titlepages ; the second has also a printed title, bearing the date.
> Part 2 had been licensed to Blount, 5 Dec., 1615 (*Stat. Reg.* iii. 579).
> B.M. (G. 10187).

[Another edition.] The History Of The Valorous and Witty-Knight-Errant, Don-Quixote, Of the Mancha. Translated out of the Spanish ; now newly Corrected and Amended. *R. Hodgkinsonne, for A. Crooke.* 1652. Fol.

> B.M. (Cerv. 334).

[Another edition.] Now newly Corrected and Amended. *For R. Scot, T. Basset, J. Wright, R. Chiswell.* 1675, 2. Fol. 2 vols.

> Vol. 2 is printed by R. Hodgkinsonne.
> B.M. (12490. k. 12).

[Stevens' revision.] The History of the most Ingenious Knight, Don Quixote De la Mancha. Written in Spanish by Michael de Cervantes Saavedra. Formerly made English by Thomas Shelton ; now Revis'd, Corrected, and partly new Translated from the Original. By Captain John Stevens. Illustrated with 33 Copper Plates, curiously Engraved from the Brussels Edition. *For R. Chiswell, R. Battersby, A. and F. Churchill, S. Smith and B. Walford, M. Wotton, and G. Conyers.* 1700. 8°. 2 vols.

> Rius, *Bibliografía crítica de las Obras de M. Cervantes Saavedra,* 613.

[Another edition.]   Translated into English By Mr. Shelton, and Mr. Blunt. And now Printed from the Quarto Edition of 1620.   With a Curious Sett of Cutts from the French of Coypell, *etc.   By and for S. Hyde and J. Dobson, and for R. Owen: Dublin,* 1733.   12°.   4 vols.

B.M. (Cerv. 82).

[Another edition.]   Translated into English by Thomas Shelton, and now printed verbatim from the 4to Edition of 1620. . . . In Four Volumes.   *For W. Knaplock, J. and B. Sprint, J. Walthoe, D. Midwinter, J. Knapton, B. Lintot, R. Robinson, B. Cowse, W. and J. Innys, G. Conyers, A. Ward, B. Motte, and T. Wotton.*   1725.   12°.   4 vols.

B.M. (12490. aaaa. 20).

[Another edition.]   *For J. Walthoe, G. Conyers, J. Knapton and T. Osborne.*   1731.   4 vols.   12°.

Rius *Bibliografía crítica de las Obras de M. de Cervantes Saavedra,* 623.

[Phillips' version.]   The History of the most Renowned Don Quixote of Mancha . . . Now made English . . . and Adorned with several Copper Plates. By J. P[hillips].   *T. Hodgkin, and are to be sold by J. Newton,* 1687.   Fol.

Some copies are "Sold by William Whitwood."

B.M. (Cerv. 336).

[Another edition.]   This Second Edition farther Revis'd and Amended. Illustrated with 33 Copper Plates Curiously Engraved from the Brussels Edition.   In Two Volumes.   *For R. Chiswell, S. and J. Sprint, R. Battersby, S. Smith, and B. Walford, M. Wotton, and G. Conyers.*   1706.   8°.   2 vols.

B.M. (12490. e. 7).

[Motteux' version.]   The History of the Renown'd Don Quixote De la Mancha . . . Translated from the Original by several Hands : And publish'd by Peter Motteux Servant to his Majesty.   Adorn'd with Sculptures.   *For S. Buckley.*   1700.   12°.   4 vols.

B.M., vol. 1 only (Cerv. 79, vol. 1).

[Another edition.]   The Third Edition.   *For S. Buckley.*   1712.   12°. 4 vols.

B.M. (12491. b. 28).

[Another edition.]   Adorn'd with New Sculptures.   The Fourth Edition. Carefully Revised . . . By J. Ozell.   *For R. Knaplock, D. Midwinter, J. Tonson, and W. Churchill; and are to be Sold by J. Brotherton and W. Meadows.*   1719.   12°.   4 vols.

B.M. (12490. cc. 8).

[Another edition.] Adorn'd with New Sculptures. The Fifth Edition. Carefully Revised . . . By J. Ozell. *For J. Knapton, R. Knaplock, J. Sprint, D. Midwinter, J. Tonson, W. Innys, J. Osborn, R. Robinson, and T. Longman.* 1725. 12°. 4 vols.

B.M. (12490. e. 20).

[Another edition.] The history of the renowned Don Quixote . . . translated . . . by Peter Motteux. *For J. Knapton [and others ?].* 1733. 12°. [4 vols. ?].

Bragge (Rius, *Bibliografia critica de las Obras de M. de Cervantes Saavedra*, 624).

[An abridgement.] The Famous History of Don Quixote de la Mancha . . . With the Merry Humours of Sancho Panca his Squire, *etc. For G. Conyers.* 1686. 8°. 𝕭.𝕷.

7 chapters.
Bodl. (Wood 259 (12)).

[A different abridgement.] The Delightful History of Don Quixot . . . Also the Comical Humours of his Facetious Squire Sancho Pancha, etc. *For B. Crayle.* 1689. 12°.

2 parts. The Dedication is signed E. S.
B.M. (12489. b. 19).

[Another edition.] The Much-esteemed History of the Ever-famous Knight Don Quixote de la Mancha . . . In Two Parts . . . Illustrated with Copper Plates, *etc. For N. Boddington.* 1699. 12°.

B.M. (12489. b. 31).

[Another edition.] *For N. & M. Boddington.* 1716. 12°.

B.M. (10817. aa. 10/2).

[A different abridgement.] The most Admirable and Delightful History of the Atchievements of Don Quixote de la Mancha . . . Done from the Spanish Edition . . . adorn'd with Cuts. *For D. Pratt.* 1721. 12°.

26 chapters.
B.M. (12490. b. 26).

[A different abridgement.] The History of the Ever-Renowned Knight Don Quixote de la Mancha, *etc. W. O[nley], and sold by H. Green.* 4°.

6 chapters.
B.M. (12490. e. 13).

The Curious Impertinent. Translated from the Spanish Original of Miguel de Cervantes Saavedra. 1720.

Don Quixote, Bk. iv., capp. 6–8.

See (in Part II) CROXALL, Samuel. A Select Collection of Novels. vol. iii.

[Another edition.] 1729.

See (in Part II) CROXALL, Samuel.   A Select Collection of Novels.   ed. 2, vol. iii.

The History of the Captive.   Translated from the Spanish Original of Miguel de Cervantes Saavedra.   1720.
Don Quixote, Bk. iv., capp. 12–14.

See (in Part II) CROXALL, Samuel.   A Select Collection of Novels.   vol. ii.

[Another edition.] 1729.

See (in Part II) CROXALL, Samuel.   A Select Collection of Novels.   ed. 2, vol. ii.

[A Continuation of Don Quixote.]   *See* (in Part II) FERNANDEZ DE AVELLANEDA, Alonso.

[Exemplary Novels.]   Exemplarie Novells; in sixe books.   The two Damosels.   The Ladie Cornelia.   The liberall Lover.   The force of bloud. The Spanish Ladie.   The jealous Husband . . .   Turned into English by Don Diego Puede-Ser.   *J. Dawson, for R. M[abbe] and are to be sold by Laurence Blaicklocke.*   1640.   Fol.
   Diego Puede-Ser is James Mabbe.   Cornelia, The Two Damsels, The Force of Blood, and The Spanish Lady were licensed to R. Mabbe, 27 Nov., 1638 (*Stat. Reg.* iv. 445).
   B.M. (C. 58. g. 10).

[Another issue.]   Delight in Severall Shapes, *etc.*   *For W. Sheares.* 1654.   Fol.
   Priv. Lib. ; Bragge (Rius 927).

[A different version.]   Select Novels : The first Six written in Spanish by Miguel Cervantes Saavedra . . .   The other by Francis Petrarch . . .   All Translated from the Originals by Dr. Walter Pope.   *For C. Brome and T. Horne.*   1694.   8°.
   The Spanish-English Lady, The Liberal Lover, The Force of Blood, Cornelia, The Rival Ladies, The Salamanca Doctor ; Patient Grissel.
   B.M. (Cerv. 368).

[A different version.]   A Collection of Select Novels, Written Originally in Castillian, By Don Miguel Cervantes Saavedra . . .   Made English by Harry Bridges, Esq., *etc. ; S. Farley, Bristol ; and Sold by F. Wall, Bath ; H. Clements, Oxford ; E. Score, Exeter ; and J. Palmer, Gloucester.*   1728.   8°.
   The Gypsie, The Dogs of Mahudez, The Deceitful Marriage, Quixaire, Princess of the Molluccoes, The Illustrious Chambermaid, and The Jealous Estremaduran.
   B.M. (12490. c. 11).

See (in Part II).   SPANISH DECAMERON.

The Fair Maid of the Inn. Translated from the Spanish Original of Miguel de Cervantes Saavedra. 1720.

See in (Part II) CROXALL, Samuel. A Select Collection of Novels. vol. ii.

[Another edition.] 1729.

See (in Part II) CROXALL, Samuel. A Select Collection of Novels. ed. 2, vol. ii.

La Gitanilla and El Zeloso Estremeno, translated by J. Ozell. 1709. 8°.
Sotheby's (Britwell sale, February, 1910, 273). Perhaps the same as the following and *El Zeloso Estremeno*, below :

[A different version ?] The Monthly Amusement. No. I., for April, 1709. Containing, La Gitanilla, The Little Gipsie, A Novel, Written by Cervantes Saavedra . . . and done from the Spanish by J. Ozell. *For D. Midwinter and B. Lintott.* 1709.
Term Cat., iii. 650. Not in Rius.

[Another edition.] The Little Gypsy. Translated from the Spanish Original of Miguel de Cervantes Saavedra. 1721.

See (in Part II) CROXALL, Samuel. A Select Collection of Novels. vol. v.

[Another edition.] 1729.

See (in Part II) CROXALL, Samuel. A Select Collection of Novels. ed. 2, vol. v.

The Jealous Gentleman of Estremadure. *For C. Blount and R. Butt.* 1681. 12°.
Term Cat., i. 461.

[A different version.] El Zeloso Estremeno : The Jealous Estremaduran. A Novel. Written by Miguel de Cervantes Saavedra. And done from the Spanish, By J. Ozell. *For D. Midwinter, and B. Lintott, and Sold by J. Morphew.* 1709. 12°.
The Monthly Amusement. Numb. III. For June, 1709.
B.M. (635. a. 43).

[A different version.] The Jealous Estremaduran, *etc.* 1720. 12°.

See (in Part II) CROXALL, Samuel. A Select Collection of Novels. vol. i.

[Another edition.] 1729.

See (in Part II) CROXALL, Samuel. A Select Collection of Novels. ed. 2, vol. i.

The Lady Cornelia.   Translated from the Spanish Original of Miguel Cervantes de Saavedra.   1721.

See (in Part II) CROXALL, Samuel.   A Select Collection of Novels.   vol. vi.

[Another edition.]   1729.

See (in Part II) CROXALL, Samuel.   A Select Collection of Novels.   ed. 2, vol. vi.

The Liberal Lover.   Translated from the Spanish Original of Miguel de Cervantes Saavedra.   1720.

See (in Part II) CROXALL, Samuel.   A Select Collection of Novels.   vol. iii.

[Another edition.]   1729.

See (in Part II) CROXALL, Samuel.   A Select Collection of Novels. ed. 2, vol. iii.

The Prevalence of Blood.   Translated from the Spanish Original of Miguel de Cervantes Saavedra.   1720.

See (in Part II) CROXALL, Samuel.   A Select Collection of Novels.   vol. iii.

[Another edition.]   1729.

See (in Part II) CROXALL, Samuel.   A Select Collection of Novels.   ed. 2, vol. iii.

The Rival Ladies.   Translated from the Spanish Original of Miguel de Cervantes Saavedra.   1720.

See (in Part II) CROXALL, Samuel.   A Select Collection of Novels.   vol. iv.

[Another edition.]   1729.

See (in Part II) CROXALL, Samuel.   A Select Collection of Novels.   ed. 2, vol. iv.

The Spanish Lady of England.   Translated from the Spanish Original of Miguel Cervantes de Saavedra.   1721.

See (in Part II) CROXALL, Samuel.   A Select Collection of Novels.   vol. vi.

[Another edition.]   1729.

See (in Part II) CROXALL, Samuel.   A Select Collection of Novels. ed. 2, vol. vi.

The Travels of Persiles and Sigismunda. A Northern History. Wherein, amongst the variable Fortunes of the Prince of Thule, and this Princesse of Frisland, are interlaced many Witty Discourses . . . The first Copie, beeing written in Spanish; translated afterward into French; and now, last, into English. *H. L[ownes], for M. L[ownes].* 1619. 4°.

B.M. (C. 59. ff. 2).

[*Supposititious.*] [Diverting Works *and* A Week's Entertainment at a Wedding.] *See* (in Part II) Montalban, Juan Perez de.

The Troublesome and Hard Adventures in Love. *See* (in Part II) Codrington, Robert.

CESPEDES Y MENESES, Gonzalo.

Gerardo the Vnfortunate Spaniard, or a Patterne for Lasciuious Louers . . . Written by an ingenious Spanish Gentleman, Don Gonçalo de Cespedes, and Meneçes, in the time of his fiue yeeres Imprisonment. Originally in Spanish, and made English by L. D. *For E. Blount.* 1622. 4°.

The dedication is signed Leonard Digges.
B.M. (12489. bb. 39).

[Another edition.] *W. Bentley, and are to be sold by W. Shears.* 1653[2]. 8°.

B.M. (E. 1234/1).

See also Part II.

CHAMBERS, Robert.

Palestina. Written By M[r]. R. C. P. and Bachelor of Diuinitie. *B. Sermartelli, Florence.* [*London?*] 1600. 4°.

B.M. (C. 25. e. 38).

CHARLES THE GREAT.

Begin : SAynt Poul doctour of veryte sayth to vs that al thynges that ben reduced by wrytyng, ben wryton to our doctryne, *etc.* 2[b]: THenne for as moche I late had fynysshed in enprynte the book of the noble & vyctoryous kyng Arthur fyrst of the thre moost noble & worthy of crysten kynges, and also had reduced in to englisshe the noble hystorye & lyf of Godefroy of boloyn kyng of Iherusalem, last of the said iij worthy Somme persones of noble estate and degree haue desyred me to reduce thystorye and lyf of the noble and crysten prynce Charles the grete kyng of Frauuce [*sic*], *etc.* *W. Caxton* [*Westminster*]. 1485. Fol. 𝕭.𝕷.

B.M. (C. 10. b. 9).

CHETTLE, Henry.

Kind-Harts Dreame ... by H. C.   *For W. Wright.*   4º.
B.M. (C. 14. a. 6).

Piers Plainnes seauen yeres Prentiship.   By H. C.   *I. Danter for T. Gosson.*
1595.   4º.   𝕭.𝕷.
Doubtfully attributed to Chettle.
Bodl. (Malone 670).

CHRISTINE DE PISE.

Here begynneth the boke of the Cyte of Ladyes, the whiche boke is
deuyded in to . iij . partes.   The fyrst parte telleth howe and by whom the
walle and the cloystre aboute the Cyte was made.   The seconde parte telleth
howe and by whom the cyte was buylded within and peopled.   The thyrde
parte telleth howe and by whom the hyghe battylmentes of the towres were
parfytely made and what noble ladyes were ordeyned to dwell in yᵉ hyghe
palayces and hyghe dongeons, *etc.*   *H. Pepwell.*   1521.   4º.   𝕭.𝕷.
B.M. (C. 13. a. 18).

Here foloweth the C. Hystoryes of Troye.   Lepistre de Othea deesse de
Prudence,   enuoyee   a   lesperit   cheualereux   Hector   de   Troye,   auec   cent
Histoires.   Nouvellement imprimee.   *R. Wyer.*   8º.   𝕭.𝕷.
"Translated out of Frenche in to Englyshe, by me.   R.W."
B.M. (C. 21. a. 34).

CHURCHYARD, Thomas.   *See* Fortunatus.

CLIDAMAS.

Clidamas, or the Sicilian Tale.   Written by J. S.   *T. Payne, and are to be
sold by I. Cowper.*   1639.   8º.
Clidamas had been licensed to Payne, 25 Feb., 1636/7 (*Stat. Reg.* iv. 373).
B.M. (12611. de. 18).

[Another edition.]   1639.   8º.
Hazlitt, II. 528.

CLODOALDUS.

A Saxon Historie, of the Admirable Adventures of Clodoaldus and his
Three Children.   Translated out of French, by Sʳ T. H.   *E. P. for H. Seile.*
1634.   4º.
B.M. (95. b. 21).

COBBLER OF CANTERBURY.

The Cobler of Caunterburie, Or An Inuectiue against Tarltons Newes out of Purgatorie. A merrier Iest then a Clownes Iigge, and fitter for Gentlemens humors, *etc.   R. Robinson.*   1590.   4°.   𝕭.𝕷.
    Bodl. (Malone 659).

[Another edition ?]
    Licensed to J. Newbery, 12 June, 1600 (*Stat. Reg.* iii. 163).

[Another edition.]   *N. Okes for N. Butter.*   1608.   4°.   𝕭.𝕷.
    B.M. (C. 30. e. 32).

[Another edition.]   The Merry Tales of the Cobler of Canterburie.   As hee passed from Billings-gate to Graues-end.   With an inuectiue against Tarltons newes out of Purgatory.   Together with his Description of the eight orders of Cuckolds.   Newly published at his owne cost without the helpe of the Shoemakers.   *For N. Butter.*   1614.   4°.   𝕭.𝕷.
    Hazlitt, I. 91 (Marquis of Bute).

[Another edition.]   The Tincker of Turvey, his merry Pastime in his passing from Billingsgate to Graues-End . . . with . . . other Mad-merry fellowes, euery-one of them Telling his Tale : . . . The Eight seuerall Orders of Cuckolds, marching here likewise in theyr Horned Rankes.   *For N. Butter.*   1630.   4°.   𝕭.𝕷.
    B.M. (C. 40. b. 5).

[Another edition.]   A Witty, Pleasant, and True Discourse of the Merry Cobler of Canterbury ; together with the pretty Conceits of Frier Bacon, with the Cobler's Song.   *Edinburgh.*   1681.   12°.
    Hazlitt, H. 317.

COLET, CLAUDE.   *See* PALMERIN.   Palladine of England.

COLONNA, FRANCESCO.

Hypnerotomachia The Strife of Loue in a Dreame.   *For S. Waterson.*   1592.   4°.   𝕭.𝕷.
    The dedication is signed R. D[allington ?].   Other copies have the imprint " for I. Busbie " (A. Lang, Claude Popelin) and " for W. Holme " (Bodl., Douce 220).   *See* the reprint by A. Lang, 1891.
    B.M. (Huth 39).

CROFTS (ROBERT).

The Lover : or, Nuptiall Love.   Written, by Robert Crofts, To please himselfe.   *B. Alsop and T. F. for R. Meighen.*   1638.   8°.
    Huth.

CUPID.

The Banishment of Cupid.   *For T. Marshe.*   8°.

Translated from the Italian by T. Hedley.   M. A. Scott, *Elizabethan Translations*, p. 29.   Watt.

[Another edition.]   1587.   12°.

M. A. Scott, p. 29.   Watt.

D., T.   *See* DELONEY, Thomas.

DARES.

The faythfull and true storye of the destruction of Troye, compyled by Dares Phrigius, which was a souldier while the siege lasted, Translated into Englyshe by Thomas Paynell.   *I. Cawood.*   1553.   8°.   𝕭.𝕷.

B.M. (79. h. 5).

DECEIT OF WOMEN.

The deceyte of Women, to the instruction and ensample of all men, yonge and olde, newly corrected.   *A. Vele.*   4°.   𝕭.𝕷.

B.M. (C. 20. c. 31/1).

DECKER, THOMAS.

A Knights Coniuring.   Done in earnest : Discouered in Jest.   By Thomas Dekker.   *T. C. for W. Barley.*   [1607.]   4°.

B.M. (C. 39. c. 3).

The Wonderfull Yeare.   1603.   Wherein is shewed the picture of London, lying sicke of the Plague.   At the end of all (like a mery Epilogue to a dull Play) certaine Tales are cut out in sundry fashions, *etc.*   *T. Creede.*   4°.   𝕭.𝕷.

B.M. (E. 1940/3).

DEGUILLEVILLE, GUILLAUME DE.

Begin : This book is intytled the pylgremage of the sowle, translated out of Frensshe in to Englysshe, Whiche book is ful of deuoute maters touchying the sowle, and many questyons assoyled to cause a man to lyue the better in this worlde, *etc.*   *W. Caxton : Westmestre.*   1483.   Fol.   𝕭.𝕷.

B.M. (IB. 55069).

DELONEY, THOMAS.

The Gentle Craft.   A most merry and pleasant Historie, not altogether vnprofitable, nor any way hurtfull : very fit to passe away the tediousnes of the long winters euenings.   *For E. White.*   1598.   4°.   𝕭.𝕷.

Both parts.   Licensed (Part 1 only ?) to R. Blore, 19 Oct., 1597 (*Stat. Reg.* iii. 93).

Hazlitt, H. 152 (no perfect copy known).

[Another edition of Part I.] A Discourse containing many matters of delight, very pleasant to be read. Shewing what famous men haue beene Shoomakers in time past in this Land, with their worthy death and great Hospitality. Declaring the Cause why it is called the Gentle Craft, and also how the prouerbe first grew; A Shoomakers sonne is a Prince borne. T.D. *For E. Brewster.* 1627. 4°. 𝕭.𝕷.

Hazlitt, H. 153.

[Another edition.] 1635. 4°.
Hazlitt, H. 153 (*Harleian Cat.*).

[Another edition of Part II.] The second Part . . . By T. D. Newly corrected and augmented, *etc. E. Purslow.* 1639. 4°. 𝕭.𝕷.

B.M. (12614. c. 7).

[Another edition of Part I.] Set forth with Pictures. . . . T. D., *etc. For J. Stafford.* 1648. 4°. 𝕭.𝕷.

Hazlitt, I. 124, may be another edition.
B.M. (12403. aaa. 11).

[Another edition.] *For J. Stafford.* 1652. 4°. 𝕭.𝕷.

Bodl. (Wood 31. c. 1).

[Another edition.] Gentle Craft. The Honour of the Gentle Craft expressed in three stories : The first of Hugh and fair Winifred, the second of Crispin and Crispianus, the third of Sir Symon Eyre, *etc. A. Clark.* 1674. 8°.

Hazlitt, H. 153.

[Another edition.] 1676. 4°. 𝕭.𝕷.
Hazlitt, H. 153.

[Another edition.] *For F. Coles.* 4°.
Hazlitt, H. 153.

[Another edition.] The First Part of the Pleasant and Princely History of the Gentle Craft . . . Set forth with Pictures . . . T. D., *etc. T. M. for W. Thackery.* 1678. 4°. 𝕭.𝕷.

B.M. (12330. g. 22).

[Another edition.] *J. Millet, for W. T*[*hackeray*], *and are to be sold by J. Gilbertson.* 4°. 𝕭.𝕷.

This is perhaps the edition of 1685 " for W. Thackeray," recorded by Hazlitt, H. 153, as in the Pepysian Library ; it is cropped and may have had a date.
Pepys 1193 (12).

[Another edition.]   The Pleasant and Princely History of the Gentle Craft.   A Discourse, Containing many matters of Delight.   Very Pleasant to Read, *etc.*   4°.   𝕭.𝕷.
> B.M. (12614. g. 15), mutilated.

[Another edition.]   *For H. Rhodes.*   4°.
> Ends on p. 51.
> B.M. (12614. g. 16).

[Another edition.]   *For H. Rhodes.*   4°.
> Ends on p. 48.
> B.M. (12316. g. 3).

[Another edition.]   *W. Wilde and sold by P. Brooksby, J. Deacon, J. Back, J. Blare, and E. Tracy.*   1696.   4°.
> Tenth Edition (*Term Cat.*, ii. 582).
> Bodl. (Douce D. 237), imperf.

[Another edition.]   [*Sold by H. Rhodes ?*]   1703.
> *Term Cat.*, iii. 342.

[Another edition.]   The Delightful, Princely and Entertaining History of the Gentle-Craft, *etc.*   *For J. Rhodes.*   1725.   12°.
> B.M. (12410. a. 18).

[Another edition.]   The Pleasant and Princely History of the Gentle-Craft, *etc.*   4°.
> Hazlitt, I. 181.

[Another edition.]   *Printed on London Bridge.*   1723.   12°.
> Hazlitt, H. 153.

[Another edition.]   *For H. Woodgate and S. Brooks.*
> Woodgate and Brooks' list, in *Argalus and Parthenia.*

[Another edition.]   The Noble and Diverting History of the Gentle-Craft : The whole Book being intermix'd with Variety of Stories . . . with a set of Pictures intirely New, *etc.*   *For A. Bettesworth, C. Hitch, R. Ware, and J. Hodges.*   1737.   12°.
> Bodl. (Douce G. 350).

[A different version.]   The Shooe-makers Glory : Or, The Princely History of the Gentle Craft . . .   The whole adorn'd with new Cuts suitable to the subject.   *W. O[nley], and are to be sold by C. Bates.*   4°.
> Bodl. (Douce R. 528).

[Another edition.]   *J. White : Newcastle.*   12°.
> B.M. (1076. l. 18/18), imperf.

[Another edition.]   *C. Brown.*   4°.

Hazlitt, I. 181.

See (in Part II) BOVINIAN.   1657.

[Jack of Newbury.]

Licensed to **T.** Millington, **7** March, 1596/7 (*Stat. Reg.* iii. 81).

[Another edition.]   The Pleasant History of Iohn Winchcomb, in his younger yeares called Iack of Newberie, the famous and worthy Clothier of England . . .   Now the eight time Imprinted, corrected, and inlarged by T. D.   *H. Lownes.*   1619.   4°.   𝕭.𝕷.

Priv. Lib.

[Another edition.]   Now the tenth time Imprinted, corrected, and enlarged by T. D.   *H. Lownes.*   1626.   4°.   𝕭.𝕷.

Bridgewater.

[Another edition.]   The eleuenth Edition, corrected and enlarged by T. D., *etc.*   *H. L[ownes]. and R. Y[oung], and are to be sold by I. Harrigat.*   1630.   4°.   𝕭.𝕷.

Bodl. (Douce D. 225).

[Another edition.]   Now the ninth time Imprinted, corrected, and inlarged, by T. D.   *R. Young, and are to be sold by C. Wright.*   1633.   4°.   𝕭.𝕷.

B.M. (1077. e. 21).

[Another edition.]   Now the tenth time imprinted, corrected and enlarged, by T. D.   *R. Young, and are to be sold by C. Wright.*   1637.   4°.

R. Hoe.

[Another edition.]   1655.   4°.

Hazlitt, H. 153.

[Another edition.]   Now the Thirteenth time Imprinted, corrected, and inlarged by, T. D., *etc.*   *E. Crouch, for T. Passinger.*   1672.   4°.   𝕭.𝕷.

Bodl. (Wood 32. c. 2).

[Another edition ?]   *For W. Thackeray.*

Thackeray's list, 1677.

[Another edition.]   The Pleasant History of John Winchcomb In his younger years called Jack of Newbery . . .   Now the Fourteenth time im-printed, corrected, and inlarged by, T. D.   *W. Wilde, for T. Passenger and W. Thackeray.*   4°.   𝕭.𝕷.

B.M. (1077. g. 35/1).

[Another edition.] The Fifteenth Edition Corrected and Inlarged, by T. D., *etc. For E. Tracy.* 4°.

> B.M. (12403. aa. 38).

[An abridgement.] A most Delightful History Of the famous Clothier of England, called, Jack of Newbery . . . Written by W. S. F. C. *H. B[rugis]. for W. Thackeray.* 1684. 8°. 𝕭.𝕷.

> Pepys 363 (1149).

[Thomas of Reading.]

> Mentioned in *Kemp's Nine Daies Wonder*, 1600. Assigned to T. Pavier by T. Millington, 19 April, 1602 (*Stat. Reg.* iii. 204).

[Another edition.] Thomas of Reading. Or, The sixe worthy yeomen of the West. Now the fourth time corrected and enlarged. By T. D. *For T. P[avier].* 1612. 4°. 𝕭.𝕷.

> B.M. (Huth 92).

[Another edition.] Now the fift time corrected and enlarged by T. D. *W. I. for T. P[avier].* 1623. 4°. 𝕭.𝕷.

> Bridgewater.

[Another edition.] Now the sixth time corrected and enlarged. By T. D. *E. Allde for R. Bird.* 1632. 4°. 𝕭.𝕷.

> B.M. (1077. f. 10).

[Another edition.] Corrected and inlarged by T. D. *For R. Bird.* 1636. 4°. 𝕭.𝕷.

> Huth.

[Another edition.] Corrected and inlarged by T. D., *etc. For W. Thackeray.* 1672. 4°.

> Bodl. (Wood 32. c. 3).

[Another edition.] *Sold by J. Deacon.*

> Advertised in the following.

[An abridgement.] The Honour of the Cloathworking Trade: or, The Pleasant and Famous History of Thomas of Reading: And other Worthy Clothiers of the West and North of England . . . Humbly dedicated to the Worshipful Company of Cloathworkers. *For J. Deacon.* 4°. 𝕭.𝕷.

> B.M. (G. 10463).

[Another edition.] *J. White: Newcastle upon Tine.* 4°.

> B.M. (12613. c. 10).

[Another edition.] *For B. Deacon.* 4°.
Bodl. (Douce R. 528).

DESMARETS DE SAINT SORLIN, Jean.

Ariana. In Two Parts. As it was translated out of the French, and presented to my Lord Chamberlaine. *J. Haviland, for T. Walkley.* 1636. Fol.
B.M. (1342. n. 2).

[Another edition.] The second Edition. *I. Dawson for T. Walkley.* 1641. Fol.
B.M. (C. 64. f. 8).

[Another edition.] *For Anne Moseley.*
Anne Moseley's list, 1663.

DIALOGI CREATURARUM.

The Dialoges of Creatures Moralysed. Applyably and edicatyfly, to euery mery and iocund mater, of late trãslated out of latyn into our Englysshe tonge right profitable to the gouernaunce of man. [*Paris?*]. *And they be to sell vpõ Powlys churche yarde.* 4°. 𝔅.𝔏.
Adapted from the Fables of Bidpai, *q.v.*
Wyer printed an edition containing only 7 dialogues, with the narrative omitted.
B.M. (C. 11. a. 26).

DICKENSON, John.

Arisbas, Euphues amidst his slumbers : Or Cupids Iourney to Hell. Decyphering a Myrror of Constancie, a Touch-stone of tried affection, begun in chaste desires, ended in choise delights : And emblasoning Beauties glorie, adorned by Natures bountie. With the Triumph of True Loue, in the foyle of false Fortune. By I. D. *T. Creede for T. Woodcocke.* 1594. 4°. 𝔅.𝔏.
B.M. (C. 57. e. 4).

Greene in Conceipt. New raised from his graue to write the Tragique Historie of faire Valeria of London . . . Receiued and reported by I. D., *etc. R. Bradocke for W. Iones.* 1598. 4°. 𝔅.𝔏.
Bodl. (Malone 575).

DOBSON, George.

Dobson's Drie Bobbes : Sonne and Heire to Skoggin. Full of mirth and delightful recreation. *V. Simmes.* 1607. 4°. 𝔅.𝔏.
T.C.C. (Capell Q. 8. 2).

DONI, Antonio Francesco. *See* Bidpai.

DURINE OF GREECE.   *See* PALMERIN.

EDWARDES, RICHARD.

[A collection of short comic stories in prose.]   1570.   𝕭.𝕷.

"Among the books of my friend the late Mr. William Collins of Chichester, now dispersed, was a collection of short comic stories in prose, printed in the black letter under the year 1570, 'sett forth by maister Richard Edwardes mayster of her maiesties reuels'. . . Among these tales was that of the *Induction of the Tinker* in Shakespeare's *Taming of the Shrew.*"—T. Warton, *History of English Poetry*, ed. W. C. Hazlitt, 1871, iv., 218.

[Another edition.   1620–1630 ?]

A fragment, containing only "The Waking Mans Dreame.   The Fifth Event" (being the story of the *Induction of the Tinker*), is described and reprinted by H. G. Norton in the *Shakespeare Society's Papers*, ii.

EGERIA.

The Aduentures of Ladie Egeria.   Containing her miserable bannishment by Duke Lampanus her husbande, through the inducement of Ladie Eldorna, the harlot, and Lord Andromus the Flatterer : who for his periurie and false insinuation, was by a wonderfull iudgement vtterly subuerted and deuoured . . .   Published by W. C. Maister of Art.   *R. Walde-graue.*   4°.   𝕭.𝕷.

Priv. Lib.

ELYOT, *Sir* THOMAS.

The boke named the Gouernour, deuised by s^r· Thomas Elyot knight.   *In edibus T. Bertheleti.*   1531.   8°.   𝕭.𝕷.

Titus and Gisippus, from the *Decameron* (x. 8), is Book ii., Cap. xii. of *The Governour.* "Tytus and Jesepus," licensed to T. Hacket in 1560-61 (*Stat. Reg.* i. 157), is probably W. Walter's poetical version.
   B.M. (G. 735).

[Another edition.]   *T. Berthelet.*   1537.   8°.   𝕭.𝕷.
   B.M. (C. 40. b. 36).

[Another edition.]   *In aedibus T. Bertheleti.*   1544.   8°.   𝕭.𝕷.
   B.M. (8006. a. 2).

[Another edition.]   *In aedibus T. Bertheleti.*   1546.   8°.   𝕭.𝕷.
   B.M. (521. a. 35).

[Another edition.]   *T. Berthelet.*   1547.   8°.   𝕭.𝕷.
   U.L.C. (Syn. 7. 53. 15).

[Another edition.]   *T. Berthelet.*   1553.   8°.   𝕭.𝕷.
   B.M. (232. a. 40).

[Another edition.]   1557.   8°.   𝕭.𝕷.

B.M. (722. a. 43).

[Another edition.]   *T. Marshe.*   1565.   8°.   𝕭.𝕷.

B.M. (8403. aa. 15).

[Another edition.]   *T. East.*   1580.   8°.   𝕭.𝕷.

B.M. (521. a. 26).

ENGLISH MERCURY.   *See* HALL, Joseph.

ERASTUS.   *See* SEVEN WISE MASTERS.

ESTIENNE, HENRI.

A World of Wonders : or, An Introduction to a Treatise touching the Conformitie of ancient and modern wonders : or, a A Preparatiue Treatise to the Apologie for Herodotus.   The Argument whereof is taken from the Apologie for Herodotus written in Latine by Henrie Stephen, and continued here by the Author himselfe.   Translated out of the best corrected French copie.   *For I. Norton.*   1607.   Fol.

B.M. (585. i. 21).

[Another issue.]   *A. Hart and R. Lawson.   Edenburgh.*   1608.   Fol.

B.M. (87. h. 16).

EULENSPIEGEL.   *See* HOWLEGLAS.

EUORDANUS.

The First and Second part of the History of the famous Euordanus Prince of Denmark.   With the strange Aduentures of Iago Prince of Saxonie : And of both theyr seuerall fortunes in Loue.   *I. R. for R. B[anckworth].*   1605. 4°.   𝕭.𝕷.

Licensed to Banckworth, 28 Feb., 1604/5 (*Stat. Reg.* iii. 283).

J.R.L.

FAUCONBRIDGE, *Lord* GEORGE.

The Famous History of George Lord Fauconbridge Bastard son of Richard Cordelion King of England.   Begotten in his Royall Tower, upon the Princely Clarabell, daughter to Don Iohn, Duke of Austria, surnamed, the Worlds faire Concubine, *etc.   I. B., and are to bee sold by I. Wright junior.* 1635.   4°.   𝕭.𝕷.

Priv. Lib.

FAUSTUS, Doctor John.

The Historie of the damnable life, and deserued death of Doctor Iohn Faustus. Newly imprinted, and in conuenient places imperfect matter amended : according to the true Copie printed at Franckfort, and translated into English by P. F. Gent. *T. Orwin, and are to be solde by E. White.* 1592. 4°. 𝕭.𝕷.

> The German original appeared in 1587. A ballad of Dr. Faustus, licensed (for 6d.) to R. Jones, 28 Feb., 1588/9 (*Stat. Reg.* ii. 516), may be a misdescription of the story.
>   B.M. (C. 27. b. 43).

[Another edition?]

> Re-licensed to White ("he hauing thinterest of Abell Ieffes thereto"), 5 April, 1596 (*Stat. Reg.* iii. 63).

[Another edition.] *I. Windet, for E. White.* 1608. 4°. 𝕭.𝕷.

> B.M. (G. 1029).

[Another edition.] *E. All–de for E. White.* 1618. 4°. 𝕭.𝕷.

> Bodl. (Douce F. 202).

[Another edition.] 1622. 4°.

> Hazlitt, H. 193 (*Harleian Cat.*).

[Another edition.] *For J. Wright.* 1636. 4°. 𝕭.𝕷.

> Hazlitt, H. 193.

[Another edition.] Translated into English by P. R. Gent. *For E. Wright.* 1648. 4°. 𝕭.𝕷.

> B.M. (C. 27. b. 44).

[Another edition.] *For W. Whitwood.* 1674. 4°. 𝕭.𝕷.

> Pepys 1192 (14).

[Another edition.] *For T. Sawbridge.* 1677. 4°.

> *Term Cat.* i. 285.

[Another edition.] *For T. Sawbridge.* 1682. 4°. 𝕭.𝕷.

> Huth.

[Another edition.] *For W. Whitwood.* [1687?]. 4°. 𝕭.𝕷.

Advertised in *The Honour of the Taylors* (Sir John Hawkwood), 1687.
>   B.M. (113. c. 26).

[Another edition.] *For W. Whitwood, and sold by T. Sawbridge.* 1690. 4°.

> *Term Cat.* ii. 326.

[Another edition.] *W. O[nley], for J. Back.* [1696]. 4°. 𝕭.𝕷.

Term Cat., ii. 607.
Mr. Quaritch.

[Another edition.] *C. Brown, for M. Hotham.* 4°.

The remainder of this was reissued in 1742 in *Winter Evening Amusements.*
B.M. (G. 1031).

[An abridgement.] The History of the Wicked Life and Damnable Death
of Dr. John Faustus, *etc.* *For T. Passinger.* 8°. 𝕭.𝕷.

13 chapters.
Bodl. (Wood 707).

[Another edition ?] *For C. Dennisson.*

Advertised in Dennisson's *The King and the Abbot of Reading.*

[A different abridgement.] The History of The Wicked Life & Miserable
End of Dr. John Faustus, who, Studying the Black Art, and Renouncing God
and Christ, gave himself, Soul and Body, to the Devil, to be served by a
Spirit, and have his Pleasure in the World for Twenty-Four Years. Also an
Account of his seeing Hell and Heaven: Traveling round the World, and
many other Pranks which he plaid, &c. Translated from the Original Copy
printed at Frankford. *W. O[nley], for J. Back.* 8°.

7 chapters.
B.M. (G. 19126).

[Another edition.] *J. White, Newcastle upon Tyne.* 4°.

Bodl. (Douce BB. 394/2).

The Second Report of Doctor John Faustus, containing his appearances,
and the deedes of Wagner, *etc.* *A. Jeffes, for C. Burby.* 1594. 4°. 𝕭.𝕷.

Bodl. (Douce MM. 475).

[Another edition.] Containing his Apparances, and the deeds of Wagner.
A. Jeffes, for C. Burby. 1594. 4°. 𝕭.𝕷.

Bodl. (Wood B. 20/4).

[Another edition.] *For W. Whitwood.* [1674?]. 4°.

Advertised in Part I., 1674.

[Another edition.] Declaring how he was amongst the Infernal Spirits,
and how he used to appear again upon the Earth, and what strange things he

did : Also very wonderful apparitions of the Infernal King and his followers. And likewise strange Exploits of Wagner and his three familiars. *For R. Smith.* 1680. 4°. 𝕭.𝕷.

B.M. (G. 1030).

[Another edition.] *For J. Conyers.* 4°.
Conyer's list.

[Another edition.] *For W. Whitwood.* [1687 ?] 4°.
Advertised in Part I, 1687.

FENTON, GEOFFREY.

Certaine Tragicall Discourses written oute of Frenche and Latin, by Geffraie Fenton, no lesse profitable then pleasaunt, and of like necessitye to al degrees that take pleasure in antiquityes or forreine reapportes. *T. Marshe.* 1567. 4°. 𝕭.𝕷.

B.M. (G. 16229).

[Another edition.] [*T. Marshe ?*] 1576. 4°. 𝕭.𝕷.
M. A. Scott, *Elizabethan Translations*, p. 18.

[Another edition.] *T. Marshe.* 1579. 4°. 𝕭.𝕷.
B.M. (C. 39. d. 12).

FLORES, JUAN DE.

Histoire de Aurelio et Isabelle . . .   Historia di Aurelio e Issabella . . . Historia de Aurelio, y de Ysabela . . .   The Historie of Aurelio and of Isabell, doughter of the Kinge of Schotlande, nyeuly translatede In foure langagies, Frenche, Italien, Spanishe, and Inglishe. *I. Steelsio, Anvers,* 1556.   8°.

B.M. (C. 12. e. 2).

[Another edition.]
Licensed to E. White, 8 Aug., 1556, in French, Italian and English (*Stat. Reg* ii. 452).

[Another edition.]
Licensed in the four languages to E. Aggas, 20 Nov., 1588 (*Stat. Reg.* ii. 507).

[Another edition.] *I. Mommart : Bruxelle.* 1608.   8°.
B.M. (1075. e. 21).

[A different version.]   A Paire of Turtle Doves : or, the Tragicall History of Bellora and Fidelio.   Seconded with the Tragicall end of Agamio, wherein (besides other matters pleasing to the Reader) by way of dispute betweene a Knight and a Lady is described this neuer before debated question. Towit : Whether man to woman, or woman to man offer the greatest temptations and allurements vnto vnbridled lust, and consequently whether man or woman in that vnlawfull act, be the greater offender.   A historie pleasant, delightfull, and witty, fit of all to be perused for their better instruction, but especially of youth to be regarded, to bridle their follies.   *For F. Burton.* 1606.   4°.   𝕭.𝕷.

Bodl. (Douce G. 245), imperf. ; Corser, *Coll. Anglo-Poet*, iv. 90–3 ; *Brit. Bib.*, iv. 210.

FORDE, EMANUEL.

The Famous Historie of Montelyon, Knight of the Oracle, and Sonne to the Renowned Persicles King of Assyria, *etc.*   *B. Alsop and T. Fawcet.* 1633.   4°.   𝕭.𝕷.

Halliwell-Phillips is said (*D.N.B.*, Art. Forde) to have possessed a copy of an earlier edition.
Huth.

[Another edition.]   *E. Alsop and R. Wood for S. S., and are to be sold by F. Coles and C. Tyus.*   1663.   4°.   𝕭.𝕷.

B.M. (12410. e. 17).

[Another edition.]   1668.   4°.

Hazlitt, H. 207.

[Another edition.]   1671.   4°.

Hazlitt, H. 207.

[Another edition.]   *A. P. for W. Thackeray and T. Passinger.*   1673.   4°. 𝕭.𝕷.

Huth.

[Another edition.]   *Sold by W. Thackeray and T. Passenger.*   1677.   4°.

Term Cat., i. 295.

[Another edition.]   *J. R. and W. W. for W. Thackeray and T. Passenger.* 1687.   4°.   𝕭.𝕷.

Bodl. (Douce D. 225).

[Another edition.]   *For W. Thackeray, and E. Tracey.*   1695.   4°.   𝕭.𝕷.

B.M. (1077. f. 13).

[Another edition.]   The Fourth Edition.   1697.   4°.
   Term Cat., iii. 31.

[Another edition.]   *W. O[nley] for E. Tracy, and C. Bates.*   4°.
   B.M. (12450. f. 4).

[An abridgement.]   The Pleasant and Delightful History of Montelion,
etc.   W. Only and sold by E. Tracy.   4°.
   B.M. (12403. aa. 39).

[Another edition?]   *For J. Blare.*   4°.
   Blare's list ; J. P. Collier, *Bibliographical and Critical Account*, ii. 242.

[A different abridgement.]   Adorned with suitable Cuts, *etc.   For Hannah
Tracy and Sarah Bates.*   1720.   12°.
   B.M. (12403. a. 19).

[Another edition.]   *For A. Bettesworth and C. Hitch, J. Osborn, S. Birt,
J. Hodges, and S. Bates.*   12°.
   B.M. (1077. e. 34).

[Another edition.]   *For H. Woodgate and S. Brooks.*   12°.
   Bodl. (Douce MM. 302).

[The Most Pleasant Historie of Ornatus and Artesia.]   4°.   𝕭.𝕷.
   Referred to in Meres' *Palladis Tamia*, 1598.
   Priv. Lib., imperf., wants title-page, etc.

[Another edition.]   The Most Pleasant Historie of Ornatus and Artesia.
Wherein is contained the vniust Raigne of Thæon King of Phrygia.   Who
with his sonne Lenon, (intending Ornatus death,) right Heire to the Crowne,
was afterwardes slaine by his own Seruants, and Ornatus after many extreame
miseries, Crowned King.   *T. Creede.*   1607.   4°.   𝕭.𝕷.
   Bodl. (Douce F. 215).

[Another edition.]   *B. Alsop and T. Fawcet.*   1634.   4°.   𝕭.𝕷.
   Huth.

[Another edition.]   Newly Corrected and Amended.   *B. A[lsop].*   1650.
4°.   𝕭.𝕷.
   B.M. (12613. c. 13).

[Another edition.]   1669.   4°.
   Hazlitt, II. 206.

[Another edition.] The Eighth Impression ; Exactly corrected and amended. *M. White, for J. Wright, J. Clark, W. Thackery, and T. Passenger.* 1683. 4°. 𝕭.𝕷.

B.M. (1077. g. 35/4).

[An abridgement.] The Famous, Pleasant, and Delightful History of Ornatus and Artesia, *etc. For B. Deacon.*

Advertised in Deacon's ed. of *The Seven Champions.*

[Another edition.] *For G. Conyers.* [1688 ?]

Advertised in Greene's *Dorastus and Fawnia,* 1688.

[Another edition.] *For J. Deacon.* [1694 ?] 4°.

Advertised in *Amadis of Greece,* 1694.

Parismus, The Renoumed Prince of Bohemia. His most famous, delectable, and pleasant Historie. Conteining his Noble Battailes fought against the Persians, his loue to Laurana, the Kings Daughter of Thessaly. And his straunge Aduentures in the Desolate Island, *etc. T. Creede for R. Olive.* 1598–9. 4°. 𝕭.𝕷. 2 vols.

Vol. 2, *Parismenos,* is printed by " T. Creede, and are to be sold by R. Olive and W. Holmes." The dedications of both parts are signed by E. Forde.

B.M. (92. b. 6).

[Another edition.] The first part of Parismus the renowned Prince of Bohemia. His most famous, delectable, and pleasant Historie, *etc. T. Creede.* 1608–9. 4°. 𝕭.𝕷. 2 vols.

Vol. 2 is "the third time imprinted, and amended."

B.M. (1077. e. 56).

[Another edition.] *T. Creede.* 1615. 4°. 𝕭.𝕷. 2 vols.

The title of vol. 2 reads "The fourth time Imprinted and amended."

B.M. (1076. f. 27).

[Another edition.] The most Famous, Delectable, and pleasant Historie of Parismus, *etc. B. Alsop and T. Fawcet, and are to be sold by T. Alchron.* 1630. 4°. 𝕭.𝕷. 2 vols.

Vol. 2 is "Newly Imprinted and Amended."

B.M. (12410. bb. 28).

[Another edition.] Newly Imprinted and amended. *B. Alsop and T. Fawcet.* 1636. 8°. 𝕭.𝕷. 2 vols.

Bodl. (Arch. Bodl. B. II. 152).

[Another edition.]   Newly Imprinted and amended.   *J. Millit, for W. Thackeray.*   1649.   4°.   2 vols.

Vol. 2 is printed by B. Alsop.
B.M. (12410. e. 16).

[Another edition.]   The Pleasant History of Parismus, Prince of Bohemia, etc.   *J. B. for C. Tyus.*   4°.   𝕭.𝕷.

Priv. Lib.

[Another edition.]   1657.   4°.

Hazlitt, H. 207 (Heber, v. 3309).

[Another edition.]   *E. Alsop and R. Wood for S. S., and are to be sold by F. Coles.*   1663.   4°.   𝕭.𝕷.

Hazlitt, I. 162.

[Another edition.]   The Seventh Impression, newly Corrected and Amended.   *G. Purslow, for F. Coles, T. Vere, W. Gilbertson, and J. Wright.* 1664.   4°.

Hazlitt, H. 207, VII. 143.

[Another edition.]   1665.   4°.

Hazlitt, H. 207.

[Another edition.]   1668–9.

Hazlitt, H. 207.

[Another edition.]   The Ninth Impression.   Newly Corrected and Amended.   *A. P. for F. Coles, T. Vere, and J. Wright.*   1671–2.   4°. 𝕭.𝕷.   2 vols.

Part 2 is printed by E. Crowch, for F. Coles, T. Vere, and J. Wright.
B.M. (1077. e. 47).

[Another edition.]   *For F. Coles, T. Vere, J. Wright and J. Clark.*   1677. 4°.   2 vols ?

Term Cat., i. 284.

[Another edition.]   *T. H. for F. Coles, T. Vere, J. Wright, J. Clarke, W. Thaceray* [sic] *and T. Passenger.*   1681.   4°.   𝕭.𝕷.   2 vols.

Vol. 2 is printed by M. White for T. Vere, J. Wright, J. Clarke, W. Thackery and T. Passenger.
Dealer's list (from Sir Mark Sykes' library).

[Another edition.] The Twelfth Impression, newly Corrected and Amended. *M. H. and J. M. for J. Wright, J. Clarke, W. Thackeray, and T. Passinger.* 1684. 4°. 𝕭.𝕷. 2 vols.

B.M. (12612. f. 16).

[Another edition.] The Thirteenth Impression, newly Corrected and Amended. *J. Millit, for W. Thackeray.* 1689. 4°. 𝕭.𝕷. 2 vols.

B.M. (12612. f. 17).

[Another edition.] The Fourteenth Impression, Corrected and Amended. *W. Wilde.* 1696. 4°. 𝕭.𝕷. 2 vols.

B.M. (12450. f. 5).

[Another edition.] The Fifteenth Impression. Corrected and Amended. *For H. Rhodes.* 1704–5. 8°. 2 vols.

B.M. (12403. aaa. 13).

[An abridgement.] The Famous and Pleasant History of Parismus, The Valiant and Renowned Prince of Bohemia. In Three Parts, *etc. W. O[nley], and sold by J. Blare and G. Conyers.* 1699. 8°.

B.M. (1077. e. 31).

[Another edition ?] *W. O[nley] for E. Tracy.* 4°.

Hazlitt, VII. 143.

[Another edition.] The Third Edition. *W. O[nley], and sold by J. Blare and G. Conyers.* 1701. 12°.

B.M. (12450. b. 20).

[Another edition.] In Two Parts, *etc. W. Onley for J. Blare, and for G. Conyers.* 8°. 𝕭.𝕷.

The title begins "Of the Famous and Pleasant History" etc.
B.M. (12450. b. 21).

[Another edition.] *W. Onley for J. Blare.* 8°. 𝕭.𝕷.

Perhaps the same as the preceding.
Hazlitt, H. 207.

[Another edition.] In Three Parts . . . The Fifth Edition. *C. Brown and T. Norris.* 1713. 12°.

B.M. (12450. b. 19).

[Another edition.] The Eighth Edition. *For H. Woodgate and S. Brooks.* 12°.

3 parts.
Priv. Lib.

[Another edition.] 1724. 18°.

Dealer's list.

[A different abridgement.] The History of Parismus, *etc. T. Norris.* 4°.

7 chapters.
Priv. Lib.

[Another edition ?] [*For J. Blare ?*] *At the Looking-Glass on London-bridge.* 12°. 𝔅.𝔏.

Hazlitt, H. 207.

FOREST OF FANCY.

The Forrest of Fancy. Wherein is conteined very prety Apothegmes and pleasaunt histories, both in meeter and prose, Songes, Sonets, Epigrams and Epistles, of diuerse matter and in diuerse manner. With sundry other deuises, no lesse pithye then pleasaunt and profytable. *T. Purfoote.* 1579. 4°. 𝔅.𝔏.

Ends: "Finis. H. C." 80 leaves. Brydges, *Restituta,* iii. 456 ("58 leaves") is probably the same as this, without leaves 2 and 3.
B.M. (C. 39. c. 36).

FORTUNATE LOVERS.

The Fortunate, the Deceived, and the Unfortunate Lovers. 1632. 4°.

M. A. Scott, *Elizabethan Translations,* p. 45.

[Another edition ?] Three excellent new Novels, containing many pleasant and delightful Histories . . . Printed in English and French. Written by the Wits of both Nations. *For W. Cadman.* 1683.

Term Cat., ii. 49.

[Another edition.] *For W. Whitwood.* 1685. 8°.

T.C.C. (Capell υ. 3).

FORTUNATUS.

[Fortunatus.]

Licensed to Field, 22 June, 1615 (*Stat. Reg.* iii. 568). Referred to by Meredith Hanmer in the Epistle Dedicatory to his Eusebius, *Ecclesiastical History,* 1576.

[Another edition ?]   The History of the Birth, Travels, Strange Adventures, and Death of Fortunatus.   4°.   𝕭.𝕷.

The two parts are not separated ;   42 chapters.
Hazlitt, I. 165 ; = B.M. (12410. bb. 8), imperf., wanting title?

[Another edition.]   With the Illustration of several New Pictures.   *T. Haly.*
1682.   4°.   𝕭.𝕷.

A note in Sawbridge's edition of the other version of the same year complains that this is a piracy.   This is, therefore, the earlier of the two.
   Pepys 1192(3).

[A different version.]   The Right, Pleasant, and Variable Tragical History of Fortunatus.   Whereby a Young-man may learn how to behave himself in all Worldly Affairs and Casual Chances.   First penned in the Dutch Tongue : There-hence Abstracted, and now First of all Published in English ;   By T. C.   *A. Purslow, for G. Saubridge.*   1676.   8°.   𝕭.𝕷.

The two parts are not separated ;   58 ("48") chapters.
   B.M. (C. 38. a. 21).

[Another edition ?]   *For G. Sawbridge.*   1679.   8°.

Term Cat., i. 362.

[A different version.]   The Right, Pleasant, and Variable Trachical [*sic*] History of Fortunatus, *etc.*   *T. B. for H. Sawbridge.*   1682.   8°.   𝕭.𝕷.

The two parts are not separated ;   46 chapters.
   B.M. (12450. b. 13).

[A different version ?]   The comical and tragical history of Fortunatus . . . The Third Edition with Additions.   *For J. Blare.*   4°.

The same version as Osborne, King, and Hodges', below ?
   Blare's list ;   J. P. Collier, *Bibliographical Account*, ii. 242.

[Another edition ?]   The Famous and Delightful History of Fortunatus, and his Two Sons : in Two Parts . . . The Fourth Edition ; to which is added, several pleasant Stories not in the former : the whole illustrated with Pictures suitable to the History.   *W. O[nley], and sold by A. Bettesworth.*
1702.   12°.

2 parts, 41 chapters.
   Bodl. (Douce F. 95).

[Another edition.]   The Seventh Edition, Illustrated with Pictures, and many pleasant Stories added, not being in the former Impressions.   *T. Norris.*
12°.

2 parts, 42 chapters.
   B.M. (12410. a. 20).

[Another edition?]   The Right, Pleasant, and Diverting History of Fortunatus ...   The Tenth Edition, Illustrated with Variety of New Pictures and New Additions.   *T. C. for J. Osborne, J. King, and J. Hodges.*   12°.

57 chapters.
Bodl. (Douce F. 84).

[Another edition ?]   *For J. Deacon.*   [1689 ?]

Deacon's list.

[Another edition ?]   *For H. Woodgate and S. Brooks.*

Woodgate and Brooks' list in *Argalus and Parthenia.*

[An abridgement.]   The Most Excellent and Delightful History of Fortunatus, *etc.*   *A. M. for J. Conyers and J. Blare.*   8°.   𝕭.𝕷.

9 chapters.
Pepys 362 (401).

FRAGOSA.

[Fragosa.]

Licensed to H. Rocket, 7 Aug. 1611 (*Stat. Reg.* iii. 462).

[Another edition.]   The First Part Of The Renowned Historie of Fragosa King of Aragon.   Together with the Strange Fortunes, and Heroicall Deedes, performed by his three Sons, and the worthy president of Love in his faire Daughter Flermia.   Right pleasant for the Aged to drive away Melancholy thoughts, and profitable for the Young to behold the often variations of the fickle World.   Written by W. C.   *B. Alsop.*   1646.   4°.   𝕭.𝕷.   2 vols.

B.M. (C. 57. b. 26).

[Another edition.]   The Renowned History of Fragosa.   In Two Parts. Written, by W. C., *etc.*   *E. Alsop.*   1656.   4°.   𝕭.𝕷.

Bodl. (Douce C. 225).

[Another edition.]   The History of the most renowned Fragosa King of Aragon, *etc.*   *E. Alsop and R. Wood.*   1663.   4°.   𝕭.𝕷.   2 vols.

An edition, "printed for Charles Tyus," was advertised in *Palladine*, 1664.
J. P. Collier, *Bibliographical Account*, i. 294.

FREDERICK OF JENNEN.

This matter treateth of a merchaûtes wyfe that afterwarde went lyke a mã and becam a great Lorde and was called Frederyke of Jennen afterwarde. *J. Dusborowghe : Anwarpe.*   1518.   4°.   𝕭.𝕷.

Britwell ; Proctor, *Doesborgh*, 17.

[Another edition.]　*R. Pynson.*　4°.　𝕭.𝕷.

Bodl. (Douce frag. e. 32).

[Another edition.]　Here begynneth a propre treatyse of a marchauntes wyfe, that afterwarde went lyke a man and became a great lorde, and was called Frederyke of Jennen.　*A. Vele.*　4°.　𝕭.𝕷.

B.M. (C. 20. c. 31/6).

G., F.

See GODWIN, Francis.

G., P. T.

See BLANCHARDINE AND EGLANTINE.

GAINSFORD, THOMAS.

The Historie of Trebizond.　In foure Bookes.　By Tho. Gainsforde Esquier.　*For T. Downe* [sic] *and E. Dawson.*　1616.　4°.

The imprints of books 2-4 are W. White for T. Downes and E. Dawson.　1 vol.
B.M. (1435. b. 1).

GARCIA, CARLOS.

The Sonne of the Rogue, or, the Politick Theefe.　With the Antiquitie of Theeves.　A worke no lesse Curious then delectable ; first written in Spanish by Don Garcia.　Afterwards translated into Dutch, and then into French by S. D.　Now Englished by W. M.　*I. D. and are to be sold by B. Langford.* 1638.　12°.

B.M. (12330. a. 31).

[Another edition.]　Lavernae, or the Spanish Gipsy . . . First written in Spanish, by Don. Garcia : Now in English by W. M.　*Not in Newgate.* 1650.　8°.

B.M. (12330. aa. 31).

GASCOIGNE, GEORGE.

[Ferdinando Ieronimi : in.]　A Hundreth sundrie Flowres bounde vp in one small Poesie, *etc.*　*H. Bynneman for R. Smith.*　[1572.]　4°.　𝕭.𝕷.

Gascoigne's Works.　·The date occurs in the preface to *Ferdinando Jeronimi,* which occupies pp. 201-293.　The name Ferdinando Jeronimi is always represented by initials, and the author's by "G. T."
B.M. (C. 13. a. 16/1).

[Another edition.]   The Posies of George Gascoigne Esquire.   Corrected, perfected, and augmented by the Authour.   1575.   *For R. Smith.*   1575. 4°.   𝕭.𝕷.

"The pleasant Fable of Ferdinando Ieronimi and Leonora de Valasco, translated out of the Italian riding tales of Bartello," occupies pp. 193-276 of "Hearbes."
B.M. (C. 34 f. 6).

[Another edition.]   The Whole woorkes of George Gascoigne Esquyre: Newlye compyled into one Volume, That is to say : His Flowers, Hearbes, Weedes . . . the Storie of Ferdinando Ieronimi, *etc.*   *A. Ieffes.*   1587.   4°. 𝕭.𝕷.

Ferdinando Jeronimi occupies pp. 193-282 of "Hearbes."
B.M. (C. 34. f. 8).

GENTLE CRAFT.

See DELONEY, Thomas.

GEORGE A GREEN.

The Pinder of Wakefield : Being the merry History of George a Greene the lusty Pinder of the North.   Briefly shewing his manhood and his braue merriments amongst his boone Companions.   A Pill fit to purge melancholy in this drooping age.   Read, then judge.   With the great Battel fought betwixt him and Robin Hood, Scarlet and little Iohn, and after his liuing with them in the Woods.   Full of pretty Histories, Songs, Catches, Iests, and Ridles.   *G. P. for E. Blackamore.*   1632.   4°.   𝕭.𝕷.

Bodl. (4°. S. 19. Art.).

[Another edition.]   *G. P. for E. Blackamoore.*   1633.   4°.
Mr. Quaritch.

[Another edition ?]
Licensed to J. Crouch, 4 Nov., 1635 (*Stat. Reg.* iv. 349).

[An abridgement ?]   The History of George A Greene, *etc.*   *For T. Norris.*   12°.
Hazlitt, H. 683.

[A different version, complete.]   The History of George A Green, Pindar of the Town of Wakefield.   His Birth, Calling, Valour, and Reputation in the Country.   With Divers Pleasant, as well as Serious Passages in the Course of his Life and Fortune.   Illustrated with Cuts.   *For S. Ballard.*   1706.   8°.

The dedication is signed N. W.
B.M. (1077. e. 32).

[Another edition.] The Second Edition. *For D. Mead, and D. Pratt.* 1715. 8°.

Hazlitt, I. 472.

GERILEON.

[Gerileon of England.]

Licensed to J. Jugge, 20 May, 1577 (for 2d.) ; to M. Jennings, 6 April, 1579 (*Stat. Reg.* ii. 312, 351).

[Another edition?] The Gallant, delectable and pleasaunt Hystorie of Gerileon of Englande : Containyng the haughtie Feates of Armes, and Knightlie Prowesse of the same Gerileon, with his Loues and other memorable Aduentures. Composed in the Frenche Tongue, by Steuen De Maison Neufue Bordelois. And now newly translated into English. *For M. Iennynges.* 1583. 4°. 𝕭.𝕷.

Bodl. (Malone 679).

The Second Part of the History of Gerileon of England. Written in French by Estienne de Maison neufve, Bordelois, and translated into English by Anthony Munday. *For C. Burbie.* 1592. 4°.

Hazlitt, H. 47. Part 2 was licensed on 8 Aug., 1592, to T. Scarlett ; parts 1, 3, 4, on 6 Oct., 1592, to A. Jeffes (*Stat. Reg.* ii. 619, 621).

GESTA ROMANORUM.

Gesta Romanorum. *Wynkyn de Worde.* 4°. 𝕭.𝕷.

St. John's Coll., Camb.

[Another edition.] [*Wynkyn de Worde.*] 4°.

Priv. Lib., frag. Bib. Soc., *Handlists.*

[Another edition.] Here after foloweth the hystorye of Gesta Romanorum. [*I.*] *Kynge.* 1557. 4°. 𝕭.𝕷.

Bodl. (Malone H. 119).

[Robinson's Record of Ancient Histories.]

In Robinson's *Eupolemia* (Royal MS. 18A. LXVI, fol. 5) is entered under 1577 :
    A Record of Ancyent Historyes intituled in Latin Gesta Romano𝔲 translated (auctore vt supponitur Iohane Leylando Antiquario) by mee perused corrected and bettered perused further and allowed by yᵉ sayde Wardens : And printed first and last by Thomas Easte in Aldersgate streete 6 tymes to this yeare 1601 cont' 21 sheetes Dedicated for 5 Impressions to the R. Honorable Lady Margaret Countess of Lyneux, who gaue me for her booke 13ˢ 4ᵈ besydes sale of 25 boks Dedicated last to the Wardens of the Lethersellers, who wᵗʰ others have gıven me xxˢ. [Marginal postscript] Dedicated last of all anno 1602 to D. Watson B of Chichester and B Almoner to the Queens Maiesty, who (not so thanckful to me as I deserued) gave me but ijˢ for my booke.

[Another edition.]   A Record of auncient Histories, intituled in Latin :
Gesta Romanorum.   Discoursing upon sundry examples for the aduaunce-
ment of vertue, and the abandoning of vice.   No lesse pleasant in reading,
then profitable in practise Now newly perused and corrected by R. Robinson,
Citizen of London.   *T. Est.* 1595. 4°. 𝔅.𝔏.

    Bodl. (Douce R. 4).

[Another edition.]   The sixth impression, *etc.*   *T. East.* 1600. 12°.

    Hazlitt, H. 227.

[Another edition.]   The Seventh Impression.   *T. East.* 1602. 12°.

    Hazlitt, H. 227.

[Another edition.]   With some thing added, by R. R.   *T. Snodham.*
1610. 8°. 𝔅.𝔏.

    Bodl. (Douce R. 3).

[Another edition.]   *W. Stansby.* 8°. 𝔅.𝔏.

    Priv. Lib.

[Another edition.]   *R. Bishop, and are to be sold by E. Blackmore.*
1648. 8°. 𝔅.𝔏.

    B.M. (12410. a. 43).

[Another edition.]   *R. Bishop.* 8°. 𝔅.𝔏.

    Bodl. (Douce R. 273).

[Another edition.]   *J. B. for A. Crook.* 1662. 8°. 𝔅.𝔏.

    Bodl. (Douce R. 1).

[Another edition.]   *J. B. for A. Crook.* 1663. 8°. 𝔅.𝔏.

    B.M. (1456. a. 2).

[Another edition.]   *A. I. for A. Crook.* 1668. 8°. 𝔅.𝔏.

    Bodl. (Douce R. 2).

[Another edition.]   *E. Crowch, for A. Crook.* 1672. 8°. 𝔅.𝔏.

    Priv. Lib.

[Another edition.]   *For F. Coles.* 1672. 8°.

    Hazlitt, H. 227.

[Another edition.]   *T. H. for R. Scott, T. Bassett, R. Chiswell, and
J. Wright.* 1681. 8°. 𝔅.𝔏.

    Bodl. (Douce R. 9).

[Another edition.]   1682.   8°.

Hazlitt, H. 227.

[Another edition.]   *For T. Basset, R. Chiswell, A. Mill, G. Conyers, and M. Wotton.*   1689.   8°.   𝕭.𝕷.

B.M. (12430. b. 13).

[Another edition.]   *R. Sanders: Glasgow.*   1696.   8°.   𝕭.𝕷.

B.M. (12403. a. 43).

[Another edition.]   *For T. Basset, R. Chiswell, A. Mill, G. Conyers and M. Wotton.*   1698.   8°.   𝕭.𝕷.

B.M. (12430. a. 14).

[Another edition.]   *For R. Chiswell, B. Walford, G. Conyers.*   1703.   12°.

B.M. (12430. a. 13).

[Another edition.]   *R. Sanders: Glasgow.*   1713.   8°.

B.M. (1456. b. 2).

[A different version.]   Gesta Romanorum : Or, Forty-five Histories Originally (as 'tis said) Collected from the Roman Records.   With Applications or Morals for the Suppressing Vice, and Encouraging Virtue and the Love of God.   Vol. I.   Newly and with Care Translated from the Latin Edition.   Printed A.D. M.D.XIV.   *R. Janeway, for T. Davis.*   1703.   12°.

B.M. (G. 17358).

[Another edition, enlarged.]   Gesta Romanorum : Or, Fifty-eight Histories Originally (as 'tis said) collected from the Roman Records.   With Applications or Morals . . .   By B. P.   Adorn'd with Cuts.   Very pleasant to read, and Profitable if practis'd.   *G. Conyers.*   12°.

B.M. (1456. a. 5).

[Another edition.]   Gesta Romanorum : containing 58 Remarkable Histories . . .   By A. B.   Adorn'd with a new Set of Cuts, proper to Illustrate and Explain the Respective Stories, *etc.*   *For T. Norris, and A. Bettesworth.*   1722.   12°.

B.M. (G. 17357).

[Another edition.]   *For H. Woodgate and S. Brooks.*

Woodgate and Brooks' list, in *Argalus and Parthenia.*

[Another edition.]   *A. Baldwin.*   8°.

Hazlitt, H. 227.

[An abridgement.]   The Young Man's Guide to a Vertuous Life.   In many Pleasant Little tales or Allegories : with Moral Explanations.   Adorned with several Cuts, *etc.   For G. and M. Conyers.*   1698.   8º.

> Bodl. (Douce R. 10).

GIFFORD, HUMPHREY.

A Posie of Gilloflowers, eche differing from other in colour and odour, yet all sweete.   By Humfrey Gifford Gent.   *For I. Perin.*   1580.   4º.   𝕭.𝕿.

> Contains "Diuers briefe histories."
> B.M. (239. g. 33).

GODFREY OF BOUILLON.

Begin : tHe hye couragyous faytes, And valyaunt actes of noble Illustrous and vertuous personnes ben digne to be recounted, *etc.   End :* Thus endeth this book Intitled the laste siege and conquest of Iherusalem with many other historyes therin comprysed, Fyrst of Eracles, and of the meseases of the cristen men in the holy londe, And of their releef τ conquest of Iherusalem, and how Godeffroy of bologne was first kyng of the latyns in that royamme τ of his deth, translated τ reduced out of ffreusshe [*sic*] in to englysshe by me symple persone Wylliam Caxton, *etc.   W. Caxton : Westmester.*   1481.   Fol.   𝕭.𝕿.

> B.M. (C. 11. c. 4).

GODWIN, FRANCIS.

The Man in the Moone : or a discourse of a Voyage thither By Domingo Gonsales The speedy Messenger.   *J. Norton, for J. Kirton and T. Warren.*   1638.   8º.

> B.M. (635. b. 27).

[Another edition.]   By F. G. B. of H.   To which is added Nuncius Inanimatus, written in Latin by the same Author, and now Englished by a Person of Worth.   The Second Edition.   *For J. Kirton.*   1657.   8º.

> B.M. (12612. a. 39).

GOMBAULD, JEAN OGIER DE.

Endimion, An Excellent Fancy first composed in French by Mounsieur Gombauld.   And now Elegantly Interpreted by Richard Hurst Gentleman.   *I. Okes for S. Browne.*   1639.   8º.

> Licensed to S. Browne, 9 May 1638 (*Stat. Reg.* iv. 418) ; probably therefore the earlier edition mentioned by Lowndes, "Endimion, an excellent Fancy, elegantly interpreted, from the French, by Richard Hurst, 1637," is a mistake for this.
> B.M. (1073. c. 24).

GONSALES, Domingo.
See GODWIN, Francis.

GOODMAN, Nicholas.
Hollands Leaguer : or an Historical Discourse of the Life and Actions of
Dona Britanica Hollandia the Arch-Mistris of the wicked women of Eutopia.
Wherein is detected the notorious Sinne of Panderisme, and the Execrable
Life of the luxurious Impudent. *A. M. for R. Barnes.* 1632. 4°.
Signed at the end.
B.M. (G. 3282).

GOSSON, Stephen.
The Ephemerides of Phialo . . . By Step. Gosson, Stud. Oxon. *T. Dawson.*
1579. 8°. 𝕭.𝕷.
B.M. (C. 12. d. 14), imperf.

[Another edition.] *T. Dawson.* 1586. 8°. 𝕭.𝕷.
B.M. (C. 12. d. 15), imperf.

GOULART, Simon.
Admirable and Memorable Histories containing the wonders of our time.
Collected into French out of the best Authors. By I. [*sic*] Goulart. And
out of French into English. By Ed. Grimeston, *etc. G. Eld.* 1607. 4°.
B.M. (12356. b. 35).

GREENE, Robert.
[Alcida.]
Licensed to John Wolfe, 9 Dec. 1588 (*Stat. Reg.* ii. 510).

[Another edition?] Alcida Greenes Metamorphosis . . . The Discourse
confirmed with diuerse merry and delightfull Histories . . . By R. G.
G. Purslowe. 1617. 4°.
B.M. (95. b. 20/4).

Arbasto, The Anatomie of Fortune. Wherin is discouered by a pithie and
pleasant Discourse, that the highest state of prosperitie, is oftimes the first
step to mishap . . . By Robert Greene Mayster of Arte. *H. Iackson.* 1584.
4°. 𝕭.𝕷.
B.M. (C. 40. e. 66).

[Another edition.] *H. Iackson.* 1594. 4°. 𝕭.𝕷.
Corser, *Coll. Anglo-Poet.* iv. 94–9.

[Another edition.]   *I. B. for R. Iackson.*   1617.   4°.

Bodl. (Malone 574), the date cut off ; Hazlitt, H. 242.

[Another edition.]   Whereunto is added a louely Poem of Pyramus and Thisbe.   *For F. Williams.*   1626.   4°.   𝕭.𝕷.

B.M. (95. b. 20/7).

The Black Bookes Messenger.   Laying Open the Life and Death of Ned Browne one of the most notable Cutpurses, Crosbiters, and Conny-Catchers, that euer lived in England . . . by R. G.   *I. Danter for T. Nelson.*   1592.   4°.   𝕭.𝕷.

The Black Book itself, which is promised in the preface, is not known to have been published.
Bodl. (Malone 575).

[Another edition.]   Ciceronis Amor. Tullies Loue. Wherein is discoursed the prime of Ciceroes youth, setting out in liuely portratures how young Gentlemen that ayme at honour should leuell the end of their affections, holding the loue of countrie and friends in more esteeme then those fading blossomes of beautie, that onely feede the curious suruey of the eye.   A worke full of pleasure, as following Ciceroes vaine, who was as conceipted in his youth as graue in his age, profitable as conteining precepts worthie so famous an Orator.   Robert Greene in Artibus magister.   *R. Robinson, for T. Newman and J. Winnington.* 1589.   4°.   𝕭.𝕷.

Corser, *Coll. Anglo-Poet.* iv. 79–80.

[Another edition.]   1592.

Cens. Lit., viii. 388.

[Another edition.]   *R. Robinson, for I. Busbie.*   1597.   4°.   𝕭.𝕷.
B.M. (G. 10454).

[Another edition.]   *For N. Lyng.*   1601.   4°.   𝕭.𝕷.
Bridgewater.

[Another edition.]   *J. R. for N. Lyng.*   1605.   4°.   𝕭.𝕷.
B.M. (1077. e. 7).

[Another edition.]   *For I. Smethwicke.*   1609.   4°.   𝕭.𝕷.
B.M. (C. 57. b. 33).

[Another edition.]   *W. Stansby for I. Smethwicke.*   1611.   4°.   𝕭.𝕷.
B.M. (95. b. 20/1).

[Another edition.]   *W. Stansby for I. Smethwicke.*   1616.   4°.   𝕭.𝕷.
    B.M. (C. 39. d. 9).

[Another edition.]   *W. Stansby for I. Smethwicke.*   1628.   4°.   𝕭.𝕷.
    B.M. (95. b. 10).

Euphues his Censure to Philautus, Wherein is presented a philosophicall
combat betweene Hector and Achylles, discouering in foure discourses, interlaced with diuerse delightfull Tragedies, The vertues necessary to be incident
in euery gentleman . . .   Robertus Greene, In artibus magister.   *I. Wolfe
for E. White.*   1587.   4°.   𝕭.𝕷.
    B.M. (95. b. 18/2).

[Another edition.]   *Eliz. Allde.*   1634.   4°.   𝕭.𝕷.
    B.M. (C. 40. d. 2).

Greene's farewell to Folly.   Sent to Courtiers and Schollers as a president
to warne them from the vaine delights that drawes youth on to repentance
. . . Robert Greene vtriusque Academiæ in Artibus magister.   *T. Scarlet for
T. Gubbin and T. Newman.*   1591.   4°.   𝕭.𝕷.
    B.M. (1077. e. 5).

[Another edition.]   *W. White.*   1617.   4°.   𝕭.𝕷.
    B.M. (1077. d. 63).

Greenes, Groats-Worth of witte, bought with a million of Repentance.
Describing the follie of youth, the falshood of makeshift flatterers, the miserie
of the negligent, and mischiefes of deceiuing Courtezans.   Written before his
death and published at his dying request.   *For W. Wright.*   1592.   4°.   𝕭.𝕷.
    B.M. (C. 57. b. 42).

[Another edition.]   *T. Creede for R. Oliue.*   1596.   4°.   𝕭.𝕷.
    "Entred for Richard Oliffes Copie Printed by Iohn Danter.   And Thomas Creede from
    tyme to tyme to print this book for Richard Oliff," 20 Oct., 1596 (*Stat. Reg.*, iii. 72).
    Hazlitt, H. 242.

[Another edition.]   1600.
    Cens. Lit., viii. 388.

[Another edition.]   1616.
    Cens. Lit., viii. 388.   Hazlitt, H. 242, " 1606," is probably the same.

[Another edition.]   Newly corrected, and of many errors purged.   *B. Alsop,
for H. Bell.*   1617.   4°.   𝕭.𝕷.
    B.M. (95. b. 20/5).

[Another edition.]   *N. O[kes] for H. Bell.*   1621.   4°.   𝕭.𝕷.
B.M. (C. 40. d. 41).

[Another edition.]   *I. Hauiland, for H. Bell.*   1629.   4°.   𝕭.𝕷.
Bodl. (Malone 572).

[Another edition.]   *For H. and M. Bell.*   1637.   4°.   𝕭.𝕷.
B.M. (95. b. 16).

[Another edition.]
Undated.   *Cens. Lit.*, viii. 388.

Gwydonius.   The Carde of Fancie.   Wherein the Folly of those Carpet
Knights is decyphered, which guyding their course by the compasse of
Cupid, either dash their Ship against most daungerous Rocks, or els attaine
the hauen with paine and perill.   Wherein also is described in the person of
Gwydonius a cruell combat betweene Nature and necessitie.   By Robert
Greene, Master of Arte, in Cambridge.   *For W. Ponsonby.*   1584.   4°.
Hazlitt, H. 237.

[Another edition.]   *For W. Ponsonby.*   1587.   4°.   𝕭.𝕷.
H. Pyne (Grosart's reprint in Huth Library).   Hazlitt, H. 237 (Heber), imperf.

[Another edition.]   *T. C. for W. Ponsonbie.*   1593.   4°.
Bodl. (Malone 573).

[Another edition.]   Greenes Carde of Fancie, *etc.*   *H. L[ownes] for*
M. Lownes.   1608.   4°.   𝕭.𝕷.
B.M. (95. b. 19/6)).

[Mamillia.]
Licensed to T. Woodcock, 3 Oct., 1580 (*Stat. Reg.*, ii. 378).

[Another edition?]   Mamillia.   A Mirrour or looking-glasse for the Ladies
of Englande . . .   By Robert Greene Graduate in Cambridge.   *For*
T. Woodcocke.   1583.   4°.   𝕭.𝕷.
Bodl. (Malone, 575*).

[Another edition.]   1593.
Cens. Lit., viii. 388.

[Mamilia, The seconde parte of the tryumphe of Pallas.]
Licensed to Ponsonby, 6 Sept., 1583 (*Stat. Reg.*, ii. 428).

[Another edition.] The second part of the triumph of Pallas . . . By Robert Greene Maister of Arts, in Cambridge. *T. C. for W. Ponsonbie.* 1593. 4°. 𝕭.𝕷.

B.M. (95. b. 19/2).

[Another edition?]

Licensed to M. Lownes, by consent of S. Waterson, 5 Nov., 1604 (*Stat. Reg.*, iii. 274).

[Menaphon.] 1587.

Cens. Lit., viii. 386. Probably an error.

[Another edition?] Menaphon Camilla's alarum to slumbering Euphues, in his melancholy Cell at Silexedra . . . Robertus Greene in Artibus magister. *T. O[rwin] for S. Clarke.* 1589. 4°. 𝕭.𝕷.

B.M. (95. b. 18/5), imperf. ; Hoe.

[Another edition.] 1599. 4°.

Cens. Lit., viii. 386.

[Another edition.] 1605.

Cens. Lit., viii. 386.

[Another edition.] Greenes Arcadia. Or Menaphon, *etc. For I. Smeth-wicke.* 1610. 4°.

B.M. (95. b. 15).

[Another edition.] *W. Stansby for I. Smethwicke.* 1616. 4°. 𝕭.𝕷.

B.M. (C. 40. e. 5).

[Another edition.] 1634. 4°.

Cens. Lit., viii. 386.

The Myrrour of Modestie, wherein appeareth as in a perfect Glasse howe the Lorde deliuereth the innocent from all imminent perils . . . By R. G. Maister of Artes. *R. Warde.* 1584. 8°. 𝕭.𝕷.

B.M. (C. 53. a. 37).

Morando the Tritameron of Loue : Wherein certaine pleasaunt conceites, vttered by diuers woorthy personages, are perfectly dyscoursed . . . By Robert Greene, Maister of Artes in Cambridge. *For E. White.* 1584. 4°. 𝕭.𝕷.

Part I.

B.M. (C. 57. b. 8/1).

[Another edition.] The first and second part . . . By Robert Greene, Maister of Arts in Cambridge. *I. Wolfe for E. White.* 1587. 4°. 𝕭.𝕷.

B.M. (95. b. 18/3).

Greenes Mourning Garment: given him by Repentance at the Funerals of Loue: which he presents for a fauour to all young Gentlemen that wish to weane themselves from wanton desires. Both pleasant and Profitable. 1590. 4°.

Hazlitt, H. 240.

[Another edition.] 1597. 4°.

Hazlitt, H. 241; Lowndes.

[Another edition.] *G. Purslowe.* 1616. 4°. 𝕭.𝕷.

B.M. (95. b. 20/3).

Greenes Neuer too late, or, A Powder of Experience: Sent to all youthfull Gentlemen . . . Decyphering in a true English historie, those particular vanities, that with their frostie vapours nip the blossoms of euerie ripe braine . . . Rob. Greene in artibus Magister. *T. Orwin for N. L. and I. Busbie.* 1590. 4°. 𝕭.𝕷.

B.M. (95. b. 18/7).

[Greene's Never Too Late, part 2.] Francescos Fortunes: Or The second part of Greenes Neuer too late, *etc.* [*T. Orwin*] *For N. L*[*ing*] *and I. Busbie.* 1590. 4°. 𝕭.𝕷.

B.M. (95. b. 18/8).

[Another edition of both parts.] Greenes Neuer too late, *etc.* *J. Roberts for N. Ling.* 1600. 4°. 𝕭.𝕷.

Bodl. (Malone 572).

[Another edition.] *For N. Ling.* 1607. 4°. 𝕭.𝕷.

B.M. (1077. e. 6).

[Another edition.] *For I. Smethwicke.* 1611. 4°. 𝕭.𝕷.

Dyce.

[Another edition.] *W. Stansby for I. Smethwicke.* 1616. 4°. 𝕭.𝕷.

B.M. (C. 40. c. 30).

[Another edition.] *For I. Smethwicke.* [1621?] 4°. 𝕭.𝕷.

B.M. (G. 10455), the date cut away; Bodl. (Douce G. 242), imperf., with a modern supplied title-page.

[Another edition.]   1631.

> *Cens. Lit.*, viii. 387.

[Another edition.]

> *Cens. Lit.*, viii. 387 ; Beloe, *Anecd. Lit.*, ii. 183 ; Roxburgh.

[Orpharion.]

> Licensed to E. White, 9 Feb., 1589/90 (*Stat. Reg.* ii. 539).

[Another edition?]   Greene's Orpharion.   Wherein is discouered a musicale concorde of pleasant Histories . . .   Robertus Greene, in Artibus Magister.   *For E. White.*   1599.   4°.   𝕭.𝕷.

> B.M. (95. b. 19/4).

A pair of Turtle Doves.   *See* FLORES, Juan de.

> This has been attributed to Greene.

Pandosto.   The Triumph of Time.   Wherein is discouered by a pleasant Historie, that although by the meanes of sinister fortune Truth may be concealed, yet by Time in spight of fortune it is most manifestly reuealed . . . By Robert Greene Maister of Arts in Cambridge.   *T. Orwin for T. Cadman.* 1588.   4°.   𝕭.𝕷.

> B.M. (95. b. 18/4).

[Another edition.]   *For G. Porter.*   1607.   4°.   𝕭.𝕷.

> Bodl. (Malone 574).

[Another edition.]   *W. Stansby.*   1609.   4°.

> Hazlitt, H. 239.

[Another edition.]   *T. C. for G. Potter, and are to be sold by J. Tap.* 1614.   4°.   𝕭.𝕷.

> B.M. (95. b. 11).

[Another edition.]   *E. Allde.*   1619.   4°.

> Hazlitt, II. 239.

[Another edition.]   *T. P[avier] for F. Faulkener.*   1629.   4°.   𝕭.𝕷.

> Bodl. (Malone 152/3).

[Another edition.]   *T. P[avier] for F. Faulkner.*   1632.   4°.   𝕭.𝕷.

> B.M. (C. 30. e. 25).

[Another edition.]   The Pleasant Historie of Dorastus and Fawnia, *etc.*
For F. Faulkner.   1636.   4°.   𝕭.𝕷.

   B.M. (C. 40. d. 3).

[Another edition.]   *For F. Faulkner.*   1648.   4°.   𝕭.𝕷.

   B.M. (C. 40. d. 4).

[Another edition.]   *For E. Blackmore.*   1655.   4°.

   T.C.C. (Capell S. 33. 2).

[Another edition.]   *R. Ibbitson for I. Wright, and are to be sold by
W. Thackery.*   1664.   4°.

   T.C.C. (Capell S. 28. 3).

[Another edition.]   1675.

   Cens. Lit., viii. 386.

[Another edition.]   *For J. Wright, and are to be Sold by J. Clarke.*   1677.
4°.   𝕭.𝕷.

   B.M. (12612. f. 20).

[Another edition.]   *H. Brugis for J. Clark, W. Thackeray and T. Passinger.*
1684.   4°.   𝕭.𝕷.

   Hazlitt, H. 239.

[Another edition.]   *For G. Conyers.*   1688.   4°.   𝕭.𝕷.

   B.M. (12403. aa. 22).

[Another edition.]   1694.   4°.

   Hazlitt, H. 239.

[Another edition.]   The Pleasant and Delightful History of Dorastus,
Prince of Sicily, and Fawnia, only Daughter and Heir to Pandosto, King of
Bohemia, *etc.   For G. Conyers.*   [1696?]   12°.

  At the end is added "The History of Josephus the Indian Prince," an abridgement of the
Philosophus Autodidactus of Abú Bakr ibn Al-Tufail.   (*See* Part II.)
  B.M. (12613. a. 14), the date 1696 supplied in MS.

[Another edition.]   *W. O*[*nley*] *for G. Conyers.*   1703.   4°.

   B.M. (12613. c. 12).

[Another edition.]   The Pleasant History of Dorastus and Fawnia, *etc.*
F. W. for G. Conyers.   4°.   𝕭.𝕷.

   Bodl. (Douce G. 515).

[Another edition.]　The Pleasant and Delightful History, *etc.*　*For*
G. Conyers.　[1704 ?]　8°.

    Bodl. (Malone 1008) ; *Term Cat.* (1704), iii. 430.

[Another edition.]　1723.

    Cens. Lit., viii. 386.

[Another edition.]　1735.

With the addition of *Hero and Leander* in prose.
    Cens. Lit., viii. 386.

[An abridgement.]　The Delightful History of Dorastus and Fawnia.
Wherein is Declared the Cruelty of Pandosto to his fair Bellaria, *etc.*　*For*
C. Dennisson.　8°.　𝕭.𝕸.

    Pepys 362 (377), the date cut away.

[Another edition ?]　*For H. Woodgate and S. Brooks.*

Abridged ?　Woodgate and Brooks' list, in *Argalus and Parthenia.*

Penelopes Web : Wherein a Christall Myrror of fæminine perfection
represents to the viewe of euery one those vertues and graces, which more
curiously beautifies the mynd of women, then eyther sumptuous Apparell, or
Iewels of inestimable valew : the one buying fame with honour, the other
breeding a kynd of delight, but with repentance . . .　Interlaced with three
seuerall and Comicall Histories.　By Robert Greene Maister of Artes in
Cambridge.　*For T. C. and E. A*[*ggas*].　1587.　4°.　𝕭.𝕸.

Licensed to E. Aggas, 26 June, 1587 (*Stat. Reg.*, ii. 472).
    Bodl. (Malone 572).

[Another edition.]　Interlaced with three seuerall and Comicall Histories.
By Robert Greene Master of Artes in Cambridge.　*For I. Hodgets.*　1601.
4°.　𝕭.𝕸.

    B.M. (95. b. 19/5.)

[Another edition.]

    Undated.　*Cens. Lit.*, viii. 389.

Perimedes the Blacke-Smith, A golden methode, how to vse the minde in
pleasant and profitable exercise . . . with certaine pleasant Histories and
tragicall tales, which may breed delight to all, and offence to none.　*I. Wolfe.*
1588.　4°.　𝕭.𝕸.

Licensed to E. White, 29 March, 1588 (*Stat. Reg.*, ii. 488).
    B.M. (1077. e. 4).

Philomela. The Lady Fitzwaters Nightingale. *R. B. for E. White.*
1592. 4°. 𝕭.𝕷.

The colophon reads : E. A. for Edwarde White.
Licensed to J. Wolfe, 1 July, 1592 (*Stat. Reg.*, ii. 614).
Hazlitt, H. 241.

[Another edition.] *G. Purslowe.* 1615. 4°. 𝕭.𝕷.

B.M. (95. b. 20/2).

[Another edition.] *G. Purslowe.* 1631. 4°. 𝕭.𝕷.

B.M. (95. b. 9).

Planetomachia : Or the first parte of the generall opposition of the seuen
Planets . . . Diuersly discouering in their pleasaunt and Tragicall histories,
the inward affections of the mindes . . . By Robert Greene, Master of Arts
and student in Phisicke. 1585. *For T. Cadman.* 1585. 4°. 𝕭.𝕷.

B.M. (95. b. 18/1).

GRIMELLO. *See* BRETON, Nicholas.

GRISELDA.

The Antient, True, and admirable History of Patient Grissel, a Poore
Mans Daughter in France. Written in French, and now translated into
English. *E. All-de.* 1607. 4°.

An history of meke and pacyent Gresell, perhaps the ballad only, was licensed (for 4d.) to
T. Colwell in 1565–6 (*Stat. Reg.*, i. 309), and again (for 8d.) in 1568–9 (i. 385).
Hazlitt, H. 245.

[Another edition.] Shewing how Maides by her example in their good
behavior may marrie rich Husbands : And likewise Wives by their patience
and obedience may gaine much glorie. Written first in French and . . . now
Translated into English, *etc.* *H. L[ownes] for W. Lugger.* 1619. 4°. 𝕭.𝕷.

B.M. (C. 34. f. 47).

[Another edition.] The True and Admirable History of Patient Grisel, *etc.*
For Eliz. Andrews. 1663. 4°. 𝕭.𝕷.

Priv. Lib.

[Another edition.] *For W. Thackeray.* 1674. 4°. 𝕭.𝕷.

Bodl. (Douce G. 256).

[Another edition.] *For W. Thackeray.* 4°. 𝕭.𝕷.

B.M. (G. 10462), the date cut.

[Another edition.] *For J. Wright, J. Clarke, W. Thackeray, and T. Passenger.* 1682. 4°. 𝕭.𝕷.

Pepys 1193 (2).

[Another edition.] *By and For W. O[nley] and are to be sold by A. Bettesworth.* 1703. 4°.

Lowndes, 2182.

[Another edition.] *T. Norris.* 4°.

Hazlitt, I. 192.

[An abridgement.] The Pleasant and Sweet History of patient Grissell. Shewing how she from a poore mans Daughter, came to be a great Lady in France, being a patterne for all vertuous Women. Translated out of Italian. *E. P. for I. Wright.* 1640. 8°. 𝕭.𝕷.

An abridged version, chapters 3–9 consisting of the ballad. The first title reads "The History of the Noble Marques."
B.M. (C. 40. a. 13), the date cut away ; Hazlitt, III. 101.

[Another edition.] *For J. Clarke, W. Thackery, and T. Passinger.* 1686. 8°. 𝕭.𝕷.

Bodl. (Wood 254/12).

See CERVANTES, M. Select Novels. 1694.

GROUNDWORKE OF CONNY-CATCHING. *See* HARMAN, Thomas.

GUICCIARDINI, LUDOVICO.

The Garden of Pleasure : Contayninge most pleasante Tales, worthy deedes and witty sayings of noble Princes & learned Philosophers, Moralized. No lesse delectable, than profitable. Done out of Italian into English, by Iames Sanford, Gent. Wherein are also set forth diuers Verses and Sentences in Italian, with the Englishe to the same, for the benefit of students in both tongs. *H. Bynneman.* 1573. 8°. 𝕭.𝕷.

B.M. (12331. a. 30/1).

[Another edition.] Howres of recreation or Afterdinners, Which may aptly be called the Garden of Pleasure : Containing most pleasant Tales, worthy deeds and witty sayings of noble Princes and learned Philosophers, with their Morals ... By Iames Sanford Gent., and now by him newly perused, corrected, and enlarged. *H. Bynneman.* 1576. 8°. 𝕭.𝕷.

B.M. (12316. aa. 27).

H., I.

See HALL, Joseph.

HAIGH FOR DEVONSHIRE.

See ROBERTS, Henry.

HALL, JOSEPH.

[Mundus alter et idem.] The Discovery of a New World, or A Description of the South Indies. Hetherto vnknowne By an English Mercury. *For E. Blount and W. Barrett.* 8°.

The attribution to Hall is doubtful. See *Gentleman's Magazine*, July, 1896.
Licensed to T. Thorpe, Jan. 18, 1609 (*Stat. Reg.*, iii. 400).
    B.M. (G. 16409).

[Another edition.] The Travels of Don Francisco De Quevedo. Through Terra Australis Incognita, Discovering The Laws, Customs, Manners and Fashions of the South Indians. A Novel. Originally in Spanish. *For W. Grantham.* 1684. 12°.

    B.M. (12315. aaa. 24).

[An abridgement.] Psittacorum Regio. The Land of Parrots: Or, The She-Lands. With a Description of other strange adjacent Countries, in the Dominions of Prince de l'Amour, not hitherto found in any Geographical Map. By one of the late most reputed Wits. *For F. Kirkman.* 1669. 8°.

    B.M. (1080. h. 36).

HAMLET.

See BELLEFOREST, François de.

HARMAN, THOMAS.

[A Caueat for Common Cursetors.]

The first edition, licensed to W. Griffith, 1566/7 (*Stat. Reg.*, i. 334), and stated in the second edition to have been in the press on Nov. 1, 1567. *See* the New Shakspere Society reprint.

[Another edition.] A Caueat for Commen Cursetors vulgarely called Vagabones, set forth by Thomas Harman, Esquier, for the vtilite and proffyt of hys naturall Countrey. Newly agmented and Imprinted. Anno Domini. M.D.LCVII, *etc. W. Gryffith.* 8 Jan., 1567 [/8]. 4°. 𝔅.𝔏.

    Bodl. (4°. R. 21. Art. Seld).

[Another edition.] A Caueat or Warening for Commen Cursetors . . . Augmented and inlarged. Anno Domini. M.D.LXVII. *etc.* *W. Gryffith.* 1567 [/8]. 4°. 𝕭.𝕷.

Huth.

[Another edition.] Newly imprinted, *etc.* *H. Middleton,* 1573.

Reprint, 1814 ; *Brit. Bibl.,* iv. 592.

[Another edition.] The Groundworke of Conny-catching . . . Done by a Iustice of Peace of great auuthoritie, who hath had the examining of diuers of them. *I. Danter for W. Barley.* 1592. 4°. 𝕭.𝕷.

With additions. It has been confused with Greene's tracts on conny-catching.
B.M. (95. b. 19/2) ; Huth, undated.

HART, ALEXANDER.

The Tragi-Comicall History of Alexto And Angelica. Containing The progresse of a zealous Candide, and Masculine Love. With a Various Mutabilitye of a feminine affection. Together with Loves Iustice thereupon. Written by Alex: Hart, Esq. *B. A[lsop] and T. F[awcet] for N. Vavasour.* 1640. 12°.

B.M. (1076. b. 9).

The True History of the Tragicke loves of Hipolito and Isabella Neapolitans. Englished. *T. Harper, and N. Field.* 1628. 8°.

B.M. (12613. a. 17).

[Another edition.] The second Edition. *T. Harper and are to be sold by R. Meighen.* 1633. 8°.

B.M. (12613. a. 18).

HAWKWOOD, *Sir* JOHN.

See VALENS, W.

See (in Part II) WINSTANLEY, William.

HELIODORUS.

An Æthiopian Historie written in Greeke by Heliodorus : very wittie and pleasaunt, Englished by Thomas Vnderdoune, *etc.* *H. Wykes for F. Coldocke,* [1569.] 4°. 𝕭.𝕷.

Licensed to Coldocke, 1568/9 (*Stat. Reg.* i. 388).
B.M. (C. 55. c. 26).

[Another edition.]   *H. Middleton for F. Coldocke.*   1577.   4°.   𝕭.𝕷.
Bodl. (Wood 599).

[Another edition.]   *For F. Coldocke.*   1587.   4°.   𝕭.𝕷.
B.M. (1074. b. 34).

[Another edition.]   *For W. Cotton.*   1605.   4°.   𝕭.𝕷.
Bodl. (90. d. 26).

[Another edition.]   *For W. Cotton.*   1606.   4°.   𝕭.𝕷.
B.M. (243. f. 2).

[Another edition, revised.]   Heliodorus His Aethiopian History : Done out of Greeke, and compared with other Translations in diuers Languages.   The Arguments and Contents of euery seuerall Booke, are prefixed to the beginning of the same, *etc.*   *F. Kyngston, for W. Barret.*   1622.   4°.
Underdown's version, revised by Barret.
B.M. (1074. l. 10).

[Another edition.]   *F. Kyngston, for W. Barret.*   1627.   4°.
Hazlitt, H. 262.

[A different version.]   The Æthiopian History of Heliodorus, in Ten Books.   The first Five translated by a Person of Quality ; the last Five by N. Tate.   To which are prefixed, The Testimonies of Writers, both Ancient and Modern, concerning this Work.   *For E. Poole.*   1686.   8°.
Term Cat., ii. 145.   Lowndes, 1033.

[Another edition.]   The Triumphs of Love and Constancy : A Romance. Containing the Heroick Amours of Theagenes & Chariclea.   In Ten Books.   The first Five Rendred by a Person of Quality, the last Five by N. Tate.   The Second Edition.   *J. Leake, for E. Poole.*   1687.   8°.
B.M. (1074. l. 22).

[A different version.]   Theagenes and Chariclia, a Romance . . .   In Two Volumes.   *For W. Taylor, E. Curll, R. Gosling, J. Hooke, J. Browne and J. Osborn.*   1717.   12°.   2 vols.
B.M. (12410. bbb. 34).

[Another edition ?]   The Reward of Chastity.   [1725 ?]
J. Roberts' and H. Curll's lists.

See also PLUTARCH.

HELYAS.

The knyght of the swanne. Here begynneth the hystory of the noble
Helyas knyght of the swanne newly translated out of frensshe into englysshe
at thynstygacyon of the puyssaunt & Illustryous Prynce lorde Edwarde Duke
of Buckyngham. *Wynkyn de Worde.* 1512. 4°. 𝕭.𝕷.

R. Hoe (on vellum). *See* Grolier Club reprint.

[Another edition.] *W. Copland.* 4°. 𝕭.𝕷.

B.M. (C. 21. c. 67.)

HEMETES.

A Paradox, Prouing by reason and example that Baldnesse is much better
than bushie haire &c. Written by that excellent Philosopher Synesius Bishop
of Thebes, or (as some say) Cyren. A Prettie pamphlet to peruse and
replenished with recreation. Englished by Abraham Fleming. Hereunto is
annexed the pleasant tale of Hemetes the Heremite, pronounced before the
Queenes Maiestie. Newly recognised bothe in Latine and Englishe by the
saide A. F. *H. Denham.* 1579. 𝕭.𝕷.

The Tale was translated by Gascoigne into Latin, French and Italian.
B.M. (C. 40. a. 14).

[Another edition, in:] The Queenes Maiesties Entertainment at Wood-
stocke. *For T. Cadman.* 1585. 4°.

See the reprint (H. Daniel and the Clarendon Press) with Introduction by A. W. Pollard. 1910.
B.M. (C. 57. b. 43), imperf., wanting leaves 1–3.

HERBERAY, Nicolas de.

See FLORES, Don.

HIND, John.

Eliosto Libidinoso: Described in two Bookes Wherein their imminent
dangers are declared who guiding the course of their life by the compasse of
Affection, either dash their ship against most dangerous shelues, or else
attaine the Hauen with extreame Preiudice. Written by John Hynd, *etc.*
V. Simmes, for N. Butter. 1606. 4°.

B.M. (C. 39. e. 4).

The most excellent Historie of Lysimachus and Varrona, daughter to
Syllanus, Duke of Hypata, in Thessalia. Wherin are contained the effects
of Fortune, the Wonders of affection, and the conquests of incertaine Time.
By J. H. R., *etc.* *T. Creede.* 1604. 4°. 𝕭.𝕷.

Bridgewater.

HIPOLITO AND ISABELLA.
See HART, Alexander.

HISTORIES.
Straunge, Lamentable, and Tragicall Hystories.
See SMYTH, Robert.

HOLLAND'S LEAGUER.
See GOODMAN, Nicholas.

HOLLYBAND, CLAUDIUS.
See SAN PEDRO, Diego de.

HONOUR'S ACADEMY.
See MONTREUX, Nicolas de.

HOWELL, JAMES.
Δενδρολογια. Dodona's Grove, or, The Vocall Forrest. By I. H., Esqr.
T. B. for H. Mosley. 1640. Fol.

B.M. (432. k. 3).

[Another edition.] The second Edition more exact and perfect then the former; with an Addition of two other Tracts, *etc.* 1644. 4°.

B.M. (E. 19/2).

[Another edition.] The third Edition more exact and perfect then the former, *etc.* *R. D. for H. Moseley.* 1645. 8°.

B.M. (968. c. 1).

[Another edition.] The last Edition much more exact and perfect than the former; with the Addition of two other Tracts, *etc.* . . . *T. W. for H. Moseley.* 12°.

Bodl. (8°. A. 6. Jur. BS.).

Δενδρολογια. Dodona's Grove, or The Vocall Forest. Second Part . . . By James Howell Esquire. *W. H. for H. Moseley.* 1650. 8°.

*_{*} A Latin version of 1646 is mentioned in the *D.N.B.*
B.M. (12614. ff. 7).

HOWLEGLAS.

[Tyll Howleglas. *J. Doesborgh : Antwerp*, 1519?]. 4°. 𝕭.𝕷.
B.M. (C. 34. f. 51), frag.

[Another edition.] Here beginneth a merye Iest of a man that was called Howleglas, and of many meruaylous thynges and Iestes that he dyd in his lyfe, in Eastland and in many other places. *W. Copland.* 4°. 𝕭.𝕷.

The second line of the title is in a type of medium size.
B.M. (C. 21. c. 53), imperf.

[Another edition.] *W. Copland.* 4°. 𝕭.𝕷.

"Imprinted at London in Tamestrete at the Vintre on the thre Craned wharfe." The second line of the title is in small type ; also the title has two variations from that of the preceding edition : "marueylous thinges" and "Eastlande."
B.M. (C. 21. c. 57).

[Another edition.] *W. Copland.* 4°. 𝕭.𝕷.

"Imprinted at London in Lothbury."
Bodl. (4° Z. 3 Art. Seld.), imperf., wanting title.

[A different version.] The German Rogue: or, the Life and Merry Adventures, Cheats, Stratagems, and Contrivances of Tiel Eulespiegle . . . Made English from the High-Dutch. 1720. 8°.

B.M. (12315. c. 20).

HUON OF BORDEAUX.

Here begynnythe the boke of duke Huon of burdeux & of them that issuyd fro him. [*Wynkyn de Worde?* 1534?]

Haigh Hall. *Cf.* E.E.T.S. reprint.

[Another edition.] The Ancient, Honorable, Famous, and delightfull Historie of Huon of Bourdeaux, one of the Peeres of Fraunce, and Duke of Guyenne . . . Being now the Third time imprinted, and the rude English corrected and amended. *T. Purfoot, and are to be sould by E. White.* 1601. 4°. 𝕭.𝕷.

Bodl. (Douce B. subt. 242) ; B.M. (C. 40. d. 42), wants title.

HURTADO, Luis.

See PALMERIN.

HURTADO DE MENDOZA, Diego.

See LAZARILLO DE TORMES.

HYPNEROTOMACHIA.

See COLONNA, Francesco.

IMAGE OF IDLENESS.

A lyttle treatyse called the Image of Idlenesse, conteynynge certayne matters moued betwene Walter Wedlocke and Bawdin Bacheler.   Trāslated out of the Troyane or Cornyshe tounge into Englyshe, by Olyuer Oldwanton, and dedicated to the Lady Lust.   *W. Seres.*   8°.   𝕭.𝕷.

Licensed to Seres, 1558–9 (*Stat. Reg.*, i. 95).
   B.M. (527. c. 37).

[Another edition?]

Licensed to A. Lawton ("which was Leonerd Maylard"), 1570–1 (*Stat. Reg.* i. 440).

[Another edition.]   Newly corrected and augmented.   *W. Seres.*   1574. 8°.   𝕭.𝕷.

   B.M. (C. 38. c. 49).

ISLE OF MAN.

See BERNARD, Richard.

J., R.

See JOHNSON, Richard.

JACK OF DOVER.

[Jack of Dover.]

Part 2 was licensed to W. Ferbrand, 3 Aug., 1601 (*Stat. Reg.*, iii. 190).

[Another edition.]   Iacke of Dover.   His Quest of Inquirie, or His priuy search for the veriest Foole in England.   *For W. Ferbrand.*   1604.   8°.

   Bodl. (Douce TT. 170).

[Another edition.]   1608.   4°.

   Bagford ; Hazlitt, H. 299.

[Another edition.]   Jacke of Dovers merry tales.   Or his Quest, *etc. I.* (?) *B. and are to be sold by R. Higginbotham.*   1615.   4°.   𝕭.𝕷.

   Bodl. (Malone 701).

JASON.

See LE FEVRE, Raoul de.

JERUSALEM.

The dystruccyon of Iherusalem by Vaspazian and Tytus.   *Wynkyn de Worde.*   4°.   𝕭.𝕷.

B.M. (C. 25. k. 5).

[Another edition.]   *R. Pynson.*   4°.   𝕭.𝕷.
U.L.C. (Sel. 5. 17).

[Another edition.]   *Wynkyn de Worde.*   1528.   4°.   𝕭.𝕷.
Priv. Lib.

JOHNSON, John.

The Academy of Love describing yᵉ folly of younge men, & yᵉ fallacy of women by Io. Iohnson, Gent.   *For H. Blunden.*   1641.   4°.

B.M. (G. 10447).

JOHNSON, Richard.

The nine Worthies of London: Explaining the honourable exercise of Armes, the vertues of the valiant, and the memorable attempts of magnanimous minds . . .   Compiled by Richard Iohnson.   *T. Orwin for H. Lownes.*   1592.   4°.   𝕭.𝕷.
B.M. (C. 38. c. 10).

The Pleasant Conceites of Old Hobson the merry Londoner, *etc.*   *For J: Wright.*   1607.   4°.
B.M. (C. 39. d. 2).

[Another edition.]   *For J. Wright.*   1634.   12°.
Bagford.

[Another edition.]   *W. Gilbertson.*   1640.   12°.
Daniel; Hazlitt, *Old English Jest Books,* vol. iii.

The Most famous History of the Seauen Champions of Christendome . . . Shewing their Honorable battailes by Sea and Land, *etc.*   *For C. Burbie.*   1596.   4°.

Licensed (part 1 only?) to J. Danter, 20 April, 1596, and both parts assigned to C. Burby soon after (*Stat. Reg.* iii. 64, 70).
Hazlitt, VII. 208.

The second Part of the famous History of the seauen Champions of Christendome.   Likewise shewing the Princely prowesse of Saint Georges three Sonnes, the liuely Sparke of Nobilitie.   With many other memoriall atchiuements worthy the golden Spurres of Knighthood.   *For C. Burbie.* 1597.   4°.   𝕭.𝕷.

Priv. Lib.

The Most Famous History of the seuen Champions of Christendome : Saint George of England, Saint Denis of Fraunce, Saint Iames of Spayne, Saint Anthony of Italie, Saint Andrew of Scotland, Saint Patricke of Ireland, and Saint Dauid of Wales ; Shewing their Honorable battailes by Sea and Land, *etc.   For E. Burbie.*   1608.   4°.   2 vols.   𝕭.𝕷.

The first part ends : " 1608.   Finis.   R. I."
B.M. (C. 57. b. 27).

[Another edition.]   Whereunto is added by the first Author, the true manner of their deaths, *etc.   W. Stansby.*   4°.   2 vols.   𝕭.𝕷.

The author dates the conclusion of part 1, 1616.
Bridgewater ;   B.M. (G. 10476), part 1 only.

[Another edition.]   *T. Snodham.*   4°.   2 vols.   𝕭.𝕷.

B.M. (12614. d. 20).

[Another edition.]   *R. Bishop.*   4°.   2 vols.   𝕭.𝕷.

B.M. (1077. e. 14).

[Another edition.]   *R. Bishop.*   4°.   2 vols.   𝕭.𝕷.

Part 2 only known.
B.M. (G. 10476).

[Another edition.]   *J. B. for A. Crooke.*   4°.   2 vols.   𝕭.𝕷.

Part 2 was printed by G. Dawson for A. Crooke.
B.M. (12403. a. 31).

[Another edition.]   *G. P. for A. Crook.*   1670.   2 vols.   𝕭.𝕷.

Part 2 is printed by E. Crowch for A. Crook.
B.M. (G. 10477.)

[Another edition.]   1675.   4°.

Hazlitt, H. 303.

[Another edition.]   1676.   4°.

Hazlitt, H. 303.

[Another edition.]   *For R. Scot, T. Basset, J. Wright, and R. Chiswell.* 1680.   4°.   2 vols.   𝕭.𝕷.

B.M. (G. 10479).

[Another edition.]   1686.   8°?

  Hazlitt, II. 303 (*Harl. Cat.*).

[Another edition.]   *For R. Scot, T. Basset, R. Chiswell, M. Wotton, and G. Conyers.*   1687.   4°.   3 vols.   𝕭.𝕷.

Part 3 is printed by J. R. for B. Harris, 1686, and the dedication is signed W. W.
W. Thackeray advertised Part 3 in 1689, and J. Deacon c. 1694.

  Pepys. 1191 (1).

[Another edition.]   *For R. Chiswell, M. Wotton, G. Conyers, and B. Walford.*   1696.   3 vols.   𝕭.𝕷.

Vol. 2 is "printed by W. Onley for R. Chiswell," etc.   Part 3 is by another printer (the imprint cut away).

  B.M. (12450. d. 1).

[Another edition.]   *W. O[nley] for G. Conyers.*   4°.   3 vols.

  B.M. (G. 10478), Part 3 only.

[Another edition.]   *For R. Chiswell, M. Wotton, G. Conyers, and B. Walford.*   1705.   4°.   2 vols.

Without Part 3.

  B.M. (G. 10478).

[Another edition.]   The Famous History of the Seven Champions of Christendom, etc.   *L. Dillon, Dublin.*   4°.   2 vols.

  B.M. (12450. d. 15).

[An abridgement.]   The Renowned History of the Seven Champions of Christendom, *etc.   A. P. and T. H. for T. Vere.*   1679.   4°.   𝕭.𝕷.

  Hazlitt, VII. 209.

[Another abridgement?]   The Illustrious and Renowned History Of the Seven Famous Champions of Christendom.   In Three Parts, *etc.   For T. Norris, A. Bettesworth.*   1719.   12°.

  B.M. (12450. a. 10).

[Another edition.]   *For T. Norris, A. Bettesworth.*   1722.   12°.

  B.M. (12410. aa. 15).

[Another edition.]   The Fifth Edition.   *For A. Bettesworth, C. Hitch, R. Ware, and J. Hodges.*   1738.   12°.

  Bodl. (2702. f. 2).

[Another abridgement.]   The Renowned History of the Seven Champions of Christendom . . . Illustrated with Variety of Pictures, *etc.   For B. Deacon.*   4°.   9 chapters.

  Bodl. (Douce R. 528).

[Another edition.]   *T. Norris.*   4°.

  Hazlitt, H. 303.

[Another edition.]   4°.   𝕭.𝕷.

  Hazlitt, H. 303.

[Another abridgement ?]   The Famous History, *etc.*   J. White, *Newcastle-upon-Tyne.*   4°.

  10 leaves.
  Hazlitt, VII. 209.

[For the Eighth Champion of Christendom :]
See (in Part II.) GURTHIE, James.

[Tom a Lincoln.]

  Licensed to W. White, 24 Dec., 1599, and part 2 also to White, 20 Oct., 1607 (*Stat. Reg.* iii. 153, 362).   It is referred to at the end of *Kemp's nine daies wonder,* 1600.

[Another edition.]   The most pleasant History of Tom a Lincolne, That renowned Souldier, the Red-Rose Knight, who for his Valour and Chiualry, was surnamed The Boast of England. . . . The sixth Impression. *A. Mathewes, and are to bee sold by R. Byrde, and F. Coules.* 1631. 4°. 𝕭.𝕷.

  Priv. Lib.

[Another edition.]   The Seventh Impression.   *A. M. and are to be sold by F. Faulkner.*   1635.   4°.   𝕭.𝕷.

  Huth.

[Another edition.]   The Ninth Impression.   *T. R. and E. M. for F. Coles.* 1655.   4°.   𝕭.𝕷.

  B.M. (1077. e. 57).

[Another edition.]   The Tenth Impression, *etc.   G. Purslow, for F. Coles.* 1668.   4°.   𝕭.𝕷.

  Priv. Lib.

[Another edition.] . . . The Twelveth [*sic*] Impression.   *H. Brugis for W. Thackeray.*   1682.   4°.   𝕭.𝕷.

  Pepys 1192 (18).

[Another edition.]   *H. B[rugis] for W. Thackery.*   1682.   4°.   𝕭.𝕸.

Bodl. (Wood 321).

[Another edition.]   *J. W. for B. Deacon.*   1703.   4°.

Called the 13th edition on the second (undated) title-page.   Part 2 is perhaps of the following edition.

Mr. Quaritch, 1908.   Hazlitt, II. 705.

[Another edition.]   The thirteenth impression.   *J. W. for B. Deacon.*
1704.   4°.   𝕭.𝕸.

Hazlitt, H. 305.

[Another edition.]   *J. W. for B. Deacon.*   1705.   4°.

B.M. (1077. e. 44).

[An abridgement.]   The Pleasant and Delightful History of Tom of
Lincoln, *etc.*   4°.

Perhaps the edition printed for J. Blare, price 2d., quoted from Blare's list by J. P. Collier, *Bibliographical and Critical Account*, ii. 242.

B.M. (12613. c. 9), imperf., title mutilated.

[Another edition?]   The History of Tom a Lincoln.   *T. Norris.*   4°.

Hazlitt, H. 305.

The History of Tom Thumbe, the Little, for his small stature surnamed,
King Arthur's Dwarfe : Whose Life and Aduentures containe many strange
and wonderfull accidents, published for the delight of merry Time-spenders.
For T. Langley.   1621.   8°.   𝕭.𝕸.

Huth.

JOSEPH OF ARIMATHEA.

Here after foloweth a treatyse takē out of a boke Whiche somtyme
Theodosius the Emperour founde in Iherusalem in the pretorye of Pylate of
Ioseph o Armathy.   *Wynkyn de Worde.*   4°.   𝕭.𝕸.

U.L.C. (Sel. 5. 32).

JOSEPHUS.

The History of Josephus the Indian Prince.   *See* Greene, Robert,
Dorastus and Fawnia.   1696.

KENNEDY, John.

The Historie of Calanthrop and Lucilla.   Conspicuously demonstrating the various mutabilities of Fortune in their Loues, with euery seuerall circumstance of joyes and crosses, fortunate exploites, and hazardous aduentures, which either of them sustained before they could attaine the prosperous euent of their wished aimes.   *J. Wreittoun, Edinburgh.*   1626.   8°.

Hazlitt, H. 315 (Farmer, Heber).

[Another edition.]   The Ladies Delight, or, The English Gentlewomans History of Calanthrop and Lucilla . . . By Iohn Kennedie.   *T. Harper for M. Sparke.*   1631.   8°.

Huth.

KINDE KIT OF KINGSTON.

See Westward for Smelts.

KNIGHT OF THE SEA.

The Heroicall Adventures of the Knight of the Sea.   Comprised in the Historie of the Illustrious & Excellently accomplished Prince Oceander, *etc.* *For W. Leake.*   1600.   4°.   𝕭.𝕷.

Huth ; Bridgewater.

LA MARCHE, Olivier de.

The Resolved Gentleman.   Translated out of Spanishe into Englyshe, by Lewes Lewkenor Esquier.   *R. Watkins.*   1594.   4°.

A translation into prose of the *Chevalier Délibéré,* from the version of Hernando de Acuna.

B.M. (C. 57. c. 7).

LARRONS.

Histoire Des Larrons, or the History of Theeves.   Written in French, and Translated out of the Originall, By Paul Godwin.   *I. Raworth, and are to be sold by T. Slater.*   1638.   12°.

B.M. (12512. b. 22).

LA TOUR LANDRY, Geoffroy de.

End : Here fynysshed the booke, whiche the knyght of the Toure made to the enseygnement and techyng of his doughters translated oute of Frenssh

in to our maternall Englysshe tongue by me William Caxton, *etc.*   *W. Caxton,*
Westmynstre.   1484.   Fol.   𝕭.𝕷.

B.M. (IB. 55085).

LAZARILLO DE TORMES.

[Lazarillo de Tormes.]

Licensed to T. Colwell in 1568-9 (*Stat. Reg.* i. 378), as The marvelus Dedes and the lyf
of Lazaro de Tormes.   The license was sold to Bynneman, 19 June, 1573.

[Another edition.]   The Pleasant History of Lazarello de Tormes, a
Spanyard, wherein is contayned his marvailous deedes and Life, with yᵉ
strange aduentures happened to him in yᵉ seruice of Sundery Masters, drawen
out of Spanish by Dauid Rowland of Anglesey.   *H. Binneman.*   1576.   8°.

Attributed to Diego Hurtado de Mendoza.
Hazlitt, H. 387 (Bagford) title only.

[Another edition.]   *A. Ieffes.*   1586.   8°.   𝕭.𝕷.

B.M. (C. 57. aa. 2).

[Another edition.]   *A. Ieffes.*   1596.   4°.   𝕭.𝕷.

B.M. (G. 10136).

The most pleasaunt and delectable historie of Lazarillo de Tormes : the
second part, translated out of Spanish by W. P.   *T. C[reed] for J. Oxenbridge.*
1596.   4°.

Bodl. (Wood 487/8), imperf., wanting title.

The Pursuit of the Historie of Lazarillo de Tormes.   By Jean de Luna.
1622.   8°.

Licensed to T. Walkley, 26 Oct. 1622 (*Stat. Reg.* iv. 83).
Hazlitt, H. 388.

[Another edition of Part 1.]   The Pleasant History of Lazarillo de Tormes
a Spanyard, *etc.*   *J. H.*   1624.   8°.

U.L.C. (Syn. 8. 63. 332/1).

[Another edition of Part 2.]   The Pursuit of the Historie, *etc.*   *G. P[urslowe]*
for R. Hawkins.   1631.   8°.

U.L.C. (Syn. 8. 63. 332/2).

[Another edition.]   The Third Edition, corrected and amended.   *E. G.*
for W. Leake.   1639.   8°.   2 vols.

Part 2 is Juan de Luna's *Pursuit of the History.*
Priv. Lib.

[Another edition.]   Lazarillo, or the excellent history of Lazarillo de Tormes, the witty Spaniard, *etc.*   *For W. Leake.*   1653.   2 vols.

Hazlitt, H. 388.

[Another edition.]   *R. Hodgkinsonne.*   1655.   8°.   2 vols.

Hazlitt, III. 60.

[Another edition.]   *B. G. for W. Leake.*   1669–70.   8°.   2 vols.

The translation revised by James Blakeston.
B.M. (12491. aaa. 20).

[Another edition.]   *For Eliz. Hodgkinson.*   1677–72.   8°.   2 vols.

Probably there were editions of both parts in 1672 and 1677.
B.M. (12491. b. 15).

[Another edition.]   The Pleasant Adventures of the Witty Spaniard, Lazarillo de Tormes . . . To which is added, The Life and Death of Young Lazarillo, Heir apparent to Old Lazarillo de Tormes, *etc.*   *J. Leake.*   1688.   12°.

Bodl. (Douce M. 166).

[Another edition?]   *For H. Rhodes.*   1693.   12°.

Term. Cat., ii. 487.

[A different version?]   The Life and Adventures of Lazarillo de Tormes, written by himself; translated from the Original Spanish; and illustrated with 20 Copper Cuts.`   In Two Parts.   *For R. Bonwicke, W. Freeman, T. Goodwin, J. Walthoe, M. Wotton, S. Manship, J. Nicholson, R. Parker, B. Tooke and R. Smith.*   1707.   12°.

Term. Cat., iii. 571.

[Another edition?]   The Second Edition, Corrected.   *For R. and J. Bonwick and R. Wilkin, J. Walthoe and T. Ward.*   1726.   12°.

B.M. (12490. aaaa. 14).

LEFEVRE, Raoul.

[The History of Jason.]   fOr as moche as late by the comaũdement of the right hye τ noble princesse my right redoubted lady, My lady Margarete, by the grace of god Duchesse of Bourgoyne Brabant τc. I translated aboke out of frensshe in to Englissh named Recuyel of the histories of Troye . . . I entende to translate the sayd boke of thistories of Iason, *etc.*   [*W. Caxton: Westminster.*   1477.]   Fol.   𝕭.𝕷.

B.M. (C. 10. b. 3).

[Another edition.] The veray trew history of the valiaūt Knight Iasō
How he conqueryd or wan the golden fles. by the Counsel of Medea. and of
many othre victoryouse and wondrefull actis and dedys that he dyde by his
prowesse and cheualrye in his tyme. *Gerard Leeu : Andewarpe.* 1492.
Fol. 𝕭.𝕷.

U.L.C. (AB. 10. 54. 2).

Begin : hEre begynneth the volume intituled and named the recuyell of the
historyes of Troye, composed and drawen out of dyuerce bookes of latyn into
frensshe by the ryght venerable persone and worshipfull man. Raoul le ffeure
. . . And translated and drawen out of frenshe into englisshe by Willyam
Caxton . . . And ended and fynysshed in the holy cyte of Colen the . xix.
day of Septembre the yere of our sayd lord god a thousand foure honderd
sixty and enleuen, ꞇct. *W. Caxton* [*and C. Mansion*] : *Bruges.* [1475 ?].
Fol. 𝕭.𝕷.

The epilogue to the third book contains Caxton's statement as to the printing.
B.M. (C. 11. c. 1).

[Another edition.] THE recuyles or gaderīge to gyder of yᵉ hystoryes of
Troye hoW it Was destroyed ꞇ brent tWyes by yᵉ puyssaunt Hercules ꞇ yᵉ
thyrde ꞇ generall by yᵉ grekes. *Wynkyn de Worde.* 1502. Fol. 𝕭.𝕷.

Some copies are dated 1503.
B.M. (G. 10509), 1503, imperf. at end ; Pepys 1996, 1502.

[Another edition.] The recuile of the Histories of Troie. First trāslated
out of latin in to Frēche by Raoul le feure in the yere from Thincarnacion
of our Sauiour Christ. .MCCCCLxiiii. and translated out of Frenche into
Englishe by Wyllyam Caxton Mercer of London, begon in the fyrst day of
Marche in the yere of our Lord god . MCCC.CLxviij and fynished in the
. xix . of Septembre in the yere mencyoned by the sayd Caxton in the ende
of the seconde booke, *etc.* *W. Copland.* 1553. Fol. 𝕭.𝕷.

Three books. Caxton's account of his translation mentioned in the title, is reprinted
at the end of Book 2.
B.M. (C. 21. d. 15).

[Another edition.] The Auncient Historie, of the destruction of Troy . . .
Translated out of French into English, by W. Caxton. Newly corrected, and
the English much amended, by William Fiston. *T. Creede.* 1596. 4°. 𝕭.𝕷.

Bodl. (Malone 626).

[Another edition.] *T. Creede.* 1607. 8°. 𝕭.𝕷.

B.M. (12450. e. 17).

[Another edition.] The fifth Edition. *B. Alsop.* 1617. 4°. 𝕭.𝕷.

B.M. (12450. e. 1).

[Another edition.]   The Sixth Edition, now newly Corrected and amended. *B. Alsop and T. Fawcet.* 1636.   4°.   𝔅.𝔏.

> Bodl. (221. g. 124.)

[Another edition.]   The Destruction of Troy, in Three Books . . . The Seventh Edition, Corrected and much amended.   *R. I. for S. S. to bee sold by F. Coles and C. Tyus.* 1663.   4°.   𝔅.𝔏.

> B.M. (1077. i. 47).

[Another edition.]   The Eight Edition, Corrected and much amended. *For T. Passenger.* 1670.   4°.   𝔅.𝔏.

> B.M. (12403. aa. 27).

[Another edition.]   The Ninth Edition, Corrected and much amended. *For T. Passenger.* 1676.   4°.   𝔅.𝔏.

> B.M. (1077. e. 15).

[Another edition.]   The Tenth Edition, Corrected and much amended. *For T. Passinger.* 1680.   4°.   𝔅.𝔏.

> B.M. (1077. f. 12).

[Another edition.]   The eleventh Edition, Corrected and much amended. *For T. Passinger.* 1684.   4°.   𝔅.𝔏.

> B.M. (G. 17515).

[Another edition.]   The Twelfth Edition, Corrected and much Amended. *For E. Tracy.* 1702.   4°.

> B.M. (1077. g. 29).

[Another edition.]   The Thirteenth Edition, Corrected and much Amended. *For E. Tracy.* 1708.   4°.

> B.M. (12612. e. 19).

[Another edition.]   *For C. Bates.*

> Bates' list, in *Hector.*

[Another edition.]   The Eighteenth Edition, Corrected and Amended. *T. Browne: Dublin.* 1738.   4°.

> B.M. (12510. e. 6).

[The New History of the Trojan Wars and Troy's Destruction, 1728, *etc.*] *See* (in Part II) Trojan Wars.

LODGE, Thomas.

An Alarum against Vsurers. Containing tryed experiences against worldly abuses. Wherein Gentlemen may finde good counsells to confirme them, and pleasant Histories to delight them . . . Heereunto are annexed the delectable historie of Forbonius and Prisceria : with the lamentable Complaint of Truth ouer England. Written by Thomas Lodge, of Lincolnes Inne, Gentleman. *T. Este, for S. Clarke.* 1584. 4°. 𝕭.𝕷.

 Bodl. (Tanner 220) ; B.M. (C. 57. d. 9), imperf.

Euphues Shadow, the Battaile of the Sences. Wherein youthfull folly is set downe in his right figure, and vaine fancies are prooued to produce many offences . . . By T. L. Gent. *A. Ieffes, for I. Busbie.* 1592. 4°. 𝕭.𝕷.

 Licensed to Busby and N. Lyng, 17 Feb., 1591/2 (*Stat. Reg.* ii. 604).
 B.M. (95. b. 17).

The Life and Death of William Longbeard, the most famous and witty English Traitor, borne in the Citty of London. Accompanied with manye other most pleasant and prettie histories. By T. L. of Lincolnes Inne, Gent. *R. Yardley and P. Short.* 1593. 4°. 𝕭.𝕷.

 Bodl. (Malone 571).

A Margarite of America. By T. Lodge. *For I. Busbie.* 1596. 4°. 𝕭.𝕷.

 B.M. (C. 14. a. 2).

The famous, true and historicall Life of Robert second Duke of Normandy, surnamed for his monstrous birth and behauiour, Robin the Diuell. Wherein is contained his dissolute life in his youth, his deuout reconcilement and vertues in his age : interlaced with many straunge and miraculous aduentures. Wherein are both causes of profite, and manie conceits of pleasure. By T. L. G. *For N. L[ing] and I. Busbie.* 1591. 4°.

 Priv. Lib.

Rosalynde. Euphues golden legacie : found after his death in his Cell at Silexedra. Bequeathed to Philautus sonnes noursed vp with their father in England. Fetcht from the Canaries. By T. L. Gent. *T. Orwin for T. G[ubbins] and I. Busbie.* 1590. 4°. 𝕭.𝕷.

 Sotheby, 25 July, 1901 ; Priv. Lib. (imperf.).

[Another edition.] *A. Ieffes for T. G[ubbins] and I. Busbie.* 1592. 4°. 𝕭.𝕷.

 B.M. (Huth 40).

[Another edition.] 1598. 4°. 𝕭.𝕷.

 Hazlitt, H. 340 (Heber, pt. 4).

[Another edition.]   *I. R[oberts], for N. Lyng.*   1604.   4°.   𝕭.𝕷.
  Priv. Lib.

[Another edition.]   *For I. Smethwick.*   1609.   4°.   𝕭.𝕷.
  B.M. (C. 30. d. 20).

[Another edition.]   Euphues Golden Legacie, *etc.*   *For I. Smethwick.*
1612.   4°.   𝕭.𝕷.
  B.M. (1076. h. 5).

[Another edition.]   *For I. Smethwick.*   1623.   4°.
  Dyce.

[Another edition.]   *For J. Smethwicke.*   1634.   4°.   𝕭.𝕷.
  B.M. (12403. a. 27/1).

[Another edition.]   *For F. Smethwicke.*   1642.   4°.   𝕭.𝕷.
  B.M. (12403. aa. 59).

LONGUS.

Daphnis and Chloe.   Excellently describing the weight of affection, the
simplicitie of loue, the purport of honest meaning, the resolution of men, and
disposition of Fate, finished in a Pastorall, and interlaced with the praises of
a most peerlesse Princesse, wonderfull in Maiestie, and rare in perfection,
celebrated within the same Pastorall, and therefore termed by the name of the
Shepheards Holidaie.   By Angell Daye.   *R. Walde-graue.*   1587.   4°.   𝕭.𝕷.
  B.M. (Huth 37).

[A different version.]   A Most Sweet, and Pleasant Pastorall Romance for
Young Ladies.   By Geo. Thornley, Gent.   *For J. Garfield.*   1657.   8°.
  B.M. (E. 1652/2).

[A different version.]   The Pastoral Amours of Daphnis and Chloe.
Written Originally in Greek by Longus, and Translated into English Adorn'd
with Cutts.   The Second Edition.   *T. Jauncy.*   1720.   12°.
  Translated by James Craggs ; the first edition had appeared in 1719.
  B.M. (11335. a. 2).

[Another edition.]   Daphnis and Chloe.   In Four Books.   Written
Originally in Greek by Longus.   Translated into English By James Craggs,
Esq. ; Adorn'd with Ten Curious Cuts.   The Fourth Edition.   *For J.
Marshall.*   1733.   12°.
  B.M. (12403. e. 9).

LUCIAN.

Certaine Select Dialogues of Lucian. Together with his True Historie, Translated from the Greeke into English By Mr. Francis Hickes. Whereunto is added the life of Lucian gathered out of his owne Writings . . . by T. H., *etc. W. Turner : Oxford.* 1634. 4°.

B.M. (1067. k. 17).

Part of Lucian made English from the Original. In the yeare 1638. By Iasper Mayne. To which are adjoyned those other Dialogues of Lucian as they were formerly translated by Mr. Francis Hicks. *H. Hall for R. Davis : Oxford.* 1664, 63. Fol.

According to the dedication Mayne's work was written in 1638, but now first published. The second title-page, " Certain Select Dialogues of Lucian . . . Translated . . . by Mr. Francis Hickes," is dated 1663.

B.M. (8461. f. 27).

Lucian's Works, translated from the Greek. To which is Prefixt, The Life of Lucian . . . By Ferrand Spence, *etc. H. Clark for W. Benbridge.* 1684, 85. 8°. 5 vols.

Vol. 2 is "printed by H. C. for T. M. and sold by W. Benbridge," vol. 3 "for W. Benbridge," and vol. 4 "and last," and 5, both dated 1685, "for T. M. and are to be sold by J. Walthoe."

B.M. (720. f. 7, 8).

[A different version.] The Works of Lucian, Translated from the Greek, by several Eminent Hands . . . with the Life of Lucian . . . Written by John Dryden, Esq. *For S. Briscoe, and sold by J. Woodward and J. Morphew.* 1711. 8°. 4 vols.

B.M. (91. i. 20).

LUNA, Jean de.

See Lazarillo de Tormes.

LYLY, John.

Euphues. The Anatomy of Wyt. Very pleasant for all Gentlemen to reade, and most necessary to remember : wherin are contained the delights that Wyt followeth in his youth by the pleasauntnesse of Loue, and the happynesse he reapeth in age, by the perfectnesse of Wisedome. By Iohn Lylly Master of Arte. Oxon. *For G. Cawood.* [1578.] 4°. 𝕭.𝕷.

Warwick Bond, Bibliography in his ed. of Lyly, 1.

B.M. (C. 40. d. 48).

[Another edition.]   Corrected and augmented.   *For G. Cawood.*   [1579.]
4°.   **B.L.**
Bond 2.
   T.C.C. (VI^d. 4. 14²), imperf.

[Another edition.]   *T. East for G. Cawood.*   1579.   4°.   **B.L.**
Bond 3.
   Bodl. (Malone 713/1).

[Another edition.]   *T. East, for G. Cawood.*   1580.   4°.   **B.L.**
Bond 4.
   U.L.C. (Syn. 7. 58. 3/1).

Euphues and his England.   Containing his voyage and aduentures, myxed
with sundry pretie discourses of honest Loue, the discription of the countrey,
the Court, and the manners of that Isle.   Delightful to be read, and nothing
hurtful to be regarded : wherein there is small offence by lightnesse giuen
to the wise, and lesse occasion of loosenes proffered to the wanton.   By
John Lyly, Maister of Arte, *etc.   For G. Cawood.*   1580.   4°.   **B.L.**
Bond 1.
Hampstead Public Library, imperf.

[Another edition.]   *T. East, for G. Cawood.*   1580.   4°.   **B.L.**
Bond 2.
   Bodl. (Malone 713/2).

[Another edition.]   *T. East, for G. Cawood.*   1580.   4°.   **B.L.**
Bond 3.
   U.L.C. (Syn. 7. 58. 3/2).

[Another edition of both parts.]   Euphues, *etc.   T. East, for G. Cawood.*
1581.   4°.   **B.L.**   2 vols.
Bond 4.
   Part 1, B.M. (G. 10437) ;   part 2 (without East's name), Bridgewater.

[Another edition.]   *For G. Cawood.*   1582.   4°.   **B.L.**   2 vols.
Part 1 undated? (wants last leaf).   Bond 5 (part 2).
   Priv. Lib.

[Another edition.]   *For G. Cawood.*   1584.   4°.   **B.L.**
Ellis, Catalogue 143.

[Another edition.]   *T. East for G. Cawood.*   1585, 86.   4°.   **B.L.**   2 vols.
Bond 6.
   Priv. Lib.

[Another edition.]   *T. East for G. Cawood.*   1587, 88.   4°.   **B.L.**   2 vols.
Bond 7.
   Hazlitt, H. 360.

[Another edition.]   *I. Roberts for G. Cawood.*   [1595?]   4°.   𝕭.𝕷.
Bond 8.
> Bodl. (2698. e. 6).

[Another edition.]   *I. Roberts for G. Cawood.*   1597.   4°.   𝕭.𝕷.   2 vols.
Bond 9.   Part 1 is undated.
> B.M. (92. b. 5).

[Another edition.]   *For W. Leake.*   1605.   4°.   𝕭.𝕷.   2 vols.
Bond 10.
> Part 1, Lowndes ; part 2, Hazlitt, I. 270.

[Another edition.]   *For W. Leake.*   1606.   4°.   𝕭.𝕷.   2 vols.
Bond 11.
> Part 1, Priv. Lib. ; part 2, B.M. (C. 40. d. 34/2).

[Another edition.]   *For W. Leake.*   1607.   4°.   𝕭.𝕷.   2 vols. ?
Bond 12.
> Part 1, B.M. (C. 40. d. 34/1) ; part 2 unknown.

[Another edition.]   *For W. Leake.*   1609.   4°.   𝕭.𝕷.   2 vols ?
Bond 12.   Part 2 only is known.
> B.M. (C. 40. d. 11).

[Another edition.]   *For W. Leake.*   1613.   4°.   𝕭.𝕷.   2 vols.
Bond 13.
> Bodl. (Malone 811) ; B.M. (G. 10438/2), part 1.

[Another edition.]   *G. Eld for W. B. and are to be sold by A. Iohnson.*
1617.   4°.   𝕭.𝕷.   2 vols.
Bond 14.
> B.M. (1077. f. 9).

[Another edition.]   *I. Beale for I. Parker.*   1623.   4°.   𝕭.𝕷.   2 vols.
Vol. 2 only is dated.
Bond 15.
> B.M. (12315. cc. 24).

[Another edition.]   *I. H. and are to be sold by I. Boler.*   1630.   4°.   𝕭.𝕷.
2 vols.
Bond 16.
> Bodl. (2698. e. 7).

[Another issue.]   *I. H., and are to be sold by I. Boler.*   1631.   4°.   𝕭.𝕷.
2 vols.
Bond 16.
> B.M. (12410. cc. 1).

[Another edition.]   *I. Haviland.*   1636.   4°.   𝕭.𝕷.   2 vols.

Bond 17.
  B.M. (12613. c. 34).

[A different version of Part 1.]   Euphues and Lucilla : or the False Friend
and Inconstant Mistress.   To which is added, Ephœbus ; or Instructions for
the Education of Youth.   With Letters upon Death etc.   Written originally
by John Lyly M.A. .... and now revis'd, *etc.*   *Sold by J. Noon, and T. Sharpey.*
1716.   4°.

Bond 18.
  Bodl. (Douce L. 59).

[Another issue.]   The False Friend and Inconstant Mistress : An Instruc-
tive Novel.   To which is added, Love's Diversion ...   By John Lyly, M.A.
One of the Refiners of the English Tongue in the Reign of Queen Elizabeth.
For J. Hooke.   1718.   8°.

Bond 18.
  B.M. (12612. a. 43).

LYSANDER AND CALISTA.

See AUDIGUIER, Vitel d'.

M., Jo.

Philippes Venus.   Wherein is pleasantly discoursed Sundrye fine and wittie
arguments in a senode of the Gods and Goddesses assembled for the expelling
of wanton Venus from among their sacred societie.   *For J. Perrin.*   1591.
4°.   𝕭.𝕷.

  Bodl. (Malone 659).

M., M.

See PARIS AND VIENNE.

MAISON–NEUVE, ESTIENNE DE.

See GERILEON.

MALORY, *Sir* THOMAS.

Colophon : Thus endeth thys noble and Ioyous book entytled le morte
Darthur, Notwythstondyng it treateth of the byrth, lyf, and actes of the
rounde table, theyr meruayllous enquestes and aduentures, thacheuyng of

the sangreal & in thende the dolorous deth & departyng out of thys world of them al, whiche book was reduced in to englysshe by Syr Thomas Malory knyght, *etc.   W. Caxton: Westmestre.*   1485.   Fol.   𝕭.𝕷.

    J. P. Morgan (formerly R. Hoe) ;   J.R.L., imperf.

[Another edition.]   *Colophon:* Here is the ende of the hoole boke of kynge Arthur, *etc.   Wynkyn de Worde: Westmestre.*   1498.   Fol.   𝕭.𝕷.

    J.R.L., imperf.

[Another edition.]   *Colophon:* Here is the ende of the hole booke of kynge Arthur and of his noble knyghtes of the rounde table, *etc.   Wynkyn de Worde.* 1529.   Fol.   𝕭.𝕷.

    B.M. (G. 10510).

[Another edition.]   The Story of the moste noble and worthy Kynge Arthur, the whiche was the fyrst of the worthyes chrysten, and also of his noble and valyaunt knyghtes of the rounde Table.   Newly imprynted and corrected.   An. MDLVII.   *W. Copland.*   1557.   Fol.   𝕭.𝕷.

    Huth ; B.M. (C. 11. b. 12) wants title, which has been supplied in a facsimile differing slightly from the above.

[Another edition.]   *T. East.*   Fol.   𝕭.𝕷.
Licensed to East, 12 March 1581/2 (*Stat. Reg.*, ii. 408).
    B.M. (G. 10511).

[Another edition.]   *T. Easte.*   Fol.   𝕭.𝕷.
    U.L.C. (AB. 10. 25).

[Another edition.]   The most Ancient and Famous History of the renowned Prince Arthur King of Britaine, *etc.   W. Stansby for I. Bloome.* 1634.   4°.   𝕭.𝕷.   3 vols.

    B.M. (C. 34. h. 38).

[An abridgement.]   Brittains Glory : Or, The History of the Life and Death of K. Arthur, And the Adventures of the Knights of the Round Table, *etc.   H. B[rugis] for J. Wright, J. Clark, W. Thackeray, and T. Passinger.* 1684.   4°.   𝕭.𝕷.

    The preface is signed J. S.
    Pepys 1192 (8).

[Another edition.]   Great Britain's Glory, *etc.   W. O[nley.]*   4°.   𝕭.𝕷.
    B.M. (12450. e. 20).

[Another edition.]   *C. Brown.*   4°.

B.M. (12450. e. 7).

MANDEVILE, *Sir* JOHN.

Here begynneth a lytell treatyse or booke named Johan Maũdeuyle knyght born in Englonde in the towne of saynt Albone ᴤ speketh of the wayes of the holy londe towarde Iherusalem, ᴤ of marueyles of Ynde ᴤ of other dyuerse coũtrees.   *Wynken de worde : Westmynster.*   1499.   4°.   𝕭.𝕿.

U.L.C. (Inc. 5. J. 1. 2.), imperf.

[Another edition.]   *Colophon :* Here endeth the boke of John Maundeuyle. knyght of wayes to Ierusalem ᴤ of marueylys of ynde and of other countrees. *Rychard Pynson.*   4°.   𝕭.𝕿.

B.M. (G. 6713).

[Another edition.]   *Wynkyn de Worde.*   1503.   4°.   𝕭.𝕿.

Bodl. (Douce frag. e. 8).

[Another edition.]   The Voyage and trauayle, of syr John Maundeuile knight, which treateth of the way toward Hierusalem, and of maruayles of Inde with other Ilands and Countryes.   *T. East.*   1568.   4°.   𝕭.𝕿.

B.M. (1045. h. 2).

[Another edition.]   Wherein is treated of the way towards Hierusalem, and of the meruailes of Inde, with other Lands and Countries.   *T. Este.* [1581 ?].   4°.   𝕭.𝕿.

Licensed to East, 12 March, 1581/2 (*Stat. Reg.*, ii. 408) as " Pre[s]ter Iohns land." Bodl. (Douce MM. 489).

[Another edition ?]   *T. Snodham.*   1612.   4°.   𝕭.𝕿.

More probably of the same version as the following. Hazlitt, I. 274.

[A different version.]   The Voyages and Trauailes of Sir John Mandeuile Knight.   Wherein is set downe the Way to the Holy Land, and to Hierusalem : as also to the Lands of the great Caane, and of Prester Iohn ; to Inde, and diuers other Countries : together with the many and strange Meruailes therein.   *T. Stansby.*   1618.   4°.   𝕭.𝕿.

With woodcuts. B.M. (G. 6715), the imprint cut away.

[Another edition.]   *T. Snodham.*   1625.   4°.

Hazlitt, H. 368.

[Another edition.] *R. B., and are to sold* [*sic*] *by A. Crooke.* 1657. 4°. 𝔅.𝔏.
  B.M. (G. 6716).

[Another edition.] 4°. 𝔅.𝔏.
  B.M. (G. 6714), imperf.

[Another edition.] *For A. Crooke.* 1670. 4°. 𝔅.𝔏.
  B.M. (10055. a. 6).

[Another edition.] *For R. Scott, T. Basset, J. Wright, and R. Chiswell.*
1677. 4°. 𝔅.𝔏.
  Pepys 1244.

[Another edition.] *For R. Scot, T. Basset, J. Wright, and R. Chiswel.*
1684. 4°. 𝔅.𝔏.
  B.M. (1045. h. 30).

[Another edition.] *For R. Chiswell, B. Walford, M. Wotton, and G.*
Conyers. 1696. 4°. 𝔅.𝔏.
  B.M. (G. 6718).

[Another edition.] *For R. Chiswell, B. Walford, M. Wotton, and G.*
Conyers. 1705. 4°.
  B.M. (1077. g. 35/2).

[Another edition.] *A. Wilde, for G. Conyers, T. Norris, and A. Bettesworth.*
1722. 4°.
  B.M. (10056. c. 22), the date cropped ; Bodl. (206. e. 3).

[A different version.] The Travels and Voyages of Sir John Mandevile,
Knt. Containing An Exact Description of the Way to Hierusalem, Great
Caan, India, the Country of Preston-John [*sic*] . . . Faithfully Collected
from the Original Manuscript, and Illustrated with Variety of Pictures. *For*
J. Osborne, and J. Hodges. 12°.
  77 chapters. Ends at chapter 103 (of the earlier editions) "A Description of the Paradise
Terrestre."
  B.M. (10055. a. 33).

[Another edition.] For *J. Hodges and J. Harris.* 8°.
  B.M. (435. a. 1).

[A different version.] The Voiage and Travaile of Sir John Maundevile,
Kt. Which Treateth of the Way to Hierusalem ; and of Marvayles of Inde,

With other Ilands and Countryes.   Now publish'd entire from an Original
MS. in the Cotton Library.   *For J. Woodman and D. Lyon, and C. Davis.*
1725.   Very large 8°.

> Reissued in 1727 with a new title-page.
>   B.M. (683. f. 18).

MARGUERITE, *de Navarre.*

The Queene of Nauarres Tales.   Containing, Verie pleasant Discourses of
fortunate Louers.   Now newly translated out of French into English.   *V. S[ims]*
for I. Oxenbridge.   1597.   4°.   𝕭.𝕷.

> The preface is signed A. B.
> Licensed to F. Norton, 1 Sept., 1600 (*Stat. Reg.* iii. 171).
>   Bodl. (Douce. M. 413).

[A different version.]   Heptameron, or the History of the Fortunate
Lovers ; Written by the most Excellent and most Virtuous Princess, Margaret
de Valoys, Queen of Navarre ...   Now made English by Robert Codrington,
master of Arts.   *F. L. for N. Ekins.*   1654.   8°.

> B.M. (E. 1468/2).

The Prudent Husband.   *See* (in Part II) D'URFEY, T.

MARKHAM, GERVASE.

The English Arcadia, Alluding his beginning from Sir Philip Sydnes ending.
By Iaruis Markham.   *E. Allde, and are to be solde by H. Rocket.*   1607.   4°.

> Book I, part 1.
>   Bodl. (Malone 633).

The Second and Last Part of the First Booke of the English Arcadia.
Making a compleate end of the first History ...   By G. M.   *N. Okes for*
T. Saunders.   1613.   4°.

> Bodl. (KK. 44. Jur.).

[*The historye of Sir Meruyn son to Ogyer the Dane one of the xij peires of*
Ffrance, translated out of Frenche.]

> Licensed to R. Jones, 3 Feb., 1595/6 (*Stat. Reg.* iii. 58).   It is referred to in Meres'
> *Palladis Tamia*, 1598.

[Another edition.]   The most Famous and renowned Historie of that
woorthie and illustrous knight Meruine, Sonne to that rare and excellent
Mirror of Princely prowesse, Oger the Dane, and one of that royail bond of

vnmatchable knighthoode, the twelue Peeres of France . . . By I. M. Gent.
R. Blower and V. Sims. 1612. 4°. 𝕭.𝕷.
    B.M. (1074. b. 35).

MARY, *of Nemmegen.*

    Here begynneth a lyttell story that was of a trwetle done in the lande of
Gelders of a mayde that was named Mary of Nēmegen yᵗ was the dyuels
paramoure by the space of .vij. yere longe. *J. Duisbrowghe: Anwarpe.*
[1518?] 4°. 𝕭.𝕷.
    Proctor, *Doesborgh*, 18.
    Britwell.

MEG, *Long, of Westminster.*

    [The Life and Pranks of Long Meg of Westminster.] *W. How, for
A. Veale.* 1582. 8°. 𝕭.𝕷.
    B.M. (12613. a. 24), imperf.

    [Another edition?]
    Licensed to T. Gubbins and T. Newman, 18 Aug., 1590 (*Stat. Reg.* ii. 559).

    [Another edition.] The Life of Long Meg of Westminster, *etc. E. All-de,
for E. White.* 1620. 4°. 𝕭.𝕷.
    The Marquis of Bute (Hazlitt I. 286).

    [Another edition.] *For R. Bird.* 1635. 4°. 𝕭.𝕷.
    Huth.

    [Another edition]. *For R. Bird.* 1636. 4°. 𝕭.𝕷.
    Hazlitt, H. 386.

MELBANCKE, BRIAN.

    Philotimus. The Warre betwixt Nature and Fortune. Compiled by
Brian Melbancke, *etc. R. Warde.* 1583. 4°. 𝕭.𝕷.
    B.M. (G. 10464).

MERVINE.

    See MARKHAM, Gervase.

MEXIA, Pedro.

The Foreste or Collection of Histories no lesse profitable, then pleasant and necessarie, dooen out of Frenche into Englishe by Thomas Fortescue. *I. Kyngston, for W. Iones.*   1571.   4°.   𝕭.𝕷.

B.M. (95. c. 8).

[Another edition.]   *J. Day.*   1476 [1576].   4°.   𝕭.𝕷.

This edition was licensed for reprinting to J. Danter, 8 Nov., 1596 (*Stat. Reg.* iii. 73).
B.M. (G. 508).

MIDDLETON, Christopher.

The Famous Historie of Chinon of England ...   With the worthy Atchieuement of Sir Lancelot du Lake, and Sir Tristram du Lions ...   By Chr. Middleton.   *I. Danter, for C. Burbie.*   1597.   4°.   𝕭.𝕷.

B.M. (C. 34. d. 58).

MIRROR OF KNIGHTHOOD.

See Ortuñez de Calahorra, Diego

MONTEMAYOR, Jorge de.

Diana of George of Montemayor: Translated out of Spanish into English by Bartholomew Yong of the Middle Temple Gentleman.   *E. Bollifant, Impensis G. B.*   1598.   Fol.

B.M. (12403. b. 7).

[Another edition.]   1738.

See Vega Carpio, Lope da.   The Pilgrim.

MONTREUX, Nicolas de.

Honours Academie.   Or the Famous Pastorall of the faire Shepheardesse, Iulietta ...   Done into English, by R. T. Gentleman.   *T. Creede.*   1610.   Fol.

The dedication is signed Robert Tofte.   The original was published by Montreux under the anagram Ollenix du Mont Sacré.
B.M. (12403. c. 10).

MORE, Sir Thomas.

Thomæ Mori Utopia, a mendis vindicata.   *W. Hall, Impensis F. Oxlad.* 1663.   24°.

First printed abroad in 1518.
B.M. (1077. a. 24).

[Another edition.] A fruteful, and pleasaunt worke of the beste state of a publyque weale, and of the new yle called Vtopia : written in Latine by Syr Thomas More knyght, and translated into Englyshe by Raphe Robynson Citizein and Goldsmythe of London, at the procurement, and earnest request of George Tadlowe Citizein *τ* Haberdassher of the same Citie. *A. Vele.* 1551. 8°. 𝔅.𝔏.

B.M. (C. 38. a. 11).

[Another edition.] A Most pleasant, fruitfull, and wittie worke, of the best state of a publique weale, and of the new Yle called Vtopia : Written in Latine, by the right worthie and famous Syr Thomas Moore Knight : and translated into English by Raphe Robinson, sometime fellow of Corpus Christi Colledge in Oxford. And now this third Edition, newly corrected and amended. *T. Creede.* 1597. 4°. 𝔅.𝔏.

B.M. (12350. aaa. 44).

[Another edition.] A frutefull, pleasaunt, & wittie worke, *etc.* *A. Veale.* 1606. 8°. 𝔅.𝔏.

Hazlitt, II. 404.

[Another edition.] Sir Thomas Moore's Vtopia : Containing, an excellent, learned, wittie, and pleasant Discourse of the best state of a Publike Weale, as it is found in the Gouernment of the new Ile called Vtopia. First written in Latine, by the Right Honourable and worthy of all Fame, Sir Thomas Moore, Knight, Lord Chancellour of England ; And translated into English by Raphe Robinson, sometime Fellow of Corpus Christi Colledge in Oxford. And now after many Impressions, newly Corrected and purged of all Errors hapned in the former Editions. *B. Alsop.* 1624. 4°.

B.M. (523 g. 26).

[Another edition.] The Commonwealth of Utopia, *etc.* *B. Alsop & T. Fawcet, and are to be sold by W. Sheares.* 1639. 12°.

B.M. (8005. a. 29).

[Another edition.] Utopia : Written in Latin by Sir Thomas More, Chancellor of England : Translated into English. *For R. Chiswell.* 1684. 8°.

Hazlitt, II. 404.

MORINDOS.

The Famous & renowned History of Morindos a King of Spaine ; Who maryed with Miracola a Spanish Witch : and of their seauen daughters,

(rightly surnamed Ladies with bleeding hearts :) their births, their liues and
their deaths. A History most wonderfull, strange, and pleasant to the
reader. *For H. R.* 1609. 4°. 𝕭.𝕷.

Bodl. (Douce MM. 478).

MUNDAY (ANTHONY).

Zelauto. The Fountaine of Fame. Erected in an Orcharde of Amorous
Aduentures. Containing a Delicate Disputation, gallantly discoursed
betweene two noble Gentlemen of Italye. Given for a friendly entertainment to Euphues, at his late arrival into England. By A. M., *etc.*
I. Charlewood. 1580. 4°. 𝕭.𝕷.

Bodl. (Douce MM. 474).

N., B.

See BRETON, Nicholas.

N., C.

See CAUSSIN, Nicolas.

NASH, THOMAS.

The Vnfortunate Traueller. Or, The life of Iacke Wilton . . . Tho. Nashe.
T. Scarlet for C. Burby. 1594. 4°. 𝕭.𝕷.

B.M. (96. b. 17/2).

[Another edition.] Newly corrected and augmented . . . Tho. Nashe.
T. Scarlet for C. Burby. 1594. 4°. 𝕭.𝕷.

Bodl. (Wood 31. C. 3) ; B.M. (C. 57. b. 52), imperf.

OLIVER OF CASTILE.

Colophon : Here endeth yͤ hystorye of Olyuer of Castylle, and of the
fayre Helayne doughter vnto the kynge of Englande. *Wynkyn de Worde.*
1518. 4°. 𝕭.𝕷.

Britwell. *Cf.* Roxburgh Club reprint, 1898.

[Another edition.]

Licensed to T. East, 12 March, 1581/2. *Oliver of Castile* is referred to in Meres' *Palladis
Tamia*, 1598.

[A different version.] The History of Olivaires of Castile, and Arthur of Dalgarve. Translated out of the Spanish into the Italian Tongue, by Francesco Portonari : And from the Italian made English. *For F. Hildyard.* 1695. 12º.

Bodl. (Douce O. 33); Huth (translated " By Mark Micklethwait, M.A. For A. and J. Churchill, and F. Hildyard ").

ORTUÑEZ DE CALAHORRA, DIEGO.

[Part 1.] The Mirrour of Princely deedes and Knighthood : Wherein is shewed the worthinesse of the Knight of the Sunne, and his brother Rosicleer, sonnes to the great Emperour Trebetio : with the straunge loue of the beautifull and excellent Princesse Briana, and the valiant actes of other noble Princes and Knightes. Now newly translated out of Spanish into our vulgar English tongue, by M. T. *T. East.* [1578.] 4º. 𝕭.𝕷.

Licensed to East, 4 Aug., 1578 (*Stat. Reg.* ii. 334).
Huth.

[Another edition.] The First Part of the Mirrour of Princely deedes and Knighthood. Wher in is Shewed the Worthinesse of the Knight of the Sunne, and his brother Rosicleer . . . Now newly translated out of Spanish into our vulgar Fnglish [*sic*] tongue, by M. T. *T. Este.* 4º. 𝕭.𝕷.

The dedication is signed Margaret Tyler.
Bodl. (Douce O. 113); Huth.

[Another edition.] *T. East.* · 4º. 𝕭.𝕷.

The Misprint "Fnglish" in the title of the preceding does not occur in this edition.
Priv. Lib. ; U.L.C. (Syn. 7. 57. 22), imperf. at end.

[Part 2.] The Second part of the first Booke of the Myrrour of Knight-hood : in which is prosecuted the illustrious deedes of the knyght of the Sunne, and his brother Rosicleer . . . Now newly translated out of Spanish into our vulgar tongue by R. P. *T. Este.* 1599. 4º. 𝕭.𝕷.

B.M. (12450. f. 7).

[Part 3.] The Third Part of the first booke, of the Mirrovr of Knight-hood. Wherein is set forth the worthie deedes of the knight of the Sunne, and his brother Rosicleer . . . Verie delightfull to the reader. Newly trans-lated out of Spanish into English by R. P. *T. Este.* 4º. 𝕭.𝕷.

The author of this part is Marco Martiñez.
B.M. (12450. f. 7).

[Parts 4, 5.] The Second part of the Myrror of Knighthood. Containing two severall Bookes, wherein is intreated the valiant deedes of Armes of sundrie worthie knights . . . Now newly translated out of Spanish into our vulgar tongue by R. P.   *T. Este.*   1583.   4°.   𝕭.𝕷.

> The author of these two parts is Pedro de la Sierra, or Marco Martiñez.
>   B.M. (12450. f. 7).

[Another edition.]   *T. Este.*   1598.   4°.   𝕭.𝕷.

> Bodl. (Douce O. 114).

[Part 6.]   The sixth Booke of the Myrrour of Knighthood. . Being The first Booke of the third Part . . . Conteining the Knightly actions and amorous conuersations of Rosicleer and Rosabel his sonne . . . Translated out of Spanish by R. P.   *E. Allde for C. Burby.*   1598.   4°.   𝕭.𝕷.

> The author is Pedro de la Sierra, or Marco Martiñez.
>   U.L.C. (Syn. 7. 57. 18).

[Part 7.]   The Seuenth Booke of the Myrrour of Knighthood.   Being the Second of the third Part.   Englished out of the Spanish language.   *T. Purfoot for C. Burby.*   1598.   4°.   𝕭.𝕷.

> The dedication is signed L. A.   The author is Marco Martiñez.
>   B.M. (12450. f. 7).

[Part 8.]   The Eighth Booke of the Myrror of Knighthood.   Being the third of the third Part.   Englished out of the Spanish tongue.   *T. Creede, for C. Burbey.*   1599.   4°.   𝕭.𝕷.

> The dedication is signed L. A.   The author is Marco Martiñez.
>   B.M. (12450. f. 7).

[Book 9.]   The Ninth part of the Mirrour of Knight-hood, Being the fourth Booke of the third part thereof.   Englished out of the Spanish tongue. [*S. Stafford*] *for C. Burbie.*   1601.   4°.   𝕭.𝕷.

> The author is Marco Martiñez.
>   U.L.C. (Syn. 7. 57. 21) ; B.M. (12450. f. 7), imperfect at end.

OSMIN AND DARAXA.   *See* ALEMAN, Mateo.

PAINTER, WILLIAM.

The Palace of Pleasure Beautified, adorned and well furnished, with Pleasaunt Histories and excellent Nouelles, selected out of diuers good and commendable authors.   By William Painter Clarke of the Ordinaunce and Armarie.   *H. Denham for R. Tottell and W. Jones.*   1566, 67.   4°.   𝕭.𝕷. 2 vols.

> Vol. 2 is printed by H. Bynneman for N. England.
>   B.M. (G. 10491, 92).

[Another edition.] *T. Marshe.* 1569. 4°. 𝕭.𝕷. 2 vols.

Bodl. (Wood 591), vol. 1 ; vol. 2, undated, *see* M. A. Scott, *Elizabethan Translations,* pp. 12, 13.

[Another edition.] Eftsones perused corrected and augmented. *T. Marshe.* 1575. 4°. 𝕭.𝕷. 2 vols.

Vol. 2 is undated.
B.M. (243. h. 5, 6).

PALATINUS, MUSAEUS.
See BRAITHWAITE, Richard.

PALESTINA.
See CHAMBERS, Robert.

PALLADINE. ⎫
PALMENDOS. ⎬ *See* PALMERIN.

PALMERIN.
Palmerin d'Oliva, the Mirrour of Nobilitie, turned into English. By Anthony Munday. *J. Charlwood.* 1588. 4°.

Continued by *Palmendos.*
Hazlitt, H. 436.

[Another edition.] [*T. Creede?* 1597.] 4°.

Priv. Lib., imperf., wanting the title.

[Another edition.] The Second Part of the honourable Historie, of Palmerin d'Oliua ... Translated by A. M., *etc. T. Creede.* 1597. 4°. 𝕭.𝕷.

Priv. Lib.

[Another edition of both parts.] *T. C[reede] and R. A. for R. Higgenbotham.* 1616. 4°.

Priv. Lib.

[Another edition.] *For B. Alsop and T. Favvcet.* 1637. 4°. 𝕭.𝕷. 2 vols.

B.M. (G. 10484).

The Honorable, pleasant and rare conceited Historie of Palmendos.
Sonne to the famous and fortunate Prince Palmerin d'Oliua, Emperour of
Constantinople and the Queene of Tharsus.   Translated out of French by
A. M., *etc. I. C[harlwood] for S. Watersonne.* 1589. 4°. 𝕭.𝕷.

The continuation of *Palmerin d'Oliva.* Continued by *Primaleon.* Licensed, with
Primaleon, to J. Charlwood, 9 Jan., 1589 (*Stat. Reg.* ii. 513).
Huth.

[Another edition.] The famous History of Palmendos son to the most
Renowned Palmerin D'Oliva, Emperour of Constantinople, And the Heroick
Queen of Tharsus, *etc. E. Alsop.* 1653. 4°. 𝕭.𝕷.

B.M. (12410. bb. 6).

[Another edition.] 1663. 4°.

Hazlitt, H. 436.

The first Booke of Primaleon of Greece. Describing the knightly deeds of
Armes, as also the memorable aduentures of Prince Edward of England.
And continuing the former History of Palmendos, brother to the fortunate
Prince Primaleon. *For C. Burby.* 1595. 4°. 𝕭.𝕷.

Continuing *Palmendos* and continued by *Palladine.* Licensed, with Palmendos, together
in seven books, to J. Charlwood. 9 Jan., 1589 (*Stat. Reg.* ii. 513). Book 4 of *Primaleon,
Durine [Dorineo] of Greece,* translated by H. W., was licensed to T. Purfoot, sen. and jun.,
8 Dec., 1598 (*Stat. Reg.* iii. 132), and Book 3 to Mistress Burby, 6 Oct., 1607 (*Stat.
Reg.* iii. 360).
Priv. Lib.

The second Book of Primaleon of Greece.   And Prince Edward of
England. Continuing the course of their rare fortunes, Knightly Aduentures,
successe in Loue, and admirable escape from verie perilous Enchantments :
As the like delightfull Historie hath sildome been heard of.   Translated out
of French by A. M.   *I. Danter for C. Burby.* 1596. 4°. 𝕭.𝕷.

Priv. Lib.

[Another edition.] The Famous and Renowned Historie of Primaleon of
Greece, *etc. T. Snodham.* 1619. 4°. 3 vols. 𝕭.𝕷.

B.M. (12613. e. 13).

[Palladine of England.]

Palladine continues *Primaleon,* and is continued (after *Platir* and *Flotir,* which were not
translated), by *Palmerin of England.*
Licensed to J. Danter, 27 Aug., 1596 (*Stat. Reg.* iii. 69).

[Another edition.] The Famous, pleasant, and variable Historie, of Palladine
of England.   Discoursing of honorable Aduentures, of Knightly deedes of

Armes and Chiualrie : interlaced likewise with the loue of sundrie noble personages . . . Translated out of French by A. M. *etc.* *E. Allde for I. Perin.* 1588. 4°. 𝕭.𝕷.

Bridgewater.

[Another edition.] *T. J. for A. Kembe and C. Tyus.* 1664. 4°.

B.M. (12450. d. 7).

[Another edition.] The excellent History of Paladine of England. *For T. Passinger.* 4°. [1685 ?]

Passinger's list in *Valentine and Orson*, 1685.

[Another edition.] *Printed and Sold by the Booksellers.* 12°.

B.M. (12410. aa. 22).

[Another issue.] The Second Edition. *J. F., and sold by J. Marshall.* 12°.

B.M. (12450. b. 18).

[An abridgement ?] The Excellent History of Paladine of England. *For E. Tracy.* 4°. [1685 ?]

Tracy's list, in *Valentine and Orson*, 1685.

[Palmerin of England, Parts 1 and 2].

Concludes the cycle. Parts 1 and 2 were licensed to J. Charlwood, 3 Feb., 1581 (*Stat. Reg.* ii. 388).

[Another edition.] [*T. Creede ?*] 1596. 4°. 2 vols.

Britwell, imperf.

[Palmerin of England, Part 3.]

Licensed to Leake, 10 March, 1594/5 (*Stat. Reg.* ii. 672).

[Another edition.] The Third and last part of Palmerin of England . . . Written in Spanish, Italian, and French, and translated into English by A. M., *etc.* *I. R[oberts]. for W. Leake.* 1602. 4°. 𝕭.𝕷.

B.M. (12403. e. 12).

[Another edition.] The First Part of the no lesse rare, then excellent and stately Historie, of the famous and fortunate Prince, Palmerin of England, *etc.* *T. Creede.* 1609. 4°. 𝕭.𝕷.

Only Part 1 is known in this edition.
B.M. (12410. dd. 7).

[Another edition.] *T. Creede, and B. Alsop.* 1616. 4°. 2 vols. 𝕭.𝕷.

Part 1, Hazlitt, H. 442 ; Part 2, B.M. (G. 10486).

[Another edition.] *B. Alsop and T. Fawcet.* 1639. 4°. 2 vols. 𝕭.𝕷.
  B.M. (12410. dd. 7).

[Another edition.] *R. I. for S. S. to bee sold by C. Tyus.* 1664. 4°.
2 vols. 𝕭.𝕷.
  B.M. (12613. b. 17).

[An abridgement.] The Famous History of the Life of the Renowned
Prince Palmerin of England : Or, The Glory of Knightly Prowess. In Three
Parts . . . Written originally in French and now faithfully done into English
. . . By J. S. *For W. Thackeray.* 1685. 4°. 𝕭.𝕷.
  Pepys 1190(1).

[Another edition.] *For W. Thackeray and J. Back.* 1691. 4°.
  Term Cat. ii. 387.

PALVIANO, *Count.*
  See ALEMAN, Mateo.

PANEDONIUS, PHILOGENES.
  See BRAITHWAIT, Richard.

PARIS AND VIENNE.
  Begin : Here begynneth thistorye of the noble ryght valyaunt ꞇ worthy
knyght Parys, and the fayr Vyēne the daulphyns doughter of vyennooys, the
which suffred many aduersytees bycause of theyr true loue or they coude enioy
the effect therof of eche other. *W. Caxton : Westmestre.* 1485. Fol. 𝕭.𝕷.
  B.M. (C. 10. b. 10).

[Another edition.] Thystorie of Parys and Vyenne. *G. Leeu : Andewarpe.*
1492. Fol. 𝕭.𝕷.
  T.C.D.

[Another edition.] [*W. de Worde.*] 4°. 𝕭.𝕷.
  Bodl. (Douce frag. f. 3).

[Another edition.] [*R. Pynson.*] 4°. 𝕭.𝕷.
  B.M. (12512. d. 14), frag.

[Another edition ?]
  Licensed to T. Purfoot, 8 Aug., 1586, as "an old booke of *the xij pairs of Ffraunce* and
of *Paris and Vienne*, vjᵈ" (*Stat. Reg.* ii. 453).

[Another edition?] The Honour of True Love and Knighthood, wherein are storied the Noble atchievements of Sir Paris of Vienna and the faire Princesse Vienna. *B. Alsop.* 1621. 4°.

Hazlitt, H. 438.

[Another edition?] Vienna. Noe Art Can Cure This hart. Where in is storied, ye valorous atchieuements, famous triumphs, constant love, great miseries, & finall happines, of the well-deseruing, truly noble and most valiant k^t, Sr Paris of Vienna and ye most admired amiable Princess, the faire Vienna. *For R. Hawkins.* 4°.

The dedication is signed M. M[ainwaring]. For the author's name see the enigmatic couplets at the end.
Bodl. (Malone 674).

[Another edition.] *For G. Percivall.* 4°.
B.M. (C. 40. c. 2).

[Another edition.] *For W. Leake.* 1650. 4°.
B.M. (12613. b. 9).

PARRY, ROBERT.

[Moderatus, The most delectable and famous Historie of the Blacke Knight.] *R. Ihones.* 1595. 4°. 𝕭.𝕷.
Bodl. (Douce PP. 212), imperf.

PARSON OF KALENBOROWE.

[The Parson of Kalenborowe.] [*J. Doesborgh : Antwerp.* 1520?]. 4°. 𝕭.𝕷.
Proctor, Doesborgh, 26.
Bodl. (Douce K. 49).

PATTERN OF PAINFUL ADVENTURES.
See APOLLONIUS.

PEELE, GEORGE.

Merrie Conceited Jests of George Peele, *etc.* 1607. 4°.
Hazlitt, *Old English Jest Books*, vol. ii.

[Another edition.] *G. P. for F. Faulkner.* 1627. 4°. 𝕭.𝕷.
B.M. (C. 40. d. 38).

[Another edition.]   *For W. Gilbertson.*   1657.   4°.   𝕭.𝕷.
B.M. (1080. i. 46).

[Another edition.]   *For H. Bell.*   4°.
S.W. Singer's reprint, 1809.

[Another edition.]   *For W. Whitwood.*   1671.   4°.   𝕭.𝕷.
Bodl. (Malone 335).

PENITENT PILGRIM.
See BRAITHWAIT, Richard.

PERICLES PRINCE OF TYRE.
See WILKINS, George.

PETRARCA, FRANCESCO.
See GRISELDA.

PETRONIUS ARBITER, TITUS.
Petronii Satyræ was licensed to the Partners in the English Stock, 22 June, 1631 (*Stat. Reg.* iv. 255.); *see* Part II.

PETTIE, GEORGE.
A Petite Pallace of Pettie his pleasure : Contayning many pretie Hystories, by him set foorth in comely colours and most delightfully discoursed. *R. W[atkins]*.   [1576].   4°.   𝕭.𝕷.
Licensed to Watkins, 6 Aug., 1576 (*Stat. Reg.*, ii. 301).
Lace border ; device fresh.
B.M. (G. 10442).

[Another edition.]   *R. W[atkins]*.   4°.   𝕭.𝕷.
R. Iugge border ; device worn.
B.M. (C. 40. d. 5).

[Another edition.]   *R. W[atkins]*.   4°.   𝕭.𝕷.
R. Iugge border ; device with shading cleared out.
B.M. (C. 27. b. 16).

[Another edition.]   *J. Roberts.*   1598.   4°.
Hazlitt, H. 455 (Warton, 1824. iv. 29).

[Another edition ?]
Licensed to F. Burton, 11 March, 1604/5 (*Stat. Reg.*, iii. 284).

[Another edition.]   *G. Eld.*   1608.   4°.   𝕭.𝕷.
B.M. (12613. b. 10).

[Another edition.]   *G. Eld.*   1613.   4°.   𝕭.𝕷.
Bodl. (Douce PP. 199).

PHILIPPES.
See M., Jo.

PIERS PLAIN.
See CHETTLE, Henry.

PILPAY.
See BIDPAI.

PILGRIM OF CASTILE.
See VEGA CARPIO, Lope da.

PISAN, CHRISTINE DE.
See CHRISTINE DE PISE.

PLUTARCH.
The Amorous and Tragicall Tales of Plutarch.   Wherevnto is annexed the Hystorie of Cariclea and Theogenes, and the sayings of the Greeke Philosophers.   Translated by Ia. Sanford.   *H. Bynneman, for L. Maylard.* 1567.   8°.   𝕭.𝕷.
B.M. (244. b. 3).

PONTHUS.
Colophon : Here endeth the noble hystory of the moost excellent and myghty prynce ꞇ hygh renowned knyght kynge Ponthus of Galyce ꞇ of lytell Brytayne.   *Wynkyn de Worde.*   1511.   4°.   𝕭.𝕷.
Bodl. (Douce PP. 214), imperf.

[Another edition.]   A History of the noble Deeds . . . of the knight Ponthus, son of the king of Gallicia, and of the beautiful Sidonia, Queen, from Britannia.   1548.   4°.   𝕭.𝕷.
Hazlitt, H. 475.

PRICE, Laurence. *See* Valentine and Orson.

PRIMALEON. *See* Palmerin.

PUTEANUS, Erycius.

Comus, siue Phagesiposia Cimmeria. Somnium. *G. Turner, impensis
H. Curteyne: Oxonii.* 1634. 12°.

The first edition was published at Louvain in 1611.
  B.M. (1193. d. 1/3).

See (in Part II) Charleton, Walter.

QUEVEDO VILLEGAS, Francisco de.

Hell Reformed or A Glasse for Favorites. Their Falls and complaints
Also the Complaints of Princes against their Favorits . . . Discovered in a
vision, by D: F: Q: V: A Spanish Knight . . . Published by E: M: Gent.
E: Griffin for S. Burton. 1641. 8°.

Bodl. (Wood 664/2).

See also Part II.

R., H. *See* Roberts, Henry

RABELAIS. François.

[Gargantua.]

Licensed to J. Danter, 4 Dec., 1594 (*Stat. Reg.* ii. 667). Referred to in R. Holland's
Holy History, 1594 (*cf. Restituta*, ii. 157), in Meres' *Palladis Tamia*, 1598, etc.

The first Book of the Works of Mr. Francis Rabelais, Doctor In Physick :
Containing five Books of the Lives, Heroick Deeds, and Sayings of
Gargantua, And his Sonne Pantagruel . . . All done by Mr. Francis Rabelais,
in the French Tongue, and now faithfully translated into English. *For
R. Baddeley.* 1653. 8°. 2 vols.

B.M. (12316. bb. 43).

[A reissue.] The Works Of the Famous Mr. Francis Rabelais Doctor in
Physick, Treating of the Lives, Heroick Deeds, and sayings of Gargantua
And his Son Pantagruel . . . Written Originally in French, and Translated
into English by Sr. Thomas Vrchard Kt. *For R. B. and are to be sold by
J. Starkey.* 1664. 8°.

Bodl. (Douce RR. 177).

[Another edition.] The Works of F. Rabelais, M.D. Or, The Lives, heroic Deeds and Sayings of Gargantua and Pantagruel. Done out of French by Sir Tho. Urchard, Kt. and others, *etc. For R. Baldwin.* 1694, 93. 12°. 5 vols.

Vol. 3 is dated 1693.
Bodl. (8°. P. 207 Art, vols. 1–3 ; 8°. N. 67, 68 Linc., vols. 4, 5) ; B.M. (1081. l. 5), vols. 1–3.

[Another edition.] The Whole Works of F. Rabelais, M.D, *etc. For J. Woodward.* 1708. 8°. 2 vols.

B.M. (12238. bb. 9).

[Another edition.] Now carefully revised, and compared throughout with the late new Edition of M. Le du Chat, By Mr. Ozell . . . Adorn'd with 15 very neat Copper-plates. *J. Hughs, for J. Brindley, and C. Corbett.* 1737. 12°. 5 vols.

Reissued in 1738.
B.M. (12235. a. 17).

RESOLVED GENTLEMAN.

See La Marche, Olivier de.

REYNARD THE FOX.

Begin : This is the table of the historye of reynart the foxe. *W. Caxton : Westmester.* 1481. Fol. 𝕭.𝕷.

[Another edition.] [*W. Caxton : Westminster.* 1489.] Fol. 𝕭.𝕷.
Pepys 1796, imperf. at end.

[Another edition.] Here begynneth the Hystorye of reinard the foxe. [*R. Pynson.*] Fol. 𝕭.𝕷.
Bodl. (Douce V. 245).

[Another edition.] [*R. Pynson.*] 4°. 𝕭.𝕷.
Signet, frag. ; Bib. Soc., *Handlist.*

[Another edition.] Here beginneth the booke of Raynarde the Foxe, conteining diuers goodlye historyes and Parables, with other dyuers pointes necessarye for al men to be marked, by the which pointes, men maye lerne to come vnto the subtyll knowledge of suche thinges as daily ben vsed ꝛ had in yᵉ counseyles of Lordes ꝛ Prelates both ghostely ꝛ wordely, ꝛ also among marchaũtes ꝛ other comen people. *T. Gaultier.* 1550. 8°. 𝕭.𝕷.

B.M. (686. d. 15).

[Another edition.]

Licensed to W. Powell, 30 Nov., 1560 (*Stat. Reg.*, i. 152).

[Another edition.]

Licensed to E. Allde, 4 Oct., 1586 (*Stat. Reg.* ii. 457).

[Another edition.]   The Most delectable History of Reynard the Fox.
Newly Corrected. . . . Also Augmented and Inlarged with sundry excellent
Moralls . . . Neuer before this time Imprinted.   *E. All-de, and are to be
solde by R. Aldred.*   4°.   𝕭.𝕷.

Bodl. (4°. M. 36. Art.).

[Another edition.]   *E. All-de.*   1629.   4°.   𝕭.𝕷.

B.M. (12410. e. 21).

[Another edition.]   *For I. Salter.*   1640.   4°.   𝕭.𝕷.

Bodl. (Ashmole 1631).

[Another edition.]   *J. Bell.*   1650.   4°.

Hazlitt, H. 501.

[Another edition.]   *J. Bell.*   1656.   4°.   𝕭.𝕷.

B.M. (12410. bbb. 18).

[Another edition.]   *A. M. and R. R. for E. Brewster.*   1681.   4°.   𝕭.𝕷.

Bodl. (70. d. 29).

[Part 2.]   The Most Pleasant and Delightful History of Reynard the Fox.
The Second Part, *etc.   A. M. and R. R. for E. Brewster.*   1681.   4°.

B.M. (1077. f. 16).

[Part 3.]   The Shifts of Reynardine The Son of Reynard the Fox . . .
Full of Variety, &c.   And may fitly be applied to the Late Times.   Now
Published for the Reformation of Mens Manners.   *T. J. for E. Brewster.*
1684.   4°.

B.M. (1077. f. 16).

[Another edition of Part 1.]   The Most Delectable History of Reynard the
Fox, *etc.   T. James, for E. Brewster.*   1694.   4°.   𝕭.𝕷.

B.M. (12410. e. 18).

[Another edition of Parts 1 and 2.]   *For E. Brewster.*   1699.   4°.

Term Cat. iii. 114.

[Another edition of Parts 1–3.]   *T. Ilive for E. Brewster.*   1701.   4°.

Part 1 only in B.M.
> B.M. (1077. f. 16, Part 1 only).

[An abridgement of Part 1.]   The most Pleasant History of Reynard the Fox, *etc.   For J. Conyers, and are to be sold by J. Blare.*   8°.   𝕭.𝕸.

> Bodl. (Wood 259/3).

[Another version.]   The most pleasing and delightful History of Reynard the Fox and Reynardine his son: in two Parts.   With the Morals, *etc.   For J. Blare.*   4°.

> Blare's list ; J. P. Collier, *Bibliographical and Critical Account*, ii. 242.

[Another version?]   To which is added, the History of Cawood the Rook : Or, The Assembly of Birds . . .   The Sixth Edition.   *For A. Bettesworth and C. Hitch, R. Ware, and J. Hodges.*   1735.   12°.

The preface is signed P. D.
> B.M. (11511. a. 24).

[Another edition of Part 1 ?]   The pleasant and delightful Historie of Reynard the Fox ; with Morals and Expositions on every Chapter.   The whole illustrated with Cuts suitable to each Story.   *J. Blare.*   4°.   𝕭.𝕸.

> Collier, *Bibliographical and Critical Account*, ii. 239.

[Another edition.]   The History of Reynard the Fox, and Reynardine his Son.   In Two Parts.   *For the Booksellers of London and Westminster.*   12°.

Without *Cawwood.*   The preface is signed D. P.
> B.M. (12430. a. 8).

REYNOLDS, John.

The Triumphs of Gods Revenege, against the crying, and execrable Sinne of Murther : or His Miraculous discoueries and seuere punishments thereof : In thirty seuerall Tragicall Histories (digested in sixe Bookes) acted in diuers Countries beyond the Seas, and neuer till now published, or imprinted in any Language . . .   Written by Iohn Reynolds.   The First Booke, *etc.   F. Kyngston, for W. Lee.*   1621, 22, 23.   4°.   3 vols.

Book 3 is printed by A. Matthewes for W. Lee.
> Book 1, Bodl. (4°. G. 29. Art.) ; Books 2, 3, B.M. (12403. d. 13).

[Another edition.]   *A. Mathewes for W. Lee.*   1629.   4°.   3 vols.?

> Lowndes, 2078.   Book 1, B.M. (12403. d. 13).

[Another edition.]   *For W. Lee.*   1635.   Fol.   6 vols.

The engraved general title and the title of Book 1 have the date 1635.   Books 2 (A. Mathewes for W. Lee), 3 (I. Haviland for W. Lee), 4 (I. Haviland for W. Lee), 5 ([A. Mathewes?] for W. Lee), and 6 (I. Haviland for W. Lee), are dated 1634.
B.M. (12403. c. 22).

[Another edition.]   *E. Griffin for W. Lee.*   1639.   Fol.

Books 2-6 have each a separate title-page.
B.M. (12403. g. 22) ; imperf.

[Another edition.]   The Second edition.   *E. Griffin, for W. Lee.*   1640. Fol.

A reissue with a new general title, and an engraved title, both dated 1640.   Parts 2-6 dated 1639.
B.M. (6055. h. 6).

[Another edition.]   The Third Edition.   Whereunto are added ...   Copper Plates.   *S. Griffin, for W. Lee.*   1657, 56.   Fol.

Books 2—6 have separate title-pages, dated 1656.
B.M. (G. 11926).

[Another edition, complete.]   The Triumphs of Gods Revenge Against the crying Sin of Murther, In thirty severall Tragicall Histories, in six Books ... By John Reynolds.   Published to undeceive the Reader, of a false Copie lately patched and pilfered out of the true Copie . . . and published by an obscure person, calling it Blood for Blood, *etc.   For W. Lee.*   1662.   8°.

B.M. (G. 19747).

[Another edition.]   The Fifth and Last Edition . . .   Whereunto are added ...   Copper Plates.   *A. M. for W. Lee, and are to be sold by G. Sawbridg, F. Tyton, J. Martin, T. Vere, R. Taylor, E. Thomas, T. Passenger, H. Broom, N. Symmons, R. Clavel, W. Crook, and J. Magnes.*   1670.   Fol.

B.M. (12403. c. 20).

[Another edition.]   The Sixth Edition, very Carefully Corrected.   To which is Added, Gods Revenge against the Abominable Sin of Adultery. Containing Ten Several Histories, Never Printed before.   Illustrated with New Sculptures.   *J. Bennet, for T. Lee.*   1679.   Fol.

(B.M. 12403. h. 1).

[Another edition.]   To which is added, God's Revenge against the abominable Sin of Adultery ;   containing several Histories never before printed.   Illustrated with new Sculptures, *etc.   For C. Passinger.*   1682.   Fol.

Term Cat. i. 480.

[Another edition.] The Seventh and last Edition. Whereunto are added the Lively Pourtraictures of the Several Persons, and resemblances of other passages mentioned therein, engraven in Copper Plates. *For C. Griffin.* 1704. Fol.

The separate parts are dated 1702.
    Hazlitt, I. 356.

[An abridgement.] Blood for Blood: or Murthers Revenged. Briefly, yet Lively set forth In Thirty Tragical Histories. To which are added Five more, Being the Sad Product of our own Times, viz K. Charles The Martyr . . . Faithfully digested for the benefit of Posterity by T. M. Esq. *For the Author: Oxford* [*London*]. 1661. 8°.

A piracy. *Cf.* the complete edition of 1662.
    B.M. (1076. k. 29).

[Another abridgement.] The Glory of God's Revenge against the Bloody and Detestable Sins of Murther and Adultery: Express'd in Thirty Modern Tragical Histories. To which are annexed, The Triumphs of Friendship and Chastity, in some Illustrious Examples. By Thomas Wright, *etc. For B. Crayle.* 1685. 8°.

Reissued in 1686.
    B.M. (836. c. 2), 1685; (G. 19743), 1686.

[Another edition?] *For B. Crayle.* 1687. 8°.
    Term Cat., ii. 187.

[Another edition?] *For B. Crayle.* 1688. 8°.
    Term Cat., ii. 226.

Gods Revenge against Adultery. For a separate edition, *see* Part II.

RICH, Barnaby.

The Aduentures of Brusanus, Prince of Hungaria, Pleasant for all to read, and profitable for some to follow. Written by Barnaby Rich, seauen or eight yeares sithence, and now published by the great intreaty of diuers of his freendes. *For T. Adames.* 1592. 4°. 𝕭.𝕷.

Licensed to T. Adams and J. Oxenbridge, 23 Oct., 1592 (*Stat. Reg.* ii. 622).
    Dulwich Coll.

A Right Exelent and plesaunt Dialogue, betwene Mercury and an English Souldier: Contayning his Supplication to Mars: Bewtified with sundry worthy Histories, rare inuentions, and politike deuises wrytten by B. Rich: Gen. 1574. [*H. Disle.* 1574]. 8°. 𝕭.𝕷.

Device and address: "The Corner Shop, at the South West Doore of Paules Church."
    B.M. (C. 58. a. 40).

Riche his Farewell to Militarie profession : conteinyng verie pleasaunt discourses fit for a peaceable tyme . . . by Barnabe Riche Gentleman. *R. Walley.* 1581. 4°. 𝕭.𝕷.

Bodl. (Tanner 213).

[Another edition.] Newly augmented. By Barnabe Riche Gentleman. *G. E[ld] for T. Adams.* 1606. 4°. 𝕭.𝕷.

Bodl. (Malone 613).

The straunge and wonderfull aduentures of Dō Simonides, a gentilman Spaniarde : Conteinyng verie pleasaunte discourse : Gathered for the recreation aswell of our noble yong gentilmen, as our honourable courtly Ladies : by Barnabe Riche gētilman. *R. Walley.* 1581. 4°. 𝕭.𝕷.

Bodl. (Malone 700).

The Second Tome of the Trauailes and aduentures of Don Simonides, enterlaced with varietie of Historie . . . Written by Barnabe Riche, Gentleman. *For R. Walley.* 1584. 4°. 𝕭.𝕷.

B.M. (12614. d. 21).

RIVERS, GEORGE.

The Heroinae : or The lives of Arria, Paulina, Lucrecia, Dido, Theutilla, Cypriana, Aretaphila. *R. Bishop, for I. Colby.* 1639. 12°.

U.L.C. (Syn. 8. 63. 316).

ROBERT THE DEVIL.

Robert the deuyll. *Wynkyn de Worde.* 4°. 𝕭.𝕷.

"Thus endeth the lyfe of Robert the deuyll
That was the seruaunt of our lorde
And of his condycyons that was full euyll
Enprynted in London by Wynkyn de Worde."

B.M. (C. 21. c. 11).

[Another edition.] *Colophon :* Here endeth the lyfe of the moost ferefullest, and vnmercyfullest, and myscheuous Roberte the deuyll whiche was afterwarde called the seruaunte of our lorde Ihesu cryst. *Wynkyn de Worde.* 4°. 𝕭.𝕷.

U.L.C. (Sel. 5. 14), imperf., wanting title.

ROBERTS, Henry.

A Defiance to Fortune. Proclaimed by Andrugio, noble Duke of Saxony . . . Whereunto is adioyned the honorable Warres of Galastino, Duke of Millaine . . . Written by H. R. *For I. Proctor.* 1590. 4°. 𝕭.𝕸.

Bodl. (Malone 659).

Haigh for Deuonshire. A pleasant Discourse of sixe gallant Marchants of Deuonshire. Their liues, Aduentures and Trauailes : With sundrie their rare showes and pastimes shewed before the King in Exeter . . . . Written by H. R. *T. Creede.* 1600. 4°. 𝕭.𝕸.

Priv. Lib.

Honours Conquest. Wherin is conteined the famous Hystorie of Edward of Lancaster . . . With the famous victories perform[ed] by the knight, of the vnconquered Castel, a gallant English knight . . . Written by H. R. *T. Creede.* 1598. 4°. 𝕭.𝕸.

Bodl. (Douce. R. 126).

Phaeander, The Mayden Knight; Describing his honourable Trauailes and hautie attempts in Armes, with his successe in loue . . . . Written by H. R. *T. Creede.* 1595. 4°. 𝕭.𝕸.

Priv. Lib.

[Another edition.] The Historie of Pheander the Mayden Knight . . . . Newly corrected and augmented. The Fourth Edition. *B. Alsop.* 1617. 4°. 𝕭.𝕸.

Priv. Lib.

[Another edition.] The famous History of Pheander the Maiden Knight, *etc. For T. Fawcet, and are to bee sold by F. Coles.* 1661. 4°. 𝕭.𝕸.

Bridgewater.

RUSH, Friar.

The Historie of Frier Rush : how he came to a house of Religion to seeke seruice, and being entertained by the Priour, was first made vnder Cooke. Being full of pleasant mirth and delight for young people. *E. Allde.* 1620. 4°. 𝕭.𝕸.

Licensed to J. Allde in 1568-9 (*Stat. Reg.* i. 389).
B.M. (C. 34. m. 23).

[Another edition.] *E. All-de, and are to be solde by F. Grove.* 1626. 4°. 𝕭.𝕸.

Bridgewater.

[Another edition.]   *Eliz. Allde.* 1629. 4°. 𝕭.𝕷.
   Huth (title only, supplied in a copy of the 1659 edition).

[Another edition.]   *Jane Bell.* 1659. 4°. 𝕭.𝕷.
   R. Hoe sale ; Huth (wanting title).

S., J.

See AMADIS ; CLIDAMAS.

S., R.

See SMYTH, Robert.

SAKER, AUSTEN.

Narbonus. The Laberynth of Libertie. Very pleasant for young Gentlemen to peruse . . . Written by Austen Saker, of New Inne. *R. Ihones.* 1580. 4°. 𝕭.𝕷. 2 vols.
   Vol. 2 is printed by W. How for R. Ihones.

SANFORD, JAMES.

See GUICCIARDINI, Ludovico.

SAN PEDRO, DIEGO DE.

The Pretie and wittie Historie of Arnalt and Lucenda : With certen Rules and Dialogues set foorth for the learner of th' Italian tong . . . By Claudius Hollyband, *etc.* *T. Purfoote.* 1575. 16°. 𝕭.𝕷.
   Italian and English. "Hollyband" was C. Desainliens.
     B.M. (C. 21. a. 57).

[Another edition.] 1591. 16°. (?)
   M. A. Scott, *Elizabethan Translations*, p. 21.

[Another edition.] The Italian Schoole-maister : Contayning Rules for the perfect pronouncing of th' italian tongue . . . And a fine Tuscan historie called Arnalt & Lucenda, *etc.* *T. Purfoot.* 1597. 8°.
   Licensed to T. Purfoot, sen. and jun., 19 Aug., 1598 (*Stat. Reg.*, iii. 124).
     B.M. (627. c. 10).

[Another edition.] *T. Purfoot.* 1608. 8°.
     B.M. (627. c. 11).

The castell of loue, translated out of Spanishe in to Englyshe, by iohan Bowrchier knight, lorde Bernis . . . The whiche boke treateth of the loue betwene Leriano and Laureola doughter to the Kynge of Masedonia. *I. Turke.* [1548?] 8°. 𝕭.𝕷.

B.M. (C. 57. aa. 36).

[Another edition.] *R. Wyer, For R. Kele.* [1550?] 8°. 𝕭.𝕷.

With a verse prologue by Andrew Spigurnell, who claims to have "newly penned the matter," "in wyll to haue it prynted agayne."

B.M. (G. 10332).

[Another edition.] *I. Kynge.* 8°. 𝕭.𝕷.

With Spigurnell's prologue, etc.

Priv. Lib.

[Another edition?]

Licensed to T. Purfoot in 1564-5 (*Stat. Reg.*, i. 265).

SAULNIER, GILBERT, *Sieur du Verdier.*

The Love and Armes of the Greeke Princes. Or, The Romant of Romants. Written in French by Monsieur Verdere, and Translated, etc. *T. Harper for T. Walkley.* 1640. Fol.

B.M. (12403. g. 14).

[Another edition?]

Anne Moseley's list, 1663.

SCOGGIN, JOHN.

[The geystes of Skoggon.]

Licensed to T. Colwell, 1565/6 (*Stat. Reg.*, i. 299).

[Another edition?] Scoggins Iestes, *etc. R. Blower.* 1613. 8°. 𝕭.𝕷.

Bodl. (Malone 388).

[Another edition.] The First and best Part of Scoggins Iests . . . Gathered by Andrew Boord, Doctor of Physicke. *For F. Williams.* 1626. 8°. 𝕭.𝕷.

B.M. (C. 38. a. 27).

[An abridgement.] Scogins Jests, *etc. For W. Thackeray, and J. Deacon.* 4°. 𝕭.𝕷.

B.M. (12315. e. 3).

SEBASTIAN, *Don.*

The True History of the late and Lamentable Aduentures of Don Sebastian, King of Portugal . . . vntil this present Day, *etc.*   *S. Stafford and I. Shaw.* 1602.   4°.

> Hazlitt, H. 478.

A continuation of the Lamentable and Admirable Aduentures of Don Sebastian, King of Portugal, *etc.   For J. Shaw.*   1603.   4°.

> Hazlitt, H. 478; *Harl. Misc.*, v. 461.

SEVEN CHAMPIONS OF CHRISTENDOM.

See JOHNSON, Richard.

SEVEN WISE MASTERS.

Here begynneth thystorye of yᵉ. vii. Wyse Maysters of rome conteyninge ryghe [*sic*] fayre ℸ ryght ioyous narracons. ℸ to yᵉ reder ryght delectable. *Wynkyn de worde.*   4°.   𝕭.𝕷.

> B.M. (C. 34. f. 46).

[Another edition.]   *W. Copland.*   8°.   𝕭.𝕷.
> Priv. Lib.

[Another edition?]
> Licensed to T. Marshe in 1558 (*Stat. Reg.*, i. 95).

[Another edition?]
> Licensed to T. Purfoot in 1565–6 (*Stat. Reg.*, i. 313).

[Another edition.]   The Hystorie of the Seaven wise Maisters of Rome. Now newly corrected, better explayned in many places, & enlarged with many pretty Pictures, liuely expressing the full History.   *T. Purfoot.*   1633. 8°.   𝕭.𝕷.
> Priv. Lib.

[Another edition.]   *J. C. for E. Blackmore.*   1653.   8°.   𝕭.𝕷.
> Bodl. (Douce R. 463).

[Another edition.]   *For J. Wright.*   1671.   8°.   𝕭.𝕷.
> B.M. (12410 aa. 25).

[Another edition.]   *For J. Wright.*   1677.   8°.   𝕭.𝕷.
> Priv. Lib.

[Another edition.] *For J. Wright.* 1682. 8°. 𝕭.𝕷.
  Bodl. (Malone 552).

[Another edition.] *For J. Wright.* 1684. 8°. 𝕭.𝕷.
  B.M. (12403. a. 23).

[Another edition.] *For M. Wotton, and G. Conyers.* 1687. 8°. 𝕭.𝕷.
  B.M. (12403. a. 25).

[A re-issue.] 1688. 8°. 𝕭.𝕷.
  Hazlitt, II. 653.

[Another edition.] Newly corrected, and better explained in many places.
R. Sanders : Glasgow. 1693. 8°. 𝕭.𝕷.
  B.M. (12450. b. 45).

[Another edition.] Now newly Corrected, better explained, *etc.* *J. W. for
G. Conyers.* 1697. 8°. 𝕭.𝕷.
  B.M. (12403. a. 24).

[Another edition.] *For J. Deacon.*
J. D.'s list.

[Another edition.] *R. Sanders : Glasgow.* 1713. 8°.
  B.M. (12450. b. 44).

[Another edition.] *J. Nicol : Aberdeen.* 1717. 8°.
  B.M. (12403. e. 11).

[A different version.] The History of Prince Erastus son to the Emperour
Dioclesian And those famous Philosophers called the Seven Wise Masters of
Rome . . . written Originally in Italian, then Translated into French, and
now rendred English by F. K. With the Illustration of Pictures, *etc.* *Anne
Johnson for F. Kirkman.* 1674. 12°.
  B.M. (1075. f. 3).

[Another edition?] Erastus, or the Roman Prince ; being a more full
Account of the famous History of the Seven Wise Masters ; with many
pleasant Additions, *etc.* *For D. Newman and B. Alsop.* 1684.
  Term Cat., ii. 71.

[A different version.] Wisdoms Cabinet Open'd : Or, The Famous History
of the Seven Wise Masters of Rome, *etc.* 4°.
  Pepys, 1192 (6), the imprint cut away.

[A different version.]   The History of the Seven Wise Masters of Rome :
Containing Seven Days Entertainment.   In many Pleasant and Witty Tales,
or Stories . . . Newly Corrected and better Explained and Enlarged.
Adorned with many Pretty Pictures, lively expressing the History.   The
Five and Twentieth Edition.   *For J. Hodges, and J. Johnston.*   8°.

    B.M. (G. 17638).

SHURLEY, J.

For parts 2 and 3 of The Honour of Chivalry, or Don Bellianis of Greece,
see BELLIANIS.

SIDNEY, *Sir* PHILIP.

The Countesse of Pembrokes Arcadia written by Sir Philippe Sidnei.   *For
W. Ponsonbie.*   1590.   4°.

   Licensed to Ponsonby 23 Aug. 1588 (*Stat. Reg.*, ii. 496).
    B.M. (C. 30. d. 22).

[Another edition.]   Written by Sir Philip Sidney Knight.   Now since the
First Edition augmented and ended.   *For W. Ponsonbie.*   1593.   Fol.

    B.M. (C. 21. d. 21).

[Another edition.]   Now the third time published, with sundry new
additions of the same Author.   *For W. Ponsonbie.*   1598.   Fol.

   With Sidney's other works.
    B.M. (C. 21. d. 16).

[Another edition.]   Now the third time published, with sundry new
additions of the same Author.   *R. walde-graue : Edinburgh.*   1599.   Fol.

    B.M. (C. 21. d. 4).

[Another edition.]   Now the Fourth Time Published, With Sundry New
Additions Of The same Author.   *For M. Lownes.*   1605.   Fol.

   Some copies are printed for S. Waterson.   The edition was licensed to them both,
5 Nov., 1604 (*Stat. Reg.*, iii. 274).
    B.M. (C. 39. h. 8), Lownes ; Bodl. (Caps. 10. 7), Waterson.

[Another edition.]   Now the Fourth time published with some new
Additions.   *H. L. for M. Lownes.*   1613.   Fol.

    Bodl. (Douce S. 818).

[Another edition.] Now the fift time published, with some new Additions. Also a supplement of a defect in the third part of this History. By Sir W. Alexander. *The Societie of Stationers : Dublin.* 1621. Fol.

Alexander's Supplement was licensed to Barrett, 31 Aug., 1616 (*Stat. Reg.*, iii. 594).
B.M. (C. 40. l. 6).

[Another edition.] Now the sixt time published. *H. L. for S. Waterson.* 1622. Fol.

Hazlitt, H. 558.

[Another edition.] Now the fifth time published. 1623. Fol.

With the note : "1623 is supposed to be a misprint for 1621."
Hazlitt, H. 557.

[Another edition.] Now the sixt time published. *H. L. for M. Lownes.* 1623. Fol.

B.M. (12403. g. 8).

[Another edition.] Now the sixt time published, with some new Additions. Also a supplement of a defect in the third part of this Historie. By Sir W. Alexander. *W. S. for S. Waterson.* 1627, 28. Fol.

With Sidney's other works. The sixth book, by R. B[eling]., is "Printed by H. L. and R. Y. 1628."
U.L.C. (Syn. 4. 62. 24).

A Sixth Booke to the Countesse of Pembrokes Arcadia. Written by R. B. Esq. *The Societie of Stationers, Dublin.* 1624. 4°.

R. B. is Richard Beling.
Licensed to Downes and Young, 18 March, 1627–8, and again to the partners in the Irish Stock, 20 Dec., 1629 (*Stat. Reg.* iv. 195, 224).
Priv. Lib.

[Another edition of the whole.] Now the seuenth time published . . . with some new Additions. With the supplement of a Defect in the third part of this History, by Sir W. A. Knight. Whereunto is now added a sixth Booke, by R. B. of Lincolnes Inne, Esq. *H. L. and R. Y., and are to be sold by S. Waterson.* 1629. Fol.

B.M. (12403. g. 10).

[Another edition.] Now the eighth time published, with some new Additions, *etc. For S. Waterson and R. Young.* 1633. Fol.

B.M. (635. l. 20).

[Another edition.] Now the ninth time published, with a twofold supplement of a defect in the third Book : the one by Sr W. A. Knight : the other,
by M^r Ja. Johnstown Scoto-Brit. dedicated to K. James, and now annexed to
this work . . . Whereunto is also added a sixth Booke, by R. B., *etc.*   *For
S. Waterson and R. Young.*   1638.   Fol.

B.M. (C. 39. h. 9).

[Another edition.]   The tenth Edition, *etc.*   *W. Du Gard, and are to bee
sold by G. Calvert, and T. Pierrepont.*   1655.   Fol.

B.M. (C. 39. h. 10).

[Another edition.]   The eleventh Edition, *etc.*   *H. Lloyd for W. Du-Gard :
and are to bee sold by G. Calvert and T. Pierrepont.*   1662.   Fol.

B.M. (12403. g. 1).

[Another edition.]   The Thirteenth Edition, *etc.*   *For G. Calvert.*   1674.
Fol.

B.M. (12410. g. 10).

[Another edition.]   The Works of The Honourable Sr Philip Sidney, kt.
In Prose and Verse.   In Three Volumes . . . The Fourteenth Edition.   *For
E. Taylor, A. Bettesworth, E. Curll, W. Mears, and R. Gosling.*   1725, 24.
8°.   3 vols.

Vols. 2 and 3 are dated 1724.
B.M. (12269. c. 18).

[A different version.]   Sir Philip Sidney's Arcadia, Moderniz'd by Mrs.
Stanley.   1725.   Fol.

B.M. (12403. k. 2).

[An abridgement.]   The Famous History of Heroick Acts : Or, The
Hononr [*sic*] of Chivalry.   Being an Abstract of Pembroke's Arcadia . . .
Illustrated and lively set forth with many curious Cuts ; the like as yet not
Extant.   *For W. Spiller.*   1701.   12°.

B.M. (1077. b. 9).

The Most Excellent History of Argalus and Parthenia.   *A. P. for T. Vere.*
1672.   8°.   𝕭.𝕷.

Hazlitt. H. 11.

[Another edition.]   The Pleasant and Delightful History of Argalus and
Parthenia.   Newly Reviv'd.   *T. H[aly] for T. Passenger.*   1683.   4°.   𝕭.𝕷.

Pepys 1192 (7).

[Another edition.] The Most Pleasant and Delightful History of Argalus and Parthenia, newly reviv'd. *J. M. for E. Tracy, and are to be sold by J. Blare.* 1691. 8°.

> B.M. (12403. aa. 26).

[Another edition.] *W. O[nley] for E. Tracy.* 4°.

> Priv. Lib.

[A different version.] The Unfortunate Lovers : The History of Argalus and Parthenia. In four Books. Adorn'd with Cuts. *W. O[nley].* 12°.

> Priv. Lib.

[Another edition.] The Fourth Edition. *T. Norris.* 12°.

> B.M. (12613. a. 33).

[Another edition.] The Fifth Edition. *For C. Hitch and L. Hawes, S. Crowder, C. Ware, and H. Woodgate and S. Brooks.* 8°.

> B.M. (12613. a. 4).

[Another edition.] *For H. Woodgate and S. Brooks.* 12°.

The title reads, "The Unfortune Lovers," etc.
> B.M. (12410. aa. 14).

For continuations of the Arcadia : *See* (in Part I) MARKHAM, Gervase ; (in Part II) WEAMYS, Anne.

SILESIO, MARIANO.

The Arcadian Princesse ; Or, The Triumph of Iustice. Prescribing excellent rules of Physicke, for a sicke Iustice. Digested into fowre Bookes, And Faithfully rendred to the originall Italian Copy, by Ri. Brathwait Esq. *Th. Harper for R. Bostocke.* 1635. 8°.

> B.M. (G. 529.)

SKELTON, JOHN.

Merie Tales Newly Imprinted & made by Master Skelton Poet Laureat *T. Colwell.* 4°.

Licensed to Colwell in 1566–7 (*Stat. Reg.* i. 339).
> Huth.

SMYTH, ROBERT.

Straunge, Lamentable, and Tragicall Hystories. Translated out of French into English by R. S. *H. Jackson.* 1577. 4°. 𝕭.𝕷.

> Bodl. (Douce HH. 207).

STRANGE FORTUNES OF TWO EXCELLENT PRINCES.

See BRETON, Nicholas.

STUKELEY, THOMAS.

The Famous History of Stout Stukley [*sic*] : or His valiant Life and Death. *R. I. for F. Grove.* 8°. 𝔅.𝔏.

Bodl. (Wood 254/13).

SURDYT.

[Surdyt King of Ireland.]   [*Wynkyn de Worde ?*]   4°. 𝔅.𝔏.

Bodl. (70. f. 1/5).

TARLTON, RICHARD.

Tarltons Jests, drawn into three parts, *etc.*   *I. H.*   1611.   4°.

~~Doubtful ; Hazlitt, I. 47.~~

[Another edition.]   *J. H. for A. Crook.*   1638.   4°.

B.M. (12331. b. 42), imperf., wanting title ; Bodl. (Malone 334).

Tarltons newes out of Purgatorie.   Onely such a iest as his Iigge, fit for Gentlemen to laugh at an houre &c.   Published by an old Companion of his, Robin Goodfellow.   *For T. G[ubbin] and T. N[ewman].*   1590.   4°.

Licensed to Gubbin and Newman, 26 June, 1590 (*Stat. Reg.* ii. 553).

B.M. (C. 40. c. 68).

[Another edition.]   *For E. White.*   4°.   𝔅.𝔏.

Bodl. (Malone 152).

[Another edition.]   *G. Purslowe, and are to be sold by F. Groue.*   1630. 4°.   𝔅.𝔏.

B.M. (C. 40. c. 31).

TAYLOR, THOMAS.

See BEARD, Thomas.

TEIXEIRA, JOSÉ.

The Strangest Aduenture that ever happened : either in the ages passed or present.   Containing a discourse concerning the successe of the King of Portugall Dom Sebastian, from the time of his voyage into Affricke, when he was lost in the battell against the infidels, in the yeare 1578. vnto the sixt of Ianuary this present 1601 . . .   All first done in Spanish, then in French, and now lastly translated into English.   *For F. Henson.*   1601.   4°.

   B.M. (1195. a. 38).

THOMAS OF READING.
   See DELONEY, Thomas.

THREE KINGS OF COLOGNE.
   The moost excellent treatise of the thre kynges of Coleyne.   *Wynkyn de Worde : Westmester* [before July, 1499].   4°.   𝕭.𝕷.

   Bodl. (Tanner 178), imperf., wants leaf 1 ; Advocates, imperf., wants last 12 leaves.

   [Another edition.]   *Wynkyn de Worde : Westmester.*   4°.   𝕭.𝕷.

   Priv. Lib. ; B.M. (IA. 55217), title supplied in facs.

   [Another edition.]   The Thre kynges of Coleyne.   *Wynkyn de Worde.*   1511.   4°.   𝕭.𝕷.

   U.L.C. (AB 4. 60. 3).

   [Another edition.]   *Wynkyn de Worde.*   1526.   4°.   𝕭.𝕷.

   Priv. Lib. (Hazlitt, H. 116 ; Bib. Soc., *Handlist*).

   [Another edition.]   *Wynkyn de Worde.*   1530.   4°.   𝕭.𝕷.

   Hazlitt, H. 116 ; Bib. Soc., *Handlist.*

TILNEY, EDMUND.
   A briefe and pleasant discourse of duties in Mariage, called the Flower of Friendshippe.   *H. Denham.*   1568.   8°.   𝕭.𝕷.

   The Epistle Dedicatorie is signed Edmonde Tilney.
   Bodl. (Malone 525).

   [Another edition.]   *H. Denham.*   1568.   8°.   𝕭.𝕷.

   The Epistle Dedicatorie is signed Edmunde Tilney.
   B.M. (8416. aa. 36) imperf., wanting title.

   [Another edition.]   *H. Denham.*   1571.   8°.   𝕭.𝕷.

   Bodl. (Tanner 133).

   [Another edition.]   *H. Denham.*   1577.   8°.   𝕭.𝕷.

   Bodl. (Wood 736).

TINKER OF TURVEY.

See COBBLER OF CANTERBURY.

TOM A LINCOLN.

See JOHNSON, Richard.

TROY.

See DARES; LE FEVRE, Raoul.

TWINE, LAURENCE.

The Patterne of Painefull Aduentures: *See* APOLLONIUS

URANO.

[The moste famous and delightfull History of Vrano otherwise called the Grene knighte and the moste bewtifull Princes Beroshia Daughter to the Kinge of Brittaine &c.]

Licensed to F. Burton, 12 Sept. 1605 (*Stat. Reg.*, iii. 300).

URFÉ, HONORÉ D'.

[Astrée.]

Licensed ("to be translated") to M. Lownes, 17 Oct., 1611 (*Stat. Reg.* iii. 470).

[Another edition.] The History of Astrea. The First Part. In Twelue Bookes. Newly Translated out of French. *N. Okes for I. Pyper.* 1620. 4°.

Bodl. (Malone 674).

[A different version.] Astrea. A Romance, Written in French, by Messire Honorè D'Urfe; And Translated by A Person of Quality. *W. W[hitwood]. for H. Moseley, T. Dring, and H. Herringman.* 1657, 58. Fol. 3 vols.

Vol. 3 is dated 1658.
B.M. (12491. u. 21).

VALENS, W.

The Honourable Prentice: Or, This Taylor is a man. Shewed in the life and death of Sir John Hawkewood, sometime Prentice of London, *etc. For H. Gosson.* 1615. 4°. 𝕭.𝕷.

The Dedication is signed W. V[alens].
Reissued in 1616.

Bodl. (4°. L. 68. Art.), 1615; (Wood 32. c. 1), 1616.

VALENTINE AND ORSON.

[Valentine and Orson.   *W. de Worde ?*]   4°.   𝕭.𝕷.

Devonshire, frag.

The Hystory of the two valyaunte brethren Valentyne and Orson, sonnes vnto the Emperour of Greece.   *W. Copland for I. Walley.*   4°.   𝕭.𝕷.

Priv. Lib.

[Another edition.]   *Begin :* All Prynces and other Lordes that take pleasure for to rede all bookes I wylle recounte vnto you thei lyfe of the two chyualrous Lordes Valentyne and Orson, sonnes of thei Emperoure of Grece, *etc.* *W. Coplande.*   4°.   𝕭.𝕷.

117 chapters.
   B.M. (C. 34. i. 17).

[Another edition ?]

Licensed to T. Purfoot, 8 Aug., 1586.

[An abridgement.]   Valentine and Orson.   The Two Sonnes of the Emperour of Greece.   Newly Corrected and amended, with new Pictures lively expressing the Historie.   *T. Purfoot.*   1637.   4°.   𝕭.𝕷.

52 chapters.
   B.M. (G. 10481).

[Another edition.]   *R. Ibbitson.*   1649.   4°.   𝕭.𝕷.

Bodl. (Malone 1007), imperf. ; Huth.

[Another edition ?]   The Famous History of Valentine and Orson, the two Sons of the Emperor of Greece.   *For C. Tyus.*

Advertised in *Palladine,* 1664.

[Another edition ?]   1677.   4°.

Hazlitt, H. 624.

[Another edition ?]   The History of Valentine and Orson, the two Sons of the Emperour of Greece.   *Sold by T. Passenger.*   1680.   4°.

Term Cat., i. 388. 410.

[Another edition.]   Valentine and Orson, The Two Sons of the Emperour of Greece.   Newly Corrected and Amended, with new Pictures, lively Expressing the History.   *T. H. for T. Passenger.*   1682.   4°.   𝕭.𝕷.

Huth.

[Another edition.] *J. R. for T. Passinger.* 1685. 4°. 𝕭.𝕷.
Pepys, 1191 (2).

[Another edition.] *J. R. for T. Passenger.* 1688. 4°. 𝕭.𝕷.
Bridgewater.

[Another edition.] *A. Purslow, for T. Passinger.* 4°. 𝕭.𝕷.
Mr. Quaritch.

[Another edition.] *J. W. for E. Tracy.* 1694. 4°. 𝕭.𝕷.
Bodl. (Douce V. 184).

[Another edition?] *J. W. for E. Tracy.* 1696. 4°.
Hazlitt, H. 624. *Term Cat.*, iii. 25.

[Price's abridgement.] The Famous History of Valentine and Orson
. . . Drawn up in a Short Volume . . . Written by Laurence Price. *For
W. Whitwood.* 1673. 8°.
Huth.

[Another edition.] Written by Lawrence Price, *etc.* *For M. W. and are to
be sold by D. Newman and B. Alsop.* 1683. 8°.
Bodl. (Wood 259/2).

[A different abridgement.] *A. M. for E. Tracy.* [1700.] 4°. 𝕭.𝕷.
42 chapters. Begins : We find it set down . . .
B.M. (1077. f. 15). *Term Cat.*, 1700, iii. 203.

[Another edition.] *E. M. for E. Tracy.* 1712. 4°.
Priv. Lib.

[Another edition.] The Famous History of Valentine and Orson . . . The
Sixteenth Edition. Newly Corrected and Amended ; with New Cuts, lively
Expressing the History. *For A. Bettesworth, C. Hitch, J. Osborn and
J. Hodges.* 1736. 12°.
B.M. (12450. b. 7).

[A different abridgement.] The New History of Valentine and Orson,
Abstracted from the French, and the best English Originals. With a new
Set of Figures, *etc.* *For E. Midwinter.* 12°.
42 chapters. Begins : Pepin, the Renowned King of France . . .
B.M. (12403. a. 21).

[Another edition.]   The Renowned History of Valentine and Orson.   The Two Sons of the Emperor of Greece.   Newly Corrected and Amended. Adorn'd with Cuts.   *D. Pratt.*   1724.   12°.

> B.M. (12450. a. 9).

[A different abridgement.]   The Famous and Renowned History of Valentine and Orson, *etc.   For C. Bates.*

> Bates' list, in *Hector.*

[Another edition.]   The Famous and Renowned History of Valentine and Orson : Sons to the Famous and Renowned Emperor of Constantinople. Containing their Marvellous Adventures in Love and Arms.   Newly Printed and Abbreviated, *etc.   T. Norris for Sarah Bates.*   4°.

> 8 chapters.
> Bodl. (Malone 689).

VEGA CARPIO, Lope da.

The Pilgrime of Casteele.   *J. Norton.*   1621.   4°.

> B.M. (C. 57. e. 23).

[Another edition.]   Written in Spanish.   Translated into English.   *E. All-de for I. N., and are to be solde by T. Dewe.*   1623.   4°.

> B.M. (12612. c. 71).

[A different version ?]   The Pilgrim, or the Stranger in his own Country ; also Diana, a Pastoral Romance, by G. de Montemajor.   1738.   12°.

> Dealer's list.

VERDIER, Gilbert.

See Saulnier, Gilbert, *Sieur du Verdier.*

VIENNA.

See Paris and Vienne.

VIRGIL.

Begin : After dyuerse werkes made, translated and achieued, hauyng noo werke in hande.   I sittyng in my studye where as laye many dyuerse paunflettis and bookys . happened that to my hande cam a lytyl booke in frenshe, *etc.   Colophon :* Here fynyssheth the boke yf [*sic*] Eneydos, compyled by Vyrgyle, whiche hathe be translated oute of latyne in to frenshe, And oute of Frenshe reduced in to Englysshe by me Wyllm̅ Caxton,

the xxii . daye of Iuyn . the yere of our lorde . M . iiij C lxxxx.   The fythe [*sic*]
yere of the Regne of kynge Henry the Seuenth.   [*W. Caxton : Westminster.*
1490.]   Fol.   𝕭.𝕷.

B.M. (IB. 55135).

Virgilius.   This boke treath of the lyfe of Virgilius and of his deth and
many meruayles that he dyd in his lyfe tyme by whychcrafte and nygramansy
thorowgh the helpe of the deuyls of hell.   *I. Doesborcke : Anwarpe.*   [1518?]
4°.   𝕭.𝕷.

Proctor, *Doesborgh*, 16.

Bodl. (Douce 40), imperf. ; Britwell.

[Another edition.]   Virgilius.   This boke treateth of the lyfe of Virgil, and
of his death, and many other maruayles that he did in his lyfe tyme by
witchecrafte and nygromancy through the deuelles of hell.   [*W. Copland ?*
1561?]   4°.   𝕭.𝕷.

Licensed to Copland in 1561 (*Stat. Reg.* i. 178).

B.M. (C. 21. c. 70), imperf.

W., G.

See WHETSTONE, George.

W., N.

See GEORGE A GREEN.

WAKING MAN'S DREAM.

See EDWARDES, Richard.

WARNER, WILLIAM.

Pan his Syrinx, or Pipe, Compact of seuen Reedes : including in one,
seuen Tragical and Comicall Arguments, with their diuers notes not impertinent : Whereby, in effect, of all thinges is touched, in few, something of the
vayne, wanton, proud, and inconstant course of the World . . . By William
Warner, *etc.*   *T. Purfoote.*   [1584.]   4°.   𝕭.𝕷.

Licensed to Purfoot, 22 Sept., 1584 (*Stat. Reg.* ii. 435).

B.M. (C. 21. c. 37).

[Another edition.]   Syrinx, or a seauenfold Historie . . .   Newly perused
and amended by the first Author, W. Warner.   *T. Purfoot.*   1597.   4°.   𝕭.𝕷.

B.M. (C. 57. b. 41).

WESTWARD FOR SMELTS.

Westward for Smelts. Or, The Water-mans Fare of mad-merry Western wenches, whose tongues albeit like Bell-clappers, they neuer leaue Ringing, yet their Tales are sweet, and will much content you. Written by Kinde Kit of Kingstone. *For I. Trundle.* 1620. 4°. 𝕭.𝕷.

An otherwise unknown edition of 1603 is referred to by Malone in Boswell's Shakespeare, 1821, vol. xiii., p. 229, *n.*

T.C.C. (Capell, Q. 8. 4).

WHETSTONE, GEORGE.

An Heptameron of Ciuill Discourses. Containing : The Christmasse Exercise of sundrie well Courted Gentlemen and Gentlewomen . . . The Reporte of George Whetstone, Gent. *R. Iones.* 1582. 4°. 𝕭.𝕷.

B.M. (1077. i. 32).

[Another edition.] Aurelia. The Paragon of Pleasure and Princely delights : Contayning The seuen dayes Solace (in Christmas Holy-dayes) of Madona Aurelia, Queene of the Christmas Pastimes . . . By G. W. Gent. *R. Iohnes.* 1593. 4°. 𝕭.𝕷.

Bodl. (4°. K. 47. Th. BS.).

The Rocke of Regard, diuided into foure parts . . . being all the inuention, collection and translation of George Whetstone Gent. *For R. Waley.* 1576. 4°. 𝕭.𝕷.

Largely in verse. Part 1, The Castle of Delight, contains the prose tale of Rinaldo and Giletta.

B.M. (1077. g. 7).

WILKINS, GEORGE.

The Painfull Aduentures of Pericles Prince of Tyre. Being the true History of the Play of Pericles, as it was lately presented by the worthy and ancient Poet Iohn Gower. *T. P. for N. Butter.* 1608. 4° 𝕭.𝕷.

B.M. (C. 34. l. 8).

WILLIAM OF PALERNE.

[Kyng Wyllyam of Palerne. *Wynkyn de Worde ?*] 𝕭.𝕷.

Priv. lib. (the Rev. J. M. Joass), frag. ; *cf. Academy,* 1893, p. 223, *Archiv. f. d. Studium d. neueren Sprachen u. Litteraturen,* vol. cxviii. 1907, p. 318.

WOTTON, HENRY.

A Courtlie controuersie of Cupids Cautels : Conteyning fiue Tragicall Histories, very pithie, pleasant, pitiful and profitable : Discoursed vppon wyth Argumentes of Loue by three Gentlemen and two Gentlewomen, entermedled with diuers delicate Sonets and Rithmes, exceeding delightfull to refresh the yrkesomnesse of tedious tyme. Translated out of French as neare as our English phrase will permit, by H. W. Gentleman. *F. Coldocke and H. Bynneman.* 1578. 4°. 𝕭.𝕷.

B.M. (12611. ee. 15), imperf. ; Bodl. (Tanner 219); Collier, *Bibliographical and Critical Account*, vol. ii., p. 543.

WROTH, *Lady* MARY.

The Countesse of Mountgomeries Urania. Written by the right honorable the Lady Mary Wroath . . . Neece to the ever famous and renowned Sʳ Phillips [*sic*] Sidney knight. And to yᵉ most exelēt Lady Mary, Countesse of Pembroke late deceased. *For I. Marriott and I. Grismand.* 1621. Fol.

B.M. (86. h. 9).

PART II.

(1643—1739.)

ENGLISH TALES AND ROMANCES.

Part II. (1643—1739).

ABÚ BAKR IBN AL-TUFAIL, Abu Jafar.

Philosophus Autodidactus siue Epistola Abi Jaafar, Ebn Tophail de Hai Ebn Yokdhan. In qua Ostenditur quomodo ex Inferiorum contemplatione ad Superiorum notitiam Ratio humana ascendere possit, Ex Arabicâ in Linguam Latinam versa Ab Edvardo Pocockio, A.M. Aedis Christi Alumno. *H. Hall: Oxonii.* 1671. 4°.

Arabic and Latin.
B.M. (479. a. 11).

[English.] An Account of the Oriental Philosophy, Shewing The Wisdom of some renowned Men of the East; And particularly, The profound Wisdom of Hai Ebn Yokdan, both in Natural and Divine things; Which he attained without all Converse with Men (while he lived in an Island a solitary life, remote from all Men from his Infancy, till he arrived at such perfection) Writ Originally in Arabick, by Abi Jaaphar Ebn Tophail; And out of the Arabick Translated into Latine, by Edward Pocok, a Student in Oxford; And now faithfully out of his Latine, Translated into English : For a General Service. 1674. 8°.

B.M. (8407. b. 25).

[Another version.] The History of Hai Eb'n Yockdan, an Indian Prince : or, the Self-Taught Philosopher. Written Originally in the Arabick Tongue, by Abi Jaafar Eb'n Tophail, a Philosopher by Profession, and a Mahometan by Religion . . . Set forth not long ago in the Original Arabick, with the Latin Version, by Edw. Pocock . M.A. and Student of Christ-church, Oxon. 1671. And now Translated into English. *For R. Chiswell and W. Thorp.* 1686. 8°.

B.M. (8407. c. 14.)

[Another version.]   [The Improvement of Human Reason ... newly Translated from the Original Arabic by Simon Ockley ...   With an Appendix.]   1708.   8°.

> B.M. (243. i. 2), the Appendix only, with a title-page dated 1708.   As the pagination in this follows on that of the *Hai Ebn Yokdhan*, there must have been an edition of the latter also in 1708.

[Another edition.]   The Improvement of Human Reason, Exhibited in the Life of Hai Ebn Yokdhan: Written in Arabick above 500 years ago, by Abu Jaafar Ebn Tophail ...   Illustrated with proper Figures.   Newly Translatad [*sic*] from the Original Arabick, by Simon Ockley ...   With an Appendix, *etc.*   *For W. Bray.*   1711.   8°.

> B.M. (243 i. 2), with the Appendix of 1708.   *See* supra.

[An abridgement.]   The History of Josephus the Indian Prince.

See (in Part I) GREENE, Robert.   The Pleasant and Delightful History of Dorastus, *etc.*   [1696 ?]

ACCOMPLISHED RAKE.

The Accomplish'd Rake: or, Modern Fine Gentleman.   Being an Exact Description of the Conduct and Behaviour of a Person of Distinction.   1727.   12°.

> Priv. Lib.

ACCOUNT.

An Account of some Remarkable Passages in the Life of a Private Gentleman.

See DEFOE, Daniel.

ADAMITE.

The Adamite, or The Loves of Father Rock, and his Intrigues with the Nuns.   A famous Novel.   Translated out of French.   *For D. Newman.*   1682.   12°.

> *Term Cat.* i. 507.

ADELAIDE.

Adellaide [*sic*], a Famed Romance.   In Four Parts.

> Advertised by Bentley and Magnes in *Nicerotis*, 1686, as in the press.   Probably *Adelaide de Champagne* (orig. ed., in 4 vols., 1680).

ADOLPHUS.

The History of Adolphus, Prince of Russia, And the Princess of Happiness. By a Person of Quality. With a Collection of Songs and Love-Verses. By several Hands, *etc. Sold by R. S.* 1691. 8°.

Priv. Lib. ; title-page, B.M. (Bagford 5972/274).

ADVENTURES.

The Adventures on the Black Mountains ; A Tale, Upon which the Plan of a Posthumous Play, call'd Double Falshood, was written Originally by W. Shakespeare. 1729.

See CROXALL, Samuel. A Select Collection of Novels, ed. 2, vol. ii.

AGIATIS.

See VAUMORIÈRE, Pierre d'Ortigue de.

ALCOFORADO, MARIANNA D'.

Five Love-Letters from a Nun to a Cavalier. Done out of French into English. *For H. Brome.* 1678. 8°.

The Letters were versified in *New Miscellaneous Poems*, 7 editions, 1713-31.
B.M. (10909. a. 8).

[Another edition.] Done out of French into English. By Sir Roger L'Estrange. *For R. Bentley, and are to be sold by S. Cownly.* 1686. 12°.
B.M. (1102. b. 8).

[Another edition.] *For R. Bentley.* 1693. 12°.
B.M. (1085. b. 20/1).

[Another edition.] The Second Edition. *For R. Wellington, and E. Rumball.* 1701. 12°.
B.M. (10909. a. 9).

Five Love-Letters Written by a Cavalier, in Answer to Five Love-Letters Written to him by a Nun. *For R. Bentley, and M. Magnes.* 1683. 12°.
Headed "The Answers of the Chevalier Del."
B.M. (1102. b. 9).

[Another edition.] *For R. Bentley.* 1694. 12°.
B.M. (1085. b. 20/2).

[Another edition, of both parts.]   Five Love-Letters, From a Nun to a Cavalier, with The Cavalier's Answers.   By Sir Roger L'Estrange.   The Fourth Edition.   To which is annex'd, The Art of Love, A Poem . . . by Mr. Charles Hopkins.   1716.   8⁰.

Prestage, Bibliography in ed. 1903.

Seven Portuguese Letters: being a second part to the Five Love-Letters from a Nun to a Cavalier.   1681.   8⁰.

Prestage.

[Another edition.]   1693.   4⁰.

Prestage.

See MANLEY, Mary de la Rivière.

ALTOPHEL AND ASTREA.

A pleasant Novel, discovering the Humours and Intrigues of a Town Gallant, in the delectable Amours of Altophel and Astrea, accompanied by Roderich [*sic*] in several adventures.   *For W. Leach.*   1678.   12⁰.

Term Cat. i. 314.

AMICORUS AND AMICANA.

Amicorus and Amicana.

The second edition was printed in 1740.

AMOROUS ABBESS.

The Amorous Abbess : or Love in a Nunnery.   A Novel.   Translated from the French by a Woman of Quality.   *For R. Bentley.*   1684.   12⁰.

In *Modern Novels*, vol. v.
B.M. (12410. c. 22).

AMOROUS CONVERT.

The Amorous Convert.   Being a True Relation of what happened in Holland.   *R. E. for R. Tonson.*   1679.   12⁰.

Bodl. (8⁰. R. 75 Art).

AMOROUS TRAVELLERS.

The Amorous Travellers, or Night Adventures.   Written originally in Spanish by a Person of Honour.   Translated into French by the exquisite pen of the Sieur Deganes, and into English by J. B.   *For A. Isted and J. Edwin.*   1671.   8⁰.

Term Cat., i. 89.   Hazlitt, II. 602 (advertised at end of W. de Brittaine, *The Interest of England*, 1672).

AMUSEMENS DE SPA.

Les Amusemens de Spa: Or the Gallantries of the Spaw in Germany . . . With Thirteen Copper-Plates . . . Translated from the Original French. The Second Edition. In Two Volumes. *Ward and Chandler, London, and at their Shops in York and Scarborough.* 1737. 12°. 2 vols.

B.M. (12512. cc. 26).

ANGLIAE SPECULUM MORALE.

See GRAHAM, Richard, *Viscount Preston.*

ANNALS OF LOVE.

The Annals of Love, Containing Select Histories of the Amours of divers Princes Courts, Pleasantly Related. *For J. Starkey.* 1672. 8°.

B.M. (12614. eee. 3).

ANTONIUS AND AURELIA.

The most excellent History of Antonius and Aurelia: or, The two Incomparable Lovers. Wherein is demonstrated the unparalel'd Constancy of true Affection to Aurelia by Antonius . . . Interlaced with Pleasant Discourses, *etc. T. Haley, and are to be sold by J. Wright, J. Clarke, W. Thackeray, and T. Passenger.* 1682. 4°. 𝕭.𝕷.

Bodl. (Douce A. 271).

ARABIAN NIGHTS.

Arabian Nights Entertainments . . . Translated into French from the Arabian MSS. by M. Galland, of the Royal Academy; and now done into English. *For A. Bell.* 1708. 12°. 8 vols.?

Term Cat., 1707, iii. 592.

[Another edition.] The Second Edition. *For A. Bell.* 1712. 12°. 6 or 8 vols.?

B.M. (12410. bbb. 32), vols. 3, 4.

[Another edition.] The Fourth Edition [*sic*]. *For A. Bell.* 1713. 12°. 6 or 8 vols.?

B.M. (12410. bbb. 32), vols. 1, 2.

[Another edition.] The Third Edition [*sic*]. *For A. Bell.* 1715. 12°. 6 or 8 vols.?

B.M. (12410. bbb. 32), vols. 5, 6.

[Another edition.]   1724.   6 vols.
Lowndes.

[Parts 9–12.]   2 vols.
Advertised, as completing the work, by D. Browne, jun., and S. Chapman, in *The Memoirs of the Baron de Brosse*, 1725.   Parts ' 5 and 6,' ' never before in English,' are advertised by Browne in Fénélon's *Fables*, 1723.

ARBUTHNOT, JOHN.

An Account of the State of Learning in the Empire of Lilliput.   Together with The History and Character of Bullum the Emperor's Library-Keeper. Faithfully Transcribed out of Captain Lemuel Gulliver's General Description of the Empire of Lilliput, *etc.   For J. Roberts.*   1728.   8°.
B.M. (12331. bb. 42/3).

[John Bull, part 1.]   Law is a Bottomless Pit.   Exemplify'd in the Case of The Lord Strutt, John Bull, Nicholas Frog, and Lewis Baboon.   Who spent all they had in a Law-Suit.   Printed from a Manuscript found in the Cabinet of the famous Sir Humphry Polesworth.   *For J. Morphew.*   1712.   8°.
Lambeth.

[Another edition.]   The Second Edition.   1712.   8°.
B.M. (8132. aa. 40/1).

[Another edition.]   The Third Edition.   *For J. Morphew.*   1712.   8°.
Bodl. (Pamph. 301/1).

[Another edition.]   The Fourth Edition.   *For J. Morphew.*   1712.   8°.
B.M. (104. a. 77).

[Another edition.]   The Sixth Edition.   *For J. Morphew.*   1712.   8°.
Bodl. (G. Pamph. 1145/6).

[Another edition.]   *Re-printed by J. Watson* : *Edinburgh.*   1712.   8°.
B.M. (12314. aa. 16).

[Part 2.]   John Bull In His Senses : Being the Second Part of Law is a Bottomless Pit, *etc.   For J. Morphew.*   1712.   8°.
B.M. (8132. a. 40/2).

[Another edition.]   The Second Edition.   *For J. Morphew.*   1712.   8°.
B.M. (8132. a. 63).

[Another edition.]   The Third Edition.   *For J. Morphew.*   1712.   8°.
B.M. (104. a. 78).

[Another edition.]   The Fourth Edition.   *For J. Morphew.*   1712.   8°.
> B.M. (E. 1984/3).

[Another edition.]   *J. Watson : Edinburgh.*   1712.
> Bodl. (55. b. 113/2).

[Part 3.]   John Bull Still In His Senses : Being the Third Part of Law is a Bottomless Pit . . .   Publish'd (as well as the two former Parts) by the Author of the New Atlantis.   *For J. Morphew.*   1712.   8°.
> The author of the *New Atlantis* was Mrs. Manley.
> B.M. (T. 2074/4).

[Another edition.]   The Second Edition.   *For J. Morphew.*   1712.   8°.
> B.M. (8132. aa. 40/3).

[Another edition.]   The Third Edition.   *For J. Morphew.*   1712.   8°.
> B.M. (G. 2233/3).

[Another edition.]   *Reprinted by J. Watson : Edinburgh.*   1712.
> Advocates'.

An Appendix to John Bull Still In His Senses : or, Law is a Bottomless-Pit.   Printed from a Manuscript found in the Cabinet of the famous Sir Humphry Polesworth : And Publish'd, (as well as the three former Parts) by the Author of the New Atalantis.   *For J. Morphew.*   1712.   8°.
> B.M. (8132. aa. 40/6).

[Another edition.]   The Second Edition.   *For J. Morphew.*   1712.   8°.
> B.M. (G. 2233/4).

[Another edition.]   The Third Edition.   *For J. Morphew.*   1712.   8°.
> With the misprint "two former parts."
> B.M. (104. a. 80).

[Another edition.]   The Fourth Edition.   *For J. Morphew.*   1712.   8°.
> Advocates'.

[Another edition.]   *J. Watson : Edinburgh.*   1712.   8°.
> Bodl. (55. b. 113/3).

[Another edition of parts 1–3, etc.]   Law is a Bottomless-pit . . .   In Three Parts ; with the Appendix, and a Compleat Key.   *J. Watson : Edinburgh.*   1712.   8°.
> Advocates'.

[Part 4.] Lewis Baboon Turned Honest, and John Bull Politician. Being the Fourth Part of Law is a Bottomless-Pit . . . Publish'd, (as well as the Three former Parts and Appendix) by the Author of the New Atalantis. *For J. Morphew.* 1712. 8°.

> B.M. (E. 1984/5).

[Another edition.] The Second Edition, Corrected. *For J. Morphew.* 1712. 8°.

> Bodl. (G. Pamph. 1145/5).

[Another edition.] *Edinburgh.* 1712.

Parts 1–4 were also printed in various editions of Swift's *Miscellanies.*
Advocates'.

The Story of St. Alb–ns Ghost, or the Apparition of Mother Haggy. Collected from the best Manuscripts, *etc.* 1712. 8°.

> B.M. (8132. aa. 40/4).

[Another edition.] The Third Edition. 1712. 8°.
> B.M. (8132. b. 49).

[Another edition.] The Fifth Edition. 1712. 8°.
> B.M. (E. 1984/8).

[Another edition.] 1612 [*sic*]. 8°.
> B.M. (G. 2233/6).

A Complete Key to the Three Parts of Law is a Bottomless-Pit, and the Story of the St. Alban's Ghost, *etc.* 1712. 8°.

> B.M. (E. 1984/6).

[Another edition.] The Second Edition Corrected. 1712. 8°.

> B.M. (E. 1984/7).

[Another edition.] A Complete Key to the Four Parts . . . The Third Edition Corrected. 1712. 8°.

> Forster.

[Another edition.] A Complete Key to Law is a Bottomless Pit . . . and Prince Mirabel . . . The Sixth Edition, Enlarged. *S. Bolton.* 1713. 8°.

> Forster.

John Bulls Last Will and Testament, as it was drawn by a Welch Attorney. With a Preface to the Ar——p of C——ry. By an Eminent Lawyer of the Temple. The second edition. *Sold by S. Popping.* 1713. 8°.

> B.M. (T. 2074/7).

A Review of the State of John Bull's Family, ever since the probat of his last will and testament. With some account of the two trumpeters, the hirelings of Roger Bold. *For J. Moor.* 1713. 8º.

B.M. (8132. aa. 20).

A Postscript to John Bull, Containing the History of the Crown-Inn, With the Death of the Widow, And what happened thereon. *For J. Moor.* 8º.

Advocates'.

[Another edition.] The Second Edition. *For J. Moor.* 8º.

B.M. (8133. aaa. 29).

[Another edition.] The Third Edition. *For J. Moor.* 8º.

B.M. (104. b. 24).

[Another edition.] The Sixth Edition. *For J. Moor.* 8º.

B.M. (G. 13520/1).

[Another edition.] The Sixth Edition. *For J. Moor.* 8º.

B.M. (8133. b. 22).

A Continuation of the History of the Crown-Inn . . . Part II. *For J. Moor.* 8º.

Advocates'.

[Another edition.] The Third Edition. *For J. Moor.* 8º.

B.M. (104. b. 24).

A Farther Continuation of the History of the Crown-Inn. Part III. Containing the present state of the Inn, *etc. For J. Moor.* 8º.

Advocates'.

[Another edition.] The Third Edition. *For J. Moor.* 8º.

B.M. (104. b. 24).

The Fourth and Last Part of the History of the Crown-Inn : With the Character of John Bull, and other Novels. Part IV. *For J. Moor.* 8º.

B.M. (104. b. 24).

[Another edition.] The Second Edition. *For J. Moor.* 8º.

B.M. (G. 13520/1).

An Appendix to the History of the Crown-Inn : With a Key to the Whole. *For J. Moor.* 8º.

B.M. (G. 13520/1).

The Present State of the Crown-Inn, For the first Three years under the New Landlord.   Wherein are Characters of some of the Chief Servants on both Sides. By the Author of the History of the Crown-Inn.   *For S. Baker.*   1717.   8°.

> B.M. (101. f. 4).

[Another issue.]   The Second Edition.   *For S. Baker.*   1717.   8°.

> B.M. (8132. b. 10).

A Supplement to the History of the Crown-Inn . . . To which is added, Some Account of an Adventure which lately happen'd at the Mitre-Inn in the same Town, *etc.   Sold by J. Moor.*   8°.

> B.M. (8132. bb. 1).

See also SWIFT, Jonathan.   [Collections.]

ARETINA.

See MACKENZIE, *Sir* George.

ARISTONOUS.

The Adventures of Aristonous.

See FÉNÉLON, François Salignac de la Mothe.   The Adventures of Telemachus.

ARLUS AND ODOLPHUS.

The Secret History of Arlus and Odolphus, Ministers of State to the Empress of Grandinsula, *etc.*   1710.   8°.

> B.M. (E. 1984. 1).

ARLUS, FORTUNATUS, AND ODOLPHUS.

The Impartial Secret History of Arlus, Fortunatus, and Odolphus, Ministers of State to the Empress of Grand Insula, *etc.*   1710.   8°.   2 vols.

> B.M. (101. c. 51), vol. 1 ;   (12314. aaa. 19), vol. 2.

ARMADORUS AND VICENTINA.

See HELVETIAN HERO.

ARMSTRONG, JOHNNY.

The Pleasant and Delightful History of the Renowned Northern Worthy, Johnny Armstrong, of Westmoreland, *etc.   W. O[nley].*   4°.

> Bodl. (Douce R. 528).

ARRAGONIAN QUEEN.

The Arragonian Queen ; a Secret History. The Second Edition.
Advertised by J. Roberts in Mrs. Haywood's *Bath Intrigues*, 1725.

ARTAXANDER AND MELLECINDA.

See UNHAPPY LOVERS.

ASSARINO, LUCA.

La Stratonica ; or The Unfortunate Queen. Written in Italian by Luke
Assarino, and now Englished. *J. Field.* 1651. 4⁰.
B.M. (E. 1621/1).

ASTERIA AND TAMBERLAIN.

See LA ROCHE GUILHEM, *Mlle.* de.

ATALANTIS MAJOR.

See DEFOE, Daniel.

AUBIN, PENELOPE.

The Life and Adventures of the Lady Lucy . . . By Mrs. Aubin. *For
J. Darby, A. Bettesworth, F. Fayram, J. Pemberton, C. Rivington, J. Hooke,
F. Clay, J. Batley, and E. Symon.* 1726. 12⁰.
B.M. (635. a 4/2).

The Life and Adventures of the Young Count Albertus . . . By Mrs.
Aubin. *For J. Darby, A. Bettesworth, F. Fayram, J. Osborn and T.
Longman, J. Pemberton, C. Rivington, J. Hooke, F. Clay, J. Batley, and
E. Symon.* 1728. 12⁰.
Bodl. (G. Pamph. 2118/2).

The Life of Madam de Beaumont . . . By Mrs. Aubin. *For E. Bell,
J. Darby, A. Bettesworth, F. Fayram, J. Pemberton, J. Hooke, C. Rivington,
F. Clay, J. Batley, E. Symon.* 1721. 12⁰.
B.M. (12613. a. 5).

The Noble Slaves : Or, The Lives and Adventures of Two Lords and Two
Ladies, who were shipwrecked and cast upon a desolate Island . . . By Mrs.
Aubin. *For E. Bell, J. Darby, A. Bettesworth, F. Fayram, J. Pemberton,
J. Hooke, C. Rivington, F. Clay, J. Batley, and E. Symon.* 1722. 12⁰.
B.M. (12511. cc. 14).

[Another edition.]   *W. Jones : Dublin.*   12°.

B.M. (12604. aa. 10).

The Strange Adventures of the Count de Vinevil and his Family.   Being
an Account of what happen'd to them whilst they resided at Constantinople . . .
By Mrs. Aubin, etc.   *For E. Bell, J. Darby, A. Bettesworth, F. Fayram,
J. Pemberton, J. Hooke, C. Rivington, F. Clay, J. Batley, and E. Symon.*
1721.   12°.

B.M. (12604. bb. 12).

AUGUSTUS.

The Secret History of the Court of Augustus.

See DESJARDINS, Marie Catherine Hortense de.

AULNOY, *la Comtesse* D'.

See LA MOTHE, Marie Catherine.

AURELIUS.

See SHURLEY, John.

AUTONOUS.

The History of Autonous.   Containing a Relation how that Young Nobleman was accidentally left alone, in his Infancy, upon a desolate Island ; where
he lived nineteen years, remote from all Humane Society, 'till taken up by
his Father.   With an Account Of his Life, Reflections and Improvements in
Knowledge, during his Continuance in that Solitary State.   The Whole, as
taken from his own Mouth.   *For J. Roberts.*   1736.   8°.

B.M. (T. 345/3).

AVERY, JOHN.

The Life and Adventures of Capt. John Avery, The Famous English
Pirate, (rais'd from a Cabbin-Boy, to a King) now in Possession of Madagascar . . .   Written by a Person who made his Escape from thence, and
faithfully extracted from his Journal.   *Sold by J. Baker.*   1709.   12°.

B.M. (1204. c. 5).

[Another edition.]   *Printed, and Sold by the Booksellers.*   1709.   8°.
B.M. (1416. c. 8).

The King of the Pirates.   *See* DEFOE, Daniel.

AYRES, Philip.

The Revengeful Mistress; Being an Amorous Adventure of an English Gentleman in Spain. In which are also contain'd three other Novels, Viz. The Wrong'd Innocence Clear'd, The Generous Impostor, and The Unfortunate Collonel . . . Writ by Ph. Ayres, Esq; *For R. Wellington.* 1696. 8°.

    B.M. (12614. e. 4).

B . . . , *the Abbot.*

    See BORDELON, Laurent.

B., J.

    See BULTEEL, John.
    See HAYWOOD, Eliza. Bath-Intrigues.

B., P.

    See BELLON, Peter.

B., R.

    See CROUCH, Nathaniel.

BAIL, *le Sieur* DU.

The Famous Chinois or The Loves of Several of the French Nobility, under borrowed Names. With a key annexed. *E. O. for T. Dring,* 1669. 8°.

    B.M. (1081. g. 24)

    See CHINA.

BANQUET.

A Banquet for Gentlemen and Ladies, Consisting of Nine Comick and Tragick Novels . . . Intermix'd with Several Pleasant and Delightful Tales and Stories. The Second Impression. *For the Author, and are to be sold by S. Harris.* 1703.

    B.M. (12613. a. 6).

[Another edition.] The Fifth Edition. *For D. Pratt.* 1718. 12°.

    B.M. (12612. a. 38).

BARKER, Jane.

The Entertaining Novels of Mrs. Jane Barker.   The Second Edition.
    A. Bettesworth's and H. Curll's lists, 1726.

[Another edition.]   The Third Edition.   *For Messrs. Bettesworth and Hitch.*   1736.   12⁰.
    B.M. (635. c. 4).

The Amours of Bosvil and Galesia.
    Advertised by E. Curll, as lately published, in *Exilius*, 1715.

Exilius: Or, The Banish'd Roman.   A new Romance.   In Two Parts:
Written After the Manner of Telemachus, For the Instruction of Some Young
Ladies of Quality.   By Mrs. Jane Barker.   *For E. Curll.*   1715.   12⁰.
    B.M. (012611. h. 25).

A Patch-Work Screen for the Ladies; or, Love and Virtue Recom-
mended, in a Collection of Instructive Novels.   Related After a Manner
intirely New, and interspersed with Rural Poems, describing the Innocence
of a Country Life.   By Mrs. Jane Barker, *etc.*   *For E. Curll and T. Payne.*
1723.   12⁰.
    B.M. (1079. d. 13).

The Lining of the Patchwork Screen; Design'd for the Farther Entertainment of the Ladies.   By Mrs. Jane Barker.   *For A. Bettesworth.*
1726.   12⁰.
    B.M. (12611. e. 4).

BARNES, Joshua.

Gerania: a new Discovery of a Little sort of People Anciently Discoursed
of, called Pygmies ...   By Joshua Barnes, *etc.*   *W. G. for O. Blagrave.*
1675.   8⁰.
    B.M. (1080. h. 35).

BARNWELL, George.

The Prentice's Tragedy: or, The History of George Barnwell: Being a
fair Warning to Young Men to avoid the Company of Lewd Women
W. O[nley].   4⁰.
    Priv. Lib.

BARON, ROBERT.

'ΕΡΟΤΟΠΑΙΓΝΙΟΝ Or the Cyprian Academy. By Robert Baron of Grayes Inne, Gent., *etc. W. W. and are to be sold by J. Hardesty, T. Huntington, and T. Jackson.* 1647. 8º.

B.M. (643. b. 19).

[A re-issue.] *W. W. and are to be sold by J. Hardesty, T. Huntington, and T. Jackson.* 1648. 8º.

B.M. (12611. e. 3).

BATEMAN'S TRAGEDY.

Bateman's Tragedy : or, the Perjur'd Bride Justly Rewarded. Being the History of The Unfortunate Love of German's Wife and young Bateman. *T. Norris, and sold by S. Bates.* 4º.

B.M. (1077. g. 33).

BATH-INTRIGUES.

See HAYWOOD, Eliza.

BAUDRIER, *le Sieur* DU.

See SWIFT, Jonathan. A new Journey to Paris.

BAYLY, THOMAS.

Herba Parietis : or, The Wall-Flower. As it grew out of the Stone-Chamber belonging to the Metropolitan Prison of London, called Newgate. Being a History which is partly True, Partly Romantick, Morally Divine . . . Written by Thomas Bayly, D.D. whilst he was a Prisoner there. Capiant qui capere possunt. *J. G., and are to be sold by J. Holden.* 1650. Fol.

B.M. (E. 1067).

[Another edition?]
Advertised by H. Herringman in 1679.

BEAR.

Beware the Beare. The strange but pleasing History of Balbulo and Rosina . . . Full of pleasant Mirth and Varietie. *For E. Crowch.* 1650. 8º.

B.M. (E. 1870/3).

BEAUTIFUL TURK.

See BREMOND, Gabriel de.   Hattige.

BEHN, APHRA.

The Histories and Novels of the Late Ingenious Mrs. Behn: In One Volume . . . Together with the Life and Memoirs of Mrs. Behn. Written by One of the Fair Sex. *For S. Briscoe.* 1696. 8°.

> Bodl. (8°. Rawl. 325).
> *Term Cat.* (1696), ii. 578, 'for R. Wellington' (the second edition?)

[Another edition?] The Third Edition. *For R. Wellington.* 1697.

> *Term Cat.*, ii. 38.

[Another edition.] The Fourth Edition, with large Additions. *For R. Wellington, and are to be sold by R. Tuckyr.* 1700. 8°.

> B. Dobell, June 1910, no. 337.

[Another edition.] The Fifth Edition, Corrected from the many Errors of former Impressions. *For R. Wellington.* 1705. 8°.

> B.M. (12613. bb. 5).

[Another edition.] The Sixth Edition, Corrected. *J. D. for M. Wellington.* 1718. 8°.

> Bodl. (Douce BB. 674).

[Another edition.] Intire in Two Volumes. Published by Mr. Charles Grindon.   The Seventh Edition, Corrected, and illustrated with Cuts, *etc. J. D. for M. P. and sold by A. Bettesworth, and F. Clay.* 1722. 12°. 2 vols.

> Bodl. (Douce B. 611, 612).

[Another edition.] The Eighth Edition, Corrected and illustrated with Cuts. *For W. Feales, R. Wellington, J. Brindley, C. Corbett, A. Bettesworth, and F. Clay, in Trust for B. Bettesworth,* 1735. 12°.

> B.M. (635. b. 24).

Two New Novels. I. The Art of Making Love . . . II. The Fatal Beauty of Agnes de Castro ; Taken out of the History of Portugal. Translated from the French by P. B. G. *For R. Bentley.* 1688. 12°.

> In *Modern Novels*, vol. v. Each has a separate title-page. *The Art of Making Love* is *The Lover's Watch*, by Mrs. Behn. P. B. G. is Peter Bellon, Gent.

Three Histories : Oroonoko, or, The Royal Slave, The Fair Jilt, or Tarquin and Miranda, and Agnes de Castro, or The Force of Generous Blood. 1688.

P. Siegel, *Aphra Behn's Gedichte u. Prosawerke* (Diss.), Leipzig, 1901. Each was advertised separately by W. Canning (*Term Cat.*, ii. 230).

[Another edition ?] 1690.

Each advertised separately by T. Walthoe (*Term Cat.*, ii. 342).

The Adventures of the Black Lady. 1684.

D.N.B. ; Siegel.

The History of the Nun, or The Fair Vow-Breaker. 1689.

Siegel. Ward, *Dramatic Poetry*, iii. 421-3.

Love Letters between a Nobleman and his Sister. *For J. Hindmarsh.* 1683. 12°.

Term Cat., ii. 49.

[Another edition.] *For J. Hindmarsh and J. Tonson.* 1693. 12°. 3 vols.

Bodl. (Art 8°. s. 89).

[Another edition.] With the History of their Adventures. In Three Parts. The Third Edition. *For D. Brown, J. Tonson, J. Nicholson, B. Tooke, and G. Strahan.* 1707. 8°.

Term Cat., iii. 576.

The Lucky Mistake : A New Novel. Written by Mrs. A. Behn. *For R. Bentley.* 1689. 12°.

In *Modern Novels*, vol. i.
B.M. (12410. c. 18).

The Deceived Lovers . . . V. The Courtezan Deceived. An Addition to the Lucky Mistake. Written by Mrs. A. Behn, 1696.

La Montre : Or the Lover's Watch. *R. H.·for W. Canning.* 1686. 8°.

B.M. (1079. d. 14).

The Unfortunate Bride : Or, The Blind Lady a Beauty. A Novel. By Mrs. A. Behn. *For S. B.* 1698. 8°.

Priv. Lib. (This copy has a second title-page dated 1700.)

BELFLOR, *Count* DE.

See LE SAGE, Alain René.

BELLAMY, DANIEL.

The Generous Mahometan.

D.N.B.

BELLON, PETER.

The Amours of Bonne Sforza, Queen of Polonia.   *T. M. for R. Bently.*
1684.   12°.

In *Modern Novels*, vol. viii.   The dedication signed P. B.
B.M. (12410. c. 25).

The Court Secret, A Novel.   *For R. Bentley and S. Magnes.*   1689.   12°.

In *Modern Novels*, vol. iii.   The dedication signed P. B.
B.M. (12410. c. 20).

The Pilgrim.   [Part 2 by P. Bellon.]   *See* BRÉMOND, Gabriel de.

The Princess of Fess : Or, The Amours of the Court of Morocco.
A Novel.   In Two Parts.   *For R. Bently and M. Magnes.*   1682.   12°.

In *Modern Novels*, vol. vii.   The dedication signed P. Bellon.
B.M. (12410. c. 24).

The Reviv'd Fugitive : A Gallant Historical Novel, *etc.*   *For R. Bentley.*
1690.   12°.

In *Modern Novels*, vol. vii.   The dedication signed P. B.
B.M. (12410. c. 24).

BENNET, LUCAS.

Memoirs of the Court of Lilliput.   Written by Captain Gulliver . . .
Published by Lucas Bennet, *etc.*   *For J. Roberts.*   1727.   8°.

B.M. (12611. k. 1/1).

[Another edition.]   The Second Edition.   1727.   8°.

Forster.

BERALDUS.

Beraldus, Prince of Savoy, A Novel, In Two Parts.   Translated out of
French by a Person of Quality.   *For W. Grantham and J. Crump.*   1675.   12°.

B.M. (12510. aaa. 5).

BERINGTON, SIMON.

The Memoirs of Sig^r Gaudentio di Lucca.   Taken from his Confession and Examination before the Fathers of the Inquisition at Bologna in Italy . . . Copied from the original Manuscript kept in St. Mark's Library at Venice . . .   Faithfully Translated from the Italian by E. T. Gent.   *For T. Cooper,* 1737.   8°.

B.M. (12613. c. 23).

BERNARD, CATHERINE.

The Count of Amboise; or the Generous Lover.   A Novel.   Written Originally in French by Madame * * * And Rendred into English by P. B. Gent., *etc.   For R. Bentley and M. Magnes.*   1689.   12°.

In *Modern Novels,* vol. xi.
Translated by P. Bellon.
B.M. (12410. c. 28).

The Female Prince ; Or, Frederick of Sicily.   In Three Parts.   *For H. Rodes.*   1682.   12°.

The dedication signed F[errand] S[pence].
B.M. (12514. a. 45).

BETHNAL GREEN, *the Blind Beggar of.*

See BLIND BEGGAR.

BEVIS.

The Famous and Renowned History of Sir Bevis of Southampton, *etc. For W. Thackeray and J. Deacon.*   1689.   4°.   𝕭.𝕷.

The Epistle to the Reader is signed S. J. [for J. S. ?]
B.M. (1077. g. 35/3).

[Another edition ?]   4°.

Advertised by J. Deacon in 1694 as "at large in 4°."

[An abridgement.]   The Gallant History of the Life and Death Of that most Noble Knight, Sir Bevis of Southampton, *etc.   A. M. for J. Deacon.* 4°.   𝕭.𝕷.

B.M. (837. e. 4).

[Another edition.]   The Gallant History, *etc.   A. M. for B. Deacon.* [1691 ?]   4°.

Term Cat., 1691, ii. 397.
B.M. (837. e. 3).

[Another edition?].   Bevis of Southampton.   *J. Nicoll: Aberdeen.*
1711.   12⁰.

Hazlitt, H. 38.

BIGNON, JEAN PAUL.

The Adventures of Abdalla, son of Hanif . . .   Translated into French
from an Arabick Manuscript found at Batavia by Mr. de Sandisson: And
now done into English by William Hatchett, Gent.   Adorn'd with Cuts.
For T. Worrall.   1729.   8⁰.

B.M. (12513. d. 31).

[An abridgement.]   The diverting History of the Adventures of Abdallah
Abridged with Cuts.   1732.

Gentleman's Magazine, April, 1732.

[Another edition.]   1733.

Gentleman's Magazine, December, 1733.

BILLY, *of Billericay, Sir.*

The Essex Champion: Or, The Famous History of Sir Billy of Billerecay,
and his Squire Ricardo.   *For J. Blare.*   4⁰.

Priv. Lib.

BIONDI, GIOVANNI FRANCESCO.

Coralbo.   A New Romance.   In Three Bookes.   Written in Italian by
Cavalier Gio. Francesco Biondi.   And now Faithfully Render'd into English.
For H. Moseley.   1655.   Fol.

The dedication signed R. G.
    B.M. (12470. k. 8).

See also Part I.

BIRINTHIA.

See BULTEEL, John.

BLACK PRINCE.

See EDWARD, *the Black Prince.*

BLACK TOM.

The Unlucky Citizen: or, A Pleasant History of the Life of Black Tom, *etc. J. M. for J. Blare.* 1686. 8°. 𝕭.𝕷.
Bodl. (Wood 254/14).

BLACKBOURN, RICHARD.

Clitie, a Novel. Written by Rich. Blackbourn, Gent. *For R. Bentley and S. Magnes.* 1688. 12°.

Edited after the author's death by Nahum Tate.
Term Cat., ii. 216, for R. Bentley and S. Magnes.
Priv. Lib.

Three Novels in one, viz.: The Constant Lovers, The Fruits of Jealousie, and Wit in a Woman. Together with Sempronia or The unfortunate Mother. By R. Blackbourn, Gent. *For G. Grafton.* 1688. 12°.
Term Cat., ii. 223.

BLAIR, BRYCE.

The Vision of Theodorus Verax. By Bryce Blair, Gentleman. *For W. Leake.* 1671. 12°.
B.M. (12350. a. 18).

BLIND BEGGAR.

The History of the Blind Beggar of Bednal-Green. *For C. Dennisson.* 1686. 8°. 𝕭.𝕷.
Pepys 362 (329).

[Another edition.] *For F. Coles, T. Vere, and J. Wright.* [4°?]
Hazlitt, H. 390.

[Another edition.] *For F. Coles, T. Vere, and J. Wright.* [4°?]
Hazlitt, H. 390.

[Another edition.] *For T. Norris.* 4°.
B.M. (12613. c. 15).

[Another edition.] *For J. Blare.* 4°.
Bodl. (Douce R. 528).

BOB.

Bob, or the Worldling's Downfall. 1731.
Gentleman's Magazine, May, 1731.

BOISROBERT, François Le Metel de.

The Indian history of Anaxander and Orazia ; wherein Are mingled the Adventures of Alcidaris of Cambaya, and the Loves of Piroxenus. Written in French by Monsieur de Boysrobert, and Translated into English, By W. G., *etc.   S. G. for J. Kirton.* 1657.   8°.

> This had been licensed to S. Waterson, 13 November, 1639 (*Stat. Reg.* iv. 488), "translated out of French into English by William Duncomb."
>
> B.M. (12613. a. 32).

BORDELON, Laurent.

A History of the Ridiculous Extravagancies of Monsieur Oufle ; Occasion'd by his reading Books treating of Magick . . . Written Originally in French, by the Abbot B——; and now Translated into English.   *For J. Morphew,* 1711.   8°.

> B.M. (12510. e. 2).

BOURSAULT, Edmé.

The Prince of Conde.   Made English.   *For H. Herringman.* 1675.   12°.

> B.M. (12512. b. 16).

BOVINIAN.

The Most Pleasant History of Bovinian.   Being An Addition to that most delightfull History of Crispine and Crispianus, never before Printed.   *For J. Stafford.*   1656.   4°.   𝔅.𝔏.

> *The History of Crispin and Crispianus* is in Deloney's *Gentle Craft* (*see* Part I).
>
> B.M. (12613. c. 14).

BOYD, Elizabeth.

The Female Page : A Genuine and Entertaining History, Relating to Some Persons of Distinction . . . In Three Parts Compleat.   By the Ingenious Mrs. Elizabeth Boyd.   *For Olive Payne.* 1737.   8°.

> B.M. (012611. g. 17).

BOYLE, Robert, *F.R.S.*

The Martyrdom of Theodora, And of Didymus.   By a Person of Honour.   *H. Clark, for J. Taylor and C. Skegnes.* 1687.   8°.

> B.M. (861. g. 4).

[Another edition.] Love and Religion Demonstrated in the Martyrdom of Theodora, and of Didymus. By the Late Honourable Robert Boyle Esq; Fellow of the Royal Society. The Second Edition Corrected. *For J. Taylor.* 1703. 12°.

B.M. (12612. b. 24).

BOYLE, ROBERT, *Captain.*

See CHETWOOD, William Rufus.

BOYLE, ROGER, *Earl of Orrery.*

English Adventures. By a Person of Honour. *T. Newcomb, For H. Herringman.* 1676. 8°.

B.M. (G. 17716).

Parthenissa: A Romance. In Six Tomes. Composed by the Right Honble The Lord Broghill, *etc. Peter de Pienne: Waterford.* 1654-5. 4°. 4 vols.

There is a transcript of the Waterford title-pages by H. Bradshaw in U.L.C.

[Another edition of Part 1.] *For R. Lownes.* 1654. 4°.

B.M. (12613. b. 8).

[A re-issue of the Waterford edition.] *For H. Herringman.* 1655. 4°. 4 vols.

Bodl. (256. e. 670-2), wanting vol. 4.

[Parthenissa, Part 5.] The Last Part. The Fifth Tome. *T. R. and E. M. for H. Herringman.* 1656. 4°

Bodl. (256. e. 673.)

[Parthenissa, Part 6.] The Last Part. The Sixth Tome. *For H. Herringman.* 1669. 4°.

Bodl. (256. e. 673).

[Another edition of the whole.] Parthenissa. That most Fam'd Romance. The Six Volumes Compleat. Composed By the Right Honourable The Earl of Orrery. *T. N. for H. Herringman.* 1676. Fol.

B.M. (86. h. 4).

BRAITHWAITE, RICHARD.

Panthalia: or the Royal Romance. A Discourse Stored with infinite variety in relation to State-Government, *etc.* *J. G. and are to be sold by A. Williamson.* 1659. 8°.

B.M. (E. 1797/1).

See also in Part 1.

BRÉMOND, GABRIEL DE.

The Apology: Or, The Genuine Memoires of Madam Maria Manchini, Constabless of Colonna, eldest Sister to the Dutchess of Mazarin. Written in Spanish by her own Hand, and afterwards made into English by a Person of Quality. *For J. Magnes and R. Bentley.* 1679. 12°.

B.M. (1417. c. 30).

The Cheating Gallant; Or, The False Count Brion. A Pleasant Novel: Translated from the French. *For J. Magnes and R. Bentley.* 1677. 12°.

In *Modern Novels,* vol. ii.
B.M. (12410. c. 19).

Gallant Memoirs: or the Adventures of a Person of Quality. Written in French, by Monsieur S. [*sic*] Bremond. And Translated into English, by P. Bellon. *For R. Bentley and M. Magnes.* 1681. 12°.

In *Modern Novels,* vol. ix.
B.M. (12410. c. 26).

The Happy Slave. A Novel. Translated from the French. By a Person of Quality. *For J. Magnes, and R. Bentley.* 1677. 12°.

Part 1 only.
Term Cat., i. 290, 1677, "The Second Part," and "The Third and Last Part."
B.M. (12512. aa. 1/1).

[Another editon.] In Three Parts compleat. The Second Edition. *For G. Cownley.* 1685. 12°.

Stated on the collective title to be in two parts. In *Modern Novels,* vol. ix.
B.M. (12410. c. 26), wanting title, which is taken from *Term Cat.,* ii. 139.

[Another edition.] *For R. Wellington and E. Rumball.* 1700. 8°.

In *A Collection of Pleasant Novels.*
Term Cat., iii. 154.

[Another version.] Translated from the French original. 1720.

See CROXALL, Samuel. A Select Collection of Novels, vol. iv.

[Another edition.] 1729.

See CROXALL, Samuel. A Select Collection of Novels, vol. iv.

Hattige : or the Amours of the King of Tamaran. A Novel. *For Simon the African : Amsterdam* [*R Bentley ? London*]. 1680. 12⁰.

A satire on Charles II and Lady Castlemaine.
   B.M. (12510. aaa. 7).

[Another edition.] *For Simon the African : Amsterdam* [*R. Bentley ? London*]. 1683. 12⁰.

In *Modern Novels*, vol. i.
   B.M. (12410. c. 18).

[Another version.] The Beautiful Turk. Translated from the French Original. 1720.

See CROXALL, Samuel. A Select Collection of Novels, vol. iii.

[Another edition.] 1729.

See CROXALL, Samuel. A Select Collection of Novels, ed. 2, vol. iii.

Ildegerte.

See LE NOBLE DE TENNELIÈRE, Eustache.

The Pilgrim. A pleasant piece of Gallantry. Written in French by M. S. [*sic*] Bremond. Translated into English by P. Bellon, Gent. *For R. Bentley and M. Magnes.* 1680–81. 12⁰. 2 vols.

Vol. 2, the Second Part, is by P. Bellon, translator of the first part.
   Priv. Lib. (vol. 2).   *Term Cat.*, i. 393, 461.

[Another edition.] *For R. Bentley and M. Magnes.* 1684. 8⁰. 2 vols. ?
   Priv. Lib. (vol. 1.)

[Another edition.] *For R. Wellington and E. Rumbail.* 1700. 8⁰.

In *A Collection of Pleasant Novels* (*Term Cat.*, iii. 154).
   B.M. (12511. bb. 8/3).

The Princess of Montferrat, a Novel ; Containing the History And the Amours of the Count de Saluces. *For R. Bentley and M. Magnes.* 1680. 12⁰.

In *Modern Novels*, vol. x.
   B.M. (12410. c. 27).

The Triumph of Love over Fortune. A Pleasant Novel. Written in French by that Great Wit of France M. St. [*sic*] Bremond. And Translated into English by a Person of Quality. *For J. Magnes and R. Bentley.* 1678. 12°.

In *Modern Novels*, vol. iv.
B.M. (12410. c. 21).

The Viceroy of Catalonia, Or, The Double Cuckold. Made English by James Morgan, Gent., *etc. J. B. for J. Magnes and R. Bentley.* 1678. 12°.

B.M. (12512. aa. 1/2).

[Another edition.] *For R. Wellington and E. Rumball.* 1700. 8vo.
In *A Collection of Pleasant Novels.* (*Term Cat.*, iii. 154).

BROSSE, *le Baron* DE.

Memoirs of the Baron de Brosse, Who was Broke on the Wheel In the Reign of Lewis XIV. Containing, An Account of his Amours. With several Particulars relating to the Wars in those Times. Collected from Authentick Authors, and an Original Manuscript. *For D. Browne, Jun., and S. Chapman.* 1725. 8°.

In two parts ; a sequel is promised.
B.M. (1201. g. 3).

[A re-issue.] The Second Edition. *For D. Browne, Jun., and S. Chapman.* 1725. 8°.

B.M. (G. 14732/2).

BROTHERS.

The Brothers : or, Treachery punish'd. Interspers'd with I. The Adventures of Don Alvarez. II. The Adventures of Don Lorenzo. III. Cupid and Bacchus, a Dramatic Entertainment. And, IV. The Adventures of Mariana, Sister to Don Alvarez. Written by a Person of Quality. *For T. Payne.* 1730. 8°.

B.M. (1459. b. 30).

BROWN, THOMAS.

The Adventure of Lindamira, a Lady of Quality. Written with her own hand to her friend in the country ; in Four Parts. Revised and corrected by T. Brown. *For R. Wellington.* 1702. 8°.

Term Cat., iii. 286, 347.

[Another edition.] The Lover's Secretary: Or, The Adventures of Lindamira... In XXIV. Letters... The Second Edition. *For R. Wellington.* 1713. 12°.

B.M. (12611. df. 25/1).

Marriage Ceremonies; As now Used In all Parts of the World ... By Seignior Gaya. The Third Edition. To which are added, large Animadversions... As also, A Looking-Glass for Married People: Or, The Fantastick Adventures of Sir E—— H———— with his Seven Wives. Written by himself, in the time of his Confinement. Put into Modern English, By Mr. Tho. Brown. For *J. Nutt.* 1704. 8°.

B.M. (8415. bbb. 15).

BRUNT, SAMUEL.

A Voyage to Cacklogallinia: With a Description of the Religion, Policy, Customs and Manners of that Country. By Captain Samuel Brunt. *J. Watson.* 1727. 8°.

B.M. (12350. e. 3).

BRUSONI, GIROLAMO.

Arnaldo, or, The Injur'd Lover. An Excellent new Romance. Written in Italian by the Excellent Pen of Girolamo Brusoni. Made English by T. S. *For T. Dring.* 1660. 8°.

B.M. (E. 1841/2).

BULL, JOHN. *See* ARBUTHNOT, John.

BULTEEL, JOHN.

Birinthea, a Romance. Written, By J. B. Gent. *T. Mabbe for J. Playfere.* 1664. 8°.

Some copies have the author's name on the title-page. *Cf.* Halkett and Laing, 225.

B.M. (635. c. 3).

BUNYAN, JOHN.

The Works of that Eminent Servant of Christ, Mr. John Bunyan, *etc. J. Hart, and sold by E. Gardner, J. Marshall, J. and J. Marshall, A. Ward, J. Clarke, and J. Oswald.* 1736-7. Fol. 2 vols.

Vol. 1 is reprinted from the edition of 1692, of which vol. 2 was not published. *The Pilgrim's Progress* (parts 1 and 2), *The Holy War,* and *The Life and Death of Mr. Badman* are in vol. 2.

B.M. (3753. e. 4).

The Holy War, made by Shaddai upon Diabolus, For the Regaining of the Metropolis of the World.   Or, the Losing and Taking Again of the Town of Mansoul.   By John Bunyan, the Author of the Pilgrim's Progress, *etc.*   *For D. Newman; and B. Alsop.*   1682.   8°.

B.M. (C. 59. a. 8).

[Another edition.]   The Holy War, made by Christ upon the Devil, For the Regaining of Man . . .   The second Edition, *etc.*   *For D. Newman.* 1684.   12°.

B.M. (4414. ee. 10).

[Another edition.]   The Holy War made by Shaddai upon Diabolus ;   For the Regaining of the Metropolis of the World, *etc.*   *The Assigns of B. A. and Sold by N. Ponder.*   1696.   12°.

Bodl. (Arch. Bodl. A. I. 48).

[Another edition.]   *For A. and J. Churchil.*   1700.   12°.
Term Cat., iii. 176.

[Another edition.]   *For N. Bodington.*   1707.   12°.
B.M. (4413. aaa. 9).

[Another edition.]   *J. Watson.*   1711.   8°.
Bodl. (141. m. 583).

[Another edition.]   *J. Moncur and J. Forrest: Edinburgh.*   1718.   8°.
B.M. (4415. bb. 8).

[Another edition.]   The Second Edition from the Original.
Advertised by J. Clarke in *Pilgrim's Progress*, part 1, 1724.

[Another edition.]   *For J. Clarke.*   1738.   12°.
Bodl. (1. g. 56).

The Life and Death of Mr. Badman, Presented to the World in a Familiar Dialogue Between Mr. Wiseman and Mr. Attentive.   By John Bunyan, the Author of the Pilgrims Progress.   *J. A. for N. Ponder.*   1680.   12°.

B.M. (C. 59. a. 7).

[Another edition.]   The Third Edition with Addition of Cuts.   *For W. P. and sold by N. Ponder.*   1696.   12°.

B.M. (4414. aaa. 15).

[Another edition.]   *For A. and J. Churchil.*   1700.
Term Cat., iii. 176.

[Another edition.]   The Third Edition.
Advertised by J. Clarke in *Pilgrim's Progress*, part 1, 1724.

[Pilgrim's Progress, Part 1.]   The Pilgrim's Progress from This World to That which is to come : Delivered under the Similitude of a Dream Wherein is Discovered, The manner of his setting out, His Dangerous Journey ; And safe Arrival at the Desired Countrey.   *For N. Ponder.*   1678.   8°.

B.M. (C. 37. d. 61).

[Another edition.]   The second Edition, with Additions, *etc.   For N. Ponder.* 1678.   12°.

B.M. (C. 25. c. 24).

[Another edition.]   The Third Edition, with Additions.   *For N. Ponder.* 1679.   12°.

With the portrait.
B.M. (C. 70. aa. 3).

[Another edition.]   The Fourth Edition, with Additions.   *For N. Ponder.* 1680.   12°.

B.M. (C. 58. a. 23).   Another copy in the B.M. (C. 37. f. 24) has an Advertisement respecting a spurious edition, then being printed by Thomas Bradyll, with the notes in Long Primer italic.

[Another edition.]   The Fifth Edition, with Additions.   *For N. Ponder.* 1680.   12°.

With an advertisement by the publisher on the cuts.
B.M. (C. 58. a. 22).

[Another   edition.]   The   Fifth   Edition,   with   Additions.   *I. Cairns : Edinburgh.*   1680.   8°.

B.M. (C. 58. a. 42).

[Another edition ?]   The Fifth Edition, with Additions.   *For N. Ponder.* 1681.   12°.

Hazlitt, II. 70.

[Another edition.]   The Sixth Edition, with Additions.   *For N. Ponder.* 1681.   12°.

B.M. (C. 59. a. 31).

[Another edition.]   The Seventh Edition, with Additions.   *For N. Ponder.* 1681.   8°.

B.M.. (C. 59. a. 32).

[Another edition.]   The Eighth Edition, with Additions.   *For N. Ponder.*
1682.   12°.

B.M. (4414. aaa. 14).

[Another edition.]   The Ninth Edition, with Additions.   *For N. Ponder.*
1683.   12°.

B.M. (C. 58. a. 38).

[Another edition.]   The Ninth Edition, with Additions.   *For N. Ponder.*
1684.   12°.

Joshua Wilson, Highbury, 1847 (*cf.* edition by G. Offor, 1847, p. cxxiii).
Hazlitt, II. 70.

[Another edition.]   By John Bunian.   The Tenth Edition, with Additions.
For N. Ponder.   1685.

Offor.

[Another edition.]   The Eleventh Edition with Additions, and the Cuts.
For N. Ponder.   1688.   12°.

B.M. (4416. aa. 14).

[Another edition.]   The Twelfth Edition.   *For N. Ponder.*   [1688 ?]
Offor.

[Another edition.]   The Thirteenth Edition with Additions, and the Cuts.
For R. Ponder, and are to be sold by N. Boddington.   1693.   12°.

B.M. (4414. de. 36).

[Another edition.]   The Fourteenth Edition, with Additions of New Cuts,
etc.   For W. P[onder].   1695.   12°.

Bodl. (Douce B. 165).

[Another edition.]   The Fifteenth Edition, with Additions of New Cuts.
For W. P[onder].   1702.   12°.

B.M. (C. 37. b. 36).

[Another edition.]   The Sixteenth Edition, with Additions of New Cuts.
For N. Boddington.   1707.   12°.

B.M. (4409. bbb. 11).

[Another edition.]   The Twentieth Edition, with Additions of New Cuts.
A. Wilde for M. Boddington.   1722.   12°.

B.M. (4414. de. 27).

[Another edition.] The One and Twentieth Edition, with Additions of New Cuts. *A. Wilde for J. Clarke.* 1724. 12°.

B.M. (C. 37. b. 35).

[Another edition of parts 1 and 2.] In Two Parts, Complete . . . The Two and Twentieth Edition, adorned with Twenty-two Copper Plates, engraven by J. Sturt. *For J. Clarke, and J. Brotherton.* 1727–8. 8°.

Part 2, printed for Clarke only, is dated 1727.

B.M. (4415. ff. 10).

[Another edition of part 1.] The Three and Twentieth Edition, with Additions of New Cuts, *etc. A. W. for J. Clarke.* 1731. 12°.

B.M. (4414. b. 15).

[Another edition.] The Four and Twentieth Edition, with Additions of New Cuts, *etc. A. W. for J. Clarke.* 1734. 12°.

B.M. (4414. aaa. 19).

[Another edition.] The Seventh Edition. *A. Carmichael, A. Miller, J. and J. Brouns: Glasgow.* 1735. 12°.

B.M.: (4414. aaa. 20).

[Another edition.] The Five and Twentieth Edition, with Additions of New Cuts, *etc. A. W. for J. Clarke.* 1738. 12°.

B.M. (4414. bb. 8).

[Pilgrim's Progress, Part 2.] The Pilgrim's Progress. From this World to That which is to come. The Second Part. Delivered under the Similitude of a Dream. Wherein is set forth the manner of the setting out of Christian's Wife and Children, their Dangerous Journey, and Safe Arrival at the Desired Country. By John Bunyan. *For N. Ponder.* 1684. 12°.

Offor (Lea Wilson, 1847).

[Another edition.] The Second Edition. *For N. Ponder.* 1686. 12°.

B.M. (C. 58. a. 19).

[Another edition.] *For N. Ponder.* 1687. 12°.

Offor.

[Another edition.] The third Edition corrected. *For R. Ponder.* 1690. 12°.

B.M. (C. 59. a. 44).

[Another edition.]   The Sixth Edition, *etc.   For R. Ponder.*   1693.   12º.
Bodl. (Arch. Bodl. A. I. 44).

[Another edition.]   The Seventh Edition, with Addition of Five Cuts. Note, The Third Part, suggested to be J. Bunyan's, is an Impostor, *etc.   For W. P[onder].*   1696.   12º.
Bodl. (Douce B. 62).

[Another edition.]   The Eighth Edition, *etc.   For W. P[onder] and to be sold by N. Boddington.*   1702.   12º.
B.M. (4413. ee. 51).

[Another edition.]   The Ninth Edition, *etc.   For N. Boddington.*   1708. 12º.
B.M. (874. d. 2).

[Another edition.]   The Ninth Edition, *etc.   For N. and M. Boddington.* 1712.   12º.
B.M. (4413. aaa. 10).

[Another edition.]   The Tenth Edition, *etc.   For N. and M. Boddington.* 1717.   12º.
B.M. (4413. ee. 21).

[Another edition.]   The Eleventh Edition, *etc.   For M. Boddington.* 1719.   12º.
B.M. (4414. de. 28).

[Another edition.]   The Twelfth Edition, *etc.   For J. Clarke.*   1723.   12º.
B.M. (C. 37. b. 34).

[Another edition.]   The Thirteenth Edition, *etc.   For J. Clarke.*   1726.   12º.
B.M. (4415. aaa. 9).

[Another edition.]   1727.
See supra, part 1.   1728.

[Another edition.]   The Fourteenth Edition, *etc.   For J. Clarke.*   1728.   12º.
B.M. (4414. b. 13).

[Another edition.]   The Fifteenth Edition, *etc.   For J. Clarke.*   1732.   12º.
B.M. (4414. bb. 7).
*** Ed. 17 is of 1743 ;   perhaps ed. 16 appeared before 1740.

[Pilgrim's Progress, Part 3.] The Pilgrim's Progress from this World to That which is to come : The Third Part. Delivered under the Similitude of a Dream . . . To which is added, The Life and Death of John Bunyan, Author of the First and Second Part, *etc.* *E. Millet for J. Deacon, J. Back, and J. Blare.* 1693, 2. 12°.

 B.M. (4415. aa. 67).

[Another edition.] 1695.
 Offor.

[Another edition.] The Third Edition. *For J. Back.* 1697. 12°.
 Term Cat., iii. 46.

[Another edition.] The Fourth Edition. *W. Onley for J. Back.* 1700. 12°.

 B.M. (4409. bbb. 4).

[Another edition.] The Sixth Edition. *W. O[nley], for A. Bettesworth and M. Hotham.* 1705. 12°.

 B.M. (4410. d. 7).

[Another edition.] The Seventh Edition. *W. O[nley], for A. Bettesworth and M. Hotham.* 1708. 12°.

 B.M. (4415. bbb. 5).

[Another edition.] The Second Edition. *R. Sanders : Glasgow.* 1717. 12°.
 B.M. (4414. a. 55).

[Another edition.] The Tenth Edition. *For A. Bettesworth.* 1722. 12°.
 B.M. (C. 37. b. 33).

[Another edition.] The Eleventh Edition. *For A. Bettesworth.* 12°.
 B.M. (4415. aaa. 62).

[Another edition.] The Twelfth Edition. *For A. Bettesworth.* 8°.
 B.M. (4415. bb. 49).

[Another edition.] The Thirteenth Edition. *For A. Bettesworth and C. Hitch.* 1738. 12°.

 B.M. (4414. aa. 60).

The Second Part of the Pilgrim's Progress. 1682. *See* S., T.

The Progress of the Christian Pilgrim. *See* CHRISTIAN PILGRIM.

BURGUNDY.

The Secret History of Burgundy.   *See* LA FORCE, Charlotte Rose de Caumont de.

BURTON, JOHN.

The History of Eriander.   Composed by John Burton.   The First Part. *R. Davenport for J. Williams.*   1661.   8°.

A second part is promised at the end.
B.M. (E. 2264).

BURTON, R.

See CROUCH, Nathaniel.

BUTLER, SARAH.

Irish Tales, by Mrs. Sarah Butler.

Advertised by E. Curll and W. Taylor in Castillo Solorzano, *The Spanish Pole Cat*, 1717.

Milesian Tales.

Advertised by E. Curll in *The Female Deserters*, 1719.

C., H.

See TRAVELS OF LOVE AND JEALOUSY.

C., S.

See CLEOCRETON AND CLORYANA; CROXALL, Samuel.

C., W.

See EGERIA; FRAGOSA; GESTA GRAYORUM

CABINET.

The Cabinet Opened, or the Secret History of the Amours of Madam de Maintenon, with the French King.   Translated from the French Copy. *For R. Baldwin.*   1690.   12°.

In *Modern Novels*, vol. xi.
B.M. (12410. c. 28).

CALPRENÈDE, *le Sieur* DE.

See COSTES, Gauthier de.

CAMPBELL, DUNCAN.

Secret Memoirs Of the late Mr. Duncan Campbel, The Famous Deaf and Dumb Gentleman. Written By Himself, who ordered they should be pub-lish'd after his Decease, *etc. For J. Millan, and J. Chrichley* [*sic*]. 1732. 8°.

Not Defoe's book, to which it alludes, but with the same portrait.
B.M. (10825. bbb. 26).

See DEFOE, Daniel ; HAYWOOD, Eliza.

CAMUS, JEAN PIERRE.

Elise, or Innocencie Guilty. A New Romance, translated into English by Jo : Jennings, Gent. *T. Newcomb for H. Moseley.* 1655. Fol.

Priv. Lib.

The Loving Enemie, Or, A famous true History Written originally in the French Tongue, by . . . J. P. Camus B. of Belley. Made English by Major Wright, *etc. J. G. and are to be sold by J. Dakins.* 1650. 8°.

B.M. (E. 1336/2).

[Another edition.] The Second Edition Revised. *For T. Rooks.* 1667. 12°.

B.M. (12510. a. 6).

Nature's Paradox : Or, The Innocent Impostor. A Pleasant Polonian History : Originally Intituled Iphigenes. Compiled in the French Tongue by the rare Pen of J. P. Camus B. of Belley. And Now English'd by Major Wright, *etc. J. G. for G. Dod and N. Ekins.* 1652. 4°.

B.M. (12510. f. 15).

A True Tragical History of Two Illustrious Italian Families ; couched under the Names of Alcimus and Vannozza. Written in French by the Learned J. P. Bishop of Belley. Done into English by a Person of Quality. *For W. Jacob.* 1677. 8°.

B.M. (12614. a. 21).

[A re-issue.] Forced Marriage. With its Fatal and Tragical Effects. Truly Represented in the Downfall of Two Illustrious Italian Families, under the Names of Alcimus and Vannozza. Done into English from the Learned Bishop of Belley . . . The Second Impression. *For W. Jacob.* 1678. 12°.

B.M. (12510. b. 4).

See also in Part I.

CARAMANIA.

See HAYWOOD, Eliza.

CAPELLO AND BIANCA.

Capello and Bianca. A Novel. Written in French; and now Englished by L. N. Gent. *For E. Wyer.* 1677. 8°.

Term Cat., i. 289.

CARA MUSTAPHA.

See PRÉCHAC, *le Sieur* de.

CARLETON, GEORGE, *Captain.*

See DEFOE, Daniel.

CARLETON, ROWLAND.

Diana, Dutchess of Mantua: Or The Persecuted Lover. A Romance. Written by R. C. Gent., *etc.   T. H., and are to be sold by H. Brome.* 1679. 8°.

B.M. (12611. c. 7).

[Another edition.] The Italian Princess, or Love's Persecutions. A new Romance, written by Row. Carleton, Gent. *For H. Bonwicke.* 1681. 8°.

Term Cat., i. 450.

CARLOS, *Don.*

See SAINT-RÉAL, César Vischard de.

CARMENI, FRANCESCO.

Nissena, an Excellent New Romance: Written Originally in Italian by Francesco Carmeni; and Now Englished by an Honorable Anti-Socordist. *For H. Moseley.* 1653[2]. 8°.

B.M. (E. 1234/2).

CARTESIUS.

See DANIEL, Gabriel.

CARTOUCHE, LOUIS DOMINIQUE.

See DEFOE, Daniel.

CASIMER.

See ROUSSEAU DE LA VALETTE, Michel.

CASTERA, LOUIS ADRIEN DUPERRON DE.

The Lady's Philosopher's Stone; Or, The Caprices of Love and Destiny: An Historical Novel.   Written in French by M. L'Abbé de Castera; And now Translated into English. *For D. Browne, Junr.; and S. Chapman.* 1725. 8°.

  B.M. (12614. dd. 19).

CASTILLO SOLORZANO, ALONSO DEL.

La Picara, Or the Triumphs of Female Subtilty . . .   Originally a Spanish Relation, Enriched with three Pleasant Novels.   Render'd into English, with some Alterations and Additions, by John Davies of Kidwelly.   *W. W., for J. Starkey.* 1665. 8°.

  B.M. (12490. b. 38).

[Another version.]   The Spanish Pole-Cat : Or, The Adventures of Seniora Rufina ; in Four Books . . .   Written Originally in Spanish, by Don Alonso De Castello Sovorcano.   Begun to be Translated by Sir Roger L'Estrange ; and Finished, by Mr. Ozell.   *For E. Curll and W. Taylor.* 1717. 8°.

  B.M. (12490. aaaa. 18).

[Another issue.]   Spanish Amusements . . .   The Second Edition.   *For H. Curll.* 1727. 8°.

  B.M. (12490. aaaa. 22).

[An abridgement.]   The Life of Donna Rosina, A Novel . . .   Originally a Spanish Relation.   In Three Parts.   Done into English, by the Ingenious Mr. E. W. a known Celebrated Author.   *B. Harris.* 12°.

  E. W. is Edward Wood.
  B.M. (12489. a. 5).

Three Ingenious Spanish Novels, *etc.* 1712. 12°.
  The novels from La Garduña de Sevilla (" La Picara ").
  The first edition, or the same as the following ?
  Dealer's list.

[Another edition?]   Three Ingenious Spanish Novels: Namely, I. The Loving Revenge : or, Wit in a Woman.   II. The Lucky Escape : Or, The Jilt Detected.   III. The Witty Extravagant : Or, The Fortunate Lover . . . Written by Don Alouso [*sic*] Savorsano . . .   Translated with Advantage. By a Person of Quality.   The Second Edition.   *For E. Tracy.* 1712. 12°.

  B.M. (12490. aaaa. 9).

See SPANISH DECAMERON.

CASTRO, Henriquez de.

Don Henriquez de Castro.   Or, The Conquest of the Indies.   A Spanish Novel.   Translated out of Spanish, by a person of Honour.   *R. E. for R. Bentley and S. Magnes.* [1686.]   12°.

In *Modern Novels*, vol. vi.   *Term Cat.*, 1686, ii. 156.
  B.M. (12410. c. 24).

CATALONIA, *Viceroy of.*

See BRÉMOND, Gabriel de.

CATULLUS.

The Adventures of Catullus, and History of his Amours with Lesbia. Intermixt with Translations of his Choicest Poems.   By several Hands. Done from the French.   *For J. Chantry.*   1707.   12°.

  B.M. (12510. bbb. 25).

CAVENDISH, Margaret, *Duchess of Newcastle.*

The Description of a New World, called The Blazing World.   Written By the Thrice Noble, Illustrious, and Excellent Princesse, the Duchess of Newcastle.   *A. Maxwell.*   1668.   Fol.

  B.M. (8407. h. 10).

Natures Pictures Drawn by Fancies Pencil to the Life.   Written by the . . . Lady Marchioness of Newcastle.   In this Volume there are several feigned Stories . . . both in Prose and Verse, *etc.   For J. Martin and J. Allestrye.* 1656.   Fol.

  B.M. (G. 11599).

[Another edition.]   The Second Edition.   *A. Maxwell.*   1671.   Fol.
  B.M. (8407. h. 12).

[Another issue?]   The Second Edition.   1674.   Fol.
  Lowndes, 1663.

CELENIA.

Celenia : Or, The History of Hyempsal, King of Numidia.   In Two Volumes, *etc.   For E. Davis.*   1736.   12°.   2 vols.

  B.M. (12612. de. 10).

CERIZIERS, RENÉ DE.

The Innocent Lady, or the Illustrious Innocence. Being an Excellent true History, and of Modern times . . . Written Originally in French, by the Learned Father de Ceriziers . . . And now Rendered into English by Sir William Lower, *etc. T. Mabb, for W. Lee.* 1654. 8°.

Bodl. (Douce C. 401).

[Another edition.] The Triumphant Lady; Or, The Crowned Innocence. A Choice and Authentick piece of the Famous, De Ceriziers, *etc. For G. Bedell and T. Collins.* 1656[5]. 8°.

B.M. (E. 1617/2).

[Another edition.] The Innocent Lady . . . The Second Edition. *For W. Lee.* 1674. 8°.

B.M. (12512. aaa. 4).

The Innocent Lord ; Or, The Divine Providence. Being The incomparable History of Joseph. Written Originally in French, and illustrated by the unparallel'd Pen of the Learned De Ceriziers, Almoner to my Lord the Kings brother. And Now rendred into English By Sir William Lowre [*sic*] Knight. *S. G. for C. Adams.* 1655[4]. 8°.

B.M. (E. 1480/3).

CESPEDES Y MENESES, GONSALO DE.

The Famous History of Auristella, Originally Written by Don Gonsalo de Cepedes [*sic*]. Together With the Pleasant Story of Paul of Segovia, by Don Francisco de Quevedo. Translated from the Spanish. *For J. Hindmarsh.* 1683. 12°.

B.M. (1075. e. 19).

See also Part I.

CHAMBERLAYNE, WILLIAM.

Eromena : Or, The Noble Stranger, A Novel, *etc. For J. Norris.* 1683. 8°.
A prose version of Chamberlayne's *Pharonnida.*

B.M. (12511. e. 20/2).

CHAMBERLEN, PAUL.

Love in its Empire, Illustrated in Seven Novels, *etc. For B. Creake, G. Harris, J. Graves, C. King, J. Stag, W. Mears, T. Corbet, W. Meadows, S. Chapman, and J. Williams.* 1721. 12°.

The dedication is signed P. Chamberlen.

Bodl. (Douce CC. 137).

CHARACTER OF LOVE.

The Character of Love, Guided by Inclination. Instanced in Two true Histories. Translated out of French. *For R. Bentley.* 1686. 12°.

In *Modern Novels*, vol. iv.

   B.M. (12410. c. 21).

CHARLES, *Duke of Mantua.*

The Loves of Charles, Duke of Mantua ; and of Margaret, Countess of Rovera. Translated out of the Italian. *H. Herringman.* 1669. 8°.

   B.M. (10629. a. 39).

[Another edition.]   The Amours, *etc.   For J. Knight and F. Saunders.* 1685. 8°.

   Term Cat., ii. 131.

CHARLETON, WALTER.

The Ephesian and Cimmerian Matrons : two remarkable Examples of the Power of Love and Wit.   [1651 ?]   4°.

The Ephesian Matron is based on Petronius.

   Lowndes, 422.

[Another edition of Part 1.]   The Ephesian Matron.   *For H. Herringman.* 1659.   12°.

   B.M. (E. 2107/1).

[Another edition of both parts.]   Two Notable Examples, *etc.   For H. Herringman.*   1668.

Part 2 has a separate title : "The Cimmerian Matron, To which is added, The Mysteries and Miracles of Love.   By P. M. Gent." The preface states that it is translated from the *Comus sive Phagesiposia Cimmeria*, of Erycius Puteanus.

   B.M. (12614. aa. 29).

[Another edition of Part 1 in Latin.]   Matrona Ephesia . Siue Lusus Serius de Amore. à Gualt. Charletono, M.D. ante decennium Anglice conscriptus, Et nunc demum Latinitate donatus à Barth. Harrisio, AM. Ejusdemq; impensis excusus.   1665.   12°.

   B.M. (12330. a. 22).

CHARON.

[Another edition.] Charon ; or, The Ferry-Boat. Dedicated to the Swiss Count ——. *Sold by W. Lewis, J. Brotherton and W. Meadows, J. Roberts, and A. Dodd.* 1719. 8°.

B.M. (12316. ee. 15/2).

[Another edition.] 1729.

See CROXALL, Samuel. A Select Collection of Novels, ed. 2, vol. ii.

CHASTE SERAGLIAN.

See PRÉCHAC, *le Sieur* de.

CHAUCER, *Junior.*

Canterbury Tales : Composed For the Entertainment of All Ingenuous young Men and Maids at their Merry Meetings . . . By Chaucer Junior. *For J. Back.* 1687. 8°.

Pepys 363 (225).

CHAVIGNY DE LA BRETONNIÈRE, FRANÇOIS DE.

The Gallant Hermaphrodite. An Amorous Novel, translated from the French of the Sieur Chavigny. *For S. Manship.* 1687. 12°.

Term Cat., ii. 206.

See INCONSTANT LOVER.

CHEATING GALLANT.

See BRÉMOND, Gabriel de.

CHEC ZADE [SHAIKZÁDAH].

Turkish Tales : Consisting of several Extraordinary Adventures : with the History of the Sultaness of Persia, and the Visiers. Written Originally in the Turkish Language, by Chec Zade . . . And now done into English. *For J. Tonson.* 1708. 12°.

Bodl. (Douce ZZ. 8).

CHETWOOD, WILLIAM RUFUS.

The Voyages and Adventures of Captain Robert Boyle, In several Parts of the World. Intermix'd with The Story of Mrs. Villars . . . To which is added, The Voyage, Shipwreck, and Miraculous Preservation of Richard Castelman, Gent. With a Description of the City of Philadelphia, and the Country of Pensylvania. The Second Edition. *Sold by A. Millar.* 1728. 8°.

> Also attributed to Benjamin Victor and to Defoe.
> B.M. (12613. f. 8).

[Another edition.] The Third Edition. *For J. Watts ; and Sold by J. Osborn.* 1735. 12°.

> B.M. (12612. b. 17).

CHEVREAU, URBAIN.

The Great Scanderbeg.

See LA ROCHE GUILHEM, *Mlle.* de.

CHEVY-CHASE.

The Famous and Renowned History of the Memorable but Unhappy Hunting on Chevy-Chase, *etc.* *W. O[nley.]* 4°.

> With the ballad.
> B.M. (1077. f. 14).

CHILDREN IN THE WOOD.

The History of the Children in the Wood, *etc.* *I. M. for J. Blare.* 1687. 8°. 𝕭.𝕷.

> Bodl. (Wood 704).

[Another edition.] The most Lamentable and Deplorable History of the Two Children in the Wood ... To which is annex'd, The Old Song upon the Same. *W. O[nley.]* 4°.

> B.M. (12612. d. 8).

[Another edition.] The History of the Two Children in the Wood. *J. White: Newcastle upon Tyne.* 8°.

> B.M. (12612. b. 15/2).

CHINA.

The History of the Court of the King of China. Out of French. *For C. Hussey.* 1681. 12°.

> Du Bail's *Famous Chinois?*
> *Term Cat.*, i. 461.

CHINESE TALES.

See GUEULLETTE, Thomas Simon.

CHOICE NOVELS.

Choice Novels, and Amorous Tales, written by the most Refined Wits of Italy. Newly translated into English. *T. N. for H. Moseley.* 1652. 8°.

Priv. Lib.

CHRISTIAN PILGRIM.

The Progress of the Christian Pilgrim, From this Present World, to The World to Come : In Two Parts. Written by way of a Dream. Discovering The Difficulties of his setting forth, the Hazards of his Journey, and his safe Arrival at the heavenly Canaan. *For the Author, and sold by the Booksellers.* 1700. 12°.

B.M. (4414. aa. 19).

[Another edition.] The Second Edition. *For the Author, and sold by the Booksellers of London and Westminster.* 1702. 12°.

Bodl. (Douce P. 79).

[Another edition.] The Third Edition. *W. O[nley] for J. Blare.* 1705. 12°.

B.M. (4413. f. 6).

CHRISTOFORO, *Armeno.*

The Travels and Adventures of Three Princes of Sarendip. Intermixed with Eight Delightful and Entertaining Novels. Translated from the Persian into French, and from thence done into English. To which is added, Amazonta, Or The Politick Wife ; a Novel. Adorn'd with Cuts. *For W. Chetwood.* 1722. 8°.

B.M. (12510. bbb. 22).

CIMMERIAN MATRON. *See* CHARLETON, Walter.

CITY JILT.

The City Jilt: Or, The Alderman turn'd Beau. A secret History, *etc.* *T. Bailey.* 4°.

B.M. (12611. ee. 3).

[Another edition.] The Second Edition. *For J. Roberts.* 1726. 8°.

B.M. (012611. e. 13).

CITY WIDOW.

The City Widow.   A Novel.

Advertised by J. Millan in *Letters from a Persian*, 1735.

CLASSIC QUARREL.

The Classic Quarrel.   A Tale.   By the Author of a proper Reply to a Lady.   *For T. Osborne.*   1733.

The quarrel must be that of Pope and Lady Mary Wortley Montagu.
Gentleman's Magazine, May 1733.

CLAUDE, Isaac.

The Count d'Soissons.   A Gallant Novel.   Translated out of French. *J. B. for R. Bentley and S. Magnes.*   1688.   12°.

In *Modern Novels*, vol. x.
B.M. (12410. c. 27).

CLEOCRETON AND CLORYANA.

The Famous and Delectable History of Cleocreton and Cloryana; Wherein is set forth The Noble and Heroick Actions of Cleocreton Prince of Hungary, His Wonderful and Warlike Atchievements in sundry Kingdoms.   Herein is also declared, His Constant Love to the most beautiful Princess Cloryana, the onely Daughter of the Emperor of Persia.   *J. B. for C. Tyus.*   4°.   **B.L.**

The dedication is signed S. C.
B.M (1077. e. 25).

CLERIO AND LOZIA.

The Loves and Adventures of Clerio and Lozia.   A Romance.   Written Originally in French, and Translated into English.   By Fra. Kirkman, Gent. *J. M. and are to be sold by W. Ley.*   1652.   8°.

B.M. (E. 1289/2).

[Another edition.]   1655.   8°.

Hazlitt, H. 112.

CLERMONT, *the Prince of.*

The Adventures of the Prince of Clermont, and Madam de Ravezan: A Novel.   In Four Parts.   By a Person of Quality.   Done from the French, by the Author of Ildegerte, *etc.* *For E. Bell, J. Darby, A. Bettesworth, F. Fayram, J. Pemberton, J. Hooke, C. Rivington, F. Clay, J. Batley, and E. Symon.* 1722. 12°.

B.M. (12511. aaaa. 14).

CLEVELAND, *Mr.*

See Prévost d'Exiles, Antoine François.

CLEVES, *the Princess of.*

See Segrais, Jean Regnauld de.

CLORANA.

The History of Clorana, the beautiful Arcadian, Or, Virtue triumphant. [*For T. Cooper.*] 1737.

Gentleman's Magazine, May, 1737.

B.M. (12614. ff. 4).

CLORIA.

Cloria and Narcissus. A Delightfull and New Romance, Imbellished with divers Politicall Notions, and singular Remarks of Moderne Transactions. Written by an Honourable Person. *S. G., and are to be sold by A. Williamson.* 1653. 8°. 2 vols.

B.M. (12613. b. 32).

[Another edition.] The Princess Cloria : or, the Royal Romance. In Five Parts . . . Written by a Person of Honour. *R. Wood, and are to be sold by W. Brooke.* 1661. Fol.

B.M. (12403. c. 18).

[Another edition.] The Second Edition. *For E. Man.* 1665. Fol.

B.M. (837. l. 13).

CODRINGTON, Robert.

The Troublesome and Hard Adventures in Love . . . Written in Spanish, by that Excellent and Famous Gentleman, Michael Cervantes ; And exactly Translated into English, By R. C. Gent. *B. Alsop.* 1652. 4°. 𝕭.𝕷.

B.M. (G. 10189).

COLE, JOHN.

The Delightful Adventures of Honest John Cole, That Merry Old Soul . . . By a Tipling Philosopher of the Royal Society. *For R. Montague and B. Dickinson, and sold by E. Nutt and others.* 1732. 8°.

B.M. (12410. bbb. 14).

COLLECTION.

A Collection of Select Discourses Out of the most Eminent Wits of France and Italy . . . Alcidalis, a Romance, by Mr. Voiture, *etc. S. R. for H. Brome.* 1678. 8°.

B.M. (836. c. 1).

COMICAL PILGRIM.

See DEFOE, Daniel.

COMPLEAT MENDICANT.

See DEFOE, Daniel.

CONDÉ, *Prince of.*

See BOURSAULT, Edmé.

CONGREVE, WILLIAM.

Incognita : Or, Love and Duty Reconcil'd. A Novel, *etc. For P. Buck.* 1692. 12°.

The dedication is signed Cleophil.
Bodl. (T. 114 Art).

[Another edition.] *For R. Wellington.* 1700. 8°.

In *A Collection of Pleasant Novels* (*Term Cat.*, iii. 154).
B.M. (12511. bb. 8/2).

[Another edition.] By Mr. Congreve. *For R. Wellington.* 1713. 8°.

Dyce.

[An abridgement, in :] Memoirs of the Life, Writings, and Amours of William Congreve Esq. . . . Compiled . . . by Charles Wilson Esq. 1730. 8°.

B.M. (275. g. 15).

CONSOLIDATOR.
See DEFOE, Daniel.

CONSTANTINI, ANGELO.
A Pleasant and Comical History of the Life of Scaramouche . . . Translated by A. R. from the French Copy : Printed at Paris, 1695. *For R. Gifford.* 1696. 12°.

Priv. Lib.

COQUETILLA.
A View of the Beau Monde : or, Memoirs of the Celebrated Coquetilla. A Real History, *etc. For A. Dodd and J. Jolyffe.* 1731. 8°.

B.M. (1080. i. 34).

COSTEKER, JOHN LITTLETON.
The Constant Lovers : Being an Entertaining History of the Amours and Adventures of Solenus and Perrigonia, Alexis and Sylvia . . . By John Littleton Costeker, Gent. *For T. Green.* 1731. 8°.

B.M. (12613. c. 19).

COSTES, GAUTHIER DE, *Sieur de Calprenède.*
Cassandra. The Fam'd Romance. Written originally in French, and now elegantly rendered into English by an Honourable Person. *For H. Moseley.* 1652. 8°.

Part 1, Books 1–3.
B.M. (12518. ccc. 8).

[Another version.] Cassandra : the fam'd. Now elegantly Rendred into English. By Sir Charles Cotterell. 1667. Fol.

Priv. Lib.

[Another edition.] The Whole Work : In Five Parts, *etc. For P. Parker.* 1676. Fol.

B.M. (86. l. 1).

[Another edition.] Cassandra, a Romance . . . Faithfully Translated into English, by Sir Charles Cotterell . . . The Third Edition, very much Corrected. *For J. Darby, A. Bettesworth, F. Fayram, J. Pemberton, J. Hooke, C. Rivington, F. Clay, J. Batley, E. Symon.* 1725. 12°. 5 vols.

B.M. (12510. b. 25).

[An abridgement.]   The Famous History of Cassandra . . . newly Translated into English, by several Hands.   *For I. Cleave, J. Pero, and E. Tracy.*
1703.   8°.   3 vols.

All five parts.
  B.M. (12512. ee. 1).

[Another edition.]   *For E. Tracy.*   1705.

  Term Cat., iii. 452.

[Cleopatra, part 1.]   Hymen's Praeludia : Or, Love's Master-Piece.   Being
the first Part of that so much admir'd Romance, intituled Cleopatra.   Written
Originally in the French, and now rendred into English By R. Loveday.
Whereunto is annexed, A succinct Abridgement of what is extant in the
succeeding Story.   By the same Hand.   *For G. Thompson.*   1652.   12°.

  B.M. (E. 1327).

[Part 2.]   The Second Part, *etc.*   *J. G. for R. Lowndes.*   1654[3].   8°.
  B.M. (E. 1459/1).

[Part 3.]   The Third Part, *etc.*   *J. G. for R. Lowndes.*   1655.   8°.
  B.M. (E. 1459/2).

[Part 4.]   The Fourth Part . . . rendred into English by J. C.   *For
J. G. and R. Lowndes.*   1656.   8°.
  B.M. (1102. c. 20).

[Part 5.]   The Fifth Part, *etc.*   *For J. G. and R. Lowndes.*   165[6].   8°.
The date appears to be misprinted 1650.
  B.M. (1102. c. 20).

[Part 7.]   The Seventh Part . . . rendred into English by J. C.   *For
H. Moseley, and J. Crook.*   1658.   8°.
Translated by John Coles.
  B.M. (E. 1827/1).

[Part 8.]   The Eighth Part . . . rendred into English By J. W.   *For
H. Moseley.*   1658.   8°.
Translated by James Webb.
  B.M. (1828/1).

[Parts 9, 10.]   The Ninth and Tenth Part . . . Rendred into English, By
J. D., *etc.*   *For H. Moseley and J. Crook.*   1659.   Fol.
Translated by John Davies.
  B.M. (12513. m. 21).

[Parts 11, 12.]   The Eleventh, Twelfth and Last Parts . . . Rendred into
English, By J. D., *etc.*   *For H. Moseley.*   1659.   Fol.
Translated by John Davies.
  B.M. (12513. m. 21).

[Another edition of parts 1–3.]   *R. D. for R. Lownds.*   1663.   8°.
　Priv. Lib.

[Another edition, complete.]   *R. D. for A. Mosely and J. Crooke.*
1665, 3.   Fol.
　Parts 7 and 8 are printed by E. M. for A. Moseley.
　　B.M. (12513. m. 21), wanting parts 9–12.

[Another edition.]   1668.   Fol.
　Lowndes, 350.

[Another edition.]   *W. R. and J. R. and are to be sold by P. Parker, and
T. Guy.*   1674.   Fol.
　B.M. (86. k. 3).

[Another edition.]   *For T. Fabian.*   1687.   Fol.
　Term Cat., ii., 202 ; Dealer's list.

[Another edition.]   1731.
J. J. Jusserand, *The English Novel in the Time of Shakespeare*, ed. 1908, p. 412.

Pharamond : Or, The History of France.   A New Romance.   In Four
Parts. · Written originally in French, By the Author of Cassandra and
Cleopatra.   And now elegantly rendred into English.   *J. Cottrell for S. Speed.*
1662.   Fol.
　Translated by John Davies.
　　Hazlitt, II. 688.

[Another edition.]   A Fam'd Romance.   In Twelve Parts.   The Whole
Work never before Englished.   Written originally by the Author of Cassandra
and Cleopatra.   Translated by J. Phillips, Gent.   *For T. Bassett, T. Dring
and W. Cademan.*   1677.   Fol.
　Parts 8–12 are by Pierre d'Ortigue de Vaumorière.
　　B.M. (86. k. 4).

COURT GALLANTS.
The Court Gallants.   In which are contained the Histories of the Fair
Jewess ; of Ismonda ; of Martis ; of the beautiful Gibsoness.   Memoirs of
Heronia, an Actress.
　Gentleman's Magazine, Dec., 1732.

COURT INTRIGUES.
See MANLEY, Mary de la Rivière.

COURT TALES.
See OLDMIXON, John.

COVENT GARDEN.

The Adventures of Covent Garden, in Imitation of Scarron's City Romance.   *H. Hills for R. Standfast.*   1699.   8°.

"Scarron's City Romance" is probably Furetière's *Roman Comique,* translated under that title in 1671.
    B.M. (12511. aa. 7).

COVERAS, Francisco de las.

The History of Don Fenise.   A new Romance, Written in Spanish by Francisco De las-Coveras.   And now Englished by a Person of Honour. *For H. Moseley.*   1651.   8°.

    Bodl. (8°. P. 17 Art. B.S.).

CRAFTY LADY.

The Crafty Lady: Or the Rival of Himself.   A Gallant Intreague. Translated out of French into English by F. C. Ph. Gent.   *For E. Vize.* 1683.   12°.

    B.M. (12511. aaaa. 42).

CRAWFORD, *Mrs.*

Mrs. Crawford's Novels.

Advertised by J. Walthoe in 1721.

CRÉBILLON, Claude Prosper Jolyot de, *fils.*

The Skimmer: or the History of Tanzai and Neadarne.   *For F. Galicke.* 1735.   12°.   2 vols.

    B.M. (12511. aa. 9).

CREIGHTON, John, *Captain.*

Memoirs of Captain John Creighton, Written by Himself.   1731.   8°.

The Advertisement to the Reader is by Swift.
    B.M. (615. c. 8).

CRISPE, Samuel, *Don.*

Don Samuel Crispe: Or, The Pleasant History of the Knight of Fond Love.   Adorned and Embellished with Sundry Rare and Delightful Adven-tures.   [*For H. Marsh?*]   1660.   4°.   𝕭.𝕷.

    Bodl. (Douce C. 214).

CROKE, Charles.

Fortune's Uncertainty, or Youth's Unconstancy.   Wherein is contained A true and impartial Account of what hapned in the space of few years to the Author, whom you will know in this ensuing Discourse by the name of Rodolphus.   *For T. Dring.*   1667.   12°.

B.M. (635. a. 2).

CRONKE, Dickory.

See Defoe, Daniel.

CROSS, R.

The Adventures of John Le Brun . . .   Being an Impartial History of his own Times . . .   The Whole Collected from a Genuine MS . . .   In Two Volumes, *etc.   For G. Hawkins, and sold by J. James.*   1739.   12°.

The preface is signed R. Cross.
B.M. (12611. e. 14).

CROUCH, Humphrey.

A New and Pleasant History of unfortunate Hodg of the South . . .   By H. Crouch.   *For T. Locke.*   1655.   8°.

Bodl. (Wood 259/6).

CROUCH, Nathaniel.

Delightful Fables in Prose and Verse ; none of them to be found in Æsop but collected from divers ancient and modern authors . . .   By R. B.   *For N. Crouch.*   1691.   8°.

Bodl. (8°. B. 163 Art.).

The Extraordinary Adventures And Discoveries of several Famous Men . . . By R. B.   1683.

B.M. (1197. b. 8/1).

[Another edition.]   1685.

D.N.B.

[Another edition.]   The Third Edition.   *For N. Crouch.*   1704.   12°.

B.M. (G. 13187).

[Another edition.]   1728.

D.N.B.

Female Excellency, or the Ladies Glory.   Illustrated In the Worthy Lives and memorable Actions of Nine Famous Women . . . By R. B.   *For N. Crouch.* 1688.   12°.

> B.M. (G. 13191).

[Another edition.]   By Robert Burton.   The Third Edition.   *For A. Bettesworth and J. Batley.*   1728.   12°.

> B.M. (10604. a. 28).

The History of the Nine Worthies of the World . . .   Being an account of their Lives and Victories : with Poems, and the Picture of each Worthy.   By R. B.   *For N. Crouch.*   1696.

> *Term Cat.*, ii. 574.

[Another edition.]   *For N. Crouch.*   1703.   12°.

> Hazlitt, II. 677.

[Another edition.]   Giving a true Historical Account of their Glorious Lives, Victories and Deaths.   *W. O[nley].*   4°.

> Mr. Quaritch.

[Another edition.]   *C. Brown.*   4°.

> Hazlitt, H. 678.

[Another edition.]   Being an Account of their glorious Lives, worthy Actions, renowned Victories, and Deaths, *etc.*   *For A. Bettesworth, and J. Batley.*   1727.   12°.

> B.M. (G. 13190).

[Another edition.]   The Fourth Edition.   *For A. Bettesworth and C. Hitch, and J. Hodges.*   1738.   12°.

> B.M. (1198. a. 1).

The Unfortunate Court Favourites of England . . . By R. B.   *For N. Crouch.*   1695.   12°.

> B.M. (10804. a. 3).

[Another edition.]   The Second Edition.   *For N. Crouch.*   1706.   12°.

> Hazlitt, I. 111.

[Another edition.]   The Sixth Edition.   *For A. Bettesworth and J. Batley.*   1729.   12°.

> B.M. (10817. a. 8/1).

The Unhappy Princesses. 1710.
D.N.B.

[Another edition.] The Unhappy Princesses. In Two Parts. Containing, First, The Secret History of Queen Anne Bullen . . . Secondly, The History of the Lady Jane Gray . . . Adorn'd with Pictures. By R. B. *For A. Bettesworth and C. Hitch, J. Hodges.* 1733. 8°.

B.M. (G. 13184).

Unparallel'd Varieties : Or, the Matchless Actions and Passions of Mankind. Displayed in near Four Hundred Notable Instances and Examples, *etc. For N. Crouch.* 1683. 12°.

Hazlitt, II. 73.

[Another edition.] The Second Edition. *For N. Crouch.* 1685. 12°.

Hazlitt, IV. 15.

[Another edition.] The Third Edition. 1697.
D.N.B.

[Another edition.] The Fourth Edition. *For A. Bettesworth and J. Batley.* 1728. 12°.

B.M. (G. 13179).

Winter Evening Entertainments . . . Containing, I. Ten pleasant and delightful Relations of many rare and notable Accidents and Occurrences. . . . By Robert Burton. The Sixth Edition. *For A. Bettesworth and C. Hitch, and J. Hodges.* 1737. 12°.

B.M. (G. 13215).

Wonderful Prodigies of Judgment and Mercy, Discovered in Above Three Hundred Memorable Histories . . . By R. B., *etc.* 1681.
D.N.B.

[Another edition.] *For N. Crouch.* 1682.
B.M. (4824. b. 7).

[Another edition.] 1685.
D.N.B.

[Another edition.] The Fifth Edition. 1699.
D.N.B.

CROWN INN.

See ARBUTHNOT, John.

CROWNE, John.

Pandion and Amphigenia : Or, The History of the Coy Lady of Thessalia. Adorned with Sculptures. By J. Crowne. *I. G. for R. Mills.* 1665. 8°.

B.M. (12611. c. 6).

CROXALL, Samuel.

The Secret History of Pythagoras : Part I. Translated from the Original Copy lately found at Otranto in Italy. By J. W. M. D., *etc. Sold by J. Brotherton and W. Meadows, J. Roberts, A. Dodd, W. Chetwood, S. Chapman, and J. Graves.* 1721. 8°.

Part 1.
B.M. (10605 c. 20).

[A re-issue.]   The Second Edition.   *For J. W. and Sold by J. Roberts, and W. Chetwood.* 1722. 8°.

Part 1.
B.M. (635. f. 11/3).

A Select Collection of Novels In Six Volumes Written by the most Celebrated Authors in several Languages. Many of which never appear'd in English before ; and all New translated from the Originals, By several Eminent Hands. *For J. Watts, And Sold by W. Mears, J. Brotherton and W. Meadows, W. Chetwood, and J. Lacy.* 1720, 21. 12°. 6 vols.

Edited by Croxall. Vols. 5 and 6 are dated 1721, the general title-page in vol. 1, 1722. Vol. I.—Huet, *The Original of Romances* ; Segrais, *Zayde* ; Macchiavelli, *The Marriage of Belphegor* ; Cervantes, *The Jealous Estremaduran.* Vol. II.—Segrais, *The Princess of Cleves* ; Cervantes, *The Fair Maid of the Inn* ; Le Sage, *The Force of Friendship* ; Cervantes, *The History of the Captive.* Vol. III.—Saint-Réal, *Don Carlos* ; Le Sage, *The History of Count Belflor and Leonora de Cespedes* ; Cervantes, *The Curious Impertinent* ; Cervantes, *The Prevalence of Blood* ; Cervantes, *The Liberal Lover* ; Brémond, *The Beautiful Turk.* Vol. IV.—Brémond, *The Happy Slave* ; Cervantes, *The Rival Ladies* ; Scarron, *The Innocent Adultery* ; *The History of the Conspiracy of the Spaniards against the Republick of Venice.* Vol. V.—Cervantes, *The Little Gypsy* ; Flaminiani, *Ethelinda* ; Aleman, *The Amour of Count Palviano and Eleonora* ; La Roche Guilhem, or Urbain Chevreau, *Scanderbeg the Great.* Vol. VI.—*The Life of Castruccio Castracani of Lucca* ; Aleman, *The Loves of Osmin and Daraxa* ; Cervantes, *The Spanish Lady of England* ; Cervantes, *The Lady Cornelia.*

B.M. (12410. c. 12–17).

[Another edition.] A Select Collection of Novels and Histories . . . The Second Edition, with Additions. Adorned with Cutts. *For J. Watts.* 1729. 12°. 6 vols.

Contents as in the first edition, with the addition of: Fénélon, *The Adventures of Melesichthon, The History and Fall of the Lady Jane Grey,* and *The Adventures on the Black Mountains,* in vol. I ; *Charon, or The Ferry-Boat,* in vol. II ; *The History of Jane Shore,* in vol. III ; *The Loves of King Henry II, and Fair Rosamond,* in vol. IV ; *The Unhappy Favourite : Or, The Fall of Robert, Earl of Essex,* in vol. V ; *The History of Massaniello, The False Duchess,* and *Memoirs of the Imprisonment and Death of Mary Queen of Scots,* in vol. VI.

B.M. (12602. aaa. 5).

CYNTHIA.

Cynthia ; with the Tragical account of the unfortunate Loves of Almerin and Desdemona. A Novel . . . Done by an English Hand. *For T. Passenger, and R. Fenner, Bookseller in Canterbury.* 1687. 12°.

Term Cat., ii. 193.

[Another edition.] 1700.

Priv. Lib.

[Another edition.] *Sold by J. Thompson, Bookseller in Mansfield.* 1703. 12°.

Term Cat., iii. 376.

[Another edition.] The Fifth Edition, Corrected. *For E. Tracy.* 1709. 12°.

B.M. (12611. de. 10).

[Another edition.] The Eighth edition, Corrected. *For J. Tracy.* 1726. 12°.

B.M. (1459. a. 6).

[Another edition.] The Tenth Edition, Corrected. *For R. Ware, C. Hitch, and J. Hodges.* 8°.

B.M. (12613. a. 8).

CYPRUS, THE GOVERNOR OF.

See VIROTTO AND DOROTHEA.

CYRANO DE BERGERAC, Hercule Savinien de.

ΣΕΛΗΝΑΡΧΙΑ. or, the Government of the World in the Moon : a Comical History.   Written by that Famous Wit and Cavaleer of France, Monsieur Cyrano Bergerac : And Done into English By Tho. St Serf, Gent.   *J. Cottrel, and are to be sold by H. Robinson.*   1659.   8°.

> B.M. (12314. a. 32).

[Another version.]   The Comical History of the States and Empires of the Worlds of the Moon and Sun.   Written in French by Cyrano Bergerac. And newly Englished by A. Lovell, A.M.   *For H. Rhodes.*   1687.   8°.

> B.M. (634. e. 4).

DANGERFIELD, Thomas.

Don Tomazo, or the Juvenile Rambles of Thomas Dangerfield.   *For W. Rumbald.*   1680.   8°.

> B.M. (12614. b. 19).

Dangerfield's Memoires, Digested into Adventures, Receits, and Expences, By his Own Hand.   *J. Bennet, for C. Brome.*   1685.   4°.

> B.M. (108. e. 26).

DANIEL, Gabriel.

A Voyage to the World of Cartesius.   Written Originally in French, and now Translated into English.   *T. Bennet.*   1692.   8°.

> B.M. (535. f. 18).

[Another edition.]   Translated into English By T. Taylor . . .   The Second Edition.   *For T. Bennet.*   1694.   8°.

> B.M. (535. f. 19).

D'AULNOY or D'AUNOIS, *la Comtesse.*

See La Mothe, Marie Catherine.

DAVYS, Mary.

The Works of Mrs. Davys : Consisting of, Plays, Novels, Poems, and Familiar Letters.   Several of which never before Publish'd.   In Two Volumes. *H. Woodfall for the Author : And sold by J. Stevens.*   1725.   8°.   2 vols.

> Dyce.

The Reform'd Coquet; A Novel. By Mrs. Davys, Author of The Humours of York, *etc. H. Woodfall, for the Author ; and sold by J. Stephens.* 1724. 12°.

    B.M. (12604. aaa. 5).

[Another edition.] The Reform'd Coquet ; Or, Memoirs of Amoranda. A Surprising Novel. By Mrs. Davys, *etc. M. Rhames, for R. Gunne: Dublin.* 1735. 12°.

    B.M. (12612. ccc. 19).

DECEPTIO VISUS.

Deceptio Visus: or Seeing and Believing are Two Things. A Pleasant Spanish History, Faithfully Translated. In Two Books. *For I. Starkey.* 1671. 8°.

    B.M. (12490. b. 22).

DEFOE, DANIEL.

An Account of some Remarkable Passages in the Life of a Private Gentleman ; With Reflections thereon. In Three Parts, *etc. J. Downing.* 1708. 8°.

    B.M. (859. h. 26).

[Another edition.] The Second Edition, with Additions from the Author's Original Papers. *J. Downing: and are to be Sold by N. Cliff and D. Jackson.* 1711. 8°.

    B.M. (859. h. 27).

Arlus, Fortunatus and Odolphus. *See* ARLUS, FORTUNATUS AND ODOLPHUS.

Atalantis Major. *Olreeky, the Chief City of the North Part of Atalantis Major [Edinburgh].* 1711. 8°.

    B.M. (1080. i. 15/7).

The Comical Pilgrim ; or, Travels of a Cynick Philosopher, Thro' the most Wicked Parts of the World, Namely, England, Wales, Scotland, Ireland and Holland, With His Merry Observations . . . Being a General Satyr on the Vices and Follies of the Age. The Second Edition. *For S. Briscoe.* 1722. 8°.

    B.M. (G. 13540).

[Another edition.] The Third Edition. *For S. Briscoe.* 1723. 8°.

    B.M. (12331. c. 23).

The Compleat Mendicant : or, Unhappy Beggar.   Being The Life of an Unfortunate Gentleman, *etc.*   *For E. Harris.*   1699.   8°.

Part I ; A second part is announced.
   B.M. (1414. b. 27).

[Another edition ?]   *For E. Harris.*   1700.   8°.
   Term Cat., iii. 170.

The Consolidator : or, Memoirs of Sundry Transactions from the World in the Moon.   Translated from the Lunar Language, By the Author of The True-born English man.   *B. Bragg.*   1705.   8°.
   B.M. (G. 13507).

[Another edition.]   With Additions.   1705.
   Lee, Chronological catalogue, in his *Daniel Defoe*, 68.

[Another edition.]   1706.   8°.
   Dealer's list.

The Dumb Philosopher ; or, Great-Britain's Wonder, containing I.   A Faithful and very Surprizing Account how Dickory Cronke, a Tinner's Son in the County of Cornwal, was born Dumb . . .   With memoirs of his Life, and the manner of his Death, *etc.*   *For T. Bickerton.*   1719.   8°.
   B.M. (112. b. 38).

[Another edition.]   The Second Edition.   1720.
   Lee 198.

The Dumb Projector, Being a Surprizing Account of a Trip to Holland made by Mr. Duncan Campbell.   With The Manner of his Reception and Behaviour there, *etc.*   *For W. Ellis, J. Roberts, Mrs. Bilingsly, A. Dod, and J. Fox.*   1725.   8°.

In the form of a letter, signed Justicia.
   B.M. (G. 13739/2).

The Fortunate Mistress : Or, A History of the Life And Vast Variety of Fortunes of Mademoiselle de Beleau, Afterwards Call'd The Countess de Wintselsheim, in Germany,   Being the Person known by the Name of the Lady Roxana, in the Time of King Charles II.   *For T. Warner, W. Meadows, W. Pepper, S. Harding, and T. Edlin.*   1724.   8°.
   B.M. (G. 13737).

The Fortunes and Misfortunes of the Famous Moll Flanders, &c. . . .
Written from her own Memorandums. *For W. Chetwood, and T. Edling.*
1721 [27 Jan., 1722]. 8°.

    B.M. (G. 13539); Lee 211.

[Another edition.] The Second Edition. *For J. Brotherton.* 1722. 8°.

    Lee 211.

[Another edition.] The Third Edition Corrected. *For W. Chetwood and
T. Edlin, W. Mears, J. Brotherton, C. King and J. Stags.* 1722. 8°.

    B.M. (1081. m. 4).

[A re-issue.] *W. Chetwood.* 1723. 8°.

    Lee 211.

[Another edition.] *Sold by C. Sympson.* 8°.

At the end are the words : The Seventh Edition. Written Originally in the Year, 1683.
Finis.
    Dyce.

[An abridgement.] The Fourth Edition. *J. Read.* 1723. 12°.

    Lee 211.

[Another abridgement.] Fortunes Fickle Distribution : In Three Parts.
Containing, First, The Life and Death of Moll Flanders . . . Part II. The
Life of Jane Hackabout . . . Part III. The Life of James Mac-Faul, *etc.
London : Printed, and Dublin : Reprinted and sold by the Booksellers.* 1730.
8°.

    B.M. (12612. b. 14).

The Four Years Voyages of Capt. George Roberts ; Being a Series of
Uncommon Events, Which befell him In a Voyage to the Islands of the
Canaries, Cape de Verde, and Barbadoes, from whence he was bound to the
Coast of Guiney . . . Written by Himself . . . Adorn'd with several Copper
Plates. *For A. Bettesworth, and J. Osborn.* 1726. 8°.

    B.M. (838. c. 5).

The Friendly Dæmon ; or, the Generous Apparition. Being a True
Narrative of a Miraculous Cure newly performed upon that famous Deaf
and Dumb Gentleman, Dr. Duncan Campbell, By a familiar Spirit, that
appeared to him in a white surplice, like a Cathedral Singing Boy.
J. Roberts. 1726. 8°.

    Lee 232.

The Highland Rogue: or, the Memorable Actions of the Celebrated Robert Mac-gregor, Commonly called Rob-Roy .... The whole Impartially digested from the Memorandums of an authentick Scotch MS. *For J. Billingsley, J. Roberts, A. Dodd, and J. Fox.* 1723. 8°.

> B.M. (C. 58. i. 8).

The History and Remarkable life Of the truly Honourable Colonel Jacque, vulgarly called Col. Jack, who was born a Gentleman, put 'Prentice to a Pick-pocket, *etc. J. Brotherton, T. Payne, W. Mears and A. Dodd, W. Chetwood, J. Graves, S. Chapman, and J. Stagg.* 1722. 8°.

> Lee 215.

[Another edition?] The History And Remarkable Life of the truly Honourable Col. Jack, *etc. J. Brotherton, etc.* 1723. 8°.

> Huth Sale, ii. 2272.

[Another edition.] The Second Edition. *Sold by J. Brotherton, T. Payne, W. Mears and A. Dodd, W. Chetwood, J. Graves, S. Chapman, and J. Stagg.* 1723. 8°.

> B.M. (12613. c. 22).

[Another edition.] The Third Edition. *J. Brotherton, etc.?* 1724. 8°.
> Lee 215.

[Another edition.] The History of the Most Remarkable Life and Extraordinary Adventures, of the truly Honourable Colonel Jaque, vulgarly call'd Colonel Jack ... Written by the Author of Robinson Crusoe. The Fourth Edition. *J. Applebee, For Ward and Chandler ... and sold also at their Shops in Coney-Street, York, and at Scarborough-Spaw.* 1738. 8°.

> B.M. (G. 13760).

[Another edition.] The Fifth Edition. 1739. 8°.
> Dealer's list.

The History of the Life and Adventures of Mr. Duncan Campbell, A Gentleman, who, tho' Deaf and Dumb, writes down any Stranger's Name at first Sight; with their future Contingencies of Fortune. Now Living In Exeter Court over-against the Savoy in the Strand. *For E. Curll: And sold by W. Mears and T. Jauncy, W. Meadows, A. Bettesworth, W. Lewis, and W. Graves.* 1720. 8°.

> B.M. (613. f. 1).

[Another edition.] The Second Edition corrected. *For E. Curll : And sold by W. Mears and T. Jauncy, W. Meadows, A. Bettesworth, W. Lewis and J. Graves.* 1720. 8°.

With *Mr. Campbell's Pacquet.*
B.M. (G. 13537).

[A re-issue.] The Supernatural Philosopher . . . exemplified in the History of the Life and surprizing Adventures of Mr. Duncan Campbell . . . By William Bond, Esq. Of Bury St. Edmond's, Suffolk. *For E. Curll.* 1728. 8°.

Lee 203.

[A re-issue.] The Second Edition. *For E. Curll.* 1728. 8°.

With "Verses to Mr. Campbell," and "A Remarkable Passage of an Apparition, 1665," appended.
B.M. (8631. eee. 14).

[A re-issue.] The Third Edition corrected. *Sold by the Men who distribute the Treatise of Husbandry, and the Voyages and Travels, etc.* 1739. 8°.

Dyce.

A Journal of the Plague Year : Being Observations or Memorials, of the most Remarkable Occurrences, As well Publick as Private, Which happened in London During the last Great Visitation in 1665. Written by a Citizen, who continued all the while in London. Never made publick before. *For E. Nutt, J. Roberts, A. Dodd and J. Graves.* 1722. 8°.

Signed H. F. at the end.
B.M. (1167. e. 3).

The King of the Pirates : being an Account of the Famous Enterprises of Captain Avery, The Mock King of Madagascar . . . In Two Letters from himself, *etc. For A. Bettesworth, C. King, J. Brotherton and W. Meadows, W. Chetwood ; and sold by W. Boreham.* 1720. 8°.

B.M. (518. f. 29).

The Life, Adventures, and Pyracies, Of the Famous Captain Singleton, *etc. For J. Brotherton, J. Graves, A. Dodd, and T. Warner.* 1720. 8°.

Published on 4 June (Lee).
B.M. (838. c. 3).

[Another edition.]

In *The Post Master or Loyal Mercury*, Exeter, from 4 Nov., 1720.
Lee 205.

[Another edition.]   *N. Mist.*   1721.

Lee 205.

[Another edition.]   The Second Edition.   *For J. King and T. King.*
1737.   12°.

B.M. (276. f. 28).

The life and Actions of Lewis Dominique Cartouche : Who was broke
Alive upon the Wheel At Paris, Nov. 28, 1721. N.S.   Relating at large His
remarkable Adventures . . . and the manner of his Execution.   Translated
from the French.   *For J. Roberts.*   1722.   8°.

B.M. (10662. cc. 21).

[Another edition.]   The Second Edition.   *For J. Roberts.*   1722.   8°.

Bodl. (G. Pamph. 58).

[Robinson Crusoe, part 1.]   The Life and Strange Surprizing Adventures
of Robinson Crusoe, Of York, Mariner : Who lived Eight and Twenty Years,
all alone in an un-inhabited Island on the Coast of America, near the Mouth
of the Great River Oroonoque ; Having been cast on Shore by Ship-wreck,
wherein all the Men perished but himself.   With An Account how he was
at last as strangely deliver'd by Pyrates.   Written by Himself.   *For W. Taylor.*
[25 April] 1719.   8°.

B.M. (C. 30. f. 6) ; Lee 191.

[Another edition.]   The Life and Strange Surprizing Adventures of
Robeson Cruso, Mariner : Who lived eight and Twenty Years alone in an
un-inhabited Island on the Coast of America, near the Mouth of the Great
River Oroonoque.   Who having been cast on Shore by Shipwreck, wherein
all the Ships Crue Perished but himself.   With an Account how he was at
last taken up and preserv'd by Pyrates.   Written by himself and deliver'd
to a Friend.   *Printed for the Book-Sellers of London and Westminster.*
1719.   12°.

A roughly-printed edition, perhaps a piracy from uncorrected proof-sheets of the first edition.
Priv. Lib.   *Cf. Athenaeum,* April 11, 18, 1903.

[Another edition.]   The Life and Strange Surprizing Adventures of Robinson
Crusoe . . . The Second Edition.   *For W. Taylor.*   [12 May] 1719.   8°.

B.M. (G. 13275) ; Lee 191.

[Another edition.]   The Third Edition.   *For W. Taylor.*   [6 June] 1719.
8°.

B.M. (12613. d. 7) ; Lee 191.

[Another edition.] The Fourth Edition. To which is added a Map of the World, in which is Delineated the Voyages of Robinson Crusoe. *For W. Taylor.* [8 August] 1719. 8°.

B.M. (12613. bb. 6) ; Lee 191.

[Robinson Crusoe, parts 1, 2.] The Life and strange Adventures of Robinson Crusoe . . . Written by himself.

In *The Original London Post, or Heathcot's Intelligence,* etc., Oct. 7, 1719–Oct. 19, 1720. 4°.
B.M. (G. 10523).

[Robinson Crusoe, part 2.] The Farther Adventures of Robinson Crusoe ; Being the Second and Last Part of his Life, And of the Strange Surprizing Accounts of his Travels Round three Parts of the Globe. Written by Himself. To which is added a Map of the World, in which is Delineated the Voyages of Robinson Crusoe. *For W. Taylor.* [20 August] 1719. 8°.

B.M. (C. 30. f. 7) ; Lee 192.

[Another edition.] The Second Edition. To which is added a Map of the World, *etc. For W. Taylor.* 1719. 8°.

B.M. (12613. d. 6).

[Another edition.] The Third Edition. *For W. Taylor.* 1719. 8°.

Huth Sale, ii. 2251.

[Another edition of part 2.] The Farther Adventures of Robinson Crusoe . . . The Fourth Edition, Adorned with Cuts. *For W. Taylor.* 1722. 12°.

B.M. (12614. a. 24).

[Another edition of parts 1, 2.] The Seventh Edition, Adorned with Cuts. In Two Volumes. *For W. Mears, and T. Woodward.* 1726. 12°. 2 vols.

Part 2 is the Fifth Edition.
B.M. (12611. ee. 4).

[Another edition.] The Eighth Edition, Adorn'd with Cuts. In Two Volumes. *For T. Woodward.* 1736. 12°. 2 vols.

Part 2 is the Sixth Edition.
Bodl. (70. b. 58, 59).

[An abridgement of part 1.] The Life And Strange Surprizing Adventures of Robinson Crusoe. . . . Written Originally by Himself, and now faithfully Abridg'd, in which not one remarkable Circumstance is omitted. *For T. Cox.* 1719. 12°.

B.M. (G. 13243).

[A different abridgement.] The Fifth Edition. 1720. 8°.

Lee 193/5.

[A different abridgement of parts 1, 2?] The Sixth Edition. 1721 8°. 2 vols.

Lee 193/6.

[Another edition?] 1722.

Lee 193/7.

[An abridgement of all three parts.] The Life and most Surprizin Adventures of Robinson Crusoe . . . The whole Three Volumes faithfull Abridg'd. [1720.]

Part 3 had been published by Taylor in 1720 as "Serious Reflections during the Life an Surprising Adventures of Robinson Crusoe : With his Vision of the Angelick Worlc Written by Himself."
Lee.

[Another edition.] The Second Edition. *For A. Bettesworth, J. Brother ton, W. Meadows, and E. Midwinter.* 1724. 12°.

B.M. (C. 58. bb. 1).

[Another edition.] The Third Edition. *For A. Bettesworth, J. Brothertor W. Meadows, and E. Midwinter.* 1726. 12°.

B.M. (12612. aa. 2).

[Another edition.] The Fifth Edition. *For J. Brotherton and W. Meadows S. Birt, C. Hitch and L. Hawes, J. Hodges, and J. Osborn.* 12°.

B.M. (12612. b. 32).

Memoirs of a Cavalier : or a Military Journal of The Wars in Germany, an The Wars in England ; From the Year 1632, to the Year 1648. Writter Threescore Years ago by an English Gentleman, *etc. For A. Bell, J. Osborr W. Taylor, and T. Warner.* [1720.] 8°.

Bodl. (25436. e. 14).

[Another edition.] *J. Lister : And sold by J. Scolfield, S. Newtor Mr. Lord, W. Edwards, and Mr. Warren : Leedes.* 8°.

Bodl. (270. f. 666).

The Military Memoirs of Capt. George Carleton. From the Dutch Wa 1672. In which he Serv'd, to the Conclusion of the Peace at Utrech 1713, *etc. For E. Symon.* 1728. 8°.

The attribution to Defoe is doubtful.
B.M. (808. e. 23).

[Another issue.] The Memoirs of an English Officer . . . By Capt.
George Carleton. *For E. Symon.* 1728. 8⁰.

Differing in the first sheet only.
  B.M. (G. 13289).

Minutes of the Negociations of Monsr. Mesnager at the Court of England,
Towards the Close of the last Reign. Wherein some of the Most Secret
Transactions of that Time, relating to the Interest of the Pretender, and a
Clandestine separate peace, are detected and laid open. Written by himself.
Done out of French. *For S. Baker.* [17 June.] 1717. 8⁰.

  B.M. (594. c. 19).

[Another edition.] The Second Edition. 1717.
  Lee 181.

[Another edition.] The Third Edition. 1731.
  Lee 181.

[Another edition.] The Second Edition. *For J. Roberts.* 1736. 8⁰.
  Lee 181 (" The Fourth Edition ").
  B.M. (8132. aaa. 2).

A New Voyage Round the World, by a Course never sailed before. Being
a Voyage undertaken by some Merchants, who afterwards proposed the Setting
up an East-India Company in Flanders. Illustrated with Copper Plates.
For A. Bettesworth, and W. Mears. 1725. 8⁰.

  B.M. (838. c. 4).

The Political History of the Devil, As well Ancient as Modern. In Two
Parts, *etc.* *T. Warner.* 1726. 8⁰.

  Huth Sale, ii. 2284. Lee 233.

[Another Edition.] The History of the Devil . . . The Second Edition.
For T. Warner. 1727. 8⁰.

  B.M. (G. 13752).

[Another edition.] The Third Edition. *J. Brindley.* 1734. 8⁰.
  Lee 233.

Some Account of the Life and most Remarkable Actions of Henry, Baron
de Goertz, Minister to the late King of Sweden. *For T. Bickerton.* 1719.
8⁰.

  B.M. (613. k. 12/4).

A True Relation of the Apparition of one Mrs. Veal, The next Day after Her Death : to one Mrs. Bargrave At Canterbury.   The 8th of September, 1705.   *For B. Bragg.*   1706.   4º.

> B.M. (101. i. 62).

[Another edition.]   Which Apparition recommends the Perusal of Drelincourt's Book of Consolations against the Fears of Death.   The Fourth Edition.

> Prefixed to an edition of Drelincourt, *The Christian's Defence against the Fears of Death.*
> B.M. (719. h. 12/8).

[Another edition.]   The Ninth Edition.   [1719.]   8º.

> Issued with Drelincourt, ed. 9 (*W. S. for R. Wilkin, etc.* 1719).
> B.M. (4408. ee. 21).

[Another edition.]   The Thirteenth Edition.   [1732.]   8º.

> Issued with Drelincourt, ed. 13 (*For D. Midwinter, etc.* 1732).
> B.M. (4408. e. 17).

[An abridgement, in Drelincourt:]   The Christian's Defence against the Fears of Death . . . abridged . . . with an Account of Mrs. Veal's Apparition to Mrs. Bargrave.   *For R. King.*   1720.   8º.

> B.M. (4412. c. 20).

DEL, *the Chevalier.*

> *See* ALCOFORADO, Marianna d'.

DELIGHTFUL FABLES.

> *See* CROUCH, Nathaniel.

DELIGHTFUL NOVELS.

Delightful and Ingenious Novels : being choice and excellent Stories of Amours Tragical and Comical, lately Related by a Club of the most refined Wits ; with Interludes.   *For B. Crayle.*   1685.   12º.

> Attributed in Crayle's list to John Reynolds.
> *Term Cat.*, ii. 113.

[Another edition.]   The Second Edition.   *For B. Crayle.*   1685.   12º.

> *Term Cat.*, ii. 139.

[Another edition.]   The Third Impression.   Enlarged with the Addition of two new Novels.   *For B. Crayle.*   1686.

> *Term Cat.*, ii. 174.

[Another edition.] Delightful Novels. Exemplifyed in Eight Choice and Elegant Histories ... The Fourth Impression, Enlarged with the Addition of Two New Novels. *For B. Crayle.* 1686. 12°.

B.M. (1081. d. 6).

DEMOCRATES.

Fatal Prudence, or Democrates, the Unfortunate Heroe. A Novell. Translated out of French. *J. Bennet for R. Bentley and M. Magnes.* 1679. 12°.

In *Modern Novels*, vol. vi.

B.M. (12410. c. 23).

DESFONTAINES, PIERRE FRANÇOIS GUYOT.

The Travels of Mr. John Gulliver, Son to Capt. Lemuel Gulliver. Translated from the French, by J. Lockman. *For S. Harding.* 1731. 8°. 2 vols.

B.M. (012611. de. 6).

DESJARDINS, MARIE CATHERINE HORTENSE DE, *Madame de Villedieu.*

The Amours of the Count de Dunois made English, *etc. For W. Cademan.* 1675. 12°.

Also attributed to Henriette Julie, Comtesse de Murat.

B.M. (12511. a. 11).

The Disorders of Love. Truly expressed in the unfortunate Amours of Givry with Mademoiselle de Guise. Made English from the French. *For J. Magnes and R. Bentley.* 1677. 12°.

The publisher's preface contains the author's initials.

Bodl. (Tanner 633).

Love's Journal : A Romance, made of the Court of Henry the II. of France. Printed with License at Paris, 1670, and now made English. *J. Ratcliff and M. Daniel.* 1671. 8°.

B.M. (12518. bbb. 53).

The Loves of sundry Philosophers And other Great Men. Translated out of French. *T. N. for H. Herringman and J. Starkey : Savoy.* 1673. 8°.

Bodl. (8°. 62 1. E. Art.).

The Memoires of the Life, and Rare Adventures of Henrietta Silvia Moliere. As they have been very lately Published in French. With Remarks. *For W. Crook.* 1672, 7. 8°. 2 vols.

> The conclusions are signed H[enrietta] S[ylvia] D[e] M[olière]. Vol. 2 is "Printed by J. C. for W. Crooke."
>
> B.M. (12511. aaaa. 24).

The Unfotunate [*sic*] Heroes : Or, The Adventures of ten Famous Men . . . Banished from the Court of Augustus Caesar. In Ten Novels. Composed by that Great Wit of France, Monsieur de Villa Dieu. Englished by a Gentleman for his Diversion. *T. N. for H. Herringman.* 1679. 8°.

> B.M. (12511. bb. 10).

[Another version.] The Secret History of the Court of Augustus. *Printed and sold by the Booksellers of London.* 1729. 8°.

> B.M. (12512. ee. 13).

The Prince of Conde. *See* BOURSAULT, Edmé.

DIAZ, RUY.

Don Carlos de lara : or the Spanish beau : translated from the Spanish of Ruy Diaz. 1731.

> *Gentleman's Magazine,* Feb. 1731.

DISGUISED PRINCE.

> *See* PRÉCHAC, *le Sieur* de.

DISORDERS OF BASSETT.

The Disorders of Bassett, a Novel. Done out of French. *For J. Newton.* 1688. 12°.

> B.M. (12510. aaa. 6).

DISTRESSED FAIR.

The Distressed Fair ; or happy Unfortunate. *For T. Cooper.* 1737.

> *Gentleman's Magazine,* Aug., 1737.

DISTRESSED ORPHAN.

The Distress'd Orphan, or Love in a Mad-House . . . The Third Edition. *For J. Roberts.* 1726. 8°.

> B.M. (12611. f. 14).

DUMB PHILOSOPHER.

See DEFOE, Daniel.

DUMB PROJECTOR.

See DEFOE, Daniel.

DUNOIS, *le Comte* DE ; *la Comtesse* DE.

See DESJARDINS, Marie Catherine Hortense de, *Madame de Villedieu.*

DUNTON, JOHN.

An Hue and Cry after Conscience : or the Pilgrim's Progress by Candle-light, in search after Honesty and Plain-Dealing.   Represented under the Similitude of a Dream . . . Written by John Dunton, Author of the Pilgrim's Guide, from the Cradle to his Death-Bed. *For J. Dunton.* 1685. 12°.

B.M. (700. a. 7/3).

The Pilgrim's Guide From the Cradle to his Death-bed : With his Glorious Passage from thence to the New-Jerusalem.   Represented to the Life In a Delightful new Allegory . . .   To which is added the Sick-Mans Passing-Bell . . .   By John Dunton late Rector of Aston Clinton.   Illustrated with Eight curious Copper Plates. *For J. Dunton.* 12°.

B.M. (700. a 7/1), the date cut away.

A Voyage Round the World : or, a Pocket Library, Divided into several Volumes.   The First of which contains the Rare Adventures of Don Kainophilus, From his Cradle to his 15th year, *etc.* *For Richard Newcome.* 1691. 8°. 3 vols.

Vol. 3 only is dated.
B.M. (G. 13723).

DU PONT, CHARLOTTA.

The Life of Charlotta Du Pont, An English Lady : Taken from her own Memoirs, *etc.*

Advertised by Bettesworth and Hitch in 1733.

[Another edition.] 1739. 8°.

B.M. (12612. ff. 19/1).

D'URFEY, THOMAS.

Stories Moral and Comical, viz. The Banquet of the Gods. Titus an Gissippus [*sic*] . . . The Prudent Husband : or Cuckoldom wittily prevented Loyalty's Glory . . . From Hints out of Italian, Spanish and French Author done into several sorts of English Verse and Prose, with large Additions an Embellishments. By T. D'urfey, Gent. *F. Leach, and sold by I. Cleav* [1706.] 8°.

The *Prudent Husband* is from the Heptameron of Marguerite of Navarre, and is in pros B.M. (1078. m. 2).

DUTCH ROGUE.

See LEBECHEA, DIOMEDES DE.

DUTCH WHORE.

See TRUMBILL.

DUVAL, CLAUDE.

See POPE, Walter.

EDWARD IV.

The Amours of Edward IV. An Historical Novel. By the Author of th Turkish Spy. *For R. Sare.* 1700. 12°.

The attribution to Giovanni Paolo Marana, author of the *Turkish Spy*, is not accepted. B.M. (12612. a. 36).

EDWARD, *the Black Prince.*

The Conquest of France, With the Life, and Glorious Actions of Edwar the Black Prince, *etc.* *A. M. for C. Bates.* 4°. 𝕭.𝕷.

B.M. (G. 1851).

A Secret History of the Amours of Edward, the Black Prince, and Alic Countess of Salisbury, etc. *T. Parcell.* 1732. 8°.

Bodl. (G. Pamph. 1154/11).

EDWARD, *Prince.*

The History of Prince Edward and Eleonora. *For T. Cooper.* 1739. *Gentleman's Magazine,* April, 1739.

EGINARDUS.

See MANLEY, Mary de la Rivière.

ELIANA.

Eliana. A new Romance : formed by an English Hand, *etc.* *T. R. for P. Dring.* 1661. Fol.

B.M. (12403. b. 6).

ELISE.

See CAMUS, Jean Pierre.

ELIZABETH, *Queen.*

The Novels of Elizabeth, *etc.*

See LA MOTHE, Marie Catherine.

The Secret History of the Duke of Alançon and Q. Elizabeth. A True History. *For Will with the Whisp, at the Sign of the Moon in the Ecliptick R. Bentley?*] 1691. 12°.

In *Modern Novels*, vol. i.
B.M. (12410. e. 18).

The Secret History of the most Renowned Q. Elizabeth and the E. of Essex. By a Person of Quality. *For Will with the Wisp, at the Sign of the Moon in the Ecliptick* [*R. Bentley*] : *Cologne* [*London*]. 1680. 12°. 2 vols.

Term Cat., i. 417 (for R. Bentley).
B.M. (G. 1515).

[Another edition.] The Second Edition. *For R. Bentley and M. Magnes.* 1681. 12°. 2 vols.

In *Modern Novels*, vol. i (part 2 only of this edition). *Term Cat.*, i. 433, 466.
B.M. (12410. c. 18).

[Another edition.] *For Will with the Wisp, at the Sign of the Moon in the Ecliptick : Cologne* [*R. Bentley, London*]. 1689. 12°.

In *Modern Novels*, vol. i (part 1 only of this edition).
B.M. (12410. c. 18).

[Another edition.] *For Will with the Wisp, at the Sign of the Moon in the Ecliptick : Cologne* [*R. Bentley, London?*].

B.M. (1417. a. 20).

[Another edition.] *For Will with the Wisp, at the Sign of the Moon in the Ecliptick : Cologne (J. Hodges, London).* 12°.

Hodges' name is printed at the end of the book.
  B.M. (12613. a. 11).

[Another edition.] *For Will with the Wisp, at the Sign of the Moon in the Ecliptick [R. Bentley?] : London.* 12°.

  B.M. (836. b. 3).

[Another edition.] *For Will with the Wisp.* 12°.

  B.M. (12612. a. 9.)

[Another edition.] The Secrct [*sic*] History of the Most Renowned Q. Elizabeth and the E. of CsseX [*sic*] By a Person of Quality. *For R. Wellington, and E. Rumball.* [1700.] 12°.

In *A Collection of Pleasant Novels.* *Term Cat.*, 1700, iii. 154.
  B.M. (12613. a. 11), the title, bound in with Hodges' edition (*supra*).

[Another edition.] *For R. Wellington.* 1703. 12°.
  Term Cat., iii. 351.

[Another edition.] 1708. 12°.
  Dealer's list.

[Another edition.] The History of the Most Renowned Queen Elizabeth, and Her Great Favourite, the Earl of Essex. In Two Parts. A Romance. *W. O[nley].* 4°.

  Priv. Lib.

[Another edition.] *W. O[nley], and sold by C. Bates.* 4°.
  B.M. (12613. d. 2).

[Another edition.] *T. Norris.* 8°.
  Dealer's list.

[Another edition.] The Secret History, *etc.* *J. Darby for Mary Poulson, and sold by A. Bettesworth and F. Clay.* 1725. 12°.

  B.M. (12603. a. 4).

[Another edition ?] The History of the Rise and Fall of that famous Favourite of Q. Elizabeth, the Earl of Essex, *etc.* [1739.]

In halfpenny parts ; part 1 advertised in *The Life of Charlotta Du Pont*, 1739.

ENGLISH ADVENTURES.

See **Boyle,** Roger, *Earl of Orrery.*

ENGLISH GUSMAN.

See **Fidge,** George.

ENGLISH MONSIEUR.

The **English** Monsieur. A Comical Novel. Wherein His Travells, Amours, and other Passages of his life, no less strange than delightful, are faithfully set down, by an Impartial hand. In Four Parts, *etc. For W. Cademan.* 1679. 12º.

Bodl. (Douce N. 25).

ENGLISH NOBLEMAN.

The **English** Nobleman : Or, Peasant of Quality. A True History, *etc. For J. Brindley, O. Payne, J. Jolliffe, A. Lyon, and C. Corbett.* 1735. 8º.

B.M. (12511. df. 12).

The pleasant Intrigues and Surprizing Adventures of an English Nobleman, at the last Carnival at Venice. By a Person of Quality. *For J. How and M. Hotham.* 1707.

Apparently a different work from the preceding.
Term Cat., iii. 571.

ENGLISH NUN.

The **English** Nun, Or A Comical Description of a Nunnery ; with the Lives and Intrigues of the Priests and Nuns. Written by an English Lady . . . The Second Edition. *For the Booksellers.* 1705. 12º.

Term Cat., iii. 438.

ENGLISH PRINCESS.

The **English** Princess, or the Dutchess Queen. A Relation of English and French Adventures. A Novel. In Two Parts. *For W. Cademan and S. Neale.* 1678. 12º.

B.M. (12614. eee. 14).

ENGLISH ROGUE.

See **Head,** Richard.

EOVAAI.

Adventures of Eovaai, Princess of Ijaveo.   A Pre-Adamitical History . .
Written originally in the Language of Nature, (of later Years but littl
understood.)   First translated into Chinese . . . and now retranslated int
English, by the Son of a Mandarin, residing in London.   *For S. Bake*
1736.   12⁰.

B.M. (12611. df. 14).

EPHESIAN MATRON.

See CHARLETON, Walter.

EROMENA.

See CHAMBERLAYNE, William.

EROTOPOLIS.

Ερωτόπολις.   The Present State of Betty-Land.   *For T. Fox.*   1684.   12
B.M.

ESSEX, *Earl of.*

Memoirs of the Unhappy Favourite : Or, the Fall of Robert Earl of Esse
1729.

See CROXALL, Samuel.   A Select Collection of Novels, ed. 2, vol. v.

ESSEX CHAMPION.

See BILLY, *of Billericay, Sir.*

EVAGORAS.

Evagoras, a Romance.   By L. L. Gent.   *For R. Clave!, and T. More*
1677.   8⁰.

B.M. (12614. aaa. 16).

EVE REVIVED.

Eve Revived, or The Fair one stark naked.   A Novel.   *Sold by J. Walthoe*
1683.   12⁰.

Term Cat., ii. 50.

EXTRAVAGANT POET.

The Extravagant Poet.   A Comical Novel, Wherein is Described his many Pleasant Follies.   Translated out of French, by G. R. Gent.   *For B. M.* [*i.e., R. Bentley and M. Magnes*] *at the Sign of Pegasus, at the Foot of Parnassus his Hill.*   1681.   12°.

> *Term Cat.*, i. 428, gives the publishers.   In *Modern Novels*, vol. viii.
> B.M. (12410. c. 25).

EXTRAVAGANT SHEPHERD.

See SOREL, Charles.

F., G.

See FIDGE, George.

F., H.

See DEFOE, Daniel.   A Journal of the Plague Year.

FAIR CONCUBINE.

See VANELLA.

FAIR EXTRAVAGANT.

See OLDYS, Alexander.

FAIR HEBREW.

See HAYWOOD, Eliza.

FAIR ONE OF TUNIS.

The Fair One of Tunis : Or, The Generous Mistres.   A new piece of Gallantry.   Out of French.   *For H. Brome.*   1674.   8°.

> Bodl. (I. 47. Art).

FALSE DUCHESS.

The False Dutchess.   Translated from the French Original.   1721.
See CROXALL, Samuel.   A Select Collection of Novels, vol. vi.

[Another edition.]   1729.
See CROXALL, Samuel.   A Select Collection of Novels, ed. 2, vol. vi.

FAMOUS CHINOIS.

See BAIL, *le Sieur* du.

FATAL PRUDENCE.

See DEMOCRATES.

FEMALE DESERTERS.

The Female Deserters. A Novel. By the Author of the Lover's Week. *For J. Roberts.* 1719. 8°.

A sequel to *The Lover's Week*, by M. H.
    B.M. (12330. cc. 11).

FEMALE DUNCIAD.

The Female Dunciad. Containing ... V. Irish Artifice ; or, The History of Clarina. A Novel. By Mrs. Eliza Haywood. *For T. Read.* 1728. 8°.

B.M. (T. 857/2).

FEMALE INCONSTANCY.

Female Inconstancy Display'd in Three Diverting Histories, Describing the Levity of the Fair Sex . . . To which is added, Several Diverting Tales and Merry Jokes . . . Dedicated to the Six Fair Maids at St. James's. *For T. Johnson.* 1732. 8°.

B.M. (12612. d. 3).

[Another edition.] The Second Edition, *etc.* *For T. Johnson.* 1732. 8°.
    B.M. (12612. d. 15).

FEMALE POLITICIAN.

The Female Politician : or the Statesman Unmask'd. A Novel. By the Author of the Prude. *J. Wilford.* 1733. 8°.

B.M. (12624. a. 16/1).

FEMALE PRINCE.

See BERNARD, Catherine.

FEMALE TUMBLER.

The Female Tumbler ; a Tale ; with a neat Frontispiece. 1737.

Gentleman's Magazine, Sept., 1737.

FÉNÉLON, François de Salignac de la Mothe.

The Adventures of Telemachus the Son of Ulysses. Translated from the French. *For A. and J. Churchil.* 1699. 12°.

At the end is a note : "The other Parts will be published in a short time." This Part ends early in Book v.
B.M. (12510. c. 9).

[Another edition.] The Second Edition. *For A. and J. Churchil.* 1700. 12°.

Term Cat., iii. 201.

[Another edition.] The Third Edition corrected. To which is added, The Adventures of Aristonous. *Sold by A. and J. Churchil.* 1701. 12°.

Term Cat., iii. 264.

[Another edition.] The Fifth [*sic*] Edition. *For A. and J. Churchil.* 1703. 12°. 2 vols.

The first Part is the same as the 1699 edition ; the second Part ends near the end of Book x.
B.M. (634. a. 12).

[Another edition.] The Fourth [*sic*] Edition, *etc. For A. and J. Churchil.* 1705. 12°.

Term Cat., iii. 470.

[Another edition.] The Sixth Edition. *For A. and J. Churchill.* 1707. 12°. 2 vols.

Bodl. (Ashmole D. 26).

[Another edition.] In Twenty-four Books . . . Done into English from the last Paris (which is the only genuine) Edition, by Mr. Is. Littlebury and Mr. A. Boyer. Adorn'd with Twenty-four Plates, and a Map of Telemachus's Travels . . . The Eleventh Edition, *etc. For J. Walthoe.* 1721. 12°. 2 vols.

Bodl. (Radcliffe, f. 176, 7).

[Another edition.] The Twelfth Edition. *For E. Symon.* 1728. 12°. 2 vols..

B.M. (12511. aaaa. 44).

[Another version.] Translated into English . . . by Mr. Ozell, *etc. For W. Innys and R. Manby, S. Birt and W. Feales.* 1735. 8°. 2 vols.

B.M. (12510. dd. 28).

See BARKER, Jane. Exilius.

See STUBBES, George. A New Adventure of Telemachus.

Fables and Dialogues of the Dead.   Written in French by the Late Archbishop of Cambray, Author of Telemachus: And done into English From
the Paris Edition of 1718, then Corrected and Revised with the Author's own
Original Manuscript . . .   The Second Edition Corrected.   *For D. Browne,
Jun., and S. Chapman.*   1723.   8⁰.

> B.M. (12304. bb. 25).

[Another version.]   Twenty Seven Moral Tales and Fables, French and
English.   Invented (For the Education of a Prince) By the late Celebrated
Archbishop of Cambray.   Author of Telemachus.   Digested . . . for the Use
of Schools, *etc.*   *For J. Wilcox, T. Worral, A. Vandenhoeck, and J. Jackson.*
1729.   8⁰.

> The translation is by Daniel Bellamy.
> B.M. (88. b. 4).

[Another version.]   The Tales and Fables Of the late Archbishop and
Duke of Cambray, Author of Telemachus, in French and English . . .
Illustrated by Twenty-nine Copper-Plates.   Engraven by George Bickham,
Junior.   *For J. Hawkins, and Sold by J. Osborn.*   1736.   8⁰.

> 17 Fables.
> B.M. (12304. aaa. 20).

The Adventures of Melesichthon.   Written Originally in French, by the
Author of the Adventures of Telemachus.   1729.
See CROXALL, Samuel.   A Select Collection of Novels, ed. 2, vol. ii.

FERNANDEZ DE AVELLANEDA, ALONSO.

A Continuation of the Comical History of the most Ingenious Knight Don
Quixote de la Mancha.   By the Licentiate Alonzo Fernandez de Avellaneda.
Being a Third Volume: Never before Printed in English.   Illustrated with
several curious Copper Cuts.   Translated by Captain John Stevens.   *For
J. Wale and J. Lenex.*   1705.   8⁰.

> B.M. (12490. e. 10).

FIDGE, GEORGE.

The English Gusman; or, the History of that Unparallel'd Thief James
Hind . . .   With several Cuts to Illustrate the Matter.   Written by G. F.
T. N. for G. Latham Junior.   1652.   4⁰.

> B.M. (E. 651/20).

[Another edition?]   The Notorious Impostor, *etc.*   1692.

> *D.N.B.*

[An abridgement.] Wit for Money, *etc.* *For T. Vere and W. Gilbertson.* [1652?] 8°. 𝕭.𝕷.

B.M. (12331. aa. 27).

Hind's Ramble, or, The Description of his manner and course of life, *etc.* *For G. Latham.* 1651. 8°.

The preface is signed G. F.
B.M. (E. 1378/4).

FIEUX, Charles de.

The French Rogue. Being a Pleasant History of His Life and Fortune, adorned with variety of other Adventures of no less Rarity. With Epigrams Suitable to each Stratagem. *T. N. for S. Lowndes.* 1672. 8°.

Bodl. (8°. M. 2 Art.).

[A different version.] The French Rogue, or The Life of Mon. Ragoue de Versailles . . . Done from the original by J. S. *For N. Boddington.* 1694. 12°.

Term Cat., ii. 522.

[Another edition.] With large Additions not in any former Impression, *etc.* *For N. Boddington.* 1704. 12°.

B.M. (12511. aaaa. 43).

[Another edition.] *For N. and M. Boddington.* 1716. 12°.

B.M. (12511. aaaa. 20).

FINISHED RAKE.

The finish'd Rake : Or, Gallantry in Perfection : Being the genuine and entertaining Adventures of a young Gent. of Fortune. *For A. Dodd.* 1733.

Gentleman's Magazine, Oct., 1733. Advertised by J. Roberts, in *The Unnatural Mother*, 1734.

FIREDRAKE, *Sir.*

The Knight Adventurer ; or, the Infamous and Abominable History of that Terrible, Troublesome, and Vain-glorious Knight, Sir Firedrake : shewing all the Passages of his Unvaliant, Courageous, and Knight-Arrant-Villainous Feats of Arms, translated by himself out of Wilde-Irish into Tame-English, because hee did not understand the Language. *R. J.* 1663. 12°. 𝕭.𝕷.

Hazlitt, H. 198.

FIVE WISE PHILOSOPHERS.

The History of the Five Wise Philosophers : Or, The wonderful Relation of the Life of Jehosaphat the Hermit, son of Avenerio, King of Barma in India . . . By H. P. Gent. *For D. Page, T. Passenger, and B. Hurlock.* 1672. 12°.

> Abridged from the old Latin Life by H. Parsons. Another version appears in Caxton's and Wynkyn de Worde's editions of the *Golden Legend.*
>
> Priv. Lib.

[Another edition.]   *For J. Tracy.*   12°.
> B.M. (12410. a. 23)

[Another edition.]   The Second Edition.   *For E. Tracy.*   8°.
> *Term Cat.*, ii. 582, iii. 32 (1696 and 1697).

[Another edition ?]   The Second Edition.   *For E. Tracy.*   1700.
> *Term Cat.*, iii. 203.

[Another edition.]   By N. H., *etc.*   *For E. Tracy.*   1703.   12°.
> *Term Cat.*, iii. 375.

[Another edition.]   *For E. Tracy.*   1711.   12°.

The preface is signed by Nich. Herick, who edited Parsons' work.
> Bodl. (Douce I. 8).

[Another edition.]   1725.
> J. Jacobs, *Barlaam and Josaphat*, 1896.

[Another edition.]   *For E. Midwinter.*   1732.   12°.
> B.M. (4805. a. 27).

FLAMINIANI.

Ethelinda. An English Novel. Done from the Italian of Flaminiani. 1721. *See* CROXALL, Samuel. A Select Collection of Novels, vol. v.

[Another edition.]   1729.   *See* CROXALL, Samuel. A Select Collection of Novels, ed. 2, vol. v.

FLORELLA AND PHILLIS.

Love a la Mode : Or, The Amours of Florella and Phillis, *etc.* *For J. Roberts.* 1732. 8°.
> B.M. (12614. g. 14).

FLORES, Don.

The Most Excellent History of the valiant, and Renowned Knight, Don Flores of Greece . . . Being, a supplement to Amadis de Gaule, Written by Mounsieur de Essule, Nicholas de Hereby . . . Translated into English by W. F. The Third Edition, *etc.* *For R. I.* 1664. 4°. 𝕭.𝕷.

An edition printed for Andrew Kembe is advertised in *Palladine*, 1664.
B.M. (12512. e. 8).

[Another edition.]
Advertised by W. Thackeray, 1677.

FLORIDON AND LUCINA.

The Pleasant and Delightful History of Floridon and Lucina, Illustrated with an admirable Description of Loves Paradice &c. never before Printed nor Published. By J. P. *T. Mabb.* 1663. 4°. 𝕭.𝕷.

Priv. Lib.

FOIGNY, Gabriel de.

See Sadeur, Jacques.

FONTAINES, Louis.

A Relation of the Country of Jansenia . . . With a Map of the Countrey. Composed in French by Lewis Fountaine, Esq. ; And newly Translated into English by P. B. *For the Author, & are sold by A. Banks and C. Harper.* 1668. 8°.

Fontaines is a pseudonym for le Père Zacharie.
B.M. (873. f. 7).

FONTANIEU, Gaspard Moïse.

.Rosalinda, A Novel . . . By a Man of Quality. Translated from the French. *For C. Davis, and Sold by J. Osborn.* 1733. 8°.

B.M. (12512. dd. 40).

FORCE OF FRIENDSHIP.

See Le Sage, Alain René.

FORCED VIRGIN.

See Lysander.

FORTUNATE TRANSPORT.

See HAYCOCK, Polly.

FORTUNE'S UNCERTAINTY.

See CROKE, Charles.

FRANCK, RICHARD.

See PHILANTHROPUS.

FRANK, JOHN.

The Birth, Life and Death of John Frank. *J. M. for J. Deacon.* 8⁰. 𝕭.𝕷.

Bodl. (Wood 259/15).

[Another edition.] *J. M. for J. Deacon, and C. Dennisson.* 8⁰. 𝕭.𝕷.

Pepys 363 (467).

FRENCH LOVERS.

The Illustrious French Lovers ; Being the True Histories of the Amours of several French Persons of Quality ... shewing the Polite Breeding and Gallantry of the Gentlemen and Ladies of the French Nation. Written Originally in French, and translated into English by Mrs. P. Aubin. In Two Volumes. *For J. Darby, A. Bettesworth, F. Fayram, J. Pemberton, C. Rivington, J. Hooke, F. Clay, J. Batley, E. Symon.* 1727. 12⁰. 2 vols.

B.M. (12511. bb. 18).

[Another edition.] The Second Edition. *For D. Midwinter, A. Bettesworth and C. Hitch, J. and J. Pemberton, R. Ware, C. Rivington, A. Ward, T. Longman, R. Hett, S. Austen, and J. Wood.* 1739. 12⁰. 2 vols.

B.M. (12511. bb. 19).

FRENCH ROGUE.

See FIEUX, Charles de.

FROLICKSOME, *Sir* HUMPHREY.

The Merry Oxford Knight. Or, the Pleasant Intrigues of Sir Humphrey Frollicksome, *etc.   A. M. for J. Bissel.* 8⁰. 𝕭.𝕷.

Pepys 363 (585).

FUGITIVE.

The Fugitive. Containing, Several very pleasant Passages, and surprizing Adventures, observ'd by a Lady in her Country Ramble . . . Now first published from her own Manuscript. *For G. Sawbridge, and Sold by J. Nutt.* 1705. 12°.

> Bodl. (Douce T. 187).

FUGITIVE STATESMAN.

The Fugitive Statesman, in Requital for the Perplex'd Prince. *A. Grover.* 1683. 12°.

> A satire on the Earl of Shaftesbury.
> B.M. (292. a. 31).

FULLER, Thomas.

Triana, Or a Threefold Romanza of Mariana Paduana Sabina. *For J. Stafford.* 1654. 12°.

> B.M. (G. 10366).

[Another issue.] Triana . . . Written by Tho. Fuller, B.D. *For J. Stafford.* 1664. 12°.

> B.M. (G. 10367).

FURETIÈRE, Antoine.

Scarron's City Romance, Made English, *etc.* *T. N. for H. Herringman.* 1671. 8°.

> Furetière's *Roman Bourgeois.*
> Bodl. (Douce S. 720/2).

See Covent Garden.

G., D.   *See* Sunday's Adventure.

GABALIS, *Count* de.   *See* Montfaucon de Villars.

GALLANT LADIES.

The Gallant Ladies, or, the Mutual Confidence. A Novel. Translated out of French, *etc.* *For R. Baldwin.* 1685. 12°. 2 vols.

> In *Modern Novels,* vol. ix.
> B.M. (12410. c. 26).

[Another edition.] The Galants : or, The Reciprocal Confidents, *etc. For J. Knight and F. Saunders.* 1685. 12⁰. 2 vols.

B.M. (12512. ccc. 16).

[Another edition.] 1697.
See NOVELS. Four Novels.

GALLANTRY UNMASKED.

Gallantry Unmasked, or Women in their proper Colours. A Novel. *For R. Bentley.* 1690. 12⁰.

Term Cat., ii. 333.

GALLIENO.

An Historical Romance of the Wars, Between the Mighty Giant Gallieno, And the Great Knight Nasonius, and His Associates. *Doublin,* 1694. 4⁰.

Gallieno and Nasonius are Louis XIV and William III.

B.M. (100. i. 64).

GAYA, LOUIS DE.

See BROWN, Thomas.

GENEROUS RIVALS.

The Generous Rivals : Or, Love Triumphant. A Novel. *For J. Morphew.* 1713. 8⁰.

B.M. (12614. ccc. 1).

[Another edition.] *For W. Hinchcliffe.* 1716. 12⁰.

Bodl. (250. q. 280).

GENTLEMAN APOTHECARY.

See VILLIERS, J. de.

GEORGE, *Saint.*

The Life and Death of The Famous Champion of England, St. George. *For W. Thackeray.* 8⁰. ▮.▮.

Bodl. (Wood 254/1).

GERMAN PRINCESS REVIVED.

See Voss, Jenny.

GIBBS, RICHARD.

The New Disorders of Love. A Gallant Novel. Written by Richard Gibbs, *etc. For R. Bentley and S. Magnes.* 1687. 12°.

In *Modern Novels*, vol. iv.
　B.M. (12410. c. 21).

GILLIAN, *of Croydon.*

The Pleasant and Delightful History of Gillian of Croydon : Containing . . . the tragical History of William and Margaret . . . Illustrated with suitable Cuts. The Whole done much after the same Method as those celebrated Novels. By Mrs. Eliza Haywood. *For A. Bettesworth.* 1727. 12°.

　B.M. (12410. a. 28).

GLANVILL, JOSEPH.

Essays on Several Important Subjects in Philosophy and Religion, *etc. J. D. for J. Baker and H. Mortlock.* 1676. 4°.

Essay vii is "Anti-fanatical Religion, and Free Philosophy. In a Continuation of the New Atlantis."
　B.M. (480. a. 14).

GOERTZ, HENRY, *Baron* DE.

See DEFOE, Daniel.

GOLDEN EAGLE.

The History of the Golden-Eagle : Being Both delightfull and profitable. Written by Philaquila. *For W. Thackeray.* 1672. 4°. 𝕭.𝕷.

　Priv. Lib.

[Another edition.] *For W. Thackeray.* 1677. 4°. 𝕭.𝕷.
　B.M. (12613. c. 11).

[Another edition.] The Famous and Delightful History of the Golden Eagle, *etc. W. O[nley].* 4°.

　Bodl. (Douce R. 528).

GOLDEN SPY.

See MONTE SOCIO, Carlo.

GOMBERVILLE, *le Sieur* DE.

See LE ROY, Marin.

GOMEZ, MADELEINE ANGÉLIQUE POISSON DE.

La Belle Assemblée: Or, The Adventures of Six Days . . . Written in French . . . by Madam de Gomez. Translated into English. Compleat, in three Parts. The Second Edition. *For D. Browne junr., and S. Chapman.* 1725. 8°. 3 vols.

> B.M. (12511. f. 25).

[Another edition.] In Two Volumes. The Second Edition. Adorn'd with Copper-Plates. *For D. Brown, W. Bickerton, and J. Pote.* 1728. 12°. 2 vols.

> B.M. (635. a. 27, 28).

[Another edition.] In Four Volumes. The Second Edition. *For D. Browne, W. Bickerton, T. Astley and F. Cogan.* 1735. 12°. 4 vols.

> B.M. (12512. c. 12), vol. 4 only.

[Another edition.] The Fourth Edition. *For J. Brotherton, J. Hazard, W. Meadows, T. Cox, W. Hinchcliffe, D. Browne, W. Bickerton, T. Astley, S. Austen, L. Gilliver, R. Willock and F. Cogan.* 1736. 12°. 4 vols.

> B.M. (12512. c. 12), vols. 1–3 only.

L'Entretien des Beaux Esprits. Being the Sequel to La Belle Assemblée . . . Written . . . by Madame de Gomez, *etc. For F. Cogan and J. Nourse.* 1734. 12°. 2 vols.

> Translated by Mrs. Haywood.
> B.M. (12512. c. 12).

The Persian Anecdotes: Or Secret Memoirs of the Court of Persia, *etc. For W. Bickerton.* 1730. 8°.

> B.M. (1080. m. 35).

GONDEZ, *Countess* DE.

See LUSSAN, Marguerite de.

GONZALEZ, ESTEVANILLO.

The Comical History of Estevanille Gonzalez, Surnamed the Merry Fellow. Translated from the Original Spanish by Monsieur Le Sage, Author of the Devil upon Two Sticks.   Done out of French.   *For W. Mears and sold by Mr. Strahan.*   1735.   12°.

B.M. (12510. bbb. 18).

See SPANISH LIBERTINES.

GOTT, SAMUEL.

Novae Solymae Libri Sex.   *Typis J. Legati.*   1648.   8°.

Attributed to Milton in the edition by W. Begley.   The author's name occurs in a publisher's list.   *Cf.* paper by S. K. Jones, in *The Library*, July, 1910.
B.M. (C. 62. a. 7).

[Another issue.]   Nova Solyma Sive Institutio Christiani, *etc.*   *Typis J. Legati et venundantur per T. Underhill.*   1649.   8°.

Begley, vol. i., p. 6.

GOVERNOR OF CYPRUS.   *See* VIROTTO AND DOROTHEA.

GRACIAN, BALTASAR.

The Critick.   Written Originally in Spanish ; By Lorenzo Gracian One of the Best Wits of Spain, And Translated into English, By Paul Rycaut Esq ; *T. N. for H. Brome.*   1681.   8°.

B.M. (836. d. 32).

GRAHAM, RICHARD, *Viscount Preston.*

Angliae Speculum Morale . . . with the Life of Theodatus, and Three Novels, viz. The Land-Mariners, Friendship Sublimed, and The Friendly Rivals.   *For H. Herringman.*   1670.   8°.

B.M. (12352. c. 40).

GRAND VIZIER.   *See* PRÉCHAC, *le Sieur* de.

GRENADINE, SEBASTIAN.

Homais Queen of Tunis, Novel.   By Sebastian Grenadine.   *For Simon the Afrikan. Amsterdam.*   [*R. Bentley: London?*]   1681.   12°.

In *Modern Novels*, vol. i.
B.M. (12410. c. 18).

GRIGG, William.

The Life and Humorous Adventures of William Grigg of Snarlton in Suffolk . . . Published from the Original Manuscript, preserved in the Grubstreet Vatican.   By a Native of Grubstreet.   *For T. Cooper.*   1733.   8°.

Part 1.
B.M. (12315. e. 30).

GRIMALKIN.

Grimalkin, or, The Rebel-Cat.   A Novell.   Representing the Unwearied Attempts of the Beasts of his Faction Against Sovereignty and Succession Since the Death of the Lyons in the Tower.   *For the Author.*   1681.   Fol.

A satire on Shaftesbury.
B.M. (12350. m. 5).

GUARDIAN'S INSTRUCTION.

See PENTON, Stephen.

GUEULLETTE, Thomas Simon.

Chinese Tales: or, the Wonderful Adventures of the Mandarin Fum Hoam.   Made English by Mr. Macky.

Advertised by J. Roberts in 1725; also by H. Curll ("translated by Mr. Stackhouse").

Mogul Tales, or The Dreams of Men Awake: Being Stories told to divert the Sultana's of Guzarat, for the supposed Death of the Sultan.   Written in French by the celebrated Mr. Guellettee [*sic*], Author of the Chinese Tales, &c.   Now first Translated into English.   In Two Volumes; adorned with proper Cuts, *etc.*   *J. Applebee, for J. Brindley, J. Jolliffe, and C. Corbett.* 1736.   8°.   2 vols.

The *Mille et une Soirées.*
B.M. (1076. i. 43).

Peruvian Tales, Related, in One Thousand and One Hours, By One of the Select Virgins of Cusco, to the Ynca of Peru . . .   Translated from the Original French, By Samuel Humphreys, Esq.   1734.   12°.

Bodl. (Douce T. 230).

GUIDO'S GHOST.

Guido's Ghost.   A Tale.   By J. H. Esq.   *For J. Brindley.*   1738.
Gentleman's Magazine, Jan., 1738.

GULLIVER, LEMUEL.

See ARBUTHNOT, John; SWIFT, Jonathan; VAIRASSE D'ALLAIS, Denys.

GURTHIE, JAMES.

The Life and Heroick Actions of the Eighth Champion of Christendom. With a Particular Account of his Combat with the Man in the Moon . . . By James Gurthie, Biographer. *For Webb.* 1739. 8°.

A political satire.
B.M. (12603. aa. 10).

GUY OF WARWICK.

[Parker's version.]
Licensed ("in prose by Martyn Parker") to Oulton, 24 Nov., 1640. Hazlitt, H. 439; *Stat. Reg., MS.*

[Smithson's version.] The Famous History of Guy Earl of Warwick. By Samuel Smithson, *etc. For F. Coles, T. Vere, J. Wright, and J. Clarke.* 8°. 𝕭.𝕴.
Bodl. (Wood 254/2).

[Another edition.] *For J. Clark, W. Thackeray, and T. Passinger.* 1686. 8°.
Pepys 362 (953).

[Shurley's version.] The Renowned History, or the Life and Death of Guy Earl of Warwick, Containing His Noble Exploits and Victories. *H. Brugis for P. Brooksby.* 1681. 4°.

The Preface is signed John Shurley.
B.M. (12403. aa. 35).

[Another edition.] *For P. Brooksby.* 1685. 4°. 𝕭.𝕴.
Pepys 1192/9.

[Another edition.] *A. M. for P. Brooksby.* 1695. 4°. 𝕭.𝕴.
Hazlitt, I. 194.

[Another edition.] 1703.
Hazlitt, H. 247 (Roxburgh).

[Another edition.] *Printed by A. M. for C. Bates, and by J. Foster.* 4°.
Bodl. (Gough Warwick 3).

[Another edition?] *For C. Bates.* 4°.
Identical with the preceding or the following?
Hazlitt, H. 247.

[An abridgement of Shurley's version.]   The History of the Famous
Exploits of Guy Earl of Warwick, *etc.   For C. Bates.*   4°.   𝕭.𝕷.

> B.M. (12450. f. 8).

[Another edition.]   *For S. Bates.*   4°.

> B.M. (12403. d. 1.)

[A different version.]   The Famous History of Guy of Warwick.   Written
by Samuel Rowland [*sic*].   *For G. Conyers.*   8°.

> Turned into prose from Rowlands' verse.
> B.M. (G. 18792/2).

[G. L.'s version.]   The Noble and Renowned History of Guy Earl of
Warwick . . .   Extracted from Authentick Records ; and the whole Illustrated with Cuts suitable to the History.   *W. O*[*nley*] *for E. B*[*rewster*].
1706.   12°.

> The Dedication is signed G. L.
> B.M. (12450. b. 16).

[Another edition.]   *W. O*[*nley*] *for E. B*[*rewster*] *and sold by A. Bettes-*
worth.   1706.   12°.

> Hazlitt, H. 247.

[Another edition.]   The Fifth Edition.   *For A. Bettesworth.*   12°.

> B.M. (12450. b. 17).

[Another edition.]   The Seventh Edition.   *For A. Bettesworth and*
C. Hitch.   1733.   12°.

> B.M. (12430. a. 9).

H., J.   *See* GUIDO'S GHOST.

H., T.
See WHITTINGTON, *Sir* Richard.

HAIRY GIANTS.
See SCHOOTEN, Hendrik van.

HANOVER TALES.
Hanover Tales, the Secret History of Count Fradonia and the unfortunate
Baritia.

> Advertised by E. Curll in *The Female Deserters*, 1719.

HAPPY SLAVE.
See BRÉMOND, Gabriel de.

HAPPY UNFORTUNATE.
The Happy Unfortunate: a Novel.   1732.

Gentleman's Magazine, March, 1732.

HARRINGTON, JAMES.
The Common-Wealth of Oceana.   *J. Streater, for L. Chapman.*   1656.   Fol.

A second title gives the author's name.
B.M. (521. k. 10).

[Another edition.]   *For D. Pakeman.*   1658.   Fol.

Bodl. (Ashm. G. 6).

[Another edition.]   The Oceana of James Harrington, and his other works. . . .   The whole Collected, Methodiz'd, and Review'd, With An Exact Account of his Life Prefix'd, By John Toland.   *Printed, and are to be sold by the Booksellers.*   1700.   Fol.

B.M. (521. m. 17).

[Another edition.]   The Oceana and other works of James Harrington Esq. . . .   To which is added, An Appendix, containing all the Political Tracts wrote by this Author, Omitted in Mr. Toland's Edition, *etc.   For A. Millar.*   1737.   Fol.

B.M. (523. m. 4).

[Another edition.]   The Oceana of James Harrington, Esq; And His Other Works, *etc.   R. Reilly, for J. Smith and W. Bruce: Dublin.*   1737.   Fol.

B.M. (12268. i. 6).

HARVIDES AND LUPELLA.
The History of Harvides and Lupella.   1733.

Probably a satire on Lord Hervey and his wife, *née* Mary Lepell.
Advertised by J. Roberts in *Mama Oello,* 1733 ; *Gentleman's Magazine,* August, 1733.

HATTIGE.
See BRÉMOND, Gabriel de.

HAWKWOOD, *Sir* JOHN.

The Honour of the Taylors ; Or, The Famous and Renowned History of Sir John Hawkwood, Knight . . .   Illustrated with Pictures, *etc.   A. Milbourn, for W. Whitwood.*   1687.   4°.

B.M. (12620. d. 5).

[Another edition.]
Advertised by W. Thackeray in 1689.

[Another edition.]   Merchant Taylors' Renown, or, The famous and delightful History of Sir John Hawkwood, Knight.

Advertised by B. Deacon in *The Seven Champions.*

See also WINSTANLEY, William.

HAYCOCK, POLLY.

The Fortunate Transport ; Or, The Secret History of the Life and Adventures of the Celebrated Polly Haycock, The Lady of the Gold Watch.   By a Creole, *etc.   For T. Taylor.*   8°.

B.M. (635. f. 11/10).

HAYWOOD, ELIZA.

Secret Histories, *etc.*   1724.   4 vols.

D.N.B.

[Another edition.]   Secret Histories, Novels and Poems.   In Four Volumes.   Written by Mrs. Eliza Haywood . . .   The Second Edition.   *For D. Browne, Jun., and S. Chapman.*   1725.   12°.   4 vols.

VOL. 1, *Love in Excess*, ed. 6, 1725 ;   VOL. 2, *The British Recluse*, ed. 3, 1725, *The Injur'd Husband*, with half-title only, *Poems*, ed. 2, 1725 ;   VOL. 3, *Idalia*, ed. 3, 1725, *The Surprise*, ed. 2, 1725, *The Fatal Secret*, ed. 3, 1725, *Fantomina*, 1725 ;   VOL. 4, *The Rash Resolve*, ed. 3, *The Masqueraders, Lasselia, The Force of Nature*, all with half-titles only.

B.M. (12612. ee. 8), the *British Recluse* in vol. 2 wanting title-page.

[Another issue of vols. 2, 3.]   *For D. Browne, jun., and S. Chapman.*   1725.   12°.   2 vols.

Vol. 1 is a duplicate of vol. 3, vol. 2 of vol. 2 of the preceding, with a new general title-page.   In vol. 2 *The Injur'd Husband* has a half-title instead of the title-page.

B.M. (12614. c. 14).

[Another edition.] The Third Edition. *For A. Bettesworth and C. Hitch,*
D. Browne, T. Astley, and T. Green. 1732. 12°. 4 vols.

VOL. 1, *Love in Excess*, ed. 7; VOL. 2, *The British Recluse*, ed. 4, *The Injur'd Husband,*
ed. 4, *Poems*, ed. 3; VOL. 3, *Idalia*, ed. 4, *The Surprise*, ed. 3, *The Fatal Secret*, ed. 4,
Fantomina, ed. 3; VOL. 4, *The Rash Resolve, The Masqueraders, Lasselia, The Force*
of Nature. The novels have half-titles only.

B.M. (012612. df. 48). *The Rash Resolve* in vol. 4 wants title-page.

The Agreeable Caledonian: or, Memoirs of Signiora di Morella . . .
Intermix'd with Many other Entertaining little Histories and Adventures
which presented themselves to her in the Course of her Travels, *etc. For*
R. King; And Sold by W. Meadows, T. Green, J. Stone, J. Jackson, and
J. Watson. 1728, 9. 8°.

The Dedication is signed Eliza Haywood.

Bodl. (Godw. Pamph. 2121/6, 7).

Bath-Intrigues: in four Letters to a Friend in London. *For J. Roberts.*
1725. 8°.

Signed J. B.   Roberts' list gives three of Mrs. Haywood's novels as by the same author.

B.M. (1080. i. 42).

The British Recluse: Or, The Secret History of Cleomira, Suppos'd Dead.
A Novel . . . The Second Edition. *For D. Brown, Jun., W. Chetwood and*
J. Woodman, and S. Chapman. 1722. 8°.

B.M. (635. f. 11/4).

The third and fourth editions are part of *Secret Histories*, 1725 and 1732; the former has
a separate title-page and imprint.

[Another edition.] The British Recluse . . . And The Injur'd Husband:
Or, The Mistaken Resentment. ·Two Novels. Written by Mrs. Eliza
Haywood . . . The Third Edition. *J. Watts: Dublin.* 1724. 8°.

B.M. (12611. f. 10).

Clarina. *See* FEMALE DUNCIAD.

Cleomelia: or, the Generous Mistress. Being The Secret History of a
Lady Lately arriv'd from Bengal . . . By Mᴿˢ· Eliza Haywood. To which is
added, I. The Lucky Rape: or, Fate the best Disposer. II. The Capricious
Lover: or, No Trifling with a Woman . . . The Second Edition. *For*
J. Millan, and sold by J. Roberts, H. Northoock, and the next Bookseller to the
Horse Guards. 1727. 4°.

Bodl. (Godw. Pamph. 1308).

The Fair Hebrew : Or, A True, but Secret History of Two Jewish Ladies, Who lately resided in London. *For J. Brindley, W. Meadows and J. Walthoe, A. Bettesworth, T. Astley, T. Worral, J. Lewis, J. Penn, and R. Walker.* 1729.   8°.

> B.M. (635. f. 1/8).

[Another edition.] The Second Edition. *For J. Brindley, W. Meadows and J. Walthoe, A. Bettesworth, T. Astley, T. Worral, J. Lewis, J. Penn and R. Walker.* 1729.   8°.

> B.M. (12614. d. 8).

Fantomima.

> Part of *Secret Histories*, 1725, with a separate title-page and imprint ; the third edition is part of *Secret Histories*, 1732.

The Fatal Secret : or, Constancy in Distress.   1725.

> *D.N.B.*

[Another edition.]   The Second Edition.

> Advertised by J. Roberts in *Bath Intrigues*, 1725.
>
> The third and fourth editions are part of *Secret Histories*, 1725 and 1732 ; the former has a separate title-page and imprint.

The Fruitless Enquiry.   Being a Collection of several Entertaining Histories And Occurrences, Which Fell under the Observation of a Lady in her Search after Happiness.   By Mrs. E. Haywood, *etc.   For J. Stephens.* 1727.   12°.

> Bodl. (8°. B. 433. Linc.).

Idalia : Or, The Unfortunate Mistress.   A Novel.   Written by Mrs. Eliza Haywood.   *For D. Browne junr ; W. Chetwood ; and S. Chapman.* 1723.   8°.

> B.M. (12614. d. 10).
> The third and fourth editions are part of *Secret Histories*, 1725 and 1732 ; the former has a separate title-page and imprint.   For a continuation of *Idalia*, see E. Gosse, *Gossip in a Library*, p. 168.

The Injured Husband, or the Mistaken Resentment.

> Advertised by W. Chetwood in 1722, also by D. Browne in Fénélon, *Fables*, 1723.

[Another edition.]   The Second Edition.

> Advertised by D. Browne and S. Chapman in *Lasselia*, ed. 2, 1724.
> The third edition (not so called) and the fourth are part of *Secret Histories*, 1725 and 1732.

Lasselia : Or, The Self-Abandoned. A Novel. Written by Mrs. Eliza Haywood . . . The Second Edition. *For D. Browne junr., and S. Chapman.* 1724. 8º.

B.M. (12613. c. 26/1).

Letters of a Lady of Quality to a Chevalier. 1724.

D.N.B.

The Life of Madam De Villesache. Written by a Lady, who was an Eye-witness of the greatest part of her Adventures, and faithfully Translated from her French Manuscript. By Mrs. Eliza Haywood, *etc. For W. Feales, and sold by J. Roberts.* 1727. 8º.

Bodl. (Godw. Pamph. 2121/4).

Love in Excess.

Advertised by W. Chetwood in 1722, and also by D. Browne, in Fénélon, *Fables*, 1723.

[Another edition.] Love in Excess, or the Fatal Enquiry. The Fourth Edition, corrected.

Advertised by D. Browne and S. Chapman in 1724.

[Another edition.] The Fifth Edition. 1724.

D.N.B.

The sixth and seventh editions are part of *Secret Histories*, 1725 and 1732 ; the former has a separate title and imprint.

The Masqueraders ; or Fatal Curiosity : being the Secret History of a Late Amour. *For J. Roberts.* 1724. 8º.

B.M. (12614. d. 14).

[Another edition. *For J. Roberts?*] 8º.

B.M. (635. f. 11/11) imperfect, wanting the title-page.

Memoirs of a Certain Island Adjacent to the Kingdom of Utopia. Written by a Celebrated Author of that Country. Now translated into English. 1725, 26. 8º. 2 vols.

B.M. (12613. g. 18).

The Mercenary Lover : Or, The Unfortunate Heiresses. Being a True Secret History of a City Amour. By the Author of Reflections on the various Effects of Love . . . The Third Edition. To which is added, The Padlock, or, No Guard without Virtue. A Novel. *For N. Dobb.* 1728. 12º.

The half-title gives the author's initials.

B.M. (12316. bbb. 38/3).

Persecuted Virtue.   A Novel.   1729.

D.N.B. ;   advertised by J. Millan, in *Letters from a Persian*, 1735.

Philidore and Placentia.   1727.

D.N.B.

The Rash Resolve : Or, The Untimely Discovery.   A Novel.   In Two Parts.   By Mrs. Eliza Haywood . . . The Second Edition.   *For D. Browne, jun*., and S. Chapman.*   1724.   8°.

B.M. (12613. c. 26/2).

The third edition is part of *Secret Histories*, 1725, but has a separate title-page and imprint.

The Secret History of the Present Intrigues of the Court of Caramania. The Second Edition Corrected.   1727.   8°.

B.M. (838. c. 7).

A Spy on the Conjurer.   Or, a Collection of Surprising and Diverting Stories, with Merry and Ingenious Letters.   By way of Memoirs of the Famous Mr. Duncan Campbell . . .   Written . . . by a Lady . . .   Revised by Mrs. Eliz. Haywood.   *For W. Ellis, J. Brotherton, J. Batty, T. Woodward, J. Fox.*   1725.   8°.

Bodl. (Hope 8°. 950).

[Another edition?]   A Collection of Stories, surprising and diverting, *etc.* 1725.   8°.

Dealer's list.

The Surprize : or Constancy Rewarded.   1725.

D.N.B. ;   advertised by J. Roberts in *Bath Intrigues*, 1725.

The second and third editions are part of *Secret Histories*, 1725 and 1732 ; the former has a separate title-page and imprint.

The Tea-Table ;   or, A Conversation between some Polite Persons of both Sexes, at a Lady's Visiting Day . . .   Interspersed with several Entertaining and Instructive Stories.   By Mrs. Eliza Haywood.   *J. Roberts.* 1725.   8°.

B.M. (635. f. 11/5).

The Unequal Conflict: Or, Nature Triumphant.   A Novel.   By Mrs. Eliza Haywood.

Advertised by J. Crokatt in Symmons' *Whimsical Lovers*, 1725.

See GILLIAN, *of Croydon.*

HEAD, RICHARD.

[The English Rogue, Part I.] The English Rogue described, in the Life of Meriton Latroon, A Witty Extravagant. Being a compleat History of the most Eminent Cheats of Both Sexes. *For H. Marsh.* 1665. 8°.

B.M. (C. 70. b. 4).

[Another edition.] *For F. Kirkman.* 1666. 8°.

Bodl. (Arch. Bodl. B. I. 75).

[Another edition.] *For F. Kirkman.* 1667. 8°.

Priv. Lib.

[Another edition.] *For F. Kirkman, and are to be sold by him and T. Dring the younger.* 1668. 8°.

Priv. Lib.

[Part 2.] The English Rogue, Continued, in the Life of Meriton Latroon, and other Extravagants. Comprehending the Most Eminent Cheats of Most Trades and Professions. The Second Part. *Printed for F. Kirkman.* 1668. 8°.

By Francis Kirkman.
The author's name occurs at the end of the dedicatory epistle.
Priv. Lib.

[Parts 1–4.] *For F. Kirkman.* 1671. 8°.

Parts 1, 4, *Term Cat.* ; Part 2, Bodl. (Malone 538) ; Part 3, Priv. Lib.

[Another edition of part 3.] *A. Johnson for F. Kirkman.* 1674. 8°.

Bodl. (Malone 539.)

[Another edition of parts 1–4.] *For F. Kirkman, and are to be sold by W. Rands.* 1680. 8°. 4 vols.

Parts 1, 2, B.M. (12613. c. 21.) ; parts 1, 4, Bodl. (Malone 538, 539) ; *cf.* D.N.B., Art. Kirkman.

[An abridgement of part 1.] The Life and Death of the English Rogue; Or, His Last Legacy to the World . . . To which is added an Alphabetical Canting Dictionary, *etc. For C. Passinger.* 1679. 4°.

Pepys 1192 (20).

[Another edition.] *T. Norris.* 4°.

Bodl. (Malone 689).

[Another edition.]   The English Rogue, Containing a brief Discovery of the most Eminent Cheats, Robberies, and other Extravagancies, by him Committed, *etc.   For J. Blare.*   1688.   8°.   𝕭.𝕴.

Bodl. (Wood 284.)

[A different abridgement of parts 1–4, with part 5.]   The English Rogue : or, Witty Extravagant : Described in the Life of Meriton Latroon . . . The Four Parts.   To which is added a Fifth Part, compleating the whole History of his Life, *etc.   For J. Back.*   1688.   12°.

The Preface is signed M.L.
Bodl. (Douce L. 545).

[Another edition.]   The Third Edition.   *For J. Back.*   1693.   12°.

Term Cat., ii. 485.

[Another edition.]   The Fourth Edition with additions.   *For J. Back.* 1697.

Term Cat., iii. 46.

[Another edition.]   The Fourth Edition, with large Additions, further compleating the whole History of his Life.   *J. Phillpott : Gosport.*   12°.

B.M. (12614. a. 15).

[Another edition.]   The Fifth Edition with large additions.   *For J. Back.* 1701.

Term Cat., iii. 279.

[Another edition.]   The Seventh Edition, with large Additions, farther compleating the whole History of his Life.   *T. Norris.*   1723.   12°.

B.M. (12611. de. 17).

The Floating Island : or, a New Discovery, relating The strange Adventure on a late Voyage, from Lambethana to Villa Franca, alias Ramallia, To the Eastward of Terra del Templo . . .   Describing the Nature of the Inhabitants, their Religion, Laws and Customs.   Published by Franck Careless, one of the Discoverers, *etc.*   1673.   4°.

B.M. (12330. e. 9).

The Life and Death of Mother Shipton.   *For W. Harris.*   1667.   4°.

Reprint, Manchester [1881].

[Another edition.]   *For B. Harris.*   1677.   4°.

Term Cat., i. 316.

[Another edition.] The Life and Death of Mother Shipton ... Strangely preserved amongst other writings belonging to an old Monastry in York-shire, and now Published for the Information of Posterity. *For B. Harris.* 1684. 4°. 𝕭.𝕷.

> B.M. (8631. aaa. 12).

[Another edition.] *For W. Harris.* 1687. 8°.

> Bodl. (Douce Adds 135/1).

[Another edition.] *For J. Back.* 1694. 4°.

> *Term Cat.*, ii. 514.

[Another edition.] *W. Onley for J. Back.* 1697. 4°. 𝕭.𝕷.

> Priv. Lib.

See also SHIPTON, Ursula, *Mother.*

The Miss Displayed, *etc.* 1683.

> Bodl. (Douce M. 511).

News from the Stars, by Meriton Latroon. 1673. 12°.

> Lowndes, 1020.

Nugæ Venales : or a Complaisant Companion. Being New Jests . . . Pleasant Novels and Miscellanies. The Third Edition Corrected, With many New Additions. By Richard Head, Author of the English Rogue. *For E. Poole.* 1686. 8°.

> B.M. (12315. a. 34).

The Western Wonder : Or, O Brazeel, An Inchanted Island discovered ; With a Relation of Two Ship-wracks in a dreadful Sea-storm in that discovery. To which is added, A description of a Place, called, Montecapernia, *etc.* *For N. C.* 1674. 4°.

> B.M. (601. f. 14/10).

HEARNE, *Mrs.*

Honour the Victory, and Love the Prize. Ten Novels.

> Advertised by H. Curll in 1726.

HECTOR.

The Famous and Renowned History of Hector, Prince of Troy. Or The Three Destructions of Troy. [*For C. Bates.*] 4°.

> Bates' list is printed at the end.
> B.M. (12612. d. 7).

HELIOTROPOLIS.

The Comical History of the Life and Death of Mumper, Generalissimo of King Charles II.'s Dogs. Written by Heliotropolis, Secretary to the Emperor of the Moon. 1704. 4°.

> *Term Cat.*, iii. 411.

HELVETIAN HERO.

The Adventures of the Helvetian Hero, with the Young Countess of Albania ; Or, The Amours of Armadorus and Vicentina : A Novel, *etc. For R. Taylor.* 1694. 8°.

> B.M. (12612. de. 11).

HENRIETTA, *Princess.*

The Amours of Madame, and the Count de Guiche. Translated into English, by a Person of Quality. *For B. C : Obedience.* 1680. 12°.

> *Term Cat.*, i. 393 (for R. Bentley and W. Cademan).
> B.M. (1080. b. 24).

HENRY VIII.

The Pleasant and Delightful History of King Henry 8th. and a Cobler, *etc. For C. Dennisson.* 8°. 𝕭.𝕷.

> Bodl. (Wood 254).

[Another edition.] The Cobler turned Courtier. Being a Pleasant Humour between King Henry the Eighth and a Cobler. *For F. Haley.* 1680. 4°.

> B.M. (12316. c. 42).

[Another edition.] The First Part of the King and Cobler, *etc. Robert Brown : Edinburgh.* 1733. 8°.

> B.M. (11621. b. 31/3).

[Another edition of both parts.] *Sold in Pearson's Close : Edinburgh.* 1734, 33. 8°. 2 vols.

> B.M. (12331. e. 43/1, 2).

The Pleasant and Delightful History of King Henry the VIII. and The Abbot of Reading, *etc. J. M. for C. Dennisson.* 8°. 𝕭.𝕷.

> Bodl. (Wood 254).

HERCULES.

The Famous and Renowned History of the Life and Glorious Actions of the Mighty Hercules of Greece, *etc.*   4°.   𝕭.𝕷.

Priv. Lib., the imprint cut away.

[Another edition.]   *For S. Bates.*   4°.

B.M. (12430. c. 13).

HERICK, Nicholas.

See Five Wise Philosophers.

HERMIT.

See Quarll, Philip.

HERO AND LEANDER.

The Famous and Renowned History of the Two Unfortunate, tho Noble, Lovers, Hero and Leander, *etc.*   *J. White : Newcastle.*   4°.

The preface is signed J. S.
B.M. (1077. g. 34).

HEROINE MUSKETEER.

See Préchac, *le Sieur* de.

HICKATHRIFT, Thomas.

The Pleasant History of Thomas Hic-ka-thrift.   *J. M. for W. Thackeray and T. Passinger.*   8°.   𝕭.𝕷.

Bodl. (Wood 259/11).

[Another edition.]   *For W. Thackeray.*   12°.   𝕭.𝕷.

Hazlitt, H. 610 ; perhaps the same as the preceding.

HIND, James.

No Jest like a true Jest : Being a Compendious Record of the Merry Life, and Mad Exploits of Capt. James Hind, The Great Rober [*sic*] of England, *etc.*   *A. P. for T. Vere.*   1674.

Reprint, 1817.

[Another edition.]   *For J. Deacon.*   8°.   𝕭.𝕷.

Pepys 363 (41).

See FIDGE, George ; YORKSHIRE ROGUE.

HIPPOLITO AND AMYNTA.

Hippolito and Amynta.

Advertised by A. Bettesworth and C. Hitch in 1733.

HIPPOLITO AND DORINDA.

The Force of Nature ; or the Loves of Hippolito and Dorinda.   A Romance.
Translated from the French Original, and never before printed in English.
R. Raikes and W. Dicey : Northampton.   1720.   8°.

The running title is : The History of Prospero, Duke of Milan.
   B.M. (1078. i. 29/2).

HYPPOLYTUS, *Earl of Douglas.*

See LA MOTHE, Marie Catherine, *Comtesse d'Aulnoy.*

HOLLAND, SAMUEL.

Don Zara Del Fogo : A Mock-Romance.   Written Originally in the Brittish
Tongue, and made English by a person of much Honor, Basilius Musophilus,
etc.   T. W. for T. Vere.   1656.   8°.

With a dedication, but no frontispiece.
   B.M. (12612. de. 9).

[Another issue.]   Wit and Fancy In a Maze . . .   A Mock-Romance . . .
Written originally in the British Tongue, and made English by a person of
much Honor.   *T. W. for T. Vere.*   1656.   12°.

With a frontispiece, but no dedication.
   B.M. (12613. a. 31).

[Another edition.]   Romancio-Mastrix, or a Romance on Romances . . .
By Samuel Holland, Gent.   *For the Author.*   1660.   8°.

   B.M. (G. 16418).

[Another edition.]   The Spaniard : or, Don Zara del Fogo : Translated
from the Original Spanish by Basilius Musopilus.   With Notes to Explain the
true Meaning of the Author, *etc.   For W. Chetwood, and R. Francklin, and
sold by J. Roberts.*   1719.   8°.

   B.M. (12490. e. 14).

HOOD, ROBIN.

The Noble Birth and Gallant Atchievements of that Remarkable Out-Law Robin Hood. Together with a true Account of the many Merry and Extravagant Exploits he play'd, in twelve severall Stories . . . Newly collected into one Volume by an Ingenious Antiquary. *For T. Vere and W. Gilbertson.* 1662. 4°. 𝕭.𝕷.

Priv. Lib.

[Another edition.] *J. M. and are to be sold by J. Deacon.* 4°. 𝕭.𝕷.

Bodl. (Wood 321).

[Another edition?]

Advertised by B. Deacon in *The Seven Champions.*

[Another edition.] The Whole Life, and Merry Exploits of bold Robin Hood : Earl of Huntington, *etc. J. Willis.* [1712?] 12°.

The date is from a MS. note.

B.M. (1077. b. 59).

[Another edition.] With the whole History of Johnny Armstrong of Westmoreland. *For A. Bettesworth, C. Hitch, R. Ware, and J. Hodges.* 1737. 12°.

Bodl. (Douce H. 41).

HOUDART DE LA MOTTE, Antoine.

One Hundred New Court Fables, Written for the Instruction of Princes, And a True Knowledge of the World . . . By the Sieur De La Motte. Made English from the Paris Edition, By Mr. Samber. *For E. Curll and T. Jauncy.* 1721. 12°.

B.M. (12305. ccc. 52).

HOWARD, Thomas.

The History of the Seven Wise Mistrisses of Rome. *For M. Wright.* 1663. 8°. 𝕭.𝕷.

* Priv. Lib.

[Another edition.] *For D. Newman, etc.* 1684. 12°.

Hazlitt, H. 660.

[Another edition.]   The History Of the Seven Wise Mistresses of
Rome. Whose Names were Halicuja, Penthesilia, Mardula, Debora,
Cicre [*sic*], Dejanira, Boadicia, *etc.   For M. Wotton, and G. Conyers.* 1686.
8°. 𝕭.𝕷.

The epistle is signed Tho. Howard.
  Pepys 364 (629).

[Another edition.]   1688.   8°.   𝕭.𝕷.

Hazlitt, H. 660.

[Another edition.]   *W. O[nley] for G. Conyers.*   8°.

B.M. (1154. d. 16).

[Another edition.]   Roman Stories : or, the History of the Seven
Wise Mistresses of Rome . . . Newly Corrected, and better Explained, and
Enlarged . . . The Two and Twentieth Edition.   *A. W. for G. Conyers.*
12°.

Bodl. (Douce R. 23).

[Another edition.]

Advertised by J. Hodges and J. Johnston, in *The Seven Wise Masters,* n.d.

HUET, PIERRE DANIEL.

Diana de Castro ; A Novel.   Written Originally in French.   By Mr. Huet,
Antient Bishop of Avranches.   *For A. Vandenhoeck.*   [1724?]   12°.

The date is taken from a MS. note.
  B.M. (12517. aa. 13).

HUSBAND.

The Husband Forc'd to be Jealous, Or The good fortune of those Women
that have jealous Husbands.   A Translation by N. H.   *For H. Herringman.*
1668.   8°.

B.M. (1081. d. 28).

I., N.

See INGELO, Nathaniel.

ILDEGERTE.

See LE NOBLE DE TENNELIÈRE, Eustache.

ILLEGAL LOVERS.

The Illegal Lovers ; a True Secret History.   Being an Amour Between A Person of Condition and his Sister.   Written by One who did reside in the Family.   *For W. Trott.*   1728.   8°.

B.M. (1079. i. 12/1).

ILLUSTRIOUS LOVERS.

The Illustrious Lovers, Or Princely Adventures in the Courts of England and France.   Containing Sundry Transactions relating to Love-Intrigues . . . Written Originaly [*sic*] in French, and now Done into English.   *For W. Whitwood.*   1686.   8°.

Hazlitt, II. 368.

ILLUSTRIOUS SHEPHERDESS.

See MONTALBAN, Juan Perez de.

INCOGNITA.

See CONGREVE, William.

INCONSTANT LOVER.

The Inconstant-Lover : An Excellent Romance.   Translated out of French. *For T. Dring.*   1671.   8°.

Perhaps a translation of Chavigny's *L'Amant parjure, ou la fidélité à l'épreuve.*

B.M. (012550. g. 17.)

INDIAN TALES.

See ZELOIDE.

INGELO, NATHANIEL.

Bentivolio and Urania, in Four Books.   By N. I. D.D.   *J. G. for R. Marriot.*   1660.   Fol.

In Four Books.

B.M. (12403. g. 2).

[Another issue.]   *J. G. for R. Marriot.*   1660, 64.   Fol.   2 vols.

The first volume is a duplicate of the preceding, except for the last two pages.   Vol. 2, containing Books 5 and 6, is new.

B.M. (635. l. 21).

[Another edition.]   In Six Books.   By Nathaniel Ingelo, D.D.   The Second Edition, *etc.*   1669.   Fol.

   Priv. Lib.

[Another edition.]   The Third Edition, with some Amendments.   Wherein all the Obscure Words throughout the Book are interpreted in the Margin, which makes this much more delightful to read than the former Editions. *T. R. for R. Marriott, and are to be sold by B. Tooke.*   1673.   Fol.

   B.M. (12612. i. 6).

[Another edition.]   The Fourth Edition, with large Amendments, *etc. A. M. and R. R. for D. Newman.*   1682.   Fol.

   B.M. (12612. i. 11).

INHUMAN HUSBAND.

See VAUDRAY, *le Chevalier* de.

INTRIGUES.

The Intrigues of Love.   A Novel.   Written originally in French, and newly translated into English by P. Lorrain.   *Sold by F. Gardiner.*   1682.   8°.

   Perhaps the *Intrigues galantes de la Cour de France*, by le Sieur Vannel.
      Term Cat., i. 476.

[Another version of the same ?]   Intrigues of Love, or The Amours and Gallantries of the French Court during the Reign of the Amorus [*sic*] and warlike Prince Henry IV . . .   Newly made English from the French, by Sir Edwin Sadleir, Baronet.   *Sold by B. Crayle.*   1689.   12°.

      Term Cat., ii. 250.

IRISH ROGUE.

The Irish Rogue, or The Comical History of the Life and Actions of Teague O'Divelley, from his Birth to This present Year, 1690.   *For G. Conyers.* [1690.]   12°.

   B.M. (1079. b. 5).

ISMENIA.   *See* PENNYMAN, *Lady* Margaret.

JACK.

Jack and the Giants.

   Advertised by C. Bates, in *Hector, Prince of Troy.*

The Second Part of Jack and the Giants. Giving A full Account of his victorious Conquests over the North Country Giants, *etc.* *J. White, Newcastle.* 1711. 12°.

  B.M. (1076. l. 18/23).

AKAYA.

See ORVILLE, Adrien de la Vieuville d'.

JAMAICA LADY.

The Jamaica Lady : Or, The Life of Bavia, *etc.* *T. Bickerton.* 1720 1719]. 8°.

The dedication is signed W. P. '1719,' MS. note.
  B.M. (12614, d. 16).

JEALOUS LOVERS.

The Jealous Lovers, or the Mistake. From the Spanish. By several hands.
Advertised by W. Mears in 1735.

JENNY.

Kick him, Jenny. A Tale. 1733.
Gentleman's Magazine, Sept., 1733.

JOURNAL OF THE PLAGUE YEAR.

See DEFOE, Daniel.

JUSTINE.

See SPANISH LIBERTINES.

K., F.

See KIRKMAN, Francis.

KEACH, BENJAMIN.

The Progress of Sin ; or the Travels of Ungodliness . . . in an apt and Pleasant Allegory . . . as also, The Manner of his Apprehension, Arraignment, Tryal, Condemnation and Execution. By B. K., *etc.* *For J. Dunton.* 1684. 2°.

  B.M. (4415. c. 39).

[Another edition.]   The Second Edition : To which is now added, Ungodliness's Voyage to Sea ; with many pleasant additions.   By B. Keach.
Illustrated with Cuts.   *For J. Dunton.*   1685.

Term Cat., ii. 118.

[Another edition.]   The Third Edition, Corrected, With some Additions
by the Author.   *For N. Boddington.*   1700.   12°.

B.M. (4414. aa. 1).

[Another edition.]   The Fourth Edition, corrected, with some additions
etc.   *For N. Boddington.*   1707.   12°.

Bodl. (1483. f. 52).

[Another edition.]   The Fourth Edition, Corrected : With some Additions
etc.   *A. W. for J. Clarke.*   1724.   12°.

B.M. (4414. b. 41).

[Another edition.]   The Fourth Edition, corrected.   *For J. Brigs and
R. Crighton : Edinburgh.*   1727.   8°.

B.M. (4413. bbb. 45/2).

The Travels of True Godliness from the Beginning of the World to this
present Day ; in an apt and Pleasant Allegory . . . By B. K., *etc.*   *For
J. Dunton.*   1683.   8°.

B.M. (4415. c. 40).

[Another edition.]   The Third Edition, carefully Corrected.   *For J. Dunton.*
1684.   12°.

Bodl. (Antiq. f. E. 1684/1).

[Another edition.]   The Fifth Edition, to which is now added Five lively
Cuts, together with True Godliness's Voyage to Sea : With many new
Additions besides.   *For J. Dunton.*   1684.   12°.

B.M. (4415. aaa. 42).

[Another edition.]   The Fourth Edition, Corrected, and with the Addition
of One whole Chapter.   By Benjamin Keach, *etc.*   *I. Dawks for N. Boddington.*   1700.   12°.

B.M. (4415. aaa. 43).

[Another edition.]   The Fifth Edition, Corrected, *etc.*   *I. Dawks, for
N. Boddington.*   1708.   8°.

B.M. (4415. c. 41).

[Another edition.] The Ninth Edition, corrected. *For J. Graham and Brigs : Edinburgh.* 1726. 8º.

B.M. (4413. bbb. 45/1).

[Another edition.] The Ninth Edition, Corrected, *etc. A. W. for Clarke.* 1733. 12º.

B.M. (4415. aa. 44).

KEPPLE, Joseph.

The Maiden-head lost by Moon-light : or, the Adventure of the Meadow. Written by Joseph Kepple. *For N. Brooke.* 1672. 4º.

P. M. Barnard.

KIRKMAN, Francis.

The English Rogue. [Parts 2–4 by Kirkman.]
See HEAD, Richard.

The Unlucky Citizen Experimentally Described in the Various Misfortunes of an Unlucky Londoner . . . Intermixed with severall Choice Novels . . . Illustrated with Pictures fitted to the severall stories. *A. Johnson for I. Kirkman.* 1673. 8º.

B.M. (G. 17717).

See (in Part I) BELLIANIS.

..., G. *See* GUY OF WARWICK.

..., L. *See* EVAGORAS.

..., S. *See* PHILARIO AND OLINDA.

LABADIE.

The Adventures of Pomponius, a Roman Knight : or, the History of Our Times. Made English from the Rome Edition of the French Original, By Mr. Macky. *For E. Curll.* 1726. 12º.

Part 1 ; no more published.
B.M. (1208. e. 2/1).

LA CHAPPELLE, Jean de.

The Unequal Match : Or, The Life of Mary of Anjou Queen o
Majorca.   An Historical Novel.   *For C. Blount and R. Butt.*   1681, 3
12°.   3 vols.

<blockquote>
In <i>Modern Novels,</i> vol. viii.   Vol. 2 is printed for R. Bentley.

B.M. (12410. c. 25).
</blockquote>

LADIES' MISCELLANY.

The Ladies Miscellany ; or travelling Adventures.   *Sold at Furnivall'*
Inn Coffee-House.   1737.

<blockquote>
Gentleman's Magazine, Aug. 1737.
</blockquote>

LADIES' TALES.

The Ladies Tales : Exemplified in the Vertues and Vices of the Quality
with Reflections.   *For F. Burleigh, A. Dod, and J. Graves.*   1714.   12°.

<blockquote>
The third edition appeared in 1741.

B.M. (12614. b. 21).
</blockquote>

LADLE, Tom.

The Pleasant History of Tom Ladle.

<blockquote>
Advertised by C. Dennisson in <i>King Henry VIII and the Abbot of Reading.</i>
</blockquote>

[Another edition.]   The Pleasant History of Tom Ladle; with the Transac
tions of Peter the Plowman and Betty his Mother.   Also How Tom wa
Avenged of the Intruding Barber, and also of the intermedling Parson, *etc*
For J. Blare.   8°.

<blockquote>
Bodl. (Wood 259/9).
</blockquote>

LA FAYETTE, *Madame de.*

See Motier, Marie Madeleine.

LA FERTÉ SENNETERRE, *la Mareschalesse* de.

The History of the Mareschaless de la Ferté.   *B. R., and are to be sold by*
R. Baldwin.   1690.   12°.

<blockquote>
In <i>Modern Novels,</i> vol. viii.

B.M. (12410. c. 25).
</blockquote>

LA FORCE, Charlotte Rose de Caumont de.

The Secret History of Burgundy : Or, The Amorous and Political Intrigues of Charles Duke of Burgundy, and Louis XI of France ... Faithfully Collected by a Person of Quality of the French Court, and now first done into English. *For J. Walthoe, T. Woodward, and sold by T. Warner.* 1723. 12°.

B.M. (12512. ccc. 24).

LAMBERTO, *Don* Juan.
See Montelion.

LA MOTHE, Marie Catherine, *Comtesse d'Aulnoy.*

The Diverting Works of the Countess D'Anois, Author of the Ladies Travels to Spain. Containing I. The Memoirs of her own Life. II. All her Spanish Novels and Histories. III. Her Letters. IV. Tales of the Fairies in Three Parts Compleat. Newly done into English. *For J. Nicholson, and J. Sprint, Andrew Bell and S. Burows.* 1707. 8°.

B.M. (12236. bb. 11).

Hypolitus Earl of Douglas ... To which is added : The Amours of Count Schlick ... By Aeneas Sylvius, *etc. For J. Woodward.* 1708. 8°. 2 vols.

The title of vol. 2 reads "The Secret History of Mack-Beth King of Scotland. Taken from a very Ancient Manuscript."

B.M. (12510. d. 9).

The Ingenious and Diverting Letters of the Lady —— Travels into Spain ... Intermixt with Great Variety of Modern Adventures and Surprising Accidents ... The Second Edition. *For S. Crouch.* 1692. 12°. 3 vols.

B.M. (10160. aa. 43).

[Another edition.] The Fourth Edition Corrected. In Three Parts Compleat. *For S. Crouch.* 1697. 8°.

B.M. (10160. aaa. 10).

[Another edition.] The Seventh Edition, *etc. For S. Crouch.* 1708. 8°.

B.M. (10169. b. 11).

[Another edition.] The Eighth Edition, *etc. For D. Browne, A. Bell, T. Darby, A. Bettesworth, J. Pemberton, C. Rivington, J. Hooke, T. Cox, T. Batley, and E. Symon.* 1717. 8°.

B.M. (10160. a. 5).

[Another edition.]   The Tenth Edition . . . In Two Volumes.   *For J. J*
and P. Knapton, D. Midwinter, A. Bettesworth and C. Hitch, J. Pemberton,
R. Ware, C. Rivington, F. Clay, J. Batley and J. Wood, A. Ward,
T. Longman and R. Hett.   1735.   12°.   2 vols.

 B.M. (10160. a. 15).

[The Novels of Elizabeth, Part 1.]   The Novels of Elizabeth Queen o[f]
England, Containing the History of Queen Ann of Bullen.   Faithfull[y]
Rendred into English by S. H.   *For M. Pardoe.*   1680.   12°.

 B.M. (G. 1516).

[Part 2.]   Containing the History of Bassa Solyman, and The Princes[s]
Eronima.   The Last Part.   Englished by Spencer Hickman.   *E. T. an[d]*
R. H., for M. Pardow.   1681.   12°.

 Term Cat., i. 416, 'for W. Cademan.'
 B.M. (12604. bbb. 14).

The Prince of Carency ; A Novel.   Written in French by the Countes[s]
D'Aunois . . . Translated into English.   *W. Wilkins.*   1719.   8°.

 B.M. (12512. dd. 41).

[Another edition.]   The History of John of Bourbon, Prince of Carency[,]
Containing a Variety of entertaining Novels . . . The Second Edition.   *Fo[r]*
J. Peele.   1723.   8°.

 B.M. (12511. f. 17).

Secret Memoirs of the Duke and Duchess of O . . .   Intermixed with th[e]
Amorous Intrigues and Adventures of the most Eminent Princes of th[e]
Court of France.   Written by Madam d'Aunoy, Author of the Ladies Travel[s]
into Spain.   Made English from the Paris Edition.   *For S. P. R. Burrough*
and J. Baker, E. Curll, E. Sanger and A. Collins, and Sold by J. Morpheu.
1708.   12°.

 B.M. (12510. aaa. 9).

Tales of the Fairys.   Translated from the French.   *For T. Cockeril.*
1699.   12°.

 Term Cat., iii. 123.

[Another edition.]   The History of the Tales of the Fairies.   Newly don[e]
from the French.   Containing, I. The Tale of Graciosa, and Prince Percine[t]
. . . II. The Blew-Bird, and Florina . . . III. Prince Avenant, and the Beaut[y]

with the Locks of Gold . . . IV. The King of the Peacocks, and the Princess Rosetta . . . V. Prince Nonpariel, [*sic*] and the Princess Brilliant . . . VII. The Orange-Tree, and its beloved Bee, *etc.*   *E. Tracy.*   1716.   12°.

> The dedication, signed B.H., mentions the 'Countess de Anois' as the author.
>   Bodl. (Douce T. 186).

[Another edition.]   A Collection of Novels and Tales of the Fairies. Written by that Celebrated Wit of France, the Countess D'Anois.   In Three Volumes . . . The Second Edition.   *For J. Brotherton, and W. Meadows, T. Edlin, and T. Astley.*   1728.   12°.   3 vols.

> B.M. (12411. aa. 3).

LANCASHIRE LOVERS.

See SIMON AND CISLEY.

LA ROBERDIÈRE, *le Sieur* DE.

Love Victorious, or The Adventures of Oronces and Eugenia.   A Novel. Written in French by the Sieur de La Roberdière, translated by J. E.   *For R. Bentley and S. Magnes.*   1685.   12°.

LA ROCHEFOUCAULD, FRANÇOIS DE, *Duc.*

The Princess of Cleves.

See SEGRAIS, Jean Regnauld de.

LA ROCHE GUILHEM, *Mlle* DE.

Almanzor and Almanzaida.   A Novel.   Written by Sir Philip Sidney, And found since his Death amongst his Papers.   *For J. Magnes and R. Bentley.* 1678.   12°.

> B.M. (635. a. 3/1).

Asteria and Tamberlain ; or, The Distressed Lovers : A Novel.   Written in French by a Person of Quality.   And rendred into English by E. C. Esq. *For R. Sollers.*   1677.   12°.

> Bodl. (V. 82 Art 2).

[Another edition.]   Royal Lovers : Or, The Unhappy Prince, *etc.*   *For R. Sollers.*   1680.   8°.

> Bodl. (Douce N. 34).

The Great Scanderbeg : A Novel.   Done out of French.   *For R. Bentley.*
1690.   12°.

In *Modern Novels*, vol. xi.   The dedication is signed N. V.
  B.M. (12410. c. 28).

Scanderbeg the Great.   Translated from the French Original.   1721.

See CROXALL, Samuel.   A Select Collection of Novels, vol. v.

[Another edition.]   1729.

See CROXALL, Samuel.   A Select Collection of Novels, ed. 2, vol. v.

Zingis : a Tartarian History.   Written in Spanish, and Translated into
English.   By J. M., *etc.*   *For F. Saunders and R. Parker.*   1692.   8°.
  B.M. (837. c. 31).

LATROON, MERITON.   *See* HEAD, Richard

LAW.

Law is a Bottomless Pit.   [John Bull.]

See ARBUTHNOT, John.

LAWSINTNEY, WILLIAM.

See WINSTANLEY, William.

LEBECHEA, DIOMEDES DE.

The Dutch Rogue or, Gusman of Amsterdam Traced from the Craddle to
the Gallows ; Being the Life, Rise, and Fall of D. de Lebechea a Decay'd
Merchant . . .   Illustrated with Copper-plates.   Out of Nether-dutch, *etc.*
A. M. for G. Hill.   1683.   12°.
  Bodl. (Douce L. 17).

LE NOBLE DE TENNELIÈRE, EUSTACHE.

Abra-Mulè, or a True History Of the Dethronement of Mahomet IV.
Written in French by M. Le Noble.   Made English by J. P.   *For R. Clavel.*
1696.   8°.
  B.M. (9136. b. 3).

Pure Love : A Novel.   Being the History of the Princess Zulima . . .
Translated from the French of Monsieur Le Noble.   *For J. Osborne, J. King,
and J. Hodges.*   12°.

The dedication is signed M.B.
  B.M. (12512. b. 15).

Ildegerte, Queen of Norway; Or, Heroick Love : A Novel. Written originally in French, by the Author of the Happy Slave, and translated into English by a Gentleman of Oxford. In Two Parts, *etc.* *For W. Chetwood.* 1721. 8°. 2 vols.

The author of *The Happy Slave* was Gabriel de Brémond.
B.M. (12511. f. 15).

[Another edition.] The Second Edition, *etc.* *For S. Illidge, W. Meadows, W. Lewis, T. Payne, B. Creake, A. Ward, and T. Butler.* 1722. 8°.

B.M. (12510. e. 20), vol. 1 only.

See CLERMONT, *the Prince of.*

LE PAYS, RENÉ.

The Drudge : Or The Jealous Extravagant. A Piece of Gallantry. *For H. Herringman.* 1673. 8°.

Zelotyde, histoire galante. The author's name occurs at the end.
B.M. (12614. aa. 14).

LE ROY, MARIN, *Sieur de Gomberville.*

The History of Polexander : in Five Bookes. Done into English by William Browne, Gent., *etc.* *T. Harper for T. Walkley.* 1647. Fol.

B.M. (12403. bb. 6).

[Another edition.] *T. Harper, for T. Walkley.* 1648. Fol.
Priv. Lib.

LE SAGE, ALAIN RENÉ.

The Bachelor of Salamanca ; Or, Memoirs of Don Cherubim de la Ronda. In Three Parts. Written originally in French by Mr. Le Sage . . . Translated by Mr. Lockman. *For A. Bettesworth and C. Hitch and C. Davis ; and G. Hawkins.* 1737, 9. 12°. 2 vols.

B.M. (12510. b. 29).

The Devil upon two Sticks : or, The Town Until'd, *etc.* *J. R.* 1708.

7 pp. ; abridges from the beginning and end of *Le Diable Boiteux.*
B.M. (1076. l. 22/25).

The History and Adventures of Gil Blas of Santillane. In Two Volumes. *For J. Tonson.* 1716. 12°.

Of the French original vols. 1, 2 appeared in 1715, vol. 3 in 1724, and vol. 4 in 1735.
Priv. Lib.

[Another edition.]   In Three Volumes . . . The Third Edition.   *For J. Tonson.*   1732.   12⁰.

   B.M. (12510. bbb. 13).

The History and Adventures of Gil Blas.   The Fourth Edition.   *For Messrs Tonson.*   1738, 42.   12⁰.   4 vols.

   Vol. 4 is of 1742, and bears no edition-number.
   B.M. (12510. aaa. 26).

The History of the Count de Belflor and Leonora de Cespedes.   Written Originally in French.   [The first novel of Le Diable Boiteux.]   1720.

See CROXALL, Samuel.   A Select Collection of Novels, vol. iii.

[Another edition.]   1729.

See CROXALL, Samuel.   A Select Collection of Novels, ed. 2, vol. iii.

The Force of Friendship.   Written Originally in French.   [The second novel of Le Diable Boiteux.]   1720.

See CROXALL, Samuel.   A Select Collection of Novels, vol. ii.

[Another edition.]   1729.

See CROXALL, Samuel.   A Select Collection of Novels, ed. 2, vol. ii.

LE VAYER DE BOUTIGNY, ROLLAND.

The Famous Romance of Tarsis and Zelie.   Digested into Ten Books. Written Originally in French, By the Acute Pen of a Person of Honour. Done into English by Charles Williams, Gent.   *For N. Ponder.*   1685.   Fol.

   B.M. (837. l. 10).

LISANDER.

Lisander Or the Souldier of Fortune, a Novel.   *H. H. for H. Faithorne, and J. Kersey.*   1681.   12⁰.

   Priv. Lib.

[Another edition.]   The History of the Loves of Lysander and Sabina ; A Novel.   *J. Taylor.*   1688.   12⁰.

   B.M. (635. a. 42).

LONDON BULLY.

The London Bully, or the Prodigal Son . . . discovered in the Life and Actions of an Eminent Citizen's Son.   *For T. Malthus.*   1683.   8⁰.   2 vols.

   Term Cat., ii. 28, 44.

LONDON JILT.   *See* OLDYS, Alexander ;   VOSS, Jenny.

LONDON PRENTICE.   *See* SHURLEY, John.

LOREDANO, GIOVANNI FRANCESCO.

The **Novells** of Gio. Francesco Loredano, a Nobleman of Venice.   Translated for diversion into English.   *For T. Fox and H. Lord.*   1682.   12°.

B.M. (1073. a. 40).

Dianea : an Excellent New Romance.   Written in Italian by Gio. Francisco Loredano a Noble Venetian.   In Foure Books.   Translated into English by Sir Aston Cokaine.   *For H. Moseley.*   1654.   8°.

B.M. (12470. bb. 8).

The **Life** of Adam.   Written in Italian by Giovanno [*sic*] Francesco Loredano, A Venetian Noble-man.   And rendered into English By J. S. *For H. Moseley.*   1659.   8°.

B.M. (E. 1909/1).

[**Another edition.**]   The History of Adam and Eve : critical and political . . . English'd from the Original Italian of the Celebrated Gio. Fran. Loredano, a Noble Venetian, *etc.   J. Read.*   8°.

Bodl. (Godw. Pamph. 405).

LOVE À LA MODE.   *See* FLORELLA AND PHILLIS.

LOVE AFTER ENJOYMENT.

Love after Enjoyment : Or, Fatal Constancy.   A Novel.   *Sold by T. Read.* 1735.

Gentleman's Magazine, May, 1735.

LOVE LETTERS.   *See* BEHN, Aphra.

LOVE UPON TICK.

Love upon Tick : or, Implicit Gallantry exemplified in some Merry Memoirs of an Extraordinary and Occasional Amour . . .   By the Author of —— . . . The Third Edition, with Additions.   *Sold by A. Bettesworth, J. Billingsley and W. Meadows, T. Worral and J. Stagg.*   1725.   8°.

B.M. (1132. c. 44).

LOVELY POLANDER.

See PRÉCHAC, *le Sieur* de.

LOVER'S WEEK.

The Lover's Week: Or, The Six Days Adventures of Philander and Amaryllis. Written by a Young Lady. The Second Edition. *For E. Curll and R. Francklin.* 1718. 8°.

The dedication is signed M. H. The sequel is *The Female Deserters,* 1719.
B.M. (1093. h. 8).

LOVES.

The Loves of Sundry Philosophers and other Great Men. *See* DESJARDINS, Marie Catherine Hortense de, *Madame de Villedieu.*

LOVE'S ACADEMY.

Love's Academy. Containing many Pleasant and Delightful Novels. Those Ladies or Gentlemen that are willing to Record Adventures in this Academy, of their own or others, are desired to send them forthwith to the Undertaker B. Lintott. *For B. Lintott.* 12°.

B.M. (12614. ee. 16).

LOVE'S EMPIRE.

Loves Empire; Or, The Amours of the French Court. *For D. Newman.* 1682. 8°.

Priv. Lib.

LOVE'S JOURNAL.

See DESJARDINS, Marie Catherine Hortense de, *Madame de Villedieu.*

LOVE'S POSY.

Love's Posie: or, A Collection of Seven and Twenty Love Letters, both in Verse and Prose; That lately pass'd betwixt a Gentleman and a very Young Lady in France. *For J. Hindmarsh.* 1686. 12°.

B.M. (10910. aa. 22).

LUCCA, GAUDENTIO DI.

See BERINGTON, Simon.

LUCINDA.

The Life and amorous adventures of Lucinda.

Advertised by E. Bell, J. Darby and A. Bettesworth, in Mrs. Aubin's *Noble Slaves*, 1722.

LUGG, PETER.

Peter Lugg : Or, Three Tales of an Old Woman of Bangor Preaching over her Liquor, *etc.   For T. Warner.*   1718.   8°.

B.M. (T. 1541/14).

LUSSAN, MARGUERITE DE.

The Life of the Countess de Gondez.   Written in her own hand in French . . . And now faithfully Translated into English by Mrs. P. Aubin.   *For J. and J. Knapton, J. Darby, A. Bettesworth, F. Fayram, J. Osborn and T. Longman, J. Pemberton, C. Rivington, F. Clay, J. Batley and A. Ward.* 1729.   12°.

B.M. (12511. aaaa. 17).

LYCIDUS.

See TALLEMANT, Paul.

LYNN, BOB.

Bob-Lynn against Franck . . . Lynn : Or, a full History of the Controversies and Dissentions in the Family of the Lynns, *etc.   J. P. for D. Reynolds.* 1732.   8°.

A satire on Walpole.
B.M. (1103. d. 37).

LYSANDER.

The Forced Virgin ; or, The Unnatural Mother.   A True Secret History. *For W. Trott.*   1730.   8°.

The dedication is signed Lysander.
B.M. (12614. d. 13).

M., P.

See CHARLETON, Walter.

M., T.

See MATTHEW, *Sir* Tobie ; NIM.

MACBETH.

See LA MOTHE, Marie Catherine, *Comtesse d'Aulnoy.*   Hippolytus, Earl of Douglas.

MACCHIAVELLI, NICCOLO.

The Divell a married man, or, The Divell hath met with his Match. [1647.]   4°.

No title-page.
  B.M. (E. 408/18).

[Another edition.]   The Marriage of Belphegor.   *See* QUEVEDO VILLEGAS, Francisco de.   Novels, 1671.

[Another edition, in :]   The Works of the Famous Nicolas Machiavel, Citizen and Secretary of Florence.   Written Originally in Italian, and from thence newly and faithfully Translated into English.   *For J. S[tarkey], and are to be sold by R. Boulter.*   1675.   Fol.

The Marriage of Belphegor, pp. 524–9.
  B.M. (521. l. 14).

[Another edition, in :]   The Works, *etc.   For J. Starkey, C. Harper and J. Amery.*   1680.   Fol.

  B.M. (12226. i. 1).

[Another edition, in :]   The Works, *etc.   For R. Clavel, C. Harper, J. Robinson, J. Amery, A. and J. Churchil.*   1694.   Fol.

  B.M. (521. m. 12).

[Another edition, in :]   The Works . . .   The Third Edition, carefully corrected.   *T. W. for A. Churchill, R. Bonwick, T. Goodwin, J. Walthoe, M. Wotton, S. Manship, B. Tooke, R. Wilkin, R. Smith, R. Robinson, and T. Ward.*   1720.   Fol.

  B.M. (521. m. 13).

[Another edition.]   1720.
See CROXALL, Samuel.   A Select Collection of Novels, vol. i.

[Another edition.]   1729.
See CROXALL, Samuel.   A Select Collection of Novels, ed. 2, vol. i.

MACDERMOT, Murtagh.

A Trip to the Moon. By Mr. Murtagh McDermot. Containing Some Observations and Reflections, made by him during his Stay in that Planet, upon the Manners of the Inhabitants. *Printed at Dublin: And Reprinted at London, for J. Roberts.* 1728. 8°.

B.M. (12350. e. 5).

MACDONALD, Donald.

The Scotch Rogue: or, the Life and Actions of Donald Macdonald A High-Land Scot, *etc. For R. Gifford.* 1706. 12°. 2 vols.

Bodl. (Douce MM. 201, 2) ; B.M. (1079. b. 6), part 1.

[Another edition.] *For A. Gifford.* 1722. 12°.

B.M. (1079. b. 7), part 1.

MACKENZIE, *Sir* George.

Aretina ; Or, The Serious Romance. Written originally in English. Part First. *For R. Broun: Edinburgh.* 1660. 8°.

B.M. (C. 57. aa. 28).

MADAM COMING-SIR.

The Rise and Fall of Madam Coming-Sir: Or, An Unfortunate Slip from the Tavern-Bar, Into the Surgeon's Powdering-Tub. *W. Thompson and T. Baily, Stamford, Lincolnshire, and St. Edmund's Bury, Suffolk.* 8°.

Not before 1740?
B.M. (12611. cc. 10).

MADAME. *See* Henrietta, *Princess.*

MAINZ.

The Siege of Mentz. Or, The German Heroin, A Novel. *For S. Briscoe.* 1692. 12°.

B.M. (635. a. 5/1).

MAMA OELLO.

The Secret History of Mama Oello, Princess Royal of Peru. A New Court Novel, *etc. For J. Dent.* 1733. 8°.

A satire on Anne, eldest daughter of George II.
B.M. (1418. d. 40).

MANCINI, Maria.

See Brémond, Gabriel.   The Apology, *etc.*

MANLEY, Mary de la Rivière.

The Adventures of Rivella ; or the History of the Author of the Atalantis. With Secret Memoirs and Characters of several considerable Persons her Cotemporaries . . .   Done into English from the French.   [*For E. Curll.*] 1714.   8º.

For the publisher see preface to the 1725 issue.
   B.M. (635. f. 11/1).

[A re-issue.]   Memoirs of the Life of Mrs. Manley.   (Author of the Atalantis.)   . . . To which is added, A Compleat Key.   The Third Edition. *For E. Curll.*   1717.   8º.

   B.M. (635. f. 11/2).

[Another re-issue.]   Mrs. Manley's History Of Her Own Life and Times. Published from Her Original Manuscript.   The Fourth Edition With a Preface concerning the present Publication.   *For E. Curll and J. Pemberton.* 1725.   8º.

   B.M. (1418. d. 44).

Court Intrigues, in a Collection of Original Letters, from the Island of the New Atalantis, *etc.*   By the Author of those Memoirs.   *For J. Morphew and J. Woodward.*   1711.   8º.

   B.M. (636. d. 10).

Letters Written by Mrs. Manley.   To which is Added A Letter from a supposed Nun in Portugal, to a Gentleman in France, in Imitation of the Nun's Five Letters in Print, by Colonel Pack.   *For R. B.*   1696.   8º.

   B.M. (1086. b. 7).

[Another edition.]   A Stage-Coach Journey to Exeter.   Describing The Humours of the Road, with the Characters and Adventures of the Company . . . To which is added, The Force of Love : or, The Nun's Complaint.   By the Hon. Colonel Pack.   *For J. Roberts.*   1725.   8º.

   B.M. (1080. i. 37).

The Power of Love : in Seven Novels . . . Never before Published.   By Mrs. Manley.   *For J. Barber and J. Morphew.*   1720.   8º.

A second volume of novels was announced by Morphew in 1720.
   B.M. (636. d. 13).

The Secret History of Queen Zarah and the Zarazians ; Being a Looking-glass for . . . . In the Kingdom of Albigion. Faithfully Translated from the Italian Copy now lodg'd in the Vatican at Rome, and never before Printed in any Language. *Albigion.* 1705. 12°. 2 vols.

> B.M. (1081. d. 11), imperfect, wanting title-page of vol. 2 ; Bodl. (22861. f. 9).

[Another edition.] Containing The True Reasons of the Necessity of the Revolution that lately happen'd in the Kingdom of Albigion. By Way of Appendix to the New Atlantis. In Two Parts. *Albigion.* 1711. 12°.

> B.M. (12614. ccc. 24).

[French.] Histoire Secrete de la Reine Zarah, et des Zaraziens. Pour servir de Miroir au . . . dans le Royaume d'Albigion . . . Seconde Edition Corrigée. *Dans le Royaume d'Albigion.* 1708. 12°. 2 vols.

> B.M. (12511. aa. 24).

[Another edition.] Histoire secrete de la reine Zarah ou la Duchesse de Marlborough démasquée . . . traduite de l'original Anglais. *Alexandre le Vertueux ; Oxford.* 1711. 12°. 3 vols.

> Bodl. (275. o. 29).

[A re-issue.] *Alexandre le Vertueux.* Oxford. 1711, 12. 12°. 3 vols.
> Vol. 3 is dated 1712.
> Bodl. (22861. f. 5).

[A re-issue.] *Alexandre le Vertueux : Oxford.* 1712. 12°. 3 vols.
> Bodl. (22861. f. 6).

[A re-issue.] *Alexandre le Vertueux : Oxford.* 1712. 12°. 3 vols.
> Bodl. (22861. f. 1).

[Another edition.] Nouvelle édition. *Albigion.* 1712. 12° 3 vols.
> Bodl. (22861. f. 7).

[The New Atalantis, part 1.] Secret Memoirs and Manners Of several Persons of Quality, of both Sexes . . . From the New Atalantis, an Island in the Mediterranean. Written originally in Italian. *For J. Morphew and J. Woodward.* 1709. 8°.

> B.M. (1081. m. 2).

[Another edition of parts 1, 2.] The Second Edition. *For J. Morphew and J. Woodward.* 1709. 8°. 2 vols.

> The first edition of part 2, which is said to be " Written in Italian, and Translated from the Third Edition of the French."
> B.M. (636. d. 8).

[Another edition.]   The Third Edition.   8°.

Vol. 1 only, "Corrected, with large additions," announced by Morphew and Woodward in vol. 2 of the second edition.

[Another edition of part 2.]   Memoirs of Europe, Towards the close of the Eighth Century . . . Written by Eginardus . . . And translated into English by the Translator of the New Atalantis, *etc.   For J. Morphew.*   1710. 8°.   2 vols.

B.M. (613. d. 12), vol. 2 only.

[Another edition.]   The Second Edition, Corrected.   *For J. Morphew.* 1711.   8°.   2 vols.

B.M. (613. d. 11), vol. 1 only.

[Another edition of parts 1, 2.]   Secret Memoirs . . .   In Four Volumes . . . The Sixth Edition.   *For J. Morphew.*   1720.   12°.   4 vols.

B.M. (1081. f. 14).

[Another edition.]   The Seventh Edition.   *J. Watson; Sold by A. Dodd.* 1736.   12°.   4 vols.

B.M. (12614. ee. 5).

MARANA, Giovanni Paolo.

See Edward IV.

MARGUETEL DE SAINT DENIS, Charles, *Seigneur de Saint Evremond.*

The Works of M. de St. Evremont.   In II Volumes.   Translated from the French.   *For A. and J. Churchill.*   1700.   8°.   2 vols.

The Ephesian Matron, from Petronius, i. 236; *A Novel (The Irish Prophet),* ii. 78.
   B.M. (12236. bb. 15).

[Another edition.]   To which are added The Memoirs of the Dutchess of Mazarin, &c.   The Second Edition, corrected and enlarged.   In Three Volumes.   *For J. and J. Knapton, J. Darby, A. Bettesworth, J. Round, E. Curl, R. Gosling, F. Fayram, G. Harris, J. Pemberton, J. Osborn and T. Longman, J. Hooke, C. Rivington, F. Clay, J. Batley, and T. Osborn.* 1728.   8°.   3 vols.

The Ephesian Matron, from Petronius, twice, i. 171 and iii. 197; *The Irish Prophet, a Novel,* i. 189; and St. Réal's *Memoirs of the Dutchess of Mazarin,* iii. 105.
   B.M. (1223. bbb. 9).

[Female Falsehood, part 1.]   Female Falsehood : or, the Unfortunate Beau. Contain'd in the genuine Memoirs of a Late French Nobleman.   Written by Monsieur S. Evremont.   And now made English.   *E. Whitlock.*   1697.   8⁰.

> B.M. (12510. d. 5).

[Another edition of both parts.]   Written by Himself in his Retirement, and Digested by Monsieur St. Evremont.   Made English.   The Second Edition.   Wherein is added the Second Part, which Compleats the Work, *etc.* *The Booksellers.*   1706, 1705.   8⁰.   2 vols.

> Vol. 2. is *Printed and to be Sold by J. Nutt,* 1705.
> B.M. (12510. d. 7).

MARINI, GIOVANNI AMBROGIO.

The Desperadoes ; an Heroick History.   Translated from the Italian of the Celebrated Marini . . .   In Four Books.   Embellish'd with eight excellent Copper Plates.   *W. R., and sold by T. Astley, J. Isted, and T. Worrall.*   1733. 12⁰.

> B.M. (12471. b. 17).

MARIVAUX, PIERRE CARLET DE CHAMBLAIN DE.

The Life of Marianne ; or, the adventures of the Countess of ＊ ＊ ＊   By M. de Marivaux.   Translated from the French Original.   *For C. Davis.* 1736, 37, 42.   3 vols.

> *Gentleman's Magazine,* June 1736, Jan. 1737, April 1742.   *See* Austin Dobson, *Samuel Richardson,* pp. 48–9.

Le Paysan Parvenu : Or, The Fortunate Peasant.   Being Memoirs of the Life of Mr. —— Translated from the French of M. de Marivaux.   *For J. Brindley, C. Corbett, and R. Wellington.*   1735.   12⁰.

> *Milord, ou le Paysan parvenu.*
> B.M. (12512. bbb. 30).

MASQUERADERS.

> *See* HAYWOOD, Eliza.

MASSANIELLO.

Memoirs of a most Remarkable Revolution in Naples : or, the History of Massaniello.   1729.

> *See* CROXALL, Samuel.   A Select Collection of Novels, ed. 2, vol. vi.

MASSEY, James.

See Tyssot de Patot, Simon.

MATTHEW, *Sir* Tobie.

The Penitent Bandito : Or the History of the Conversion & Death of the most Illustrious Lord Signor Troilo Sauelli, a Baron of Rome.   The second Edition more correct.   By Sir T. M. Knight.   1663.   12°.

B.M. (865. a. 8).

MAZARINE, *The Duchess.*

See Marguetel de Saint Denis, Charles, *Seigneur de Saint Evremond.* The Works, *etc.* 1728 ; Saint Réal, César Vischard de.

M-D-LLA.

The Secret History of M-d-lla.   Containing a faithful Account of her Birth and Parentage ; her Amour with a Gentleman of Ireland, *etc.*   1733.

Gentleman's Magazine, May, 1733.

MEMOIRS.

Memoirs of a Certain Island.

See Haywood, Eliza.

MERCENARY LOVER.

See Haywood, Eliza.

MEROVEUS.

Meroveus, a Prince of the Blood-Royal of France.   A Novel.   *For R. Bentley and M. Magnes.*   1682.   12°.

In *Modern Novels,* vol. xi.

B.M. (12410. c. 28).

MESSALINA.

The Amours of Messalina, late Queen of Albion, *etc.*   1689.   2 vols.

Vol. 2 (part 4) is entitled "The Amours of the French King with the late Queen of Albion, being the fourth and last part.

B.M.

MILISTRATE AND PRAZIMENE.

Two Delightful Novels ; Or, The Unlucky Fair One. Being the Amours of Milistrate and Prazimene . . .   Translated from the French, by a Person of Quality. *E. Tracy.*   12º.

B.M. (12512. aa. 20).

MIRABEL, *Prince.*

The History of Prince Mirabel's Infancy, Rise and Disgrace : With the sudden Promotion of Novicius . . .   Collected from the Memoirs of a Courtier lately Deceas'd. *For J. Baker.* 1712.   8º.   3 vols.

A satire on the Duke of Marlborough.

B.M. (1417. e. 23).

[Another edition of vol. 1.] The Second Edition. *For J. Baker.* 1712. 8º.

B.M. (12611. g. 16).

The Perquisite-Monger : or the Rise and Fall of Ingratitude.   Being One of the Stories, which the Monks of Godstow were wont to divert Fair Rosamond with, and which may serve to clear up several Absurdities in the History of Prince Mirabel.   Made Publick from an Original Manuscript lately found in the Ruines of Woodstock-Bower.   1712.   8º.

B.M. (T. 2118/3).

MISCELLANEA AUREA.

Miscellanea Aurea : or the Golden Medley.   Consisting of I. A Voyage to the Mountains of the Moon under the Æquator, or Parnassus reform'd. II. The Fortunate Shipwreck, or a Description of New Athens . . . by Morris Williams Gent . . .   IV. The Secret History of the Amours of Don Alonzo, Duke of Lerma, Grandee of Spain, . . .   VII. An Account of Bad and Good Women . . .   Among which is the Story of the Spartan Dame, the Subject of Mr. Southern's Play, *etc.*   *For A. Bettesworth and J. Pemberton.*   1720.   8º.

B.M. (12330. e. 25).

MISTAKEN HUSBAND.

The Mistaken Husband.

Advertised by Bentley and Magnes in 1677.

MOCK-CLELIA.

See SUBLIGNY, Adrien Thomas Perdou de.

MODERN AMOURS.

Modern Amours : Or, A Secret History of the Adventures of some Persons of the first Rank.   Faithfully related from the Author's own Knowledge of each Transaction.   With a Key prefixed, *etc.*   1733.   8°.

B.M. (012612. df. 21).

MOLIÈRE, HENRIETTA SILVIA DE.

See DESJARDINS, Marie Catherine Hortense de, *Madame de Villedieu.*

MONEY, *Mistress.*

The Death and Burial of Mistress Money, *etc.   A. Clark, and are to be sold by T. Vere and J. Clark.*   1678.   8°.   𝔅.𝔍.

Pepys 363 (563).

MONTALBAN, JUAN PEREZ DE.

Aurora, & the Prince : By Don Juan Perez de Montalvan.   Oronta The Cyprian Virgin : By Sign^r Girolamo Preti . . .   Translated by T. S. Esq. *For H. Moseley.*   1647.   8°.

From *Successos e Prodigios de Amor.*
B.M. (E. 1146/1).

[Another edition.] Translated by Thomas Stanley, Esq ; The Second Edition, with Additions.   *W. Wilson for H. Moseley.*   1650.   8°.

B.M. (E. 1422/3).

The Illustrious Shepherdess.   The Imperious Brother.   Written originally in Spanish : Now made English, And Dedicated to the Marchioness of Dorchester, And the Countess of Strafford, by E. P.   *J. C. for N. Brook.* 1656.   8°.

From *Successos e Prodigios de Amor.*   Each has a separate title-page.
B.M. (E. 1588/1), *The Illustrious Shepherdess* only ; (E. 1569/2), *The Imperious Brother* only, with the collective title.

The Diverting Works of the Famous Miguel de Cervantes, Author of the History of Don Quixot.   Now first Translated from the Spanish.   With an Introduction by the Author of the London-Spy.   *J. Round, E. Sanger, A. Collins, T. Atkinson and T. Baker.*   1709.   8°.

From *Para Todos.*
B.M. (12490. e. 8).

[A re-issue.]   A Week's Entertainment at a Wedding.   Containing Six Surprising and Diverting Adventures, *etc.   J. Woodward.*   1710.

B.M. (Cerv. 445).

MONTELION.

[Don Juan Lamberto, part 1.]   Don Juan Lamberto, or a Comical History of the Late Times.   The First Part.   1643.   4°.

Hazlitt, II. 457.

[Another edition of part 1.]   *Sold by H. Marsh.*   1661.   4°.   𝔅.𝔏.

B.M. (E. 1048/6.)

[Another edition of both parts.]   The second Edition Corrected. *J. Brudenell for H. Marsh.*   1661.   4°.   𝔅.𝔏.   2 vols.

Vol. 2 was printed by T. Leach for H. Marsh.

B.M. (G. 4132.)

[Another edition.]   The third Edition corrected.   *For H. Marsh.*   1664. 4°.   𝔅.𝔏.

Bridgewater.

[Another edition.]   *For H. Marsh.*   1665.   4°.   𝔅.𝔏.

Hazlitt, H. 458.

[Another edition.]

Advertised by W. Thackeray in 1677.

MONTE SOCIO, Carlo.

The Golden Spy : or, a Political Journal of the British Nights Entertainments of War and Peace, and Love and Politics : Wherein are laid open, The Secret Miraculous Power and Progress of Gold, in the Courts of Europe, *etc.   For J. Woodward and J. Morphew.*   1709.   8°.

B.M. (12614. cc. 21).

[Another edition.]   1710.   8°.

Published serially.

B.M. (12614. ee. 7), the first two nights only.

The New Metamorphosis, or the Pleasant Transformation : being the Golden Ass of Lucius Apuleius of Medaura, alter'd and improv'd to the

Modern Times and Manners . . .   Written in Italian by Carlo Monte Socio, *etc.*   1708.   8°.   2 vols.

Dealer's list.

[Another edition.]   Adorned with Cuts : In Two Volumes.   The Second Edition, corrected.   *For D. Brown, G. Sawbridge, E. Sanger, S. Brisco, and J. Baker.*   1709.   8°.   2 vols.

B.M. (1080. m. 5).

[Another edition.]   Also the Golden Spy, *etc.*   *For S. Briscoe.*   1724. 12°.   2 vols.

B.M. (1079. d. 18).

MONTFAUCON DE VILLARS.

The Count of Gabalis : Or, The Extravagant Mysteries of the Cabalists . . . Done into English, By P. A. Gent., *etc.*   *For B[entley] and M[agnes].* 1680.   12°.

Term Cat., i. 373, " for J. Magnes and R. Bentley, and R. Harford " ; i. 393, " for R. Harford."   In *Modern Novels*, vol. ii.

B.M. (12410. c. 19).

[Another version.]   The Count of Gabalis : Or, Conferences about Secret Sciences.   Rendered out of French into English.   With an Advice to the Reader.   By A. L. A.M.   *For R. Harford.*   1680.   12°.

The " Advice to the Reader " states that the translation was ready and the book delayed by the publisher, and that meanwhile the other translation appeared.

B.M. (8907. a. 31).

[Another version.]   Being a Diverting History of the Rosicrucian Doctrine of Spirits . . .   Done from the Paris Edition, *etc.*   *For B. Lintott and E. Curll.* 1714.   8°.

The half-title reads " The Count de Gabalis.   Very necessary for the Readers of Mr. Pope's Rape of the Lock."

B.M. (C. 70. bb. 1/2), bound after *The Rape of the Lock*, 1714.

MONTFERRAT, *the Princess of.*

See BRÉMOND, Gabriel de.

MONTPENSIER, *the Princess of.*

See SEGRAIS, Jean Regnauld de.

MORGAN, Schon ap.

The Wonderful Adventures and Happy Success of Young Schon ap Morgan, the only Son of Sheffery ap Morgan, *etc.* *For J. Deacon.* 8°. 𝕭.𝕷.

Pepys 363 (297).

MORGAN, Sheffery ap.

The Life and Death of Sheffery ap Morgan, Son of Shon ap Morgan. *For J. Deacon.* 8°. 𝕭.𝕷.

Pepys 362 (977).

[Another edition.] The Life and Death of Sheffery Morgan, *etc.* *For J. Deacon.* 8°. 𝕭.𝕷.

Bodl. (Wood 259/14).

MOROCCO, *the Emperor of.*

An Historical Account of the Amours of the Emperor of Morocco; shewing by what Methods he attempted the Marriage of the Princess Dowager of Conti. Writ, by way of Letters, to a Person of Quality, by the Count of ——. Done out of French into English. *Sold by E. Mallet.* 1702. 12°.

Term Cat., iii. 320.

MOTIER, Marie Madeleine, *Comtesse de la Fayette.*

The Princess of Cleves. The Princess of Montpensier. Zayde.

See Segrais, Jean Regnauld de.

MOULINET, Nicolas de, *Sieur de Parc.*

See Sorel, Charles.

HUMPER.

See Heliotropolis.

MURAT, Henriette Julie, *Comtesse de.*

See Desjardins, Marie Catherine Hortense de, *Madame de Villedieu.*

MUSOPHILUS, Basilius.

See Holland, Samuel.

NARZANES.

Narzanes: Or, the injur'd Statesman. Containing the most important Negotiations, and Transactions Of that Great Minister, Whilst He presided over the Affairs of Persia. *For T. Payne.* 1731. 8°.

B.M. (101. f. 64).

NAZARENES, *the Prince of the.*

The Secret History of the Prince of the Nazarenes and Two Turks. To which is added, The Fatal Amour between a Beautiful Lady, and a Young Nobleman, *etc. For J. Moore.* 1719. 8°.

B.M. (114. l. 63).

[Another edition.] The Third Edition. *For J. Moore.* 1721. 8°.

Bodl. (Godw. Pamph. 1852/6).

NEAPOLITAN.

The Neapolitan, or The Defender of his Mistress. Done out of French by Mr. Ferrand Spence. *For R. Bentley.* 1683. 12°.

B.M. (1073. a. 41).

NEVILE, HENRY.

The Isle of Pines, or, A late Discovery of a Fourth Island in Terra Australis, Incognita. Being A True Relation of certain English persons, Who in the dayes of Queen Elizabeth, were cast away . . . And now lately Anno Dom. 1667. a Dutch Ship . . . have [*sic*] found their Posterity, *etc. S. G. for A. Banks and C. Harper.* 1668. 4°.

The narrative of George Pine alone.
B.M. (B. 671/9).

A New and further Discovery of The Isle of Pines In A Letter from Cornelius Van Sloetton, *etc. For A. Bankes and C. Harper.* 1668. 4°.

The narrative of Van Sloetten alone. The " Relation printed at London " is referred to on pp. 1 and 6, and is omitted.
B.M. (10491. b. 36).

[Another edition of the whole.] The Isle of Pines . . . By Henry Cornelius Van Sloetten, *etc. For A. Banks and C. Harper.* 1668. 4°.

B.M. (838. d. 24).

The Parliament of Ladies. Or Divers remarkable passages of Ladies in Spring-Garden, in Parliament Assembled. 1647. 4°.

B.M. (1080. i. 60).

[Another edition.]

Without title or imprint.
B.M. (E. 1143).

[Another edition.] Together with certaine Votes of the unlawfull Assembly at Kates in Coven Garden . . . The second Edition corrected by the originall, *etc.* 1647. 4°.

B.M. (E. 388/4).

The Ladies, a Second Time, Assembled in Parliament. A Continuation of the Parliament of Ladies, *etc.* 1647. 4°.

B.M. (E. 406/23).

NEW ATALANTIS.

See MANLEY, Mary de la Rivière.

NEW VOYAGE ROUND THE WORLD

See DEFOE, Daniel.

NEWCASTLE, MARGARET, *Duchess of.*

See CAVENDISH, Margaret.

NICEROTIS.

The History of Nicerotis, A Pleasant Novel. *For R. Bentley and S. Magnes.* 1685. 8°.

B.M. (12611. a. 7).

[Another edition.]

A fragment, occupying pp. 235-321 of vol. 1 (?) of a collection, not yet identified.
B.M. (12330. aaa. 6/4).

NICOSTRATUS.

Nicostratus. 12°.

Advertised by Bentley and Magnes in 1680.

NIM.

The Life of a Satyrical Puppy called Nim. Who worrieth all those Satyrists he knowes, and barkes at the rest. By T. M. *For H. Moseley.* 1657. 8°.

> B.M. (1418. c. 12).

NINE PIOUS PILGRIMS.

See PHILANTHROPUS.

NINE WORTHIES.

See CROUCH, Nathaniel.

NORTHERN ATALANTIS.

See YORK SPY.

NOVA SOLYMA.

See GOTT, Samuel.

NOVELS.

A Curious Collection of Novels, *etc.   For J. Billingsley.* 1731. 8°.

> B.M. (1093. h. 19).

Four Novels in one Vol. Viz. The Gallants, or, The Reciprocal Confidents. In Two Parts. The Amours of the Sultana of Barbary. The Amours of Philantus and Bellamond, *etc.   For F. Saunders.* 1697. 12°.

> The novels (*q.v.*) had previously appeared in 1685, 1689 and 1690 respectively.
> B.M. (Bagford 5986, 133), title only.

A Select Collection of Novels. In Two Volumes. *For J. Brotherton.* 1732.

> *Gentleman's Magazine*, Aug.–Sept. 1732.

See CROXALL, Samuel.

Select Novels. 2 vols. Advertised by E. Bell, J. Darby and A. Bettesworth, in Mrs. Aubin's *Noble Slaves*, 1722.

NUNNERY TALES.

Nunnery Tales; written by a Young Nobleman, and translated from his French Manuscript into English. 1727. 8°.

> Dealer's list.

OBLIGING MISTRESS.

The Obliging Mistress: or, the Fashionable Gallant. A Novel . . . **By** a Person of Quality. *For J. Magnes and R. Bentley.* 1678. 12°.

In *Modern Novels*, vol. vii.

B.M. (12410. c. 24).

O'DIVELLEY, Teague.

See Irish Rogue.

OLDMIXON, John.

Court Tales: Or, A History of the Amours of the Present Nobility, *etc.* *For J. Roberts.* 1717. 8°.

B.M. (12613. cc. 1).

OLDYS, Alexander.

The Fair Extravagant, or The humorous Bride. An English Novel. *For C. Blount.* 1681. 12°.

Term Cat., i. 461.

The London Jilt: or, The Politick Whore . . . Interwoven with several pleasant Stories of the Misses Ingenious Performances. *For H. Rodes.* 1683. 12°.

Priv. Lib.

[Another edition.] The Second Edition Corrected. *For H. Rodes.* 1684. 12°.

Term Cat., ii. 89.

[Another edition.] The Female Gallant or, the Wife's the Cuckold. A Novel. *For S. Briscoe.* 1692. 12°.

Bodl. (8°. B. 174. Art.)

OLIVIER, *l'Abbé.*

Memoirs of the Life and Adventures of Signor Rozelli . . . Done into English, from the Second Edition of the French ; and adorn'd with several curious Copper-Cuts. *For J. Morphew.* 1709. 8°.

B.M. (G. 13510).

[Another edition.]   The Second Edition corrected, enlarged with an Appendix of two whole Sheets, and adorn'd with curious Cutts.   *For J. Morphew and J. Woodward.*   1713.   8°.

B.M. (G. 13512/1).

[Another edition.]   The Third Edition, corrected ; and adorn'd with Curious Copper-Cutts.   *For F. Fayram, J. Bowyer, and A. Roper, aud sold by J. Isted.* 1725.   8°.

B.M. (1451. f. 14/1).

A Continuation of the Life and Adventures of Signor Rozelli . . .   Written by himself . . .   Adorn'd with Curious Copper-Cutts.   *For W. Taylor and T. Butler.*   1724.   8°.

B.M. (G. 13511).

ONEBY, *Major.*

The Life of Major Oneby.

Advertised by J. Loveall in 1728.

ORRERY, *the Earl of.*

See BOYLE, Roger, *Earl of Orrery.*

ORVILLE, ADRIEN DE LA VIEUVILLE D'.

The Adventures of Prince Jakaya : Or, the Triumphs of Love over Ambition . . .   Translated from the Original French.   In Two Volumes. *For A. Bettesworth, C. Hitch, W. Innys, and R. Manby.*   1733.   12°.

B.M. (12491. b. 33).

OTTOMAN GALLANTRIES.

Ottoman Gallantries : Or the Life of the Bassa of Buda.   Done out of French.   *For R. Bentley and S. Magnes.*   1687.   12°.

In *Modern Novels,* vol. vi.   The dedication is signed B. Berenclow.
B.M. (12410. c. 23).

OUFLE, *Monsieur.*

See BORDELON, Laurent.

P., *Lord.*

The Moral State of England, with the several Aspects it beareth to Virtue and Vice.   With the Life of Theodatus, And Three Novels, Viz. The Land

Mariners, Friendship Sublimed, The Friendly Rivals. By the Lord P. *For R. Bentley and D. Brown.* 8694 [1694]. 8°.

Sion College.

P., J.

See FLORIDON AND LUCINA ; SIMON AND CISLEY.

P., L.

See PRICE, Laurence.

P., W.

See JAMAICA LADY.

PACK, RICHARDSON.

See MANLEY, Mary de la Rivière. Letters, *etc.*

PAMPHILUS, HESYCHIUS.

The History of Moderation ; Or, The Life, Death and Resurrection of Moderation . . . Written by Hesychius Pamphilus : And now faithfully translated out of the Original. *For T. Parkhurst.* 1669. 8°.

At the end are " The Outlandish Names in this Discourse Englished." The dedication and preface signed N. S.

B.M. (12611. e. 1).

PANTHALIA.

See BRAITHWAIT, Richard.

PANTON, EDWARD.

Speculum Juventutis : Or, A true Mirror . . . Portrayed to the Life in the Legend of Sisaras and Vallinda. By Capt. Edward Panton, Patrophilus. *For C. Smith, and T. Burrell.* 1671. 8°.

B.M. (1031. d. 2).

PARC, *le Sieur* DE.

See SOREL, Charles.

PARISIAN MAID.

See PRÉCHAC, *le Sieur* de.

PARKER, Martin.

See Guy of Warwick.

PARSONS, H.

See Five Wise Philosophers.

PARTHENISSA.

See Boyle, Roger, *Earl of Orrery.*

PASQUIN.

Pasquin risen from the dead : Or, His own Relation of a late Voyage He made to the Other World, in a Discourse With his Friend Marforio. *J. C. for N. C.* 1674. 8°.

> B.M. (12331. aaa. 31).

Pasquiniana; or an Account of Pasquin's Travels, Dialogues with Marphorio and Seraphino, &c. *B. Bragg.* 1708. 4°.

> B.M. (838. h. 1).

PASTIME ROYAL.

The Pastime Royal; Or, The Gallantries of the French Court. In Two Parts. By a Person of Quality. *J. Harefinch for H. Rodes.* 1682. 12°. 2 vols.

> B.M. (12511. aaaa. 18).

PATRICK, *Saint.*

The Delightful History of the Life and Death of That Renowned & Famous St. Patrick, Champion of Ireland, Containing His Heroick Actions, and Valorous Atchievments in Europe, Asia, and Africk. With other Remarkable Passages, from his Cradle to his Grave. *For D. Newman.* 1685. 8°.

> B.M. (G. 5720).

PATRICK, Simon.

The Parable of the Pilgrim : Written to a Friend. By Symon Patrick, B.D. *R. White for F. Tyton.* 1665. 4°.

> B.M. (858. g. 14).

[Another edition.]   *R. White for F. Tyton.*   1667.   4°.
> B.M. (4415. dd. 33).

[Another edition.]   *R. White for F. Tyton.*   1670.   4°.
> B.M. (4399. g. 2).

[Another edition.] The Fourth Edition. *R. White for F. Tyton.* 1673. 4°.
B.M. (4408. f. 9).

[Another edition.] The Fifth Edition. *R. White for F. Tyton.* 1678. 4°.
B.M. (858. g. 15).

[Another edition.] The Sixth Edition Corrected. *For R. Chiswell.*
687. 4°.
B.M. (4414. f. 23).

PAUSANIAS AND AURORA.

See PENNYMAN, *Lady* Margaret.

PEGO.

The History of Pego the Great. *For T. Cooper.* 1733.
Gentleman's Magazine, Dec. 1733.

PENNYMAN, *Lady* MARGARET.

Ismenia and the Prince ; or the Royal Marriage : being a sequel to Prince
Titi, done from the Italian original. *E. Curll.* 1736. 8°.
This and the following were reprinted in 1740 in the author's *Miscellanies.*
Dealer's list ; *Gentleman's Magazine,* April, 1736.

Pausanias and Aurora, or the Royal Marriage : being a sequel to Prince
Titi, done from the Italian original. *E. Curll.* 1736. 8°.
Dealer's list.

See SAINT-HYACINTHE, Hyacinthe Cordonnier de.

PENTON, STEPHEN.

The Guardian's Instruction, Or, The Gentleman's Romance. Written for
The Diversion and Service of the Gentry. *For the Authour, and sold by
S. Miller.* 1688. 12°.
B.M. (1030. b. 11/3).

PEPPA.

Peppa : or, The Reward of Constant Love. A Novel. Done out of
French . . . By a Young Gentlewoman, *etc. For W. Crooke.* 1689. 12°.
The dedication is signed A. C.
B.M. (12331. a. 4).

PEREZ, ANDREAS. *See* SPANISH LIBERTINES.

PERFIDIOUS BRETHREN.

The Perfidious Brethren, Or, The Religious Triumvirate : Displayed in Three Ecclesiastical Novels.   I. Heathen Priestcraft : Or the Female Bigo ...   II. Presbyterian Piety : or the Way to get a Fortune.   III. The Cloven-Foot : Or the Anabaptist Teacher Detected, *etc.*   *T. Bickerton W. Meadows and J. Brotherton, and A. Dodd.*   1720.   8°.

The dedication is signed A. B.
B.M. (12611. g. 9).

PERFIDIOUS P - - -.

The Perfidious P - - -   Being Letters from a Nobleman to Two Ladies under the Borrow'd Names of Corydon, Clarinda & Lucinda.   With the Ladies Answers.   1702.   12°.

B.M. (12611. ccc. 16).

PERICLES.

Pericles of Greece.

Advertised by J. Phillpott, Gosport, in Head's *English Rogue*, n.d. [after 1688].

[Another edition.]   The most Renowned History of the Invincible Pericles Prince of Greece, *etc.*   *For J. Blare.*   1702.   12°.

Term Cat., iii. 302.

[Another edition.]   12°.

B.M. (12403. a. 35).

PERJURED CITIZEN.

The Perjured Citizen : Or, Female Revenge, *etc.*   *For C. Corbett.*   1732.   8°

B.M. (12614. d. 7).

PERPLEXED DUCHESS.

The Perplex'd Dutchess : or, Treachery Rewarded.   Being some Memoir of the Court of Malfy.   In a Letter ...   To which is added Innocence Preserv'd.   A Novel.   *S. Powell, for G. Risk and W. Smith : Dublin*   1727.   12°.

Dealer's list.

PERPLEXED PRINCE.

The Perplex'd Prince. *For R. Allen.* [1682?] 12°.

A libel on the Duke of York, on behalf of the Duke of Monmouth. The dedication is signed T. S.
B.M. (292. a. 34).

[Another edition.] *For R. Allen.* 12°.

Corrected. In *Modern Novels*, vol. ii.
B.M. (12410. c. 19).

See FUGITIVE STATESMAN.

PERPLEXED PRINCESS.

The Perplex'd Princess, or The famous Novel of Donna Zagas. Written originally in Spanish. Tome I. *For T. Malthus.* 1683. 12°.

Term Cat., ii. 28.

PERQUISITE-MONGER.

See MIRABEL, *Prince.*

PERRAULT, CHARLES.

Tales of Mother Goose, translated by Mr. Samber. *For J. Pote.* 1729.

Advertised in the *Monthly Chronicle*, March 1729 ; *cf.* Perrault, ed. Lang, 1892, p. xxxiv.

PERRON, JACQUES DAVY DU.

The Miscellaneous Remains of Cardinal Perron, President Thuanus, Monsr. St. Evremont, &c. Abridged, and done into English, *etc. For T. Osborne, and S. Butler.* 1707. 12°. 2 vols.

Arlequiniana is contained in vol. 1, pp. 281–329.
B.M. (12518. aa. 9).

PERSECUTED VIRTUE.

See HAYWOOD, Eliza.

PERSIAN AND TURKISH TALES.

See PÉTIS DE LA CROIX, François.

PERUVIAN TALES.

See GUEULLETTE, Thomas Simon.

PÉTIS DE LA CROIX, François.

The Persian and the Turkish Tales, Compleat.   Translated formerly from those Languages into French, by M. Petis de la Croix . . . and now into English from that Translation, by the late Learned Dr. King, and several other hands . . .   In Two Volumes.   *For W. Mears and J. Browne.*   1714. 12°.   2 vols.

Les Mille et Une Soirées; in collaboration with Le Sage.
B.M. (12513. b. 37).

[Another version.]   The Thousand and One Days : Persian Tales . . . Translated from the French.   By Mr. Philips . . .   The Third Edition.   *For J. Tonson.*   1722.   12°.   3 vols.

The third volume contains additional tales.
B.M. (12512. b. 33).

PETRONIUS ARBITER, Titus.
[Satirae.]

Petronii Satyrae had been licensed to the Partners in the English Stock, 22 June, 1631 (*Stat. Reg.*, iv. 221).

The Satyr of Titus Petronius Arbiter, A Roman Knight.   With its Fragments, recover'd at Belgrade.   Made English by Mr. Burnaby of the Middle Temple, and another Hand.   *For S. Briscoe.*   1694.   8°.

B.M. (11306. b. 27).

[Another version.]   The Satyrical Works of Titus Petronius Arbiter, In Prose and Verse.   In Three Parts.   Made English by Mr. Wilson, Mr. Burnaby, Mr. Blount, Mr. Tho. Brown, Capt. Ayloff, and several others. And adorn'd with Cuts, *etc.   For S. Briscoe, and are to be Sold by B. Bragge.* 1708.   8°.

B.M. (11306. d. 4).

[Another edition.]   The Works of T. Petronius Arbiter, *etc.   For S. Briscoe, and Sold by J. Woodward, and J. Morphew.*   1710.   8°.

Bodl. (Radcliffe e. 138).

[Another edition.]   Translated by several Hands.   With a Key by a Person of Honour . . .   The Fourth Edition . . .   The whole Adorn'd with Cuts.   *For S. Briscoe.*   1712.   8°.

Re-issued in 1713 and 1714 with new titles : *for S. Briscoe, and Sold by J. Morphew and J. Woodward* ; and *for S. Briscoe and Sold by W. Taylor, W. Brand and J. Kent* ; *J. Graves.* Part 1 "made English by Mr. Wilson . . . and several others" ; part 2 "by Mr. Burnaby, Mr. Tho. Brown, Capt. Ayloff, and Others."
1712, dealer's list ; 1713, B.M. (1080. m. 7) ; 1714, B.M. (1080. m. 8).

[Another version.] Translated from the Original Latin, By Mr. Addison, etc. *For J. Watts ; and sold by J. Osborne.* 1736. 12º.

B.M. (98. a. 10).

The Ephesian Matron.

See CHARLETON, Walter ; MARGUETEL DE SAINT DENIS, Charles, *Seigneur de Saint Evremond.*

PHILANTHROPUS.

The Admirable and Indefatigable Adventures of the Nine Pious Pilgrims, Devoted to Sion by the Cross of Christ ; and Piloted by Evangelist to the New Jerusalem. Written in America, in a time of Solitude and Divine Contemplation ; by a Zealous Lover of Truth, *etc. For R. Hartley.* 1707. 8º.

By Richard Franck. The preface is signed Philanthropus. Franck's *Philosophical Treatise of the original and production of things* was "writ in America in a time of solitudes." B.M. (4413. cc. 39).

[Another edition.] *For J. Morphew.* 1708. 12º.

Priv. Lib.

PHILANTUS AND BELLAMOND.

The Amours of Philantus and Bellamond. A French History. *For F. Saunders.* 1690. 12º.

B.M. (Bagford 5986, 127), title only.

[Another edition.] 1697. *See* NOVELS. Four Novels, *etc.*

PHILAQUILA. *See* GOLDEN EAGLE.

PHILARIO AND OLINDA.

The Amours of Philario and Olinda : or the Intrigues of Windsor. A Genuine History. *For F. Cogan.* 1730. 8º.

The preface is signed S. L.
B.M. (12614. d. 11).

PHILOXYPES AND POLYCRITE.

The History of Philoxypes and Polycrite, As it was told by Leontides to the great Cyrus. Englished out of French, by an Honourable Anti-Socordist, *etc. For H. Moseley.* 1652. 8º.

B.M. (1074. b. 41).

PIKE.

The Pike.   A Tale.   *Sold by J. Penn.*   1733.

Gentleman's Magazine, Dec. 1733.

PILGRIM.

The Pilgrim ; or, the Stranger in his own Country.   In several Historical Novels.   *Sold by D. Farmer.*   1738.   12°.

Gentleman's Magazine, June 1738.

PINES, *the Isle of.*

See NEVILE, Henry.

PLANTIN, ARABELLA.

Two Novels. viz. I. The Ingrateful : Or, The just Revenge.   II. Love led Astray: Or, The Mutual Inconstancy.   By Mrs. Arabella Plantin.   1727.   12°.

Issued in *Whartoniana*, 1727, and again [1731 ?] in the same, with the title "The Poetical Works of Philip Duke of Wharton . . . also Two Entertaining Novels, by the Celebrated Mrs. Arabella Plantin."

B.M. (12614. c. 1), separate ; (11607. bbb. 18), [1731?]

PLAYER'S TRAGEDY.

The Player's Tragedy.   Or, Fatal Love, a New Novel.   *R. Taylor.*   1693. 12°.

B.M. (635. a. 5/2).

PLEASANT COMPANION.

The Pleasant Companion, or Tryall of Wits, being a choice Collection of . . . Stories, *etc.*   1684.

Univ. Lib., Chicago.

[Another edition.]   The Pleasant Companion : or, Wit in all Shapes, *etc. For J. Brooks.*   1734.   12°.

Bodl. (Douce N. 134).

PLEASURES OF MATRIMONY.

The Pleasures of Matrimony, Intermix'd with Variety of Merry and Delightful Stories.   *A. G. for H. Rhodes.*   1688.   12°.

Priv. Lib.

[Another edition.]   The Second Edition.   *For H. Rhodes.*   1689.   12°.
  Term Cat., ii. 294.

[Another edition.]   The Fourth Edition.   *For H. Rhodes.*   1693.   12°.
  Term Cat., ii. 487.

LESS, *Mr.*

Memoirs of the life and misfortunes of Mr. Pless . . . by a lady.   1731.
  Gentleman's Magazine, Feb. 1731.

OLEXANDER.

See LE ROY, Marin, *Sieur de Gomberville.*

OMERANO, CASTALION.

See BRAITHWAITE, Richard.

OMPONIUS.

See LABADIE.

OPE, ALEXANDER.

A Full and True Account of a Horrid and Barbarous Revenge by
oison, On the body of Mr. Edmund Curll, Bookseller : With a faithful
opy of his Last Will and Testament.   Published by an Eye Witness.
old by J. Roberts, J. Morphew, R. Burleigh, J. Baker, and S. Popping.
716.]   Fol.
  B.M. (816. m. 19/70).

A Further Account of the most Deplorable Condition of Mr. Edmund
urll, Bookseller, since his being poison'd on March 28.   1716.   8°.
  T. C. D.

See SWIFT, Jonathan.   [Collections], and Memoirs of the Life of Scriblerus.

OPE, WALTER.

The Memoirs of Monsieur du Vall, containing the History of his Life and
eath ; with his last Speech and Epitaph.   *For H. Brome.*   1670.   4°.
  B.M. (1132. g. 62).

PORTOCARRERO, Luis Manuel, *Cardinal.*

The History, Political and Gallant, of the Famous Card. Portocarrero
Archbishop of Toledo, Done out of French. *W. R., and to be sold b*
J. Nutt. 1704. 12º.

    B.M. (12511. c. 16).

PORTUGUESE NUN.

See Alcoforado, Marianna d'.

POWEL, Robert.

See Second Tale of a Tub.

PRACTICAL PART OF LOVE.

The Practical Part of Love. Extracted out of the Extravagant and Lasci
vious Life of a Fair but Subtle Female. 1660. 8º.

    Priv. Lib.

PRÉCHAC, *le Sieur* DE.

The Amours of Count Teckeli And the Lady Aurora Veronica de Serini . .
Translated out of French. *For R. Bentley and S. Magnes.* 1686. 12º.

    B.M. (12511. de. 24/1).

The Chaste Seraglian: or Yolanda of Sicily. A Novel. In two parts
Done out of French by T. H. Gent. *For R. Bentley and S. Magnes.*
1685. 12º.

In *Modern Novels*, vol. vii.

    B.M. (12410. c. 24).

The Grand Vizier: Or the History of the Life of Cara Mustapha, Who
Commanded the Turkish Army at the Siege of Vienna, In the year 168,
etc. *H. Hills, Jun. for J. Whitlock.* 1685. 12º.

    B.M. (1450. a. 21).

[Another edition.] The True History of Cara Mustapha. Late Grand
Vizier . . . Written Originally in French by a Person of Quality, and now
translated into English by Francis Philon. Gent. *For L. Curtiss and*
H. Rodes. 1685. 12º.

    B.M. (10605. de. 19).

The Heroin Musqueteer, or The female Warrior. A true History, very delightful and full of pleasant Adventures in the Campagnes of 1676, 1677. Translated out of French. *For J. Magnes and R. Bentley, and R. Tonson.* 678. 12°. 4 vols.

Histoire véritable de Mlle. Christine, Comtesse de Meyrac.
    Term Cat., i. 300, 320, 330. Vols. 3 and 4 are also for J. Tonson.

[Another edition.] *J. Orme, for R. Wellington.* 1700. 8°.

In *A Collection of Pleasant Novels.*
    B.M. (12511. bb. 8/1).

The Illustrious Parisian Maid, or The secret Amours of a German Prince. A History true and full of Gallantry. From the true French copy, printed at Paris, 1679, *etc. For J. Amery.* 1680. 12°.

    Term Cat., i. 393.

[Another version.] The Disguis'd Prince : or, the Beautiful Parisian. A True History. Translated from the French. *For T. Corbett ; and Sold by J. Roberts.* 1728. 8°.

The dedication is signed Eliza Haywood.
    B.M. (12511. h. 5).

[Another edition.] The Second Edition. *For T. Corbett, and sold by J. Roberts.* 1733. 8°.

    Bodl. (Godw. Pamph. 1231/4).

The Lovely Polander. A Novel. *For J. Kidgell.* 1681. 12°.

    Term Cat., i. 461.

The Serasquior Bassa. An Historical Novel of the Times : containing all that passed at the Siege of Buda. Done out of French. *For H. Rodes.* 1685. 12°.

    Term Cat., ii. 124.

PRENTICE'S TRAGEDY.

See BARNWELL, George.

PRÉVOST D'EXILES, ANTOINE FRANÇOIS.

The Life of Mr. Cleveland, natural son of Oliver Cromwell : written by himself. 1731. 2 vols.

Le Philosophe Anglais.
    Gentleman's Magazine, April, 1731.

[Another edition.]   In Four Volumes, *etc.   For T. Astley.*   1734, 35.   12⁰
5 vols.

The fifth volume is dated 1735.

B.M. (12516. de. 23).

[Another edition.]   In Two Volumes.   *S. Powell, for W. Heatley : Dublin*
1736.   12⁰.   2 vols.

B.M. (12511. b. 6).

Memoirs of a Man of Quality.   Written originally in the French Tongue
by himself, after his Retirement from the World.   Now first published in
English.   *J. Wilford.*   1738.   12⁰.

B.M. (837. b. 5).

PRICE, LAURENCE.

The Witch of the Woodlands : Or, The Coblers New Translation.   Written
by L. P., *etc.   For J. Stafford.*   1655.   8⁰.   𝕭.𝕷.

Bodl. (Wood 704).

[Another edition.]   *J. Millet and Sold by J. Gilbertson.*   8⁰.   𝕭.𝕷.

Bodl. (Wood 707).

[Another edition.]   *For W. T[hackeray] and are to be sold by C. Passinger*
[1677 ?]   8⁰.

Bodl. (Douce P. 653), the date partly cut away.

[Another edition.]   *A. P. for W. Thackeray.*   8⁰.   𝕭.𝕷.

B.M. (C. 40. b. 12).

Witty William of Wilt-shire.   His birth, Life, and Education, and strange
adventures : with his unmatcheable Cheats . . .   With merry songs and
sonnets.   *For C. Passinger.*   1674.   8⁰.   𝕭.𝕷.

Huth.

PRUDE.

The Prude.   A Novel.   Written by a Young Lady.   The Third Edition.

Advertised by J. Roberts, in Mrs. Haywood's *Bath Intrigues,* 1725.

PSITTACORUM REGIO.

See (in Part I) HALL, Joseph.

*PYLADES AND CORINNA.

Pylades and Corinna, or Memoirs.   1731.

Gentleman's Magazine, July 1731.

The Honourable Lovers, or second volume of Pylades and Corinna.   1732.

Gentleman's Magazine, Feb. 1732.

*PYTHAGORAS.

See CROXALL, Samuel.

QUARLL, PHILIP.

The Hermit : Or, the Unparalled [*sic*] Sufferings And Surprising Adventures of Mr. Philip Quarll, An Englishman.   Who was lately discovered by Mr. Dorrington a Bristol Merchant, upon an uninhabited Island in the South-Sea, *etc.   J. Cluer and A. Campbell for T. Warner and B. Creake.* 1727.   8°.

B.M. (635. f. 16).

[Another edition.]   The Sufferings and Surprizing Adventures of Mr. Philip Quarll, *etc.   Sold by the Booksellers of London and Westminster.*   4°.

B.M. (12410. f. 19).

QUEVEDO VILLEGAS, FRANCISCO DE.

The Novels of Dom Francisco de Quevedo Villegas, Knight of the Order of St. James.   Faithfully Englished.   Whereunto is added, The Marriage of Belphegor, An Italian Novel.   Translated from Machiavel.   *For J. Starkey.* 1671.   8°.

Bodl. (Douce QQ. 26).

The Comical Works of Don Francisco de Quevedo, Author of the Visions . . .   Translated from the Spanish.   *J. Morphew.*   1707.   8°.

B.M. (12330. cc. 40).

[Another edition.]   *For J. Woodward.*   1709.   12°.

B.M. (12230. b. 9).

The Life and Adventures of Buscon The Witty Spaniard.   Put into English by a Person of Honour.   To which is added, The Provident Knight. By Don Francisco de Quevedo, A Spanish Cavalier.   *J. M. for H. Herringman.*   1657.   8°.

B.M. (E. 1585/2).

[Another edition.]   The second edition.   *For H. Herringman.*   1670.   8°
  B.M. (1074. d. 24).

[Another edition.]   Paul of Segovia.

See CESPEDES Y MENESES, Gonzalo de.   The Famous History of Auristella.
1683.

The Travels of Don Francisco de Quevedo.   Through Terra Australis
Incognita.

See (in Part I) HALL, Joseph.

See also Part I.

QUINTANA, FRANCISCO DE.

The most Entertaining History of Hippolyto and Aminta . . .   Translated
from the Original Spanish ; Written by that celebrated Wit, Don Francisco
de Quintana.   *For A. Bettesworth, J. Batley, and W. Boreham.*   1718.   12°.
  B.M. (12490. c. 17).

[Another edition.]   Translated . . . by Capt. Stevens.   The Second Edition.
For A. Bettesworth, and J. Batley.   1729.   12°.

  B.M. (12490. dd. 16).

RAKE.

The Rake's Adventures, or a trip through the Bills of Mortality.

  Gentleman's Magazine, March 1731.

The Progress of a Rake : Shewing the Various Intrigues and Dangers he
met with, *etc.*   *For N. Cox.*   1732.   8°.

  Another edition of the preceding ?
  B.M. (12330. ccc. 34/6).

RAMSAY, ANDREW.

The Travels of Cyrus.   In Two Volumes.   To which is annex'd, A
Discourse upon the Theology and Mythology of the Ancients.   By the
Chevalier Ramsay, *etc.*   *Sold by T. Woodward and J. Peele.*   1727.   8°.   2 vols.

  The dedication is signed Andrew Ramsay.
  Bodl. (8°. E. 143, 4 Linc).

[Another edition.]   The Third Edition.   *T. Woodward and J. Peele.*
1728.   8°.   2 vols.

  B.M. (89. a. 13).

[Another edition.] The Fourth Edition much Enlarged. *Sold by T. Woodward, and J. Peele.* 1730. 8°. 2 vols.

B.M. (12511. f. 26).

[Another edition.] The Travels of Cyrus. Fourth Edition. *J. Bettenham.* 1730. 4°.

A very large 4to.

B.M. (635. l. 3).

[Another edition.] The Sixth Edition. *J. Bettenham, and sold by A. Bettesworth and C. Hitch.* 1739. 12°.

B.M. (634. a. 1).

REVIVED FUGITIVE. *See* BELLON, Peter.

REYNOLDS, JOHN.

The Flower of Fidelitie. Displaying In a Continuate Historie, The various Adventures of Three Foraign Princes. By John Reynolds, Author of that Excellent Historie Entituled (God's Revenge against Murther). *T. M. and A. C. for G. Badger.* 1650. 8°.

B.M. (E. 1236/1).

[Another edition.] *For R. Horne.* 1660. 8°.

Hazlitt, II. 518.

[Another edition.] The Garden of Love, and Royal flowers of Fidelity : a pleasant History written by Mr. John Reynolds . . . Now much amplified by several hands. The Fourth Edition, with Amendments and Alterations. *For N. Boddington, and J. Back.* 1692.

Term Cat., ii. 405.

[Another edition.] The Seventh Edition, with Amendments and Alterations. *For T. Norris, and M. Boddington.* 1721. 12°.

B.M. (12614. aaa. 29).

[Another edition.] The Eighth Edition, with Amendments and Alterations. *For A. Bettesworth and C. Hitch, and J. Clarke.* 1733. 12°.

B.M. (12613. a. 30).

[Another edition.] The Ninth Edition, with Amendments and Alterations. *For H. Woodgate, and S. Brooks.* 8°.

B.M. (12612. b. 35).

God's Revenge Against the Crying and Execrable Sin of Adultery, Express'd in Ten several Tragical Histories . . . The whole Illustrated with . . . proper Cuts to each History. By John Reynolds. *For J. How, and A. Bettesworth.* 1708. 12°.

    B.M. (12613. a. 29).

For God's Revenge against Murder, *and editions of* God's Revenge against Adultery *appended to it, See* Part I.

See DELIGHTFUL NOVELS.

RIVAL MOTHER.

The Rival Mother ; a late True History : Digested into a Novel. *For R. Baldwin.* 1692. 12°.

    Bodl. (S. 178 Art).

RIVAL PRINCESSES.

The Rival Princesses : Or, The Colchian Court : A Novel. *For R. Bentley.* 1689. 12°.

    In *Modern Novels*, vol. x.
    B.M. (12410. c. 27).

ROBERTS, *Captain* GEORGE.

See DEFOE, Daniel.

ROCK, *Father*.

See ADAMITE.

RODOLPHUS.

See CROKE, Charles.

ROSALINDA.

See FONTANIEU, Gaspard Moïse.

ROSAMOND, *Fair*.

The Life and Death of Rosamond, King Henry the Second's Concubine. And how she was Poysoned to Death by Queen Elenor. *For F. Coles, T. Vere, J. Wright, J. Clarke, W. Thackeray, and T. Passinger.* 8°. **B.L.**

    Pepys 362 (25).

[Another edition.]   *For W. Thackeray and T. Passenger.*   8°.   𝕭.𝕷.
  Bodl. (Wood 254/3).

The Loves of King Henry II, and Fair Rosamond.   1729.

See CROXALL, Samuel.   A Select Collection of Novels, ed. 2, vol. iv.

ROUSSEAU DE LA VALETTE, MICHEL.
  [Casimer, King of Poland.   Part 1.   *For R. Bentley?*]   8°.
  In *Modern Novels*, vol. ii.
    B.M. (12410. c. 19), imperfect.

The Life of Count Ulfeld, Great Master of Denmark, And of the Countess
Eleonora his Wife: Done out of French, *etc.*   1695.   8°.
    B.M. (G. 14778).

ROVER.
  The Rover.
  Serially, in *The British Mercury*, from 14 July, 1714.
    C. Morgan, *Rise of the Novel of Manners*, p. 213, n.

ROXAS, FERNANDO DE.
  Celestina, The Bawd of Madrid.   1707.
  See SPANISH LIBERTINES.

ROYAL LOVES.
  See ASTERIA AND TAMBERLAIN.

ROZELLI, *Signor*.
  See OLIVIER, *l'Abbé*.

S., J.
  See CHILDREN IN THE WOOD; SHURLEY, John.

S., N.
  See PAMPHILUS, Hesychius.

S., T.

The Second Part of the Pilgrims Progress, from This present World of Wickedness and Misery, to An Eternity of Holiness and Felicity ; Exactly Described under the Similitude of a Dream.   *T. H.*   1682.   12°.

> By T. S., who signs the dedication, not by Bunyan.
> B.M. (C. 58. aa. 5).

[Another edition.]   *For T. Malthus.*   1683.   12°.

> Hazlitt, II. 530.

[Another edition.]   *The Heir of Andrew Anderson : Edinburgh.*   1684.   12°.

> Hazlitt, II. 530.

See LISANDER ; PERPLEXED PRINCE.

SADEUR, JACQUES.

A New Discovery of Terra Incognita Australis, or the Southern World. By James Sadeur a French-man.   Who Being Cast there by a Shipwrack, lived 35 years in that Country . . .   Translated from the French Copy, Printed at Paris, By Publick Authority.   *For J. Dunton.*   1693.   12°.

> By Gabriel de Foigny.
> B.M. (838. a. 1).

SAINT ALBAN'S GHOST.

See ARBUTHNOT, John.

SAINT EVREMOND, *le Seigneur* DE.

See MARGUETEL DE SAINT DENIS, Charles.

SAINT-HYACINTHE, HYACINTHE CORDONNIER DE.

Histoire du Prince Titi, A.R.   The History of Prince Titi, a Royal Allegory.   Translated by a Lady, *etc.   For E. Curll.*   1736.   12°.   2 vols.

> B.M. (12513. a. 25), imperf., wanting vol. 2 (part 4) ; dealers' list.

[Another version.]   The Memoirs and History of Prince Titi.   Done from the French by a Person of Quality.   *For A. Dodd.*   1736.   12°. 2 vols.

> For the relation of this with Prince Frederick, *cf. D.N.B., art.* Ralph, James.
> (B.M. (12511. cc. 2), imperf., wanting vol. 2 (part 4) ; dealer's list.

For the sequel, *See* PENNYMAN, *Lady* Margaret.

SAINT JORY, Louis Rustaing de.

The Adventures of Malouka, The Beautiful Arabian : or, The Triumph of Virtue and Innocence over Malice, Corruption and Perjury. Translated from the French of the Chevalier de St. Jory ... By Charles Forman, Esq. *For J. Huggonson.* 1738. 8°.

La Bienaimée du Prophète.
B.M. (012551. e. 16).

SAINT RÉAL, César Vischard de.

Don Carlos : Or, An Historical Relation of the Unfortunate Life, and Tragical Death of that Prince of Spain, Son to Philip the II^d. Written in French, Anno 1672. and newly Englished by H. I. *T. N. for H. Herringman, and J. Crump.* 1674. 12°.

B.M. (10632. aa. 4).

[Another edition.] The second edition. *For H. Herringman and J. Crump.* 1676. 12°.

Term Cat., i. 259.

[Another edition.] Don Carlos. An Historical Novel. Written originally in French by the Abbé de St. Real. 1720.

See Croxall, Samuel. A Select Collection of Novels, vol. iii.

[Another edition.] 1729.

See Croxall, Samuel. A Select Collection of Novels, ed. 2, vol. iii.

The Memoires of the Dutchess Mazarine. Written in French by her Own Hand, and Done into English by P. Porter ... Together with the Reasons of her Coming into England, *etc. Sold by W. Cademan.* 1676. 8°.

B.M. (1417. c. 46).

[Another edition.] The Third Impression with Additions. *For R. Bentley.* 1690. 12°.

B.M. (12510. aaaa. 28/1).

[Another edition.] Written in Her Name by the Abbot of St. Real. With a Letter containing a True Character of her Person and Conversation, *etc.* 1713. 8°.

Bodl. (8°. F. 63 Jur.).

See Marguetel de Saint Denis, Charles, *Seigneur de Saint Evremond.* The Works ... To which are added the Memoirs of the Dutchess of Mazarin, *etc.* 1728.

SALAS BARBADILLO, Alonso Geronimo.

The Fortunate Fool. Written in Spanish by Don Alonso Geronimo de Salas Barbadillo of Madrid. Translated into English by Philip Ayres, Gent. *M. Pitt.* 1670. 8°.

> B.M. (1074. d. 29).

SALISBURY, *the Countess of.*

The Countess of Salisbury; Or, The Most Noble Order of the Garter. An Historical Novel. In Two Parts. Done out of French by Mr. Ferrand Spence. *For R. Bentley and S. Magnes.* 1683. 12°.

In *Modern Novels*, vol. iii.
> B.M. (12410. c. 20).

SALTON, W. (SALTONSTALL, Wye?)

[Somnia Allegorica : or Dreams expounded. A Novel. By W. Salton, of Magd. Coll. in Oxon. The Second Edition.] 1661.

" In the year 1661 was the second edit. of a book entit. *Somnia Allegorica : or Dreams expounded. A Novel*, being the first written in this way, published under the name of W. Salton, whom I take to be the same with Wye Saltonstall, tho' in the title 'tis said he was of Magd. Coll. in Oxon, but false." à Wood, *Athen. Oxon.*, ed. Bliss, 1813-20, vol. ii., col. 677.

SANDISSON, *Monsieur* DE. *See* BIGNON, Jean Paul.

SARENDIP. *See* CHRISTOFORO, *Armeno.*

SAVELLI, Troilo. *See* MATTHEW, *Sir* Tobie.

SCANDERBEG. *See* LA ROCHE GUILHEM, *Mlle.* de.

SCARAMOUCHE. *See* CONSTANTINI, Angelo.

SCARBOROUGH.

A Journey from London to Scarborough, in several Letters from a Gentleman there, to his Friend in London. *For C. Ward and R. Chandler : London . . . And sold at their shop in Scarborough.* 8°.

> B.M. (12330. k. 12/3).

SCARRON, PAUL.

The whole comical Works of Mons. Scarron ; containing, 1. His comical Romance of a company of Stage players, in Three Parts compleat.   2. All his Works and Histories.   3. His select Letters, Characters, etc. : a great part of which never before in English.   Translated by Mr. Tho. Brown, Mr. Savage. and Others.   *For S. and J. Sprint, J. Nicholson, R. Parker, and B. Tooke.* 1700.   8°.

> B.M. (1074. k. 10).

[Another edition.]   The Second Edition, revised and corrected.   *For S. and J. Sprint, J. Nicholson, R. Parker and B. Tooke.*   1703.   8°.

> B.M. (12237. bbb. 27).

[Another edition.]   The Third Edition, Revised and Corrected.   *For J. Nicholson, J. and B. Sprint, R. Parker, and B. Tooke.*   1712.   8°.

> Bodl. (Douce S. 419).

[Another edition.]   The Fourth Edition, Revis'd and Corrected.   *For J. and J. Knapton, J. and B. Sprint, R. Robinson, T. Sanders, B. Motte, and A. Ward.*   1727.   12°.   2 vols.

> B.M. (12237. aaa. 20).

Scarron's Comical Romance : Or, A Facetious History of a Company of Strowling Stage-Players . . .   Written originally in French by the Famous and Witty Poet Scarron, and now turn'd into English.   *J. C. for W. Crooke.* 1676.   Fol.

> B.M. (12510. i. 2).

Scarron's Novels.   Viz.   The Fruitless Precaution.   The Hypocrites. The Innocent Adultery.   The Judge in his own Cause.   The Rival Brothers. The Invisible Mistress.   The Chastisement of Avarice.   Rendred into English, with some Additions, by John Davies of Kidwelly.   *For T. Dring.* 1665.   8°.

> According to the *D.N.B.*, Davies published three of Scarron's novels separately in 1657, then four more in 1662.
> Bodl. (Bliss 2. 2114).

[Another edition.]   *For T. Dring.*   1667.   8°.

> Bodl. (Douce S. 720).

[Another edition.]   *Sold by W. Freeman.*   1682.   8°.

> *The Unexpected Choice* is added to the list of contents ; it had appeared separately since the first edition of this collection.
> Term Cat., i. 514.

[Another edition ?]

> Advertised by J. Walthoe in 1721.

The Innocent Adultery. Translated from the French Original of Monsieur Scarron. 1720.

See CROXALL, Samuel. A Select Collection of Novels, vol. iv.

[Another edition.] 1729.

See CROXALL, Samuel. A Select Collection of Novels, ed. 2, vol. iv.

The Unexpected Choice, A Novel. By Monsieur Scarron. Rendred into English, with Addition and Advantage. By John Davies of Kidwelly, Gent. *For J. Martyn,* 1670. 12°.
Plus d'Effets que de Paroles.
B.M. (1073. d. 52).

Scarron's City Romance.

See FURETIÈRE, Antoine.

SCHOOTEN, HENDRIK VAN.

The Hairy Giants : Or, A Description of Two Islands in the South Sea, Called by the name of Benganga and Coma : Discovered by Henry Schooten of Harlem ; In a Voyage began January 1669, and finished October 1671. Written in Dutch by Henry Schooten ; and now Englished by P. M. Gent. *A. Maxwell for J. Watson, and are to be sold by J. Collins.* 4°.
B.M. (G. 7076), the date cut away.

SCOTCH ROGUE.
See MACDONALD, Donald.

SCUDÉRY, MADELEINE DE.

Almahide ; or the Captive Queen. An Excellent New Romance, Never before in English. The whole Work. Written in French by the Accurate Pen of Monsieur de Scudery . . . Done into English by J. Phillips Gent, *etc.* *J. M. for T. Dring.* 1677. Fol.
B.M. (12403. i. 6).

Amaryllis to Tityrus. Being the First Heroic Harangue of the Excellent Pen of Monsieur Scudery. A Witty and Pleasant Novel. Englished by a Person of Honour. *For W. Cademan.* 1681. 8°.
B.M. (1458. a. 19).

Artamenes or the Grand Cyrus, An excellent new Romance. Written by that famous Wit of France, Monsieur de Scudery Governour of Nostre-Dame. And now Englished by F. G. Gent. *For H. Moseley and T. Dring.* 1653-5. Fol. 5 vols.
B.M. (86. k. 16).

[Another edition.]   *J. Darby, and sold by R. Roberts, B. Griffin, and R. Everingham.*   1691.   12°.   10 vols.

> *Term Cat.*, ii. 362.

[Clelia, parts 1, 2.]   Clelia.   An excellent new Romance dedicated to Mlle. de Longueville.   Written in French by the Exquisite Pen of M. de Scudery, *etc.   For H. Moseley and T. Dring.*   1655, 56.   Fol.   2 vols.

> Bodl. (fol. BS. 143).

[Parts 1–5.]   Clelia, *etc.   For H. Mosely and T. Dring.*   1656–61.   Fol. 5 vols.

> Parts 1–3 translated by J. Davies, 4 and 5 by G. Havers.
> B.M. (12403. c. 23).

[Another edition.]   *To be sold by H. Herringman, D. Newman, T. Cockerel, S. Heyrick, W. Cadman, S. Loundes, G. Marriot, W. Crook, and C. Smith.* 1678, 77.   Fol.   5 vols.

> Vols. 2, 3 and 4 are "Printed for D. Newman and T. Cockerel," vol. 5 for H. Herring-man.   Vols. 4 and 5 are dated 1677.
> B.M. (837. m. 20).

Ibrahim.   Or the Illustrious Bassa.   An excellent new Romance.   The Whole Work, in Foure Parts.   Written in French by Monsieur de Scudery, and now Englished By Henry Cogan, Gent.   *For H. Moseley, W. Bentley, and T. Heath.*   1652.   Fol.

> B.M. (837. l. 15).

[Another edition.]   *J. R., and are to be sold by P. Parker.*   1674.   Fol.

> B.M. (12403. i. 10).

See ZELINDA.

SEBASTIAN, *Don.*

Don Sebastian King of Portugal.   An Historical Novel.   In Four Parts. Done out of French by Mr. Ferrand Spence.   *For R. Bentley and S. Magnes.* 1683.   12°.

> In *Modern Novels*, vol. v.
> B.M. (12410. c. 22).

SECOND TALE OF A TUB.

A Second Tale of a Tub : or, The History of Robert Powel the Puppet-Show-Man.   *For J. Roberts.*   1715.   8°.

> B.M. (1079. m. 14).

SEGRAIS, JEAN REGNAULD DE.

Five Novels.   Translated from the French of M. Segrais . . . viz.   I. The Beautiful Pirate ; or The Constant Lovers.   II. Eugenia ; or, The Force of Destiny.   III. Bajazet ; or, The Imprudent Favourite.   IV. Montrose ; or, The Happy Discovery.   V. Mistaken Jealousy ; or, The Disguised Lovers. *For D. Browne, jun*ʳ.   1725.   12°.   2 vols.

> Vol. 2 has the title " The power of Jealousy Exemplify'd in two Novels," *etc.*
>   B.M. (12511. aaa. 23).

The Princess of Cleves.   The most fam'd Romance.   Written in French by the greatest wits of France.   Englished by a Person of Quality, at the request of some friends.   *For R. Bentley and M. Magnes.*   1679.

> By Segrais, the Comtesse de la Fayette, and the Duc de Rochefoucauld.
>   *Term Cat.*, i. 349.

[Another edition.]   *For R. Bentley and S. Magnes.*   1688.   12°.

> B.M. (12512. ee. 6).

[Another version.]   1720.
See CROXALL, Samuel.   A Select Collection of Novels, vol. ii.

[Another edition.]   1729.
See CROXALL, Samuel.   A Select Collection of Novels, ed. 2, vol. ii.

The Princess of Montpensier, written originally in French, and now newly rendered into English.   1666.   8°.

> By Segrais and the Comtesse de la Fayette.
>   B.M. (12512. aaa. 36).

Zayde, a Spanish History, being a Pleasant and Witty Novel.   In Two Parts, Compleat.   Originally Written in French, by Monsieur Segray.   Done into English by P. Porter, Esq.   *T. Milbourn for W. Cademan.*   1678.   8°. 2 vols.

> By Segrais and the Comtesse de la Fayette.
>   B.M. (12510. c. 8).

[Another edition.]   The Second Edition Corrected.   *For F. Saunders.* 1690.   8°.

> B.M. (12511. aa. 20).

[Another version.]   1720.
See CROXALL, Samuel.   A Select Collection of Novels, vol. i.

[Another edition.] 1729.

See CROXALL, Samuel. A Select Collection of Novels, ed. 2, vol. i.

SERASQUIOR BASSA.

See PRÉCHAC, *le Sieur* de.

SETHOS.

See TERRASSON, Jean.

SFORZA, BONA.

See BELLON, Peter.

SHEPPARD, SAMUEL.

The Loves of Amandus and Sophronia, Historically Narrated. A Piece of rare Contexture, Inriched with many pleasing Odes and Sonnets . . . By Samuel Sheppard. *G. D. for I. Hardestie.* 1650. 8°.

B.M. (1081. d. 3).

SHIPTON, URSULA, *Mother.*

The History of Mother Shipton, *etc.* 4°.

Bodl. (Douce BB. 394).

The Strange and Wonderful history of Mother Shipton . . . With an exact collection of all her famous Prophecys, *etc.* *For W. H[arris] and sold by J. Conyers.* 1686. 8°.

Not the same as the preceding, or as Head's narrative.
Reprint, Manchester [1881], the size given there as 4°; Pepys, 362/1201, the imprint cut away.

See also HEAD, Richard.

SHORE, JANE.

The Life and Character of Jane Shore collected From our best Historians, chiefly from the Writings of Sir Thomas More; Who was Her Cotemporary, and Personally knew Her. Humbly Offer'd to the Readers and Spectators of Her Tragedy Written by Mr. Rowe. Inscrib'd to Mrs. Oldfield. *Sold by J. Morphew and A. Dodd.* 1714.

Rowe's play produced also a *Life and Death of Jane Shore,* not a romance, in the same year.
B.M. (T. 1092/3).

The History of Jane Shore.   1729.

See CROXALL, Samuel.   A Select Collection of Novels, ed. 2, vol. iii.
A different work, also dedicated to Mrs. Oldfield.

SHURLEY, JOHN.

The Famous History of Aurelius, The Valiant London-Prentice . .
Written for Incouragement of Youth. By J. S.   *For J. Back.*   8°.   𝔅.𝔏.
   Pepys 362 (307).

[Another edition ?]   [*For W. Thackeray and T. Passinger ?*]   8°.   𝔅.𝔏.
   Bodl. (Wood 254/7), frag.

[Another edition.]
Advertised by B. Deacon, in *The Seven Champions.*

[Another edition.]   *J. White: Newcastle.*   1711.   12°.
   B.M. (12612. b. 15/1).

[Another edition ?]   London's Glory : or, the History of the Famous and
Valiant London Prentice, *etc.*   *W. O[nley] and sold by E. Tracy.*   4°.
   Bodl. (Douce R. 528).

See GUY OF WARWICK.

SIDEN, *Captain.*
   See VAIRASSE D'ALLAIS, Denis.

SIDNEY, *Sir* PHILIP.
   Almanzor and Almanzaida.
   See LA ROCHE GUILHEM, *Mlle* de.

SIMON AND CISLEY.

The Merry Conceits and Passages of Simon and Cisley, two Lancashire
Lovers . . .   By J. P.   *H. B[rugis] for J. Clark, W. Thackery, and T. Passinger.*
8°.   𝔅.𝔏.
   Pepys 362 (1227).

SKIMMER.
   See CRÉBILLON, Claude Prosper Jolyot de, *fils.*

SLOETTEN, HENRY CORNELIUS VAN.
  See NEVILE, Henry.

SMITH, ALEXANDER.
  The Comical and Tragical History of the Lives and Adventures Of the most
Noted Bayliffs In and about London and Westminster . . .   Written by
Captain Alexander Smith. *For S. Briscoe.* 1723. 8°.
    B.M. (12314. f. 7).

SMITHSON, SAMUEL.
  See GUY OF WARWICK.

SOISSONS, *the Count* DE.
  See CLAUDE, Isaac.

SOREL, CHARLES.
  The Extravagant Shepherd. The Anti-Romance : or, the History of the
Shepherd Lysis. Translated out of French. *For T. Heath.* 1653. Fol.
    B.M. (12403. b. 11).

  [Another edition.] An Anti-Romance ; Written originally in French, and
Now made English. *T. Newcomb for T. Heath.* 1654. Fol.
    Bodl. (Douce R. 205).

  [Another edition.] In XIV. Books . . . Published the Second time. *For
T. Bassett.* 1660. Fol.
    B.M. (12403. b. 12).

  The Comical History of Francion. Wherein The variety of Vices that
abuse the Ages are Satyrically limn'd in their Native Colours. Interwoven
with many pleasant Events . . . By Monsieur De Moulines, Sieur de Parc,
a Lorain Gentleman . . . Done into English by a Person of Honour. *For
F. Leach, and are to be sold by R. Lowndes.* 1655. Fol.
    B.M. (12510. h. 30).

  [Another version.] Satyrically exposing Folly and Vice, in Variety of
Humours and Adventures . . . Translated by Several Hands, and Adapted
to the Humour of the Present Age. *For R. Wellington.* 1703. 8°.
    Hazlitt, II. 169.

[Another edition.] The Second Edition, very much Corrected, and Adorn'd with Cuts, *etc.* *For M. Poulson, and sold by J. Darby, A. Bettesworth, F. Fayram, J. Pemberton, C. Rivington, J. Hooke, F. Clay, J. Batley, and E. Symon.* 1727. 12°. 2 vols.

Revised and altered. The Preface is signed W. A.

Bodl. (Douce P. 516, 7).

SPANISH AND FRENCH HISTORY.

The Spanish and French History: Or, Love out of Season . . . Out of French, *etc.* *For W. Hull.* 1689. 12°.

B.M. (12510. df. 33).

SPANISH DECAMERON.

The Spanish Decameron : Or, Ten Novels. Viz. The Rival Ladies. The Mistakes. The Generous Lover. The Libertine. The Virgin Captive. The Perfidious Mistress. The Metamorphos'd Lover. The Impostour Out-Witted. The Amorous Miser. The Pretended Alchymist. Made English by R. L. *For S. Neale.* 1687. 8°.

The translator is L'Estrange. The first five novels are, *The Rival Ladies, Cornelia, The Liberal Lover, The Force of Blood,* and *The Spanish-English Lady,* from Cervantes' *Exemplary Novels ;* the sixth, seventh and eighth are the novels from Solorzano's *Garduña de Sevilla ;* the ninth and tenth are the latter half of Book 1 and Book 2 of the same.

B.M. (12490. bbb. 24).

SPANISH LIBERTINES.

The Spanish Libertines ; or, the Lives of Justina, The Country Jilt ; Celestina, The Bawd of Madrid ; and Estevanillo Gonzales . . . Written by Eminent Spanish Authors, and now first made English by Captain John Stevens. *S. Bunchley.* 1707. 8°.

La Picara Justina, by Francisco de Ubeda (Andreas Perez), selected and adapted. Celestina is the tragicomedy.

B.M. (12491. f. 30).

[Another edition.] *For J. Woodward.* 1709. 8°.

Priv. Lib.

STANHOPE, HUGH.

The Fortunate and Unfortunate Lovers : Or, The History of the Lives, Fortunes, and Adventures of Dorastus and Fawnia, Hero and Leander. Made English from the Originals, Written in the Bohemia and Grecian Tongues by a Gentleman, *etc.* *For A. Bettesworth and C. Hitch, R. Ware, and J. Hodges.* 1735. 12°.

The preface is signed Hugh Stanhope.

B.M. (12611. d. 22).

STEVENS, John.

　The Ungrateful Fair, by Capt. John Stevens. 1731. 8°.

　　B.M. (12614. d. 12), imperf. ; dealer's list.

STITCH, Tom.

　Wanton Tom : or, The Merry History of Tom Stitch the Taylor. *For R. Butler, and sold by R. Kell.* 1685. 8°. 𝔅.𝔏.

　　Pepys 362 (281).

STUBBES, George.

　A new Adventure of Telemachus. By the Author of the Dialogue on Beauty, in the Manner of Plato. *W. Wilkins.* 1731. 8°.

　　First published in *The London Journal* for 1724.
　　B.M. (12511. c. 28).

SUBLIGNY, Adrien Thomas Perdou de.

　The Mock-Clelia. Being a Comical History of French Gallantries, and Novels, in imitation of Don Quixote. Translated out of French. *For L. Curtis.* 1678. 8°.

　　B.M. (12611. g. 11).

SULTANA OF BARBARY.

　The Amours of the Sultana of Barbary. A Novel, in Two Parts. The Story finished. *To be sold by R. Baldwin.* 1689. 12°.

　　A satire on the Duchess of Portsmouth.
　　B.M. (G. 13992).

　[Another edition.] 1697. *See* Novels. Four Novels.

SUMMERS, Will.

　A Pleasant History of the Life and Death of Will Summers. How he came first to be known at Court, and by what means he got to be King Henry the Eighth's Jester, *etc. For T. Vere, and J. Wright.* 1676. 4°. 𝔅.𝔏.

　　Bodl. (Douce S. 176).

SUNDAY'S ADVENTURE.

A Sundays Adventure, or, Walk to Hackney. Being a Description of an Amorous Intrigue Acted there. *For J. Kidgel.* 1683. 12°.

The dedication is signed D. G.
Priv. Lib.

SWIFT, Jonathan.

[Collections.] Miscellanies by Dr. Jonathan Swift . . . To all which is prefix'd, A Complete Key to the tale of a Tub. *For E. Curll.* 1711. 8°.
B.M. (12350. b. 16).

Miscellanies in Prose and Verse. *For J. Morphew.* 1711. 8°.
Contains the Bickerstaff-Partridge series.
B.M. (838. g. 1).

[Another edition.] The Second Edition. *For J. Morphew.* 1713. 8°.
B.M. (633. g. 20).

[Another edition.] The Fourth Edition, with . . . Additions, *etc.* *S. Fairbrother : Dublin.* 2721 [1721]. 8°.
B.M. (12269. aa. 4).

Miscellaneous Works, Comical & Diverting : by T. R. D. J. S. D. O. P. I. I. In two parts. I. The Tale of a Tub . . . II. Miscellanies in Prose & Verse. *etc. Printed by Order of the Society de propagando, &c.* 1720. 8°.
Contains *The Tale of a Tub, The Battle of the Books,* and the Bickerstaff-Partridge series.
B.M. (12331. bb. 10).

Miscellanies in Prose and Verse. *For B. Motte.* 1727. 8°. 3 vols.
Contains in vol. 1 the Bickerstaff-Partridge series, in vol. 2 Arbuthnot's *John Bull* and Pope's *Memoirs of P. P., Parish Clerk.* For vol. 3, see *infra,* 1732.
B.M. (12269. dd. 2).

[Another edition.] *For B. Motte.* 1728. 8°. 3 vols. ?
Only vol. 1 is known.
Forster.

[Another edition.] *S. Fairbrother : Dublin.* 1728. 3 vols.
Bodl. (St. Am. 370), vol. 3 of the 1732-3 Dublin edition.

[Another edition.] *For B. Motte.* 1732. 8°. 3 vols.
Forster.

[Another edition.] *For S. Fairbrother : Dublin.* 1732, 33. 3 vols. 12°.
T. C. D.

[Another edition.] *For B. Motte.* 1733. 12°. 3 vols.
Vol 2 is called "Second Edition."
Dyce.

[Another edition.] *For B. Motte.* 1736, 38. 12°. 3 vols.
Vol. 1 is undated.
Forster.

Miscellanies. The Third Volume. *For B. Motte and L. Gilliver.* 1732.
8°.

Not the same as vol. 3 of the 1737 *Miscellanies*, according to W. S. Jackson (Bibliography in Swift's *Prose Works*, ed. Temple Scott, vol. 12). Contains Pope's *Narrative of Dr. Robert Norris concerning the Frenzy of Mr. J——n D——is*, *Poisoning of Edmund Curll*, and *Condition of Edmund Curll*, and Arbuthnot's *Circumcision of Edmund Curll.*
B.M. (12269. dd. 2), in the 1727 set, with which it is uniform.

[Another edition.] *For B. Motte and L. Gilliver.* 1732. 12°.
Dyce.

[Another edition.] *For B. Motte and L. Gilliver.* 1733. 12°.
Dyce.

[Another edition.] *For B. Motte and L. Gilliver.* 1736. 12°.
Forster.

[Another edition.] *For B. Motte and L. Gilliver.* 1738. 12°.
Forster.

Miscellanies. Consisting chiefly of Original Pieces in Prose and Verse.
By D . . n S . . . t. Never before Published in this Kingdom. *Dublin Printed. London : Re-printed for A. Moore.* 1734. 8°.
Contains *The History of Martin.*
W. S. Jackson, Bibliography in Swift's *Prose Works*, ed. Temple Scott, vol. 12.

The Works of J. S., D.D, D.S.P.D. in Four Volumes, *etc.* *G. Faulkner : Dublin.* 1735. 8°. 4 vols.
Contains, in vol. 1 the Bickerstaff-Partridge series, in vol. 3 *Gulliver's Travels.*
B.M. (632. d. 36).

[Another issue.] *For G. Faulkner : Dublin.* 1735. 8°. 6 vols.
Volumes were added in 1741, 1742 and 1746.
T. C. D. ; Bodl. (Radcliffe e. 235, 6), vols. 5, 6.

The History of John Bull. And Poems on several Occasions, by Dr. Jonathan Swift with several Miscellaneous Pieces, by Dr. Swift and Mr. Pope. *Sold by A. Midwinter and A. Tonson.* 12º.

Contains Arbuthnot's *John Bull*, Pope's *Dr. Norris' Narrative of the Frenzy of Mr. J——n D——is*, *The Poisoning of Edmund Curll*, and *The Condition of Edmund Curll*, and Arbuthnot's *Circumcision of Edmund Curll.*

B.M. (12611. d. 20).

[Another edition, with additions.] A Supplement to Dr. Swift's and Mr. Pope's Works, *etc.   S. Powell, For E. Exshaw : Dublin.* 1739.   12º.

B.M. (12269. aa. 7).

[Single tales.] [The Accomplishment of the First of Mr. Bickerstaff's Predictions. Being an Account Of the Death of Mr. Partridge, the Almanack-maker. Upon the 29th instant. In a Letter to a Person of Honour. 1708.]

No copy known.

See also supra : [Collections].

A Vindication of Isaac Bickerstaff Esq ; against What is Objected to Him by Mr. Partridge, in his Almanack for the Present Year 1709. By the said Isaac Bickerstaff Esq. 1709. 8º.

A sequel to *Predictions for the year 1708*, and *The Accomplishment of the First of Mr. Bickerstaff's Predictions.*

B.M. (1080. i. 58).

See also supra : [Collections].

The Battle of the Books.

See supra : [Collections], and *infra :* The Tale of a Tub.

The History of Martin. Giving an Account of his Departure from Jack . . . By the Rev. D——n S——t, *etc.   For J. Temple.* 8º.

B.M. (1080. i. 25/6), the date cut away.

See also supra : [Collections].

Memoirs of the Life of Scriblerus . . . By D. S——t. *Printed from the Original Copy from Dublin ; and Sold by A. Moore.* 1723. 8º.

B.M. (12316. ee. 15/3).

A New Journey to Paris : Together with some Secret Transactions Between the Fr . . . h K . . . g, and an Eng . . . Gentleman. By the Sieur du Baudrier. Translated from the French. *For J. Morphew.* 1711. 8º.

B.M. (8132. a. 21).

[Another edition.] The Second Edition Corrected. *For J. Morphew.* 1711. 8°.

Advocates ; Guildhall.

[Another edition.] The Third Edition. 1711. 8°.

W. S. Jackson, Bibliography in Swift's *Prose Works*, ed. Temple Scott, vol. 12.

A Tale of a Tub. Written for the Universal Improvement of Mankind . . . To which is added, An Account of a Battel between the Antient and Modern Books in St. James's Library. *For J. Nutt.* 1704. 8°.

B.M. (C. 58. d. 16).

[Another edition.] The Second Edition Corrected. *For J. Nutt.* 1704. 8°.

B.M. (1079. m. 13).

[Another edition.] The Third Edition Corrected. *For J. Nutt.* 1704. 8°.

B.M. (12315. e. 45).

[Another edition.] The Fourth Edition Corrected. *For J. Nutt.* 1705. 8°.

Forster.

[Another edition.] The Fourth Edition Corrected. *Dublin, Reprinted ; and are to be Sold only at Dick's and Lloyd's Coffee-Houses, and at the Printing Press in Fishamble-Street.* 1705. 8°.

B.M. (012314. ee. 58).

[Another edition.] The Fifth Edition : With the Author's Apology and Explanatory Notes. By W. W..tt..n, B.D. and others. *For J. Nutt.* 1710. 8°.

Bodl. (Douce SS. 292).

[Another edition.] 1711. 12°·

B.M. (12330. a. 32).

[Another edition.] The Sixth Edition, *etc. For S. Tooke and B. Motte.* 1724. 12°.

B.M. (1079. h. 6).

[Another edition]. The Seventh Edition, *etc. For B. Motte.* 1727. 8°.

B.M. (12330. bb. 37).

[Another edition.] A New Edition, *etc.* 1734. 8°.

B.M. (1079. h. 7).

See also supra : [Collections].

A Complete key to the Tale of a Tub, *etc. For E. Curll.* 1710. 8°.

 B.M. (1080. i. 66).

See also supra : [Collections].

Travels into several Remote Nations of the World. In Four Parts. By Lemuel Gulliver, First a Surgeon, and then a Captain of several Ships, *etc. For B. Motte.* 1726. 8°. 2 vols.

 The Preface to the Reader signed ' Richard Sympson.'
 Ed. A. pp. xvi., 148 ; [vi.], 164 ; [vi.], 155 [6] ; [viii.], 199 [200].
 B.M. (C. 59. e. 11).

[Another edition.] *For B. Motte.* 1726. 8°. 2 vols.

 Ed. AA. pp. xii., 148 ; [vi.], 164 ; vi., 155 [6] ; viii., 199 [200].
 B.M. (12612. d. 23), vol. 1 only ; Forster.

[Another edition.] *For B. Motte.* 1726. 8°. 2 vols.

 Ed. B. pp. xii., 310 ; vi. 353.
 B.M. (12610. f. 10) vol. 1 only ; Forster.

[Another edition.] *For B. Motte.* 1726. 12°. 2 vols.

 Bodl. (8°. E. 111. 2 Linc).

[Another edition.] *J. Hyde : Dublin.* 1726. 12°. 2 vols.

 W. S. Jackson, Bibliography in Swift's *Prose Works,* ed. Temple Scott, vol. 12.

[Another edition.] *For B. Motte.* 1726. 8°. 2 vols.

 B.M. (12612. d. 23) vol. 2 only ; T. C. D.

[Another edition. 1726–7.] In *Parker's Penny Post,* Nos. 246 (Nov. 28, 1726) — 390 (Nov. 3, 1727).

 W. S. Jackson, Bibliography in Swift's *Prose Works,* ed. Temple Scott, vol. 12.

[Another edition.] *For B. Motte.* 1727. 12°. 2 vols.

 B.M. (12604. bb. 19).

[Another edition.] To which are prefix'd. Several Copies of Verses Explanatory and Commendatory ; never before printed ... The Second Edition. *For B. Motte.* 1727. 8°.

 B.M. (12612. d. 22).

[Another edition.] *For G. Risk, G. Ewing, and W. Smith : Dublin.* 1727. 8°.

 B.M. (12611. h. 5).

[A re-issue of the 12° edition of 1727.] *For B. Motte.* 1731. 12°. 2 vols.
   B.M. (12614. bbb. 7).

[Another edition.] Travels into several Remote Nations of the World,
etc. 4°.
   Not abridged, as sometimes stated.
   B.M. (12613. h. 7).

See also supra : [Collections.]

[An abridgement.] Faithfully Abridged. *For J. Stone, and R. King.*
1727. 12°. 2 vols.
   A piracy, defended in the publishers' preface.
   B.M. (12604. bb. 1), imperf., wanting quire A (title, etc.) of vol. 2.

[A key to Gulliver's Travels.] Lemuel Gulliver's Travels Into Several
Remote Nations of the World Compendiously methodized, *etc.* 1726. 8°.
   "A Key with Observations."
   B.M. (12612. d. 24).

See BENNET, Lucas ; CREIGHTON, *Captain* John ; DESFONTAINES, Pierre
François Guyot ; VAIRASSE D'ALLAIS, Denis.

A Description of the Kingdom of Absurdities.—A Voyage into England,
by a Person of Quality in Terra Australis incognita, translated from the
Original.
   Announced in *The Tale of a Tub*, 1711 and 1734, as by the same author. Probably
   neither had any existence.

SYMMONS, *Mr.*
   The Whimsical Lovers : Or, Cupid in Disguise. A Novel. By Mr. Symmons.
For J. Crokatt. 1725. 8°.
   B.M. (12614. ff. 18).

TACHMAS.
   Tachmas, Prince of Persia : An Historical Novel . . . Render'd into
English by P. Porter, Esq. *For D. Newman.* 1676. 8°.
   B.M. (12511. e. 20/1).

TALLEMANT, Paul.

Lycidus : or the Lover in Fashion.   Being an Account from Lycidus to Lysander, of his Voyage from the Island of Love.   From the French.   By the same Author Of the Voyage to the Isle of Love, *etc.*   *For J. Knight and F. Saunders.*   1688.   8°.

The dedication is signed A. Behn.
  B.M. (1077. f. 91).

TANZÄI AND NEADARNE.

See CRÉBILLON, Claude Prosper Jolyot de, *fils.*

TARSIS AND ZÉLIE.

See LE VAYER DE BOUTIGNY, Rolland.

TAXILA.

Taxila, or Love Prefer'd before Duty.   A Novel.   By D. W. Gent.   *For T. Salusbury.*   1692.   12°.

B.M. (12614. ccc. 7).

TECKELI, *Count.*

See PRÉCHAC, *le Sieur* de.

TELEMACHUS.

A new Adventure of Telemachus.

See STUBBES, George.

TERRASSON, Jean.

The Life of Sethos.   Taken from Private Memoirs of the Ancient Egyptians. Translated from a Greek Manuscript into French.   And now faithfully done into English from the Paris Edition ;   By Mr. Lediard.   In Two Volumes. *For J. Walthoe.*   1732.   8°.   2 vols.

B.M. (89. a. 26).

THEOBALD, Lewis.

The History of the Loves of Antiochus and Stratonice . . .   By Mr. Theobald.   *For J. Browne.*   1717.   12°.

B.M. (12613. a. 35).

THEODORA.

See BOYLE, Robert, *F.R.S.*

THEOPHANIA.

Theophania : or severall Modern Histories Represented by way of Romance : and Politickly Discours'd upon ; by An English Person of Quality. *T. Newcomb for T. Heath.* 1655. 4°.

B.M. (12613. c. 18).

THIBAULT, *Mons., Gouverneur de Talmont.*

The Life and Adventures of Pedrillo del Campo. Intermix'd with several Entertaining and Delightful Novels. Written Originally in French, by Mons. Thibault, G. D. T. From thence Translated into English, by Ralph Brookes, M.D. *For T. Corbett.* 1723. 12°.

B.M. (12490. aaa. 12).

THOUSAND AND ONE DAYS.

See PÉTIS DE LA CROIX, François.

TIT-BIT.

The Tit-bit. A Tale. *For T. Cooper.* 1738.

Gentleman's Magazine, March, 1738.

TITI, *Prince.*

See SAINT-HYACINTHE, Hyacinthe Cordonnier de ; PENNYMAN, *Lady* Margaret.

TOMAZO, *Don.*

See DANGERFIELD, Thomas.

TRAM, TOM.

Tom Tram of the West, Son-in-Law to Mother Winter. Shewing his Merry Jests . . . To which is added divers Merry Tales, *etc. For W. T[hackeray], and are to be sold by J. Gilbertson.* 8°. 𝔅.𝔏.

Bodl. (Wood 259/8).

[Another edition.] *For W. T[hackeray], and sold by J. Deacon.* 8°.

Pepys 362 (881).

TRAVELS.

The Travels of an Adventurous Knight through the Kingdom of Wonder. 1731.

Gentleman's Magazine, May, 1731.

The Travels of Love and Jealousie.   A Novel, In Two Parts.   By H. C., Gent.   *For R. Bentley and D. Brown.*   1693.   8º.

Term Cat., ii. 477.

TREACHEROUS CONFIDANT.

The Treacherous Confident: or, Fortune's Change   A Novel, *etc.* *S. Powell: Dublin.*   1728.   12º.

B.M. (12431. a. 29/1)

TRIANA.

See FULLER, Thomas.

TRIUMPH OF FRIENDSHIP.

The Triumph of Friendship, and The Force of Love.   Two new Novels from the French.   *For D. Brown and J. Walthoe.*   1684.   12º.

Term Cat., ii. 96.

TROJAN TALES.

Trojan Tales, Related by Ulysses, Helenus, Hector, Achilles, and Priam. *For F. Burleigh, J. Groves, J. Richardson, J. Browne, and A. Dodd.* 1714.   12º.

B.M. (837. a. 2).

TROJAN WARS.

The New History of the Trojan Wars and Troy's Destruction.   In Four Books, *etc.*   *For C. Bates.*   1728.   12º.

Only the second part, containing the " Tragicomedy of the Siege of Troy," is dated.
B.M. (12450. b. 8).

[Another edition.]   *For C. Bates.*   "1603."   12º.

This edition almost exactly resembles that of 1728.
B.M. (12403. aa. 20).

[Another edition.] *For J. Hodges and J. Fuller.* 4°.
Priv. Lib.

[Another edition.] *For Sarah Bates, and J. Hodges.* 1735. 12°.
B.M. (12612. a. 37), imperf.

TRUMBILL.

The Dutch Whore; or, The Miss of Amsterdam. Being a New Discovery of the Humours and Intreagues of Bullies, Pimps, Bauds, Cracks and their Cullies, *etc.* 1690. 12°.

In some copies the dedicatory epistle is without the name of the author.
Priv. Lib.

TUDOR, Owen.

Tudor Prince of Wales. An Historical Novel. In Two Parts. *For J. Edwin.* 1678. 12°.

Term Cat., i. 312.

TURKISH SECRETARY.

See Vignau, *le Sieur* du.

TURKISH TALES.

See Chec Zade [Shaikzádah].

TYSSOT DE PATOT, Simon.

The Travels and Adventures of James Massey. Translated from the French. *For J. Watts.* 1733. 12°.

B.M. (12511. c. 30).

UBEDA, Francisco Lopez de [Andreas Perez].

See Spanish Libertines.

ULFELD, *Count.*

See Rousseau de la Valette, Michel.

UNEQUAL MATCH.

See La Chappelle, Jean de.

UNFORTUNATE DUCHESS.

The Unfortunate Duchess : or, The Lucky Gamester.   A Novel.   Founded on a true Story.   *For T. Read.*   1739.   8º.

B.M. (012611. k. 11).

UNFORTUNATE NEAPOLITAN.

See OLIVIER, *l'Abbé.*

UNFORTUNATE HEROES.

Unfortunate Heroes, or the Adventures of Famous Men, viz., Ovid, Lentalus [*sic?*], Horace, Agrippa, and others, in Ten Novels, Englished by a Gentleman for his diversion.   1679.   8º.

Dealer's list.

UNHAPPY LOVERS.

The Unhappy Lovers : Or, The Timorous Fair One.   A Novel.   Being the Loves of Artaxander and Mellecinda.   In a Letter to the most Charming Cordelia.   *For R. Bentley.*   1694.   12º.

B.M. (12611. de, 6).

See WELSTON, James.

UNLUCKY CITIZEN.

See BLACK TOM ; KIRKMAN, Francis.

UNLUCKY FAIR ONE.

See MILISTRATE AND PRAZIMENE.

UNNATURAL MOTHER.

The Unnatural Mother and Ungrateful Wife, A Narrative : Founded on true and very Interesting Facts.   Contain'd in Three Letters, *etc.   For J. Jefferies, and Mrs. Windbush.*   8º.

B.M. (12614. d. 15).

The Unnatural Mother : Or, Innocent Love Persecuted, *etc.   For J. Roberts.* 1734.   8º.

Not the same as the preceding.
B.M. (11775. bbb. 13).

UNSATISFIED LOVERS.

The Unsatisfied Lovers. A new English Novel. *Sold by J. Partridge.* 1683. 12º.

Term Cat., ii. 44.

UTOPIAN MEMOIRS.

See HAYWOOD, Eliza.

VAIRASSE D'ALLAIS, DENIS.

The History of the Sevarites or Sevarambi : A Nation inhabiting part of the third Continent, Commonly called, Terrae Australes Incognitae. With an account of their admirable Government, Religion, Customs, and Language. Written by one Captain Siden, *etc. For H. Brome.* 1675, 79. 8º. 2 vols.

B.M. (836. b 5).

[Another edition.] The History of the Sevarambians : a People of the South-Continent. In Five Parts . . . Translated from the Memoirs of Captain Siden, Who lived fifteen years amongst them. *For J. Noon.* 1738. 8º.

B.M. (12611. h. 4).

Travels into several remote Nations of the World, by Capt. Lemuel Gulliver. Vol. III. 1727. 8º.

A forgery, largely translated from the *Histoire des Sevarambes.*
Swift, *Prose Works*, 1899, vol. 8, p. xxxi.

VANELLA.

The Fair Concubine : Or, The Secret History Of the Beautiful Vanella . . . The Second Edition. *For W. James.* 1732. 8º.

B.M. (635. f. 11/9).

VANNEL, *le Sieur.*

See INTRIGUES.

VAUDRAY, *le Chevalier* DE.

See VERGI, *la Comtesse* de.

VAUMORIÈRE, Pierre d'Ortigue de.

Agiatis, Queen of Sparta, Or, The Civil Wars of the Lacedemonians, in the Reigns of the Kings Agis and Leonidas.   In Two Parts.   Translated out of French.   *R. E. for R. Bentley and S. Magnes.*   1686.   8°.

B.M. (12510. bb. 1).

The Grand Scipio, an Excellent New Romance.   Written in French by Monsieur De Vaumoriere.   And Rendered into English by G. H.   *For H. Mosely, T. Dring and H. Herringman.*   1660.   Fol.

B.M. (12510. g. 27).

Pharamond, Parts 8–12.

See Costes, Gauthier, *Sieur de Calprenède.*

VEAL, *Mrs.*   *See* Defoe, Daniel.

VENETIAN TALES.

Venetian Tales; or, a Curious Collection of entertaining Novels, designed for the Amusement of the Fair Sex.   Translated from the Italian.   *For T. Cooper.*   1737.

Gentleman's Magazine, May, 1737.

VERGI, *la Comtesse* de.

The Tragical History of the Chevalier de Vaudray, and the Countess de Vergi.   In Two Parts.   To which is annexed, A short Novel, Intitled, The Inhumane Husband.   Done from the French.   By J. M.   *For A. Bettesworth.* 1726.   12°.

La Comtesse de Vergi.
B.M. (12517. aa. 20).

VICTOR, Benjamin.

The Voyages and Adventures of Captain Robert Boyle, *etc.*

See Chetwood, William Rufus.

VICTORIOUS LOVERS.

[The Victorious Lovers; Or, Love Victorious over Fortune.   *R. Bentley?*]   12°.

In *Modern Novels*, vol. iv.
B.M. (12410. c. 21), imperf.

VIGNAN, *le Sieur* DU.

The Turkish Secretary, Containing the Art of Expressing ones Thoughts, without Seeing, Speaking, or Writing to One another; With the Circumstances of a Turkish Adventure ... Translated by the Author of the Monthly Account. *J. B. and sold by J. Hindmarsh and R. Taylor.* 1688. 4°.

B.M. (1053. i. 36).

VILLA DIEU, *Monsieur* DE; and
VILLEDIEU, *Madame* DE.

See DESJARDINS, Marie Catherine Hortense de, *Madame de Villedieu.*

VILLAINS.

The Lives of sundry notorious Villains, memorable for their base and abominable Actions. Together with a Novel, as it really happened at Roan in France. *For S. Crouch.* 1677. 12°.

Term Cat., i. 289.

VILLIERS, J. DE.

The Gentleman Apothecary. Being a late and true story; turn'd out of French. *For H. Brome.* 1670. 8°.

B.M. (1081. i. 2).

[Another edition.] With several Letters. *Sold by H. Brome.* 1678. 8°.

Term Cat., i. 294 (1677; *see* ed. of 1726).

[Another edition.] The Gentleman 'Pothecary. A True Story. Done out of French, by Sir Roger L'Estrange, Knt. in the Year 1678. The Second Edition. *For E. Curll.* 1726. 12°.

B.M. (12511. df. 15).

[Latin.] Nobilis Pharmacopola . Historia Si non vera, jucunda tamen, Nunc demum Latinitate donata; Cum nonnullis Epistolis. *Ex Officina M. C.* 1693. 12°.

B.M. (1081. i. 1).

VIROTTO AND DOROTHEA.

The Governor of Cyprus, or The Loves of Virotto and Dorothea. A Novel. *For J. Knapton.* 1689. 12°.

Term Cat., ii. 286.

VIRTUE REWARDED.

Vertue Rewarded; Or, The Irish Princess.   A new novel.   *For R. Bentley.*
1693.   12°.

In *Modern Novels*, vol. xii.
   B.M. (12410. c. 29).

VOITURE, VINCENT DE.

[Alcidalis, in :]   The Works of Mr. de Voiture.   Translated by Mr. Ozell.
In Two Volumes.

Advertised by H. Curll in 1726.

[Another edition.]   The Works of Monsieur Voiture.   In Two Volumes.
Containing, Letters . . .   Alcidalis and Zelida.   A Romance . . .   The
Third Edition, Revised and Corrected throughout of the last Edition
Printed at Paris, *etc.*   *For A. Bettesworth, E. Curll, and J. Pemberton.*
1736.   12°.

   B.M. (1085. f. 10).

[Another edition.]   Alcidalis, a Romance.

See COLLECTION.   A Collection of Select Discourses.

See ZELINDA.

VOSS, JENNY.

The German Princess revived ; or the London Jilt ; being a true Account
of the Life and Death of Jenny Voss.   1684.   4°.

   Lowndes, 2795.

VOYAGE.

A Voyage Round the World.   *See* DUNTON, John.

A Voyage up the Thames.   *See* WEDDELL.

W., D.
See TAXILA.

W., J.
See CROXALL, Samuel.

WANTON FRIAR.

The Wanton Fryer, Or The Irish Amour. A new Novel. *Sold by R. Baldwin.* 1689. 12°.

   Term Cat., ii. 251, 286.

WEAMYS, ANNE.

A Continuation of Sir Philip Sydney's Arcadia: Wherein is handled The Loves of Amphialus and Helena Queen of Corinth, Prince Plangus and Erona . . . Written by a young Gentlewoman, M^iss A. W. *W. Bentley, and are to be sold by T. Heath.* 1651. 8°.

   B.M. (E. 1288/2).

[Another edition.] The Second Edition. *For W. Miller.* 1690. 8°.

   Term Cat., ii. 316.

WEDDELL.

A Voyage up the Thames. *Sold by J. Roberts.* 1738. 8°.

   B.M. (838. h. 2).

WELSTON, JAMES.

The Unhappy Lovers: Or, The History of James Welston, Gent. Together with his Voyages and Travels, *etc. J. Hughs, for T. Dormer, T. Warner, J. Crichley, W. Hinton, and E. Nutt.* 1732. 8°.

   B.M. (12316. bbb. 38/4).

WESTERN WONDER.

See HEAD, Richard.

WHARTON, ROBERT.

Historiæ Pueriles. By Robert Wharton. *For T. Wotton.* 1734. 12°.

   B.M. (12809. aaa. 72).

WHIG, *Saint.*

The Life and Glorious Actions of St. Whig . . . with the Lives of his Principal Friends and Enemies. Writ by a Fryar at Geneva; and printed by a Jesuit at Edinburg. 1708. 8°.

   Term Cat., iii. 571 ("sold by S. Bunchley.")
   B.M. (T. 1584/5).

WHITTINGTON, *Sir* RICHARD.

The Famous and Remarkable History of Sir Richard Whittington . . .
Written by T. H.   *W. Wilson, and are to be sold by F. Coles.*   1656.
8°.   𝕭.𝕷.

B.M. (12431. aa. 38).

[Another edition.]   *A. P. and T. H. for T. Vere and J. Wright.*   1678.
4°.   𝕭.𝕷.

B.M. (12410. bb. 9).

[Another edition.]   *For W. Thackeray and T. Passinger.*   4°.

Pepys 1192 (12).

[Another edition.]   8°.   𝕭.𝕷.

Bodl. (Wood 254), mutilated.

[Another version.]   The Excellent and Renowned History of the Famous
Sir Richard Whittington, *etc.*   8°.   𝕭.𝕷.

Pepys 363 (735), the imprint cut away.

[Another edition ?]

Advertised by G. Conyers in Greene's *Dorastus and Fawnia*, 1688.

[Another version.]   The History of Sir Richard Whittington, thrice Mayor
of London.   *I. Lane : Durham.*   1730.

Villon Society, ed. 1885, p. xxv.

[Another edition.]   *I. Lane : Durham.*   12°.

Not before 1740 ?
B.M. (1076. l. 18/2).

WINSTANLEY, WILLIAM.

The Honour of Merchant-Taylors, Wherein is set forth the Noble
Acts, Valliant Deeds, and Heroick performances of Merchant-Taylors in
former Ages.   Their Honourable Loves, and Knightly Adventures . . .
Written by William Winstanley.   *P. L. for W. Whitwood.*   1668.   4°.
𝕭.𝕷. in part.

B.M. (12410. bb. 12).

WINTER EVENING TALES.

Winter Evening Tales. Being a Collection of Entertaining Stories, Related in an Assembly Of the most Polite Persons of the French Nation. *For F. Cogan.* 1731. 12°.

A second volume is promised at the end, should the present receive sufficient support.
B.M. (12614. ccc. 14).

WISDOM REVEALED.

Wisdom revealed: or the Tree of Life discovered. A Tale. To which is added The Crabtree, or Sylvia discover'd. By a studious enquirer into the mysteries of Nature. *For W. Shaw.* 1732.

Gentleman's Magazine, Dec. 1732.

WIT AND FANCY.

Wit and Fancy in a Maze. *See* HOLLAND, Samuel.

WITTY WILLIAM OF WILTSHIRE.

See PRICE, Laurence.

WRIGHT, THOMAS.

The Triumphs of Friendship and Chastity.

See (in Part I) REYNOLDS, John. The Glory of God's Revenge against Murder and Adultery.

XENOPHON *Ephesius.*

[Greek and Latin.] ΞΕΝΟΦΩΝΤΟΣ ἐφεσιου τῶν κατὰ Ἀνθίαν καὶ Ἀβροκόμην Εφεσιακῶν λόγοι πέντε. Xenophontis Ephesii Ephesiacorum libri v. de amoribus Anthiae et Abrocomae. Nunc primum prodeunt e vetusto codice Bibliothecae Monachorum Cassinensium Florentiae cum Latina interpretatione Antonii Cocchii Florentini. *G. Bowyer.* 1726. 8°.

B.M. (1074. l. 11).

[Another edition of Book 1, in Greek and Latin.] Xenophontis Ephesii Ephesiacorum libri v . . . Cum Animadversionibus . . . Curante E. P., *etc. Apud T. Field, ex Typographia J. Haberkorn.* 8°.

B.M. (1074. l. 12/1).

[English.]   Xenophon's Ephesian History : or the Love-Adventures of Abrocomas and Anthia.   In Five Books.   Translated from the Greek.   By Mr. Rooke.   *For J. Millan.*   1727.   8°.

B.M. (1074. l. 12/2).

[Another edition.]   The Third Edition.   *For J. Millan.*   1727.   8°.
Bodl. (Douce XX. 5).

[Italian.]   Di Senofonte Efesio Degli Amori di Abrocome ed' Anthia Libri v. Tradotti Da M. Salvini.   *G. Pickard.*   1723.   12°.

B.M. (1074. b. 30/1).

YOLANDA.

See PRÉCHAC, *le Sieur* de.

YORK SPY.

The Northern Atalantis : or, York Spy.   Displaying The Secret Intrigues and Adventures of the Yorkshire Gentry ; more particularly the Amours of Melissa, *etc.*   *For A. Baldwin.*   1713.   8°.

Bodl. (Hope 8°. 1107).

YORKSHIRE ROGUE.

The Yorkshire Rogue, or Captain Hind Improved.   1684.   8°.

Lowndes, 3019.

ZACHARIE, *le Père.*

See FONTAINES, Louis.

ZADE, CHEC.

See CHEC ZADE [SHAIKZÁDAH].

ZAGAS, *Donna.*

See PERPLEXED PRINCESS.

ZARAH, *Queen.*

See MANLEY, Mary de la Rivière.

ZAYDE.

See SEGRAIS, Jean Regnauld de.

ZELINDA.

Zelinda : An Excellent New Romance.   Translated from the French of Monsieur De Scudery.   By T. D. Gent. *etc.*   *T. R. and N. T. for J. Magnes and R. Bentley.*   1676.   12°.

In *Modern Novels*, vol. vii.   Not by Scudéry ; the plot is from Voiture's *Alcidalis et Zélide*. B.M. (12410. c. 24).

ZELOIDE.

Indian Tales, or the Adventures of Zeloide and Amanzarifdine.   A novel, done from the Paris edition, *etc.*   *For A. Bell, J. Osborn, and J. Brotherton and W. Meadows.*   1718.   12°.

Les Mille et Une Faveurs.
B. Dobell, cat. 209, no. 635.

ZINGIS.

See LA ROCHE GUILHEM, *Mlle.* de.